Feminist Readings of Antigone

SUNY Series in Gender Theory

Tina Chanter, editor

Feminist Readings of Antigone

Edited by

FANNY SÖDERBÄCK

SUNY PRESS

Cover art: Bracha L. Ettinger, *Eurydice* no. 50
Oil on paper mounted on canvas (25.3 x 31.1 cm), 2006–2007

Published by State University of New York Press, Albany

Printed in the United States of America

For information, contact State University of New York Press, Albany, NY
www.sunypress.edu

Production by Eileen Meehan
Marketing by Michael Campochiaro

Library of Congress Cataloging-in-Publication Data

Feminist readings of Antigone / edited by Fanny Söderbäck.
p. cm. — (SUNY series in gender theory)
Includes bibliographical references and index.
ISBN 978-1-4384-3279-3 (alk. paper)
ISBN 978-1-4384-3278-6 (pbk. : alk. paper)
1. Sophocles. Antigone. 2. Feminism and literature—Greece. 3. Antigone (Greek mythology) in literature. 4. Women in literature. 5. Sex role in literature. 6. Tragedy. I. Söderbäck, Fanny, 1978–

PA4413.A7F46 2010
882'.01—dc22 2010005120

10 9 8 7 6 5 4 3 2 1

For Jonna, my sister, who has the courage of Antigone.
And for all women who fight for the right to speak in their own voice.

Contents

Acknowledgments ix

Introduction: Why Antigone Today? 1
Fanny Söderbäck

Prologue: Nomadic Antigone 15
Moira Fradinger

I. Between Past and Future: Feminist Politics in the Private and Public Realms

1. After Antigone: Women, the Past, and the Future of Feminist Political Thought 27
Catherine A. Holland

2. On the Body of Antigone 45
Adriana Cavarero

3. Impossible Mourning: Sophocles Reversed 65
Fanny Söderbäck

4. The Performative Politics and Rebirth of Antigone in Ancient Greece and Modern South Africa 83
Tina Chanter

5. The Eternal Irony of the Community 99
Luce Irigaray

6. "the celestial Antigone, the most resplendent figure ever to have appeared on earth": Hegel's Feminism 111
J. M. Bernstein

II. Incestuous Desire: Sexuality, Kinship, and Psychoanalytical Approaches

7. Promiscuous Obedience — 133
Judith Butler

8. Antigone's Line — 155
Mary Beth Mader

9. Beyond Pleasure: The Other History of Sexuality — 173
Cecilia Sjöholm

10. Transgressing With-In-To the Feminine — 195
Bracha L. Ettinger

11. Antigone: Limit and Horizon — 215
Julia Kristeva

Bibliography — 231

Contributors — 241

Index — 245

Acknowledgments

Editing a book is both a solitary and deeply collective endeavor. This volume not only gathers a series of dialogues and debates in a particular academic field but it is also—like most books—the result of conversations with colleagues, teachers, students, and friends. It is impossible for me to properly thank all those who have contributed along the way. Let me nevertheless attempt to mention a few.

First and foremost, I want to express my gratitude to two individuals without whom this book would not exist: J. M. Bernstein, my mentor, in whose seminar on tragedy and philosophy my passion for Antigone was born; and Tina Chanter, whose tireless work on this figure is a source of inspiration, and who supported my proposal from the outset. Their ongoing encouragement made this project possible.

Great thanks go, as well, to all of the participating authors, whose contributions brought this book into existence, and who were simply wonderful to work with throughout the various stages of the process. I want to thank Ella Brians, who kindly lent me her sharp eyes as I prepared the manuscript for publication. My gratitude also goes to the two anonymous readers at SUNY Press, who provided helpful feedback and comments, and to Jane Bunker, Michael Campochiaro, and Eileen Meehan at SUNY Press for their invaluable assistance. I am indebted to Matt Hackett and Anne Marsella for helping me edit Julia Kristeva's essay, and to Christina Kkona for guidance with Greek transliterations. I owe special thanks to Claudia Baracchi for providing keys to unlock the world of ancient Greece.

I cannot properly thank Matt Hackett for the tireless work he has put into this project. His philosophical depth and language skills have been an invaluable resource, and his generosity a sign of true friendship. Finally, I would like to thank Ben Goldfarb for giving me courage in the early stages of the project; Rocío Zambrana, Stina Bergman, and my parents for their unfailing love and support; and Tana Ross and Anne Thulin, who so generously welcomed me into their home, providing the abode in which this book came to life.

Generous funding has been provided through J. M. Bernstein by the Philosophy Department of the New School for Social Research and by the Lars Hiertas Minne Foundation in Sweden.

Introduction

Why Antigone Today?

As I write this introduction, the world is both a darker and a brighter place than it has been in a long time. We are faced with a financial crisis of unknown measure, haunted by post-9/11 fear that has prompted us to launch preemptive wars, while global warming threatens the very survival of our planet. At the same time, the citizens of the United States have elected their first African-American president, and people around the world, surprised and moved, are celebrating this historic event. The mantra throughout the presidential campaign was "Change We Can Believe In." People are thirsty for change, not just change in the political agenda or the voices behind that agenda, but also, and perhaps more important, change in the very manner in which politics is conducted. At a moment of global crisis we allow ourselves to dream: Can we seize this moment to redefine the political as such? Could this—our sudden capacity for dreaming—have been possible only because the president is now a man of color? Has the simultaneous candidacy of a woman and a black man for what is arguably the most powerful position in the world incited the need to remap the field of politics, to redraw the demarcation lines that, until now, have defined the political as we know it?

These questions are present in my mind as I once again read the story of Antigone. Hegel compared her to Socrates and Jesus. Like them, she made the most extraordinary sacrifice for her commitments. But rather than highlighting (and thus fetishizing?) the martyrdom of these figures, what seems more important is that they represent, each in their own way, what we dream of doing today: They changed not only the content of philosophy, religion, or politics, but also, and more crucially, they revolutionized the very stakes and conditions of these respective fields. Each one of them embodies novelty and change: Socrates rejected a school of thinking that saw the task of philosophy to be rhetorical in nature—the Sophistic desire to master the art of argumentation—and embarked instead on a dialectical search for truth; Jesus inscribed forgiveness and reconciliation into the very heart of a religious discourse thitherto marked by a logic of vengeance and duty; and Antigone? Oh, Antigone. Not only did she attempt the impossible, but she herself seems impossible to label, to define. Who is she, this enigmatic figure? What are the implications of her story? What motivated her to sacrifice her own life to honor her dead brother? And why, I ask myself as I revisit her story, do we continually return to this figure in our attempts to grapple with the struggles and crises of our own times?

Like all great Greek tragedies, *Antigone* presents us with existential questions similar to those addressed by Socrates and Jesus. In the choral ode to man (the perhaps most famous passage from this drama), human existence is characterized as wondrous, riddle-like, uncanny. Human beings are natural and rational at once, bound by necessity yet gifted with freedom, mortal yet capable of transcending the mere necessities of life and survival, the doers of good and evil, makers and breakers of laws and city walls. Although the story of Antigone addresses these universal and timeless contradictions and perplexities of humankind, it simultaneously tells the story of a singular individual: Antigone, a woman who defies King Creon's edict without any fear, doubts, or regrets. This courageous woman, the fruit of incest, has fascinated philosophers in the nineteenth century, inspired playwrights in the twentieth century, and intrigued feminist thinkers and activists for decades.

This book collects some of the most interesting and thought-provoking examples of feminist engagements with this enigmatic figure—some have been published elsewhere, others have been written specifically for this volume. In recent years we have seen a flood of interpretations and performances of this ancient drama, and today Antigone is the subject of countless conferences and college courses around the world. In order to understand the role she plays in contemporary political debates (and more specifically feminist debates), and in order to provide a comprehensive resource for those currently working on this topic as teachers, scholars, artists, or activists, I envisioned a volume that would gather the relevant texts considered "classics" in this field, alongside some newly written chapters that tarry with or move beyond the most well-known readings. Needless to say, this book covers only a slice of all the creative, provocative, and subtle feminist readings of *Antigone* that have been published in recent years. With this in mind, the bibliography in this volume lists many of the interpretations that could not be included.

My ambition is to offer a selection of chapters by authors who are concerned with the various instances in which Antigone figures in contemporary debates about the role of women in our society. Why, we ask, has Antigone become such an important figure? As modern women and men, what can we learn from her? Can a feminist politics that turns to this ancient heroine be progressive, or is it bound to romanticize the past? To claim that feminists turn to the figure of Antigone simply because she is a heroic woman is oversimplistic. Greek tragedy gives us many remarkable and inspiring female figures, most of whom have drawn the attention of contemporary feminists in various fields, although none matches the allure of Antigone. What is it about *her* story that so compels us? How is it that this fictitious woman, at the center of a drama written 2,500 years ago, continues to shed light on the specific problems of every historical generation?

The chapters in this volume set out to confront these questions. In doing so, they address an extraordinary range of topics relevant to women and feminists today: female subjectivity and sexuality; questions of race and gender; the role and place of the body in our culture; the tension between and interdependence of the private and the public spheres; ethical and moral conduct; the possibility of a different future; the misogyny (or feminism?) of preeminent thinkers such as Jacques Lacan and G. W. F. Hegel; kinship, reproduction, and maternal origins; the emancipatory status and role of art and aesthetics; the tension and relationship between culture and nature, humans and animals; issues concerning freedom, citizenship, and democracy; the mechanisms that replicate taboos, normativity, and pathology; the challenges involved in intersubjective relations; and the intersection between sexism and other forms of oppression. The story of Antigone permits us to tackle these matters in a variety of ways, and I hope this collection will not only provide readers with interesting and compelling interpretations of her story, but that it can also function as a source of inspiration for feminist thought and practice at this time of crisis and potential change.

In her prologue, "Nomadic Antigone," Moira Fradinger assumes the ambitious task of tracing the global journey of Antigone as it unfolds in the second half of the twentieth century. From Greece to Australia, via Brazil, Argentina, Cuba, Puerto Rico, Nigeria, Ghana, South Africa, India, Indonesia, Ireland, Poland, Spain, Egypt, Turkey, Colombia, Mexico, and beyond—is there *any* country in the world she has not visited in one of her many guises? Whatever alias she assumes—Antígona Vélez, Mariana, Antígona Pérez, Akwele, Odale, Clara Luz, Antígona Furiosa, Sofia, Melissa, Anita, Tègònni—she always challenges authority in the specific form it takes. Whenever and wherever civil liberties are endangered, when the rights or existence of aboriginal peoples are threatened, when revolutions are under way, when injustices take place—wherever she is needed, Antigone appears. And although the details and context may vary, certain elements of the story always remain the same: the lone individual fighting against state power, the kinship burial rites, and, interestingly, her status as a woman. Because whatever group or interest Antigone is brought in to defend—religious, cultural, or racial minorities; guerilla fighters; spiritual leaders; war-torn people; the economically oppressed—it is always as a woman (or, in some cases, where female actors are not available, in feminine attire) that she appears on stage. Sexual difference stood at the center of the original

Sophoclean drama, and sexual difference continues to mark her story as she is stubbornly resurrected.

But we must ask, is this eternal return of Antigone not a sign that we lack new imaginaries? If she is summoned in times of political turmoil and change, is the very repetition of her story not an indication of the static nature of political affairs? And should we, as feminists, really turn to a heroine of the past in our attempts to formulate a different future? These questions inform Catherine A. Holland's chapter, "After Antigone: Women, the Past, and the Future of Feminist Political Thought," which raises the issue of "the symbolic significance of the past within contemporary feminist political theory." If Fradinger reveals the recurrence and relevance of Antigone in modern history, Holland insists instead on her *difference* from us and articulates the political stakes in underlining such a difference or distance.

Holland begins by examining three early feminist readings of *Antigone*: Jean Bethke Elshtain's "Antigone's Daughters" (1982), which argues that the *family* has been eclipsed in current political life; Mary Dietz's "Citizenship with a Feminist Face: The Problem with Maternal Thinking" (1985), which instead suggests that *politics* (understood in terms of citizenship) has been eclipsed; and, finally, Linda Zerilli's "Machiavelli's Sisters: Women and 'the Conversation' of Political Theory" (1991), which puts forth the view that above all, the *maternal body* has been eclipsed. All three see in Antigone the possibility of recovering these lost grounds. Holland worries that each of them, in different ways, nostalgically idealizes a long lost past and consequently risks accepting a variety of problematic premises handed down by the very tradition that they set out to contest.

Her own reading of the play focuses on the way Antigone "shows us how we may innovate from within a tradition." Drawing from Froma I. Zeitlin's "Thebes: Theater of Self and Society in Athenian Drama" (1990), which offers an analysis of Thebes as a city cursed by its own past, contrary to the dynamic politics of its neighbor Athens, Holland examines the way Antigone herself, as a consequence of her incestuous lineage, indeed is paralyzed by the past. She goes on to show, however, that Antigone's actions nevertheless allow her to overcome the fateful repetition inherent in this lineage, thus allowing for new beginnings that are both personal and collective. In this sense, Antigone does not retrieve a long-lost eclipsed past but—by introducing difference into a logic of sameness—rather puts an end to the repetitive character of the past, thereby pointing to the possibility of a different future. Holland seems to suggest that what we can learn first and foremost from the figure of Antigone is precisely the importance of avoiding an idealization of past figures and the need to, instead, develop a feminist politics grounded in the specificity of our own times and our future to come.

The next two chapters—Adriana Cavarero's "On the Body of Antigone" and my "Impossible Mourning: Sophocles Reversed"—are concerned with a set of related themes, although these themes are addressed in quite distinct ways and with different interpretive tools: What, we ask, is the significance of the binary oppositions that structure the play? How are these very oppositions constitutive of the way in which "the political" is construed? And what consequences can be drawn from the fact that woman, within a binary logic, repeatedly finds herself on the *outside* of politics—an excluded other that, ironically, nevertheless functions as the hidden ground upon which the founding fathers may begin their work of constructing a polis? While Cavarero addresses these questions by examining the ambiguous tension between the body politic and the human body through a close engagement with Plato, I consider the relationship between the public and the private realms in critical dialogue with Hannah Arendt.

Cavarero describes a tradition in which the female body has been excluded from a political sphere that, precisely in order to establish itself as political, has expelled the body altogether because our bodies unavoidably confront us with our animal origins. In the tragedy of *Antigone*, the city bans the burial of Polyneices, leaving his dead unmourned body exposed to the elements, and fatally banishes the body of Antigone to the darkness of a cave. This very expulsion, Cavarero suggests, should bring our attention to the complicated and intimate way in which the physical body and the "stately body" have been linked throughout human history. Why, she asks, do both Antigone and Creon occupy themselves with the *body* of a dead man, in a cultural context that so sharply separates body from soul and, moreover, privileges the soul because the immortality of the latter is elevated over the finitude of the former? For the ancients, she argues, the soul alone is capable of being a principle for action, and, therefore, also an object of enmity. But the enemy in *Antigone* strangely appears as sheer body—the dead body of Polyneices. Herein lies the paradox of the play: In its connection with the animalistic and female elements of human life, the body is inherently *apolitical*; but insofar as it becomes a locus of enmity, it is turned into a site for political contestation. "The politics that banishes the body from within its walls speaks indeed, from beginning to end, only in the grammar of the body," Cavarero notes. We may thus speak of a *body politic* in a literal way. But while the male body ultimately returns to the polis—be it as enemy or friend—the female body remains constitutively excluded, deeply estranged from the city that buries it alive.

In my own reading of the play, I scrutinize the way in which our heroine has been commonly understood as a representative of the family, divine law, and a mythical past, whereas Creon has been assumed to represent the state, human law, and a political present. Through an engagement with Arendt's analysis of the distinction between private and public in ancient Greece, I trace what I call a "Sophoclean reversal" at the heart of the play, suggesting that Antigone lays the ground for a political space where action and speech can take place, whereas Creon embodies the private sphere of household economy. If Cavarero focuses on our carnal and maternal beginnings, my main interest lies rather in the way in which Antigone embodies a *new beginning*—the beginning of the political as we know it. The paradox, however, is that Antigone, as a woman, is denied access to the very sphere that she has founded, and this paradox points not only to a well-known blind spot in Arendt's thinking, but also to the enigmatic role that women in general play within political life.

Tina Chanter shares this interest in seeing Antigone as the constitutively excluded of the polity—an idea that runs through much of feminist scholarship on *Antigone*—in her chapter "The Performative Politics and Rebirth of Antigone in Ancient Greece and Modern South Africa." Chanter, however, emphasizes that this logic extends well beyond the question of sexual difference. Her chapter is an attempt to point out "how exclusionary logics reiterate themselves," whether the excluded other is marked by gender, sexuality, race, class, nationality, religion, or some other contingency. Her chapter echoes Holland's in seeing Antigone as "calling for a renewal of the political itself." And in this regard her own reading is performative: she turns to a contemporary adaptation of the drama (*The Island*, 1973), inscribing the legacy of Antigone into a relatively current discussion about political discourses on race (the play is staged in apartheid South Africa), and by introducing race as another constitutive outside of politics she simultaneously renews and broadens a feminist discourse that has too long remained blind to its own others, to its own constitutive outside. Just as Antigone was buried alive for a crime that was not a crime, the black prisoners on Robben Island are excluded from their polis because of their racial identity, by a political regime whose existence and structure depends on this very exclusion.

In a sense Chanter's text does exactly what I call for at the end of my chapter: on her reading, Antigone redraws "the lines of the polity, so that it is no longer able to cast her out as its excluded outside," thus "calling into being a future polity that does not rely on the political exclusion of some of its members." The figure of Antigone, according to Chanter, thus challenges the very logic of a polity whose necessary condition for representation is exclusion—be it of women, people of color, or other marginalized subjects.

The last two chapters of the first part of the book engage with G. W. F. Hegel's (in)famous reading of *Antigone*. Luce Irigaray's chapter "The Eternal Irony of the Community" (first published in *Speculum of the Other Woman* in 1974) is a classic within feminist scholarship on *Antigone* (Heidi M. Ravven has called it "daring," "almost midrashic"), while J. M. Bernstein's " 'the celestial Antigone, the most resplendent figure ever to have appeared on earth':

Hegel's Feminism," presents us with an altogether different Hegel than the one we find in Irigaray's influential chapter (and, for that matter, in most feminist readings). Hegel's discussion of *Antigone* appears in the chapter on Spirit in the *Phenomenology of Spirit* (1806) and has been the focus of attention for a host of feminist interpreters. While some commentators, like Seyla Benhabib, Patricia Jagentowicz Mills, and Kelly Oliver among others, have raised concerns about Hegel's division between family and state (and his association of woman with the former and man with the latter), others, such as Kimberly Hutchings, Alison Stone, and Laura Werner, have argued that these criticisms misread the context of Hegel's account. The two chapters included here are, to my mind, the best representatives of each of these positions.

Irigaray's chapter from 1974 marks the beginning of her lifelong interest in the figure of Antigone, to whom she returns time and again—sometimes going so far as identifying with her—and seeing her as illustrative of key aspects of her own philosophy of sexual difference. Articulating a feminist critique of Hegelian dialectics, Irigaray suggests that it is founded on a system of oppositional duality. This dichotomous logic, she argues, reaches its climax in Hegel's discussion of *Antigone*, where the relation between the sexes, on her account, is conceived in terms of polar opposition. One must overcome the other for the dialectical movement to proceed, and what is lost on this journey is not only the specificity of female subjectivity, but also the very possibility for women to claim selfhood. Woman, in this system, is reduced to a mere blood-giver who provides man with the vitality he needs to attain universality. The tomb where Antigone dies comes to represent the very space in which femininity is sacrificed and lost, and this tomb consequently also becomes the cave in which the maternal-material—repressed, unconscious, and dumb—is washed away in the waters of oblivion, making way for true Spirit.

In his feminist defense of Hegel, Bernstein traces a very different narrative in the *Phenomenology*. On his account, Hegel's reading is first and foremost concerned with the disparity between an (ideal) ethical world and (actual) ethical action. In contrast to the German celebration (from Kant to the Romantics) of Greek culture as a model of a harmonious, nonconflictual community (a world marked by "beauty"), Hegel turns to Antigone to find a figure who reveals the inherent contradictions embedded in such an idealized world. Hegel's criticism of Greek *Sittlichkeit* (morality), Bernstein argues, is based on his view that structures of what ought to be purely spiritual relations secretly (and wrongly!) depend on natural distinctions, above all the distinction between male and female. One immediate consequence of this is that individuals are reduced to their social positions. Through her transgressive act Antigone, in contrast, emerges as the first individual to express self-determining subjectivity beyond her social role. The drama thus "enacts the transition from world to action." But Antigone is, tragically, an individual that Greek social life had no way of recognizing. Bernstein understands Hegel's chapter on Spirit as an attempt at recognizing her. The notion of true Spirit, which Irigaray identifies as a "Hegelian dream," is thus on Bernstein's account something that Hegel himself wanted to do away with—the idealized dream or fantasy of his post-Kantian contemporaries. That dream depends on what Bernstein calls "the social metaphysics of gender complementarity," and what he aims to demonstrate is that Hegel, in fact, "unequivocally and emphatically shares" Irigaray's view that such gender complementarity is what ultimately causes the collapse of that ideal world. What feminist readers have seen as an oppositional logic in Hegel's account of ethical life must, therefore, be read as a report of Creon's views within the play—views that Hegel categorically opposes.

Although Bernstein's reading presents a feminist Hegel whose views begin to look similar to those of Irigaray, some central differences between the two remain. True, Hegel wants to bar sexual identity from having a determining role in spiritual life, meaning that—contrary to what most feminist critics have assumed—he would grant women access to the spiritual realm from which Creon wants to exclude them. But Hegel's argument nevertheless hinges on the *sublation* of sexual difference, and for Irigaray, Bernstein notes, this "might be thought to entail a worse repression and a deeper androcentrism than the social metaphysics of gender complementarity." While Hegel wants to rid ethical life from sexual difference altogether, Irigaray wants to articulate an ethics of sexual difference, understood in noncomplementary terms. Hegel's critique of the social metaphysics of gender complementarity is, moreover, by no means a critique of patriarchy (on a sociopolitical level Hegel was, no doubt, as much of a misogynist as his contemporaries), but it is rather a critique of Spirit represented as an ethical whole, a harmonious and beautiful ideal. His argument is thus ontological, not ethical, but it is precisely this, in Bernstein's mind, that gives it critical depth: "Any sexual division of spiritual labor must necessarily undermine the categorical requirements of individuality for any possible self-consciously self-determining community." The condition of possibility for singularity—a category central to Irigaray's own thought—is thus the elimination of social roles that reduce individuals to their sexual being.

Part two opens with two chapters that address questions involving kinship and reproduction. Judith Butler's chapter "Promiscuous Obedience" (first published as the final chapter of her book *Antigone's Claim: Kinship between Life and Death* in 2000) situates the figure of Antigone "within a contemporary context in which the politics of kinship has brought a classical western dilemma into contemporary crisis." In line with her previous work on gender and sexuality, Butler speaks of kinship not as a form of *being*, but rather as a form of *doing*.

In the chapter that follows, "Antigone's Line," Mary Beth Mader organizes her argument around this performative and socially contingent conception of kinship. But whereas Butler offers an interpretation of Antigone as a figure whose incestuous genealogy allows her to question, challenge, and transgress kinship norms ("the norms that govern legitimate and illegitimate modes of kin association might be more radically redrawn"), Mader will, contrarily, show that Antigone, in fact, *reestablishes* the very boundaries that have been transgressed by the incestuous relationship of her own parents, and that she does so precisely by performing relations of kinship (by *making* her brother into a brother). Her act is, therefore, "restorative or reparative" rather than transgressive.

Echoing her own groundbreaking book *Gender Trouble* (1990), Butler speaks about "kinship trouble" at the heart of the Sophoclean drama. She examines the interdependence of state power and kinship, wondering, on the one hand, if kinship can flourish without the support and mediation of the state and, conversely, if the state can thrive—even exist—without the family providing this very support and mediation. Although most commentators see a conflict between the forces of kinship and those of state power as represented by Antigone and Creon respectively, Butler points to various ways in which Antigone in fact *departs* from kinship. Her incestuous lineage makes regarding her as a simple representative of the sacred family difficult. But what sort of kinship, Butler asks, does Antigone represent? And what is her role within the field of politics? Can a feminist/queer politics of kinship be derived from the figure of Antigone?

Butler sees in Antigone's act a fatal challenge to normative heterosexuality, one that allows us to question Jacques Lacan's dependence on a heterosexual conclusion to the Oedipal drama, that is to say, the psychoanalytic view that a presocial law (the law of the Father) limits the variability of social forms; a constraint which is "understood to be beyond social alteration." Any psychoanalytic theory that takes Antigone (a character who clearly fails to produce heterosexual closure for the drama) as its point of departure, might challenge not only psychoanalytical norms but also those that structure and shape our own contemporary society—be it in terms of racial aspects of kinship, or with regard to queer kinship, single mothers, adoptive parents, or other figurations that challenge the norms or posit themselves as the essential "perversions" that the norm depends on but nevertheless fails to include. Although Antigone most certainly is no queer heroine, she allows us to rethink kinship on the basis of aberration and the displacement of gender, making visible the inherently performative aspects of kinship, consequently showing that "kinship founders on its own founding laws."

In her chapter, Mader turns to these laws to make sense of the enigmatic and controversial passage in which Antigone claims that she would not do for husband or child what she was willing to do for her brother. This statement, Mader suggests, can be understood only as an attempt to differentiate between those kin generated by oneself and those generated by another. It is a distinction that, in Antigone's own family, has been blurred: by marrying his mother, Oedipus becomes the father of his own siblings. And this is the transgression his daughter-sister, Antigone, is trying to undo. Her own transgression, on Mader's reading, is thus a necessary yet impossible effort at *restoring* her family's distorted genealogy: "Her burial of her brother is the making of a brother as something that 'cannot' be made by oneself; it is an attempt to make a 'can not' of an 'ought not,' to impart on a supposed social or moral necessity the strength of an ontological necessity." The law that Antigone wants to establish expresses the "cannot-must not" of certain kin relations. While it is possible to get oneself both a brother and a husband or child, the former is the kind of action that one can, but ought not, perform. Antigone's only chance at establishing a nonincestuous family is to recognize those family members she did not beget. Her brother must, therefore, rank over husband and child. The tragedy of the drama, however, is that Antigone cannot undo her father's violation of the incest taboo without simultaneously undoing herself.

Another important theme that runs through feminist scholarship on *Antigone* is that of sexuality and female desire. As is made clear in Mader's chapter, Antigone must sacrifice her own future as a lover, wife, and mother, in order to undo the perversions committed by her father-brother Oedipus. She has often been described as a character married to death, and her husband-to-be Haemon even joins her in a deathly embrace that puts an end to all future erotic relations. And yet this suicidal virgin-widow has prompted several discussions about the nature and status of female desire, two of which are included here. Both Cecilia Sjöholm ("Beyond Pleasure: The Other History of Sexuality") and Bracha L. Ettinger ("Transgressing With-In-To the Feminine") view female sexuality in terms of destructive forces and death. They do not, however, reduce female desire to some dark desire for death. They see it rather as a question of freedom and subject-formation. While these two chapters treat the figure of Antigone in a somewhat marginal manner, they speak to the interpretive resources that Antigone offers for thinking about a wide range of concepts important to feminist theory. These two chapters shed light on the ways in which the story of Antigone can function, on the one hand, as a springboard for alternative readings of the history of concepts such as desire, freedom, sexuality, and vulnerability (Sjöholm) and, on the other hand, for innovating a radically different approach to current theories of subject development and psychic structures (Ettinger).

Sjöholm, who has written a book on the subject of female desire using the story of Antigone as her point of departure (*The Antigone Complex: Ethics and the Invention of Feminine Desire*, 2004), provides an alternative to both the Foucauldian history of sexuality conceived from the point of view of a male subject and to the standard view of femininity that runs through a philosophical discourse dominated by a male perspective. In turning to tragedy, she seeks to establish eros as "a form of sexuality that has more to do with weakness than virility, with exposure rather than active agency," yet drawing from Friedrich Schelling she defines this very vulnerability not as a weakness understood in negative terms—as lack—but rather in terms of human freedom. In her engagement with the Greeks, Sjöholm not only turns to Sophocles' *Antigone* and Euripides' *Hippolytus*, but also to some lyrics by Sappho, the renowned female poet from the seventh century BCE. If Foucauldian eros is conceived in terms of pleasure and mastery of the self, tragic eros, as it appears in Sappho, is not merely pleasurable, but also exceeds control. Sexuality "is linked to the forms of negativity that manifest the limits of human agency and willpower." And "man manifests his freedom, according to Schelling, through the exposure to sexuality." In Schelling, sexuality thus becomes defined as "the embodied force of human freedom." What is important, for Sjöholm, is that tragic eros, as described by Sappho and Schelling, undermines the demarcation between culture and nature, active and passive, subject and object. This allows her to regard sexuality beyond its determination by gender hierarchies, "associating it with a freedom that takes us well beyond the categories of social domination."

If freedom is at stake for Sjöholm, Ettinger pursues the question of female desire in a way that allows us to understand it in positive terms and not merely as an inaccessible enigma. She thus challenges a recurrent theme of psychoanalytic discourse—a theme perhaps best illustrated by Sigmund Freud's infamous "What do women want?"—moving instead beyond the Oedipal paradigm and its mystification of women with the aid of our Theban princess. In critical dialogue with Lacan's claim that feminine sexuality is radically unknown to women and men alike, Ettinger argues that his claim only holds within a logic that presupposes the male Oedipal paradigm (one that sees woman as supplementary and derivative of man) as the sole valid model for subjectivity. This standard psychoanalytic account forecloses difference understood otherwise than in terms of phallus-presence and castration-lack and is bound to view woman as an excessive surplus. Ettinger proposes that we, instead, depart "from a difference which is feminine from the onset"—from the psychical sphere that she, elsewhere, has named matrixial (*The Matrixial Borderspace*, 2006). Such a move allows us to understand feminine desire without having to fit it into the phallic order, which, in turn, would render knowledge of feminine sexuality possible. The matrixial sphere is essentially transgressive and relational (being-born-of), and it reinscribes the maternal body and prenatal incestuous relations into the very foundation of subject-formation.

Ettinger, who speaks of early transsubjectivity rather than intersubjectivity, chooses two figures to illustrate this process: Tiresias, who according to myth was transformed into a woman for seven years and then back into his original sex; and Antigone, who transgresses the frontiers between life and death. Both characters, on Lacan's account, perform the impossible; the former in extracting knowledge of the feminine, and the latter in coming to know death in the domain of life. Echoing Lacan, Ettinger draws a parallel between woman and death, connecting the two with aesthetic and ethical experience (art, on her account, is what makes possible the transgression to the "other side") yet contrary to Lacan, she views the transgression with-in-to the feminine (and death?) not as impossible, but rather as the condition of possibility for a subjectivity constituted outside of and different from already established phallic norms and laws.

A central aspect of Ettinger's work is the significance she attributes to the *mother* in her notion of the matrixial psychic space. Irigaray, in her chapter, points to the important link between Antigone and the maternal womb that has birthed her. Mader notes, in turn, that the incestuous crime that marks Antigone's family depends on the importance of maternal filiation. And Cavarero, as we have seen, proposes that the horror produced by the body be understood as a fear precisely of our maternal-material roots, of the fact of our being born. Oedipus is undoubtedly the figure that has drawn the most attention in interpretations of the cycle that bears his name, but Jocasta—the mother-grandmother—is a central figure in numerous feminist readings. Importantly, Julia Kristeva—a thinker who has written extensively on the figure of Oedipus in her psychoanalytic work—chooses to emphasize the role of this maternal figure as she, for the first time, engages in an extended discussion of *Antigone*. While Butler skillfully demonstrates that Antigone "occupies, linguistically, every kin position *except* 'mother,' " and while Cavarero notes that Antigone inhabits the position of sister and daughter, and not wife and mother (a rare phenomenon in Greek drama), Kristeva—in the final chapter of this volume ("Antigone: Limit and Horizon")—argues that it is precisely the maternal position that our heroine desires to inhabit. For although Antigone dies unwedded and childless, Kristeva brings our attention to the uncanny moments in which she mirrors Jocasta, noting her desire to fulfill the maternal vocation of tenderness and care; of sublimation.

Like several of the chapters in this volume, Kristeva's reading of *Antigone* draws from Lacan's analysis of the play, but her engagement with him is less critical than that of, for instance, Ettinger. Lacan discussed the figure of Antigone in his seminar *The Ethics of Psychoanalysis* (1959–1960). One of the central aspects of Lacan's reading, and one that Kristeva follows and develops in her chapter, turns around a familiar theme from Greek tragedy, namely that of a *limit experience*. Antigone, the transgressor, is situated *between* worlds: she is caught between life and death, public and private, inside and outside. She is an ambiguous and oxymoronic figure who brings our attention to boundaries exactly by transgressing and destabilizing them: loyal to the brother who has launched a civil war; a member of a city that excludes her; incestuous offspring;

a divine yet exceptionally human figure. Kristeva examines the enigmatic nature of Antigone at length (thus differentiating herself from Ettinger, who rejects the view that Antigone is enigmatic or "impossible"), and positions her both as, at, and beyond the limit, as someone who exceeds herself and lacks a fixed identity, but who nevertheless knows exactly what she wants and how to pursue it. She makes her own laws, sets her own standards. And insofar as she inhabits the place of the mother, she gives birth to an imaginary universe: a "world in which life is possible at the limit."

Perhaps it is exactly this insight that we can draw from Antigone at this moment in history, in this time of crisis and change: the possibility of giving birth to imaginary universes, of imagining a world different from the one we know. Universes where life is possible at the limit, and where life beyond that limit is not condemned to exclusion, madness, or a loss of subjectivity. As Kristeva puts it, "Those who step past this threshold usually sink into madness, lose their human contours, and pass away. Not Antigone." Perhaps this is our task for the future: To challenge and exceed limits, like Antigone, while nevertheless maintaining our human contours, our human rights, our dignity, and our own voice.

Fanny Söderbäck, May 2009

Prologue

Nomadic Antigone

Moira Fradinger

It is a challenge to one's stamina to follow the traces of this 2,500-year-young Theban princess, who looks younger every day. She is indefatigable, as all the undead seem to be. Sophocles had King Creon leave her corpse unburied, like that of Polyneices, not realizing—or perhaps precisely realizing—that the representation of such a lack of funeral rites would contaminate 2,500 years of Western imagination, much in the way Polyneices' corpse had began contaminating Thebes. This lack of ritual, a certain lack in symbolization, might well be what propelled Antigone's travels through both fictional and real life theaters around the world.

Relentlessly summoned by the undead, she traveled throughout her native and neighboring lands in antiquity and later along the shores of "modern" Europe. On her way she found famous admirers who were dazzled by her and sought to follow and document the tricks with which her undead spirit managed to tell her story time and again. By the nineteenth century, she had made numerous transoceanic voyages to visit places she had never heard of or dreamt of visiting, where she shared the drama of the political theft that had incited her own anger back home. Her geographic range expanded dramatically in the twentieth century, especially after the great European wars, and the invitations she received around the world enticed her to new dialogues, taught her new ideas, offered her new outfits, opened new ways of linking her ancient drama to the modern undead.

Here are only some of the travels that led her through the ashes of post-1945 Europe to voice with renewed force the warning at the heart of her story around the globe. The end of the war finds her in Spain; she learns Portuguese in 1946; she traverses the German Black Forest to arrive in socialist Berlin in 1947; and in 1951, she finds herself back in her native Greece consoling a compatriot in solitary confinement during the civil war, which gives her an occasion to meditate on the history of her war-torn homeland and the illusions of her young leftist comrades. As she quickens her pace through the devastation of Europe, she wonders how her ancient warning to Ismene—"sister, do you not realize that the evils of our enemies are coming upon our own people"—can be so timely.

Maybe because she cannot perform on stage for her own people, that same year she decides to cross the Atlantic to embody Antígona Vélez in the Argentine Pampas, torn by the nineteenth-century war between conquering Christians and Indians, where she is sacrificed and pierced by Indian arrows as she is cast out and forced to ride a horse into their territory. She soon comes back, undead, to life in the warmer climate of the northern coast of Colombia, summoned to give advice on the display of the tension between tradition and modernity in the town that will later be known to the world as having endured one hundred years of solitude. She stays around in the Caribbean to learn Haitian Creole in 1953, and perhaps becoming a deified Haitian Vodou spirit gives her the extra agility needed to cross the Atlantic again, stopping in Portugal in 1954, to reach Cataluña in 1955. She is accompanied by a hunchback slave on her road to death and then heads back to the Americas. In 1957 she lands as Mariana in Afro Brazil, where in the midst of the staging of an 1842 anticolonial struggle she leaves her brother unburied, thereby saving her lover and herself as well. Full of energy in 1958, she travels first to Nicaragua to demand that her brother be exhumed from a mass grave and then back south to a small town in northern Argentina where she incarnates the nineteenth-century real-life heroine Doña Fortunata, who in 1841 buried a soldier who had been impaled in the town's plaza. Perhaps it is the rigidity of Argentine historical solemnity that prompts her in 1961 to jump out of her tragic corset and try on a lighter, satirical outfit, in the Caribbean, where she appears dressed as a bourgeois Dominican lady, who defends her brother in front of her husband while quoting Sophocles.

But she finds the satirical corset too tight: In just a few months she travels twice behind the Iron Curtain to Stalinist Slovenia; first to a recreation of a Nazi concentration camp during the final years of the war, where the inmates help her to bury the body of a political comrade; and then to another setting, where she lends her myth (although not her presence onstage) to protest the killing of Slovenian guards by Communist authorities. Having engaged with antitotalitarian movements, she cannot miss the anticolonial struggle, though on her way to Africa she wonders how her story can still be so vital. In 1962 she joins the Pan-African movement in Ghana when, invited to see the imaginary geography of Africa spanning through the territories of forced African migration, she becomes Akwele or Odale and speaks to her African sisters about her choice to fight for justice. Though the Parisians call her back in 1965, asking her to claim Polyneices' right to the throne, in 1966 the Caribbean tempts her again, this time with the grotesque, as she embodies an eighty-year-old Venezuelan woman in search for her sister Ismene's corpse, which has been stolen by a multinational corporation that sells bodies on the international market. In 1967 she converses with every character in the Sophoclean myth while entombed alive in Mexico. She is rescued from this tomb by an avant-garde theater in New York staging a war dance between Thebes and Argos, a reference to the Vietnam War that includes an invitation to the audience to become members of the Argive army.

The New York dance puts her in shape for the heat of 1968, when she personifies three revolutionaries in the convulsed Americas: She is Antígona Pérez in Puerto Rico, defying none other than the anticommunist Dominican dictator Trujillo by burying two political subversives; she is Clara Luz in Cuba, where she refuses the order to bury her brothers who have betrayed the revolution, and is saved by the people who kill Creon; and back in Mexico she refuses to plant a bomb, claiming that her revolutionary comrades have forgotten that man is not an instrument of man. She walks away, toward Brazil, where she embodies Marta, who during the 1789 anticolonial rebellion had been too poor to bury her revolutionary son and left his rotting corpse on the plaza as a lesson about injustice.

She had tried cinematic lights before, but only in Greek attire. In 1971 she is offered a modern look and a trip to a war-torn Italian city of the future where she finds a companion to help her bury her unburied brother. Once back in her native Mediterranean, she stops in 1973 to mourn her dead in Turkey, and then traverses the African continent to apartheid South Africa where on Robben Island she inspires two male prisoners to rehearse her drama for an audience of inmates. In 1974 she boards a ship through the Indian Ocean to Suharto's Indonesia where she learns from the villagers of a small Javanese village the art of "ketoprak," a rural Javanese popular operetta form from the 1920s that uses humor to voice protest. The oceans cradle her again, as she once more grapples with the surprise she feels at the pressing need for her story to be retold.

Perhaps traversing the Pacific to accelerate her trip, she reaches the Caribbean again in 1975, dressed as a "capresse," two-thirds black and one-third white, speaking French to a Creole-speaking executioner in Martinique. With the 1980s come two countries that seem to be at the center of her tribulations. She tours Spain five times: In 1980, 1983, 1986, 1988, and in one of two scenarios presented in 1983, she grotesquely buries a chicken that stands in for the corpse of her brother and defies the king declaring she would even have buried a lizard had it only been forbidden. She tours Ireland four times during that "Orwellian year" of 1984, which saw worrisome restrictions in civil liberties. First she stops in Belfast, then twice in Dublin, where during a performance copies of the Criminal Justice Bill infringing on Irish civil liberties are distributed among the audience; during another performance she defiantly declares, "I have decided not to die." She also stars in a film in which she incarnates a housekeeper working for Robert Emmet, a member of the United Irishmen whom the British executed in 1803: Here she defies the British forces by attempting to perform a Catholic burial for a dead male body.

How she manages in that same year to cross from Ireland through the Baffin Sea to Alaska, British Columbia and Los Angeles escapes us. But indeed, 1984 finds her living in an Eskimo town, learning Yup'ik mythology, in order to perform in the Winter Ceremony at which traditional songs and stories told by old men are punctuated by masked dancers and drums; and then in Canada, attempting to perform funeral rites for a dead bird in an insane asylum; only to end up in Los Angeles, where she learns the basics of Japanese Noh theater and performs a ritualized masked dance ending in a hara-kiri as she strips her Noh robes and reveals her white kimono stained with blood.

Back in Buenos Aires in the guise of Antígona Furiosa in 1986, she reveals that she is unable to die: she first undoes the noose on her neck and ends by furiously hanging herself again as she proclaims she will return a thousand times to bury her dead. Across the Andes and through Chile on her way to Texas in 1987, she picks an attire custom-made for her to embody the Greek peasant Sofia, who is given the choice to surrender and save her grandson's life—instead, she lets the child and herself be killed. In 1988, as Melissa, an expatriate from the imaginary African country of Amandla (which means "power to the people"), she tells ancient African stories to an audience in England. In 1992 the possibility of engaging in a dialogue with women attracts her to a stage in Lisbon where she meets three fellow travelers: Juliette, Inés de Castro, and Medea. Across the Atlantic again, she travels through the United States, first landing in New York in 1993 as Anita, a Puerto Rican immigrant inhabiting the space of the doomed homeless urban underclass by living in a park, where she tries to properly bury her lover. After passing through Maine and trying on Mayan headdresses in 1994, she flies to Atlanta, where in an imaginary town in northern Nigerian Yorubaland, she arrives along with Yoruba goddess Yemoja to observe how her African sister Tègònni relives her drama in nineteenth-century British colonized Nigeria. She tells Tègònni's sister that she has come to see her because she "has traveled the same route before." She cannot but be puzzled by how times both have and have not changed as she is obliged to contend at once with the modern and ancient technologies of power and zones of undeath.

Lost in thought about the uncanny resemblance of her routes, in 1995 she arrives in India to sit in Manipur in front of a banner with the image of Manipur's first king, symbol of the nationalist resistance to Hinduization and Indianization. Perhaps the meditation on her persistence prompts her to take a rest and in 2000 she decides to let a Peruvian Ismene tell the story from her own point of view. But eclectic and electric as she has always been, she does not wait until the end of that same year to wake up from her nap to learn how to play electric guitar, spray graffiti on the walls, and sing rock songs in a future 2015 Los Angeles. In 2002 she takes up tango lessons in an economically panicked Buenos Aires, a city she knows so well; she then experiments with modern dance and Chinese music as she meets the three Fates at the beginning of time in New York; and finally makes another visit to Catalonia, where Creon kills her with his own hands.

The year 2003 brings her a thrilling surprise: She is taken for the first time to meet the legendary Scheherazade in Egypt, a woman with whom she has for centuries so much longed to share the fearful solitude in the face of death that she knows they have both experienced like no one else. Perhaps it is Scheherazade who suggests she take two trips that same year: first to perform in Ireland according to a Middle Eastern scenario projecting the Palestine conflict on a megascreen at the back of the stage; followed by an appearance in Gujarat, India, against the backdrop of screens with images of the Gujarat holocaust. She is horrified at the vandalism against Muslim mosques and the pogroms against the Muslim population, which remind her of those in Germany against the Jews, and so she joins the banished Muslim victims in a refugee camp set in a Muslim graveyard. In 2004 she incarnates a persecuted Arab woman in Damascus; challenges her own multiple Creons and Ismenes in Tokyo; addresses the whole noble globe pointing at the modern presences of the ancient undead from a stage in Ireland; and then tours the United States from California—where she learns from her Asian cast tai chi, wushu, kung fu, Falun Gong exercises, and Chinese opera in a Berkeley theater—to New York—where she performs in five short pieces whose narratives incorporate characters as diverse as an African widow condemned to die by stoning in accord with Islamic law and a black woman asking to be given a war medal for her dead brother in order to have something to bury in his place. She ends up at the Mexican border, where she tries to bury her sister, a female worker who has joined the victims of what is now known as the "femicide" in Ciudad Juárez.

Never having forgotten her German sojourn in 1947, she decides in 2006 to stop by Northern Italy, at the so-called "Gothic Line" the Nazis built in World War II to defend their ranks from the Allies coming from southern Italy. She then stops in Turkey, distraught by finding a solution to the Kurdish minority problem; moves on to Ramallah, fifteen kilometers northeast of Jerusalem, to witness war-torn Palestine; and finally makes it all the way to Colombia, doubling herself to protest both class, racial, and gender conflicts all at once. As I write this prologue in 2008, she watches Ismene on stage in Chicago; she brings the peasant widow Sofia to the stage of New York; and she takes a long wanted trip to Australia trying on Maori features to defend the long-lasting struggle for the human rights of the continent's indigenous peoples.

I am most certain that Antigone would disapprove of my not having exhausted all the scenarios she has visited in the last five decades, as well as my closing this prologue without finding out where in the world she is at this very moment, no doubt still deep in thought about the uncanny familiarity that she feels between our time and her ancient story. In closing this prologue, I want to say to her, wherever she is, that I, too, cannot help but feel unsettled at our apparent need to awaken her again and again. That is why I will continue trying, like so many other women and men, to imagine a world in which Antigone can cease being undead: A world where she can either rest in peace—or live.

Works Mentioned

The works cited in the following list, which are in order of appearance, are not exhaustive, but rather a representative selection for the purposes of this prologue. I have included the author's country of origin wherever this is different from the place of publication, and the year in which the text was originally written in cases where this differs from the year of publication. All references are dramatic texts unless otherwise noted. I wish to thank, in alphabetical order, Nadia Altschul, Inês Alves Méndez, Verónica Azcue Castillón, Onur Bakiner, Geetanjali Chanda, Kamari Clarke, Helene Foley, Margaret Litvin, John MacKay, Erin Mee, Edgar Melgar, Esteban Restrepo, Montserrat Roser-i-Puig, and Josefina Vázquez Arco, for their help in tracing Antigone's journeys; and last, but not least, Fanny Söderbäck, for inviting me to participate in this collection.

Pemán, José María. *Antígona*. In *Antígona y Electra*. Madrid, Spain: Ediciones Alfil, 1953 (1945).

Dantas, Júlio. *Antígona: Peça em 5 atos*. Lisbon, Portugal: Livraria Bertrand, 1946.

Brecht, Bertold. *Antigonemodell*. Berlin, Germany: Gebrüder Weiss, 1949 (1947).

Alexandrou, Aris. *Antigone*. In *Not Mincing Words (1937–1975)*, 19–72. Athens, Greece: Vergos 1977 (1951).

Marechal, Leopoldo. *Antígona Vélez*. Buenos Aires, Argentina: Editorial Sudamericana, 1970 (1951).

García Márquez, Gabriel. *La Hojarasca* (novella). Barcelona, Spain: Mondadori, 3rd ed., 2000 (Colombia, 1951).

Morisseau-Leroy, Félix. *Antigòn an Kreyòl*. Nendeln, Liechtenstein: Kraus Reprint, 1970 (Haiti, 1953).

Pedro, António. *Antígona*. In *Teatro Completo*, edited by António Brás Oliveira, 255–330. Lisbon, Portugal: Impr. Nacional-Casa da Moeda, 1981 (1954).

Espriu, Salvador. *Antígona*. Barcelona, Spain: Editorial Empúries, 1985 (1955).

Andrade, Jorge. *Pedreira das almas: Peça em dois atos e quatro quadros*. Rio de Janeiro, Brazil: AGIR, 1960 (1957).

Steiner, Rolando. *Antígona en el infierno*. León, Nicaragua: Universidad Nacional, 1965 (1958).
de Zavalía, Alberto. *El límite*. Buenos Aires, Argentina: Librería Huemul, 2nd ed., 1973 (1958).
Domínguez, Franklin. *Antígona-Humor*. In *Teatro: Espigas Maduras*, 81–128. Santo Domingo, Dominican Republic: Sociedad de Autores y Compositores Dramáticos, 1968 (1961).
Karvaš, Peter. *Antigone a tí Druhí*. Bratislava, Slovakia: Slovenský spisovatel', 1962 (Greece, 1961).
Smole, Dominik. *Antigone*. Ljubljana, Slovenia: Društvo slovenskih pisateljev, 1988 (1961).
Kamau Brathwaite, Edward. *Odale's Choice*. Ibadan, Nigeria: Evans Brothers, 1967 (Barbados, 1962, written in Ghana).
Wybot, Roger. *Antigone*. Paris: Denoël, 1965.
Rengifo, César. *La fiesta de los moribundos*. Caracas, Venezuela: Asociacíon de Escritores Venezolanos, 1970 (1966).
Zambrano, María. *La tumba de Antígona* (prose drama). Madrid, Spain: Mondadori, 1989 (1967, written in Mexico).
Brecht, Bertolt. *Antigone*. Translated by Judith Malina. New York: Applause Theatre Books, 1990 (performed by The Living Theatre of Judith Malina and Julian Beck in the United States, 1967).
Rafael Sánchez, Luis. *La pasión según Antígona Pérez*. Río Piedras, Puerto Rico: Editoral Cultural, 1983 (1968).
Triana, José. *Detrás queda el polvo*. Unpublished manuscript (Cuba, 1968).
Fuentes Mares, José. *La joven Antígona se va a la guerra*. In *Teatro: La emperatriz*, 57–105. Mexico City, Mexico: Editorial Jus, 1969 (1968).
Andrade, Jorge. *As Confrarias*. São Paulo, Brazil: Editôria Perspectiva, 1970 (1969).
Cavani, Liliana. *I cannibali* (motion picture). Italy: 1971.
Demirel, Kemal. *Antigone*. Istanbul, Turkey: Tekin Publishing, 1973.
Fugard, Athol, John Kani, and Winston Ntshona. *Statements: Sizwe Banzi Is Dead, the Island, and Statements after an Arrest Under the Immorality Act*, 45–77. New York: Theater Communications Group, 1986 (South Africa, 1973).
Rendra, Willibrordus Surendra Broto. *Antigone*. In *Antigone / Sophokles; diterjemahkan oleh Rendra*. Jakarta, Indonesia: Pustaka Jaya, 1976 (1974).
Chamoiseau, Patrick. *Une manière d'Antigone*. Unpublished manuscript (Martinique, 1975).
de la Rica, Carlos. *La razón de Antígona*. Madrid, Spain: El Toro de Barro, 1980.
Bergamín, José. *La sangre de Antígona*. In *Obra esencial*, edited by Nigel Dennis, 335–373. Madrid, Spain: Turner, 2005 (1983).
Elizondo, José Martín. *Antígona entre muros*. Madrid, Spain: Sociedad General de Autores España, 1988.
Comamala, Romà. *Antígona*. In *Teatre*. Barcelona, Spain: Publicacions de l'Abadia de Montserrat, 1988 (1986).
Riaza, Luis. *Antígona . . . ¡Cerda!*. Madrid, Spain: La Avispa, 1986 (1983).
Paulin, Tom. *The Riot Act*. London: Faber and Faber, 1985 (Ireland, 1984).
Matthews, Aidan Carl. *Antigone*. Unpublished manuscript (Ireland, 1984).

Kennelly, Brendan. *Antigone*. Newcastle upon Tyne, UK: Bloodaxe Books, 1986 (Ireland, 1984).

Murphy, Pat. *Anne Devlin* (motion picture). Ireland: 1984.

Hunsacker, Dave. *Yup'ik Antigone*. Unpublished manuscript (United States, 1984).

Doi, Yuriko. *Antigone*. Unpublished manuscript (Japan, 1984, written in the United States).

Watson, Sheila. "Antigone." *In Five Stories*, 49–65. Toronto, Canada: Coach House, 1984.

Gambaro, Griselda. *Antígona furiosa*. In *Teatro*, 195–217. Buenos Aires, Argentina: Grupo Editorial Norma, 2002 (1986).

Dorfman, Ariel, and Tony Kushner. *Viudas*. Buenos Aires, Argentina: Ediciones de la Flor, 1996 (Chile/United States, 1987). Adaptation from the novel *Viudas* by Ariel Dorfman. Mexico City, Mexico: Siglo XXI, 1981.

Bemba, Sylvain. *Noces posthumes de Santigone*. In *Theater and Politics: An International Anthology*, edited by Sylvain Bemba and Erika Munk, 1–70. New York: Ubu Repertory Theater, 1990 (Congo, 1988).

Dionísio, Eduarda. *Antes que a noite venha*. Lisbon, Portugal: Cotovia, 1992.

Glowacki, Janusz. *Antigone in New York*. New Haven, CT: Yale University Press, 1995 (Poland, 1993, written in the United States).

Stump, Walter R. *Oh Antigone*. Unpublished manuscript (United States, 1994).

Òsófisan, Fémi. *Tègònni: An African Antigone*. Lagos, Nigeria: Concept Publications, 2007 (1994, first performed in the United States).

Premchand, Nongthombam (director). *Antigone*. Unpublished manuscript (Manipur, India, 1995).

Watanabe, José. *Antígona: versión libre de la tragedia de Sófocles*. Lima, Peru: Yuyachkani: Comisión de Derechos Humanos, 2000.

Kurup, Shishir. *An Antigone Story: A Greek Tragedy Hijack*. Unpublished manuscript (United States, 2000).

Huertas, Jorge. *Antígonas: linaje de hembras*. Buenos Aires, Argentina: Editorial Biblos, 2002.

Wellman, Mac. *Antigone*. Manuscript available online at http://www.macwellman.com/images/antigone.pdf (United States, 2002).

Coca, Jordi. *Antígona*. Barcelona, Spain: Edicions Proa, 2002.

Yehya Effat, and Amel Fadji. *Once Upon a Time*. Unpublished manuscript (Egypt, 2003).

Morrison, Conall. *Antigone*. Unpublished manuscript (Ireland, 2003).

Kapur, Anuradha, and Ein Lall. *The Antigone Project*. Unpublished manuscript (Gujarat, India, 2003).

Sa'ad, Jihad. *Antigone's Emigration*. Unpublished manuscript (Syria, 2004).

Miyagi, Satoshi. *Antigone*. Unpublished manuscript (Japan, 2004).

Heaney, Seamus. *The Burial at Thebes*. London: Faber and Faber, 2004 (Ireland, 2004).

Lee, Cherylene. *Antigone Falun Gong*. Unpublished manuscript (United States, 2004).

Hartman, Karen, Chiori Miyagawa, Caridad Svich, Lynn Nottage, and Tanya Barfield. *The Antigone Project*. Unpublished manuscript (United States, 2004).

de la Rosa, Perla. *Antígona: las voces que incendian el desierto*. In *Cinco Dramaturgos Chihuahuenses*, edited by Guadalupe De la Mora. Juárez, Mexico: Fondo Municipal Editorial Revolvente-Municipio de Juárez, 2005 (2004).

Zeta, Archivio. *Antigone*. Unpublished manuscript (Italy, 2005).
Tekand, Şahika. *Euridice'nin Çığlığı* ("Eurydice's Cry"). Unpublished manuscript (Turkey, 2006).
Abul Su'ood, Mohamed. *Antigone in Ramallah . . . in Beirut*. Unpublished manuscript (Egypt, 2006).
Ariza, Patricia. *Antígona*. Unpublished manuscript (Colombia, 2006).
Menekseoglu, Jeremy. *Ismene*. Unpublished manuscript (United States, 2008).
Dorfman, Ariel. *Widows*. London: Sceptre, 1997 (Chile, performed in the United States).
Kohn, Chris (director), Seamus Heaney (author). *The Burial at Thebes* (performed in Australia, 2008).

Part I

Between Past and Future

Feminist Politics in the Private and Public Realms

1

After Antigone

Women, the Past, and the Future of Feminist Political Thought

Catherine A. Holland

"The task of the theoretical imagination," as Sheldon Wolin wrote nearly thirty years ago, "is to restate new possibilities."[1] Wolin's formulation is especially apt for the concerns that prompt this chapter because it captures the sense in which political theorists revisit the thought of former eras and seemingly distant problems, only to turn that thought and those problems toward more current affairs. Such an activity is not without its complications, of course. As Wolin also observed, whenever we mine past texts as resources for evaluating contemporary concerns, the danger is that the "persistent and contemporaneous influence" of those texts can limit our political vision and thus narrow our political horizons, a danger that the past will overfill the present, shrinking rather than expanding the space of political possibility.[2]

The ambiguity of past texts, their ability both to enable and to foreclose political vision, is of particular concern to feminist political theorists, who are committed at minimum to the belief that women matter politically because within the Western theoretical tradition the figure of Woman appears not to open up political possibility, but on the contrary to preclude it. This is especially true in the modern tradition, where women hold the paradoxical place of representing both the necessary condition of politics and its prepolitical, even antipolitical, other.

A longer version of this chapter was originally published in *American Journal of Political Science,* vol. 42, no. 4 (1998). This modified version has been approved by the author. Reprinted with permission of the publisher.

Beginning in the late eighteenth century and continuing up until the present day, *Antigone* has served as the theoretical stage for reflection on a variety of conflicts and ambivalences seen as endemic to the modern condition: between the old and the new, family and state, conviction and obedience, sentiment and reason, women and men. And ironically enough, feminists have turned to *Antigone* in their efforts to engage and contest the marginal place assigned to women in the Western political tradition as an occasion to reflect on both the perils and the promise of trying to speak as feminists from within a tradition that does not easily accommodate feminist thought.

This chapter examines three readings of *Antigone* by feminist political theorists Jean Bethke Elshtain, Mary Dietz, and Linda Zerilli, each of whom sees in Antigone's acts a model for very different kinds of feminist politics. Interpreting Antigone as, in turn, the representative of an antiauthoritarian social feminism, a radical democracy with a feminist face, and a feminism of irreducible discursive otherness, their debate dramatizes both the generative power of Sophocles' tragedy and the rich and multivalent nature of feminist political speech. However, in deploying Antigone as the model for contemporary feminist politics, an archetypal figure from the distant past who can be transported into the present as the enabling ground of feminism, I argue that all three readings ultimately normalize the past, attenuating our distance from it by overlooking the profound degree to which Antigone is, in fact, unlike us. And Antigone's difference from us, her very strangeness to our present, is, on my reading, of greatest critical value to feminist thinkers of today.

This emphasis on Antigone's difference from us is what allows me to raise a series of questions about the symbolic significance of the past within contemporary feminist political theory. To what extent is feminist political thought dependent on securing an ontological ground from which we may speak? How might the project of identifying that ground in the past limit and constrain feminist political vision at least as much as it enables it? Finally, how can feminist political theorists "restate new possibilities" without reinstating the past? The remainder of the chapter seeks to answer these questions by reading *Antigone* in yet another way. Central to my reinterpretation of the play are two linked claims. First, the significance of Antigone's actions should be read against the place that her city, Thebes, occupied in Athenian tragedy. Thebes' role as the symbolic other of Athens throws new light on the nature of Antigone's dispute with Creon, and it also clarifies what is at stake in that dispute. Second, precisely because of the way in which Antigone speaks—without authority, in the vernacular of her city—her words and actions have the effect of opening up the space of the political in Thebes. I argue that it is to Antigone's "unwomanly" acts that contemporary feminist thinkers might turn in their own attempts to articulate a specifically feminist political vision.

Three Feminisms, Three Antigones, Three Pasts

Jean Bethke Elshtain opened the feminist debate about the meaning of *Antigone* for contemporary feminism in 1982, hoping to "advance a note of caution" against the feminist embrace of the state as exemplified by the National Organization of Women's initiative to have women included in the military draft.[3] The allure of inclusion, she suggests, is itself the consequence of an ancient defeat, namely, of the usurpation of power from "older, less universal forms of authority" like the family that value women as full "participant[s] in social life" (55). To embrace the public order without simultaneously contesting its terms, Elshtain insists, is to ignore the ancient wisdom of Antigone, "the woman who [threw] sand into the machinery of arrogant public power" (55). Antigone's defiance of her king marks a final, fatal attempt to defend the prerogatives of family and household against the "imperious demands and overweening claims of state power [that] run roughshod over deeply rooted values" (56). For Elshtain, *Antigone* chronicles the "final suppression of traditional female social worlds" (46); and in her view, a feminism that pursues assimilation not only bolsters state power but also violates a "primordial family morality" that "precedes and overrides the laws of the state" (53).

The task Elshtain proposes for modern feminists is "to see ourselves as Antigone's daughters" (59), as "maternal thinkers" (58–59) who reject amoral statecraft by working to preserve "the arena of the social world where life is nurtured and protected from day to day" (55). She counsels contemporary feminists to heed Antigone's challenge to her sister, Ismene: "And now you can prove what you are: A true sister, or a traitor to your family" (53). For Elshtain, Antigone's actions exemplify a social feminist defiance of the "impersonal, abstract, and rational standards" of statesmen, a feminism that tempers and chastens arrogant state power by humanizing and repersonalizing social life (51). Drawing on a tradition of activism that runs from Jane Addams through the Argentine Mothers of the Plaza de Mayo, Elshtain urges feminists to "break out of the rigidities into which current feminist discourse has fallen" (57), and to act in public on behalf of the concerns of household and family, of "human good and civic necessity."[4]

While Elshtain shows how the perspectives engendered by the concerns of the private sphere may be marshaled by feminists to campaign for limits on the power of the state, Mary Dietz questions the wisdom of Elshtain's renegotiation of the public-private divide. In failing to recognize the primacy of the political, Dietz argues, Elshtain ends up reinforcing and gendering an already exaggerated and "abstract split between the public and private realms."[5] Dietz shares Elshtain's criticism of the hierarchy and depersonalized bureaucracy of a centralized state that has exchanged participation for administrative efficiency.

However for Dietz, politics, not the family, is "primary to all other human activities, be they public or private" (27); feminists who reject the public realm to embrace the family forget that it is an engaged citizenry that "collectively and perpetually determine[s] the forever shifting boundaries of what is private and public" (28). Elshtain's designation of the household as the privileged space of feminist action misses, indeed, *dis*misses the very venue of public politics that, Dietz argues, holds out the promise of feminist freedom and women's equality. In doing so, Elshtain inadvertently reduces politics to the activity of the state and thus reconfines women within the family and the household, idealizing those spaces as locations of women's power only by ignoring the myriad inegalitarian relationships that have historically prevailed within them. Oppressive political institutions such as the administrative state, Dietz insists, are best challenged not by "the language of love and compassion, but only [by] the language of freedom and equality" (34).

It follows, then, that Dietz's interpretation of *Antigone* sees in the heroine's actions a model for a more public and participatory "citizenship with a feminist face" (as in the title of her essay). In Dietz's reading, Creon has launched a concerted assault on Thebes' ancient democratic order, and Antigone acts not so much to defend the prerogatives of the family as to preserve "the customs and traditions of a collective civil life" (28–29). Read this way, Antigone "emerges not simply as a 'sister' whose familial loyalties pit her against a King, but as a citizen of Thebes whose defense of her brother is rooted in a devotion to the gods and to the ways and laws of her city" (29). The challenge, therefore, for contemporary feminists is to politicize rather than maternalize women's consciousness, and for Dietz this means that feminism must be guided by overtly public commitments.

The seemingly irremediable opposition between Elshtain's social feminism and Dietz's "citizenship with a feminist face," Linda Zerilli maintains in her own contribution to the debate, is not so much a split *within* feminism as it is a function of Elshtain's and Dietz's too ready adoption of the existing vocabulary of political thought. For Zerilli, their undertaking is an object lesson in the risks involved with feminist attempts to speak from within an established canon that forces them to "translate . . . the foreign, dissonant voice of Antigone into the more familiar, reassuring voice of mothers and/or citizens."[6] Both positions represent what Zerilli calls "counterfeit utterances" (257), problematic for their overdetermination in or by the discourse of the "political theory fathers" and thus for their bland inability to transmit the "more radical tones of feminist discourse" (258). Elshtain's turn to family and household, Zerilli maintains, embraces rather than challenges a patriarchal vision of female domesticity, and in the name of social feminism it contents itself with a mere shadow of the power women once held. Dietz's devotion to an Aristotelian language of civic friendship requires her to subsume all concern for the specificity of the feminine within sexual difference in order to argue for a model of citizenship that can be at best only occasionally and incidentally feminist. In the end, neither Elshtain's maternalist social feminism nor Dietz's finally sexually undifferentiated model of civic friendship manages to escape from the received categories of the Western theoretical tradition.

How, then, can feminists speak simultaneously within and against the traditions in which they work? What alternative modes of speaking does the tradition offer those who seek not to maintain it but to transform it? Such questions, Zerilli suggests, may be partially answered by rereading Sophocles' tragedy in yet another way. Drawing heavily on the work of Luce Irigaray, Zerilli reads the conflict between Antigone and Creon as "more tragic, more mutually exclusive" (256) than either Elshtain or Dietz can allow because Antigone preserves and deploys the last vestiges of a prepatriarchal past. Her actions memorialize an ancient matricide, a matricide most powerfully depicted by Aeschylus in his *Oresteia* trilogy. For Zerilli, the tale of the murder of Clytemnestra by her son, Orestes, recounts the final suppression of a matrilineal world, once secured by the "visible bond of blood," by an emerging patriarchy that reorganizes "family and state . . . around the invisible: the legal fiction of paternity" (256). In light of the events of the *Oresteia*, Zerilli concludes, Antigone's "discourse is not only criminal but suicidal in a political city which recognizes only the masculine voice" (256).

Central to Zerilli's argument is the conviction that while the language of the fathers of political theory obscures and suppresses its roots in this ancient matricide, it can never finally extinguish the violent terms of its own founding. Insofar as feminist political thinkers must speak in the terms made available by a tradition of discourse, they can never speak *simply* within those terms because feminist speech maintains other commitments. For Zerilli, feminists speak specifically as feminists only insofar as their speech, like that of Antigone, remembers and memorializes their "material beginnings in the original home of the mother" (262). Zerilli suggests a variety of discursive strategies that maintain this complex relation to a lost past: from the use of masks that demonstrate and exploit the ambiguities of political speech; to a mimesis that converts the terms of female subordination into feminist affirmation; and, finally, an evocative and provocative heteroglossia by which feminist speech resonates with multiple levels and strategies of meaning. Feminist politics thus conceived would both bring to light the original injury women have suffered at the hands of patriarchal power and demand redress through the revaluation of a once-suppressed feminine symbolic.

Although I agree with Zerilli that feminists "cannot *reclaim* but must transform a political conversation that inscribes their absence" (270) and that the positions promoted by Elshtain and Dietz fall too easily into the received categories of the Western canon, there is a sense in which Zerilli's project also moves in a reclamationist rather than a transformative direction. And it does so, curiously enough, in ways not so very different from Elshtain and Dietz.

Without minimizing the substantial differences among them, I want to suggest that a common critical strategy nonetheless runs throughout their readings: In distinct ways and to different degrees, each identifies in Antigone's actions the remnant of a lost past, a past that may serve as the ontological ground of feminist politics and thus inform and invigorate contemporary feminist practice. In each case, what is valued in Antigone's action is its ability to help us recall an almost prelapsarian moment of resistance unsullied by statist, antidemocratic, or patriarchal power. Put differently, Antigone's stance is understood to contain and command a prior moment, a past that feminist action in the present might to some degree reinstate. For these three feminists, the act of reading becomes an attempt to recapture what has been lost with Antigone in the past, and to return it to us in the present as a feminist politics. For Elshtain, Antigone draws on a "primordial family morality [that] precedes and overrides the laws of the state" in ways that contemporary feminists, too, may take up as "an affirmation of the dignity of the human person," and a reminder that "public policy has an impact on real human beings" (53, 59). For Dietz, the polis (not the family) has been eclipsed, and here Antigone represents and defends the "customs and traditions of a collective civil life" (53). Accordingly, Dietz urges modern feminists to look to a tradition of civic friendship "for a model of the kind of bond we might expect from, or hope to nurture in, democratic citizens" (32).[7] Finally, for Zerilli, Antigone "refuses to forget . . . a repressed matricide which haunts the terms of discourse in Creon's patrilineal and patriarchal state" (256), and Zerilli invites contemporary thinkers to reconsider their vocation "from the position of the woman who speaks but who refuses to forget or deny her material origins in the house" (254).

Of course, these three thinkers are not unique in taking recourse to an imagined past because such a device is a frequent strategy of radical feminism as well as a whole variety of nationalism.[8] However, while feminists have long debated the character of some prepatriarchal, pretyrannical past, little attention has been devoted to examining the consequences of such a strategy for feminist vision, for our ability, that is, to act to reshape the present and the future in explicitly feminist terms. This strategic reinstatement of the past does not serve feminism well because it overcommits feminists to a backward-looking and reclamationist rather than a transformative imagination. In their various attempts to resurrect Antigone as a model for contemporary feminism, neither Elshtain, nor Dietz, nor even Zerilli allow her disruptive course of action to remain disruptive. On the contrary, each discovers in Antigone's acts a register of order that echoes the past, and each embraces that past as a counterprinciple of order, seeking to reinstate it as the ground of a feminist politics that might redeem our present.

The allure of ancient texts for contemporary thinkers is, as Friedrich Nietzsche put it, their untimeliness, their capacity for "acting counter to our time and thereby acting on our time and, let us hope, for the benefit of a time to come."[9] The figure of Antigone is a powerful one because it provides contemporary feminists with a set of possibilities now foreclosed, a language of politics no longer in use, although importantly, not yet completely forgotten. Yet, however much this strategy of mining the past for critical resources enables Elshtain, Dietz, and Zerilli to think outside the limits of the present, I am concerned that they do so in ways that unnecessarily—and paradoxically—normalize the past, eliding what is most distinctive about it. The attempt to recover the past for the present risks losing sight of the important distinctions between past and present that motivated their inquiry in the first place. By escorting an ancient heroine into the present moment, they make familiar what initially attracted them by its strangeness, assimilating past with present by reasserting the past as the ontological ground for contemporary feminism.

If we are concerned with developing a transformative feminist politics, one that enables us to think and act in ways that take place within, but do not reinstate, the terms and constraints of either the past or the present, then we need to cultivate the ability to view the past differently, to establish a relation of difference with the past in ways that retain its strangeness and its unfamiliarity. We will find that such a strategy helps us to view not only the past, but also the present, as strange, as problematic, as something other than the given, logical, or even necessary culmination of prior events. Feminists cannot afford to forget that the most politically charged of all moments is the present, that the connection between past and present is neither logical nor chronological but *political.* As it happens, the tragedy of *Antigone*, read differently, may help us to understand this point and to think differently about the way we resort to the past in our attempts to transform politics in the present.

In this regard, we should try to understand both *Antigone* and "the past" its heroine comes to represent in other, more radical—feminist and democratic—terms. Antigone's actions may be read as a mobilization of the past that does not reinstate it but instead relegates it to the past once and for all. Antigone does not so much represent an idyllic past as exemplify her distance from it and her differences with it. Antigone's actions neither reinstate nor memorialize the past but rather resignify it. Her actions do not preserve and restore but instead refocus and reorient the traditions of her House and her city. In *Antigone* there is redemption neither *of* nor *from* the past; rather, the tragedy shows us what it means to disclose a political *present.*

Athens' Thebes

If mistaking Antigone for a figure who speaks for some familial, pretyrannical, or prepatriarchal past is all too easy, this may be due at least in part to the place that she occupies within her city and the place, moreover, that her city occupies in the Athenian tragic imagination. As Froma I. Zeitlin has suggested, the cities of Thebes and Argos, the respective settings of the *Oedipus* and the *Oresteia* cycles, hold special significance in Athenian tragedy. Both are theaters for the staging of distinctly non-Athenian, nondemocratic political possibilities and their fateful consequences.[10] Of the three cities, Thebes is by far the most corrupt. It is, on Zeitlin's account, beyond redemption. Those who remain in Thebes are mired in a place where the endless repetition of the past makes escaping it impossible, and for this reason Zeitlin denominates Thebes the city of "Eternal Return" (150). "Time in Thebes," she observes, "returns always and again to its point of departure, since it can never generate new structures and new progeny that can escape the paradigmatic patterns of the beginning." The "past inevitably rules" over the future, over the possibility of new beginnings, over the city's prospects of departing from its endless cycle of self-identical repetition (153).

That the crises of family and state; of identity and citizenship; and of past, present, and future dramatized in Sophocles' *Oedipus* cycle should take place not in Athens but in Thebes is no coincidence. The problems in Thebes, as Zeitlin puts it, "started at the very beginning," in Thebes' autochthonous founding (141).[11] Beginnings, in fact, lie at the heart of Thebes' problems, problems that cycle through one generation only to be reconstituted and repeated by the next: In contrast to the Athenians, who imagined a democratic future by negotiating a break from the past and their myths of origin,[12] Thebans are caught perpetually in their own past, unable to break with it, unable to even see the need to break free.

In Thebes, the past suffocates the present, it suffocates politics. Thebans have developed no viable political institutions, and they adhere to no canon of law (147). Consequently, they have no means of engaging the tensions between identity and difference. "Unable to incorporate outsiders into its system and locked into the priority of the blood relations of the *genos* [family], Thebes endlessly shuttles between the extremes of rigid inclusions and exclusions on the one hand and radical confusions of difference on the other," Zeitlin writes (148). In many ways, the problems within the House of Laius condense and contain the larger, more collective ills of the city. Indeed, Thebes' place in Athenian tragedy can be brought into greater focus in terms of the tale of Oedipus.

Oedipus' actions effectively collapse all boundaries—spatial, temporal, and finally moral—because his crimes are committed as much against the polis as the House. In patricide, Oedipus commits regicide as well; in incest, he recirculates his parents' blood through his mother once more, (re)producing in greater concentration within the next generation Apollo's original curse on his family and his city. As Peter Euben puts it, Oedipus "occupies two generations at once" and thus lives not "in a progress of years, but on a coincident plane of diachrony and synchrony."[13] Like his city, Oedipus is self-engendering: Husband to his mother, he becomes his own father, and brother to his own children. Thebes, the city that "respects no laws or institutions" (147), and Oedipus, the man who "collapses space and time into perverse singularity,"[14] come together in a shared principle of reproduction that privileges the selfsame as both origin and destination. Autochthony and incest have in common the ideal of a self-originary, self-referential, self-generating, self-identical, self-continuous, and finally, self-enclosed narrative of beginnings that has nowhere to go except back to its original starting point. Oedipus, a seeker of "a place where he might be at home, where he might truly belong" (131–132), finds in Thebes a place that is at once too much of and yet not enough of a home—too much because his "adopted" family and city turn out to have been his original abode all along; not enough because in Oedipus' case the embrace of that home not only fails to bring him redemption, but introduces him deeper into precisely those crimes from which he must be redeemed. Finally, it is to Athens rather than Thebes that Oedipus must retreat in search of redemption for his crimes, and it is in Athens that Oedipus, like Orestes before him, gains the necessary distance from home that enables him to develop his sense of justice.

Events in Thebes are especially significant for Athenians because this theatrical Thebes is the site onto which Athenians displaced their deepest and most profound concerns about their own polis; in short, Thebes represented what Athens might become if its citizens failed to engage the problems of democracy in thoughtful and creative ways. I want to suggest, as well, that within Athens' Thebes, the figure of Antigone holds a special significance because her speech and actions partake of the Theban tradition in ways that complexly reorder them.

Thebes' Antigone

The *Oedipus cycle* dramatizes the degree to which change in a place such as Thebes is as impossible as it is unthinkable, yet its concluding work, *Antigone*, may be read as a meditation about unthinkable change and the terms in which it might in fact be made possible. In it, Antigone and Creon each produce a competing discourse of kinship and citizenship, of family and polis, and by doing so each promotes a distinct vision of the city's future that attempts to alter the course of Theban time. In neither case, however, is the language of family as fully opposed to that of city as Elshtain and Dietz would have it, rather their respective discourses negotiate—to radically different effect—the peculiar relationship between the two that pertains in Thebes. In the end, neither Antigone nor Creon emerges victorious; however, while Creon's failures may be seen as the defeat of an attempt to impose a wholly new order on the city, Antigone's work to different effect. Where Creon fails in his attempt to rebuild Thebes on a foundation of distinctions that are rigid, and rigidly gendered, Antigone's speech and actions deploy difference, particularly sexual difference, in novel ways. Although Zerilli is right to claim that Antigone's speech recalls what we might call the "old" ways, far from reinstating the past her actions suggest the possibility of a new beginning and offer to Thebans the opportunity to set aside a past that is otherwise inescapable.

Creon, son of the House of Menoeceus and brother of Jocasta, ascends to power under what the chorus calls "the new conditions given by the gods"[15]—as the warrior who oversaw the defense of Thebes against its Argive attackers. In his opening speech, Creon traces the lines of succession on which he rests his claim: from Laius to Oedipus, from Oedipus to Eteocles, and then on to himself, "by reason of my kinship with the dead" (19). Yet Creon cannot assume power in precisely the same terms as had his nephews, for the nature of Creon's kinship to the House of Laius is different; it is affinal rather than ancestral. The Greek text denotes a break in Creon's genealogy, indicating a gap in lineage between Oedipus and his sons on the one hand, and Creon on the other. Into this break the Lloyd-Jones translation inserts the phrase, "with my sister as his wife" (19). This inserted passage not only smoothes over and obscures the discontinuities in Creon's genealogy, but it also points to what is novel about Creon's new order. The appearance of an unbroken line from Laius to Creon is achieved by Creon's replacement of ties of blood and ancestry with the legal fiction of marriage, and his new order thus instrumentalizes kinship as a function of law. These "new conditions given by the gods," but pronounced by Creon, regard women as passive conduits of kinship: not Jocasta but her marriage(s) link Creon to Laius and his House. Creon's new order relies on the formal exclusion of women from both political and familial authority.

It replaces the rule of tradition with the rule of law by transforming the terms of kinship that organize family and city. In the new Thebes, kinship no longer signifies a shared ancestry, but instead establishes the links that relate men to one another through marriage—links that not only depend on and formalize women's presence, but that also require and enforce their invisibility in both House and city. Where the law of marriage links men, it also establishes juridical distinctions between men and women. As the founder of this new order, Creon enshrines himself as the enforcer of a whole series of distinctions conferred by the state: woman and man, old and new, dead and living, enemy and friend. Creon's law seeks to simplify and untangle the dense web of relations and events that characterized the Thebes of Oedipus' rule. But where the Thebes of the House of Laius muddled all distinctions, the Thebes of Creon's making draws them too sharply. This new order is too orderly, marked as it is by distinctions that are really oppositions, politically congealed in and through Creon's law, impervious to reason, human action, or even death. "An enemy is never a friend, even when he is dead," Creon insists to Antigone (51).

Creon imprisons himself within his oppositions, and his intransigence and inflexibility foster only failure. The gods do not reward him in his brash attempt at imposing a new order, but instead remind him painfully of his own affective commitments to family, as well as to those he has declared traitors, enemies, and transgressors. Not the living but the dead bring down Creon's rule: Only in light of his son's and, later, his wife's suicide does Creon come to recognize his own investments in the House. "Woe for the errors of my mistaken mind, obstinate and fraught with death," he laments, bearing Haemon's body back into the city. "Ah, my son, young and newly dead, alas, alas, you died . . . through my folly . . ." (119). By their deaths, Haemon and Antigone strike directly at the foundations of Creon's new order, namely, the power of the state to regulate kinship through marriage, because they consummate their marriage not with the imprimatur of Creon's state but instead "in the house of Hades" (117). Creon is condemned to live out his days bereft of kin, "an animated corpse" (111) reproached by the dead for crimes from which there can be no expiation.

If, in his attempt to rid Thebes of its curse, Creon initiates a fundamental reorganization of the House, of kinship, and of the state, his antagonist, Antigone, might well be understood as the defender of the old ways, as the spokesperson for a past that has been superseded by Creon's new order. The important interpretive question, however, is not *whether* Antigone's speech recalls the past—indeed, her speech calls on multiple and perhaps competing pasts—but rather how her speech effects something new, something decisively unfamiliar to Athens' Thebes. Antigone's actions, in effect, break the cyclical course of Theban time even if her words seem to reiterate it. Her acts deploy difference—and sexual difference—in ways that both undercut and overflow Creon's rigid simplifications and gendered distinctions of home and state, and in doing so Antigone effects a departure from, rather than a repetition of, the past that her speech recalls.

Antigone's difference, her departure from the eternally repetitive spiral in which her city is caught, is carefully articulated in the vernacular of her city, her people, and their gods. Significantly, her acts entail both a repetition and an inversion of Orestes' in the *Oresteia* and of Oedipus' in *Oedipus at Colonus*. Unlike those tragic heroes before her, both of whom must travel to Athens to achieve the distance necessary to see things differently, Antigone finds a language that is specifically Theban, articulated in terms internal to the discourse of her city. Throughout the play Antigone defends, variously, her brother, her family, her city and its citizens, and their gods. Her language restates the entirety of the Theban tradition, yet she does not reinstate the prior order. Rather, she reassembles what is most familiar in Theban discourse in ways that heighten its strangeness, as well as her own, for any woman who speaks, who acts publicly in Creon's order, is "unwomanly."[16] Unable to claim the ground to speak for either the House or the polis, Antigone speaks her city's tradition complexly, with a difference, in terms that heighten the irony and liminality of her own position with regard to both House and polis.

By speaking and acting as she does, where she does, in ways that transgress the limitations placed on women in the Theban (as well as the Athenian) order, Antigone interferes in an instance where she has no formal right or standing. Her actions position her as a stranger, as one who acts without fully occupying the ground on which her actions take place. As Creon puts it, Antigone "act[s] apart,"[17] she "think[s] differently" (49) from other Thebans; for her part, Antigone likens herself to Niobe, "the Phrygian stranger" once married to a Theban king (81).[18] Yet her deployment of the multivocal traditions at work within Thebes position her as not an absolute but a *familiar* stranger to her own people, and her actions, although undertaken alone, work to open up and restore the public space.[19]

Antigone's speech has the effect not of reinstating a lost past, an old order that has been supplanted by Creon's edicts, but of reorienting the distinctively Theban order. Her complex reiteration of Theban traditions produces what Foucault calls a "minute deviation"[20] from them, a tiny difference that in this case makes a world of difference because her mobilization of an otherwise immobile past fundamentally alters the terms of that past and, thus, the terms of the Theban present and future. While Zeitlin's denomination of Thebes as the city of "Eternal Return" (150–167) may be an entirely appropriate description of that city under the rule of Laius, Oedipus, and his sons, it misses the effects of Antigone's deployment of sexual difference, which lends to her acts an irreducible and nonsimple dimension that affects their meaning in important ways. A woman, Antigone acts in ways that are explicitly *un*womanly (although not manly), in ways that contest and defy the highly constrained limitations placed on women's movements, in ways that compound and confound the orderliness of gender in Creon's Thebes.

Unwomanly acts such as Antigone's cannot simply be lost in past crimes; they cannot be confused with past rivalries of father and son, or brother with brother, because they are constitutively nonsimple. Even as her condemnation and disavowal of her sister echoes parricide, Antigone's insistence on securing her brother's place in Hades reverses, or at least tempers, the effects of another act of parricide. Furthermore, she does not—cannot—claim the power of the throne. As Euben has put it, her actions are "an-archic": They do not establish her as the new leader of Thebes, nor do they install her as the origin of a new order.[21] Not until Antigone's actions have transformed her from familiar to stranger can the curse of her House—and a course of action set into motion by a stranger who is and becomes a familiar—be broken. Where Oedipus' incest, his hyperfamiliarity, both shapes and destroys the polis, Antigone's strangeness—her groundlessness, her rhetorical stance, her defiance of Creon, her suicide—repeals the Oedipal order. In the end, Antigone's death returns to Thebans the possibility—if only the possibility—of acting and speaking freely, freedoms doubly obliterated by the tyranny first of Oedipus and later of Creon.

Antigone's actions bring to an end Thebes' otherwise endless cycle of beginnings. Her death strikes a note as paradoxical as her life: She who lived "neither among the mortals nor as a shade among the shades, neither with the living nor with the dead" (83) is sent, "unwept, friendless, unwedded" (85) to her "strange tomb" (83). Although Antigone's words and actions are worked out in distinctively Theban terms, they produce fundamentally different effects because they do not introduce another generation into the cycle of Theban time.[22] Rather, Antigone takes with her to her grave the curse on Thebes and its ruling House. Of her doomed family she is "the last" (87)[23] and in this sense, even her name is significant, for Anti-gone translates to mean "anti-generation."[24] Its significance resides, not in its announcement of Antigone's renunciation of gender as Arlene Saxonhouse suggests, but precisely in the connotations of sexual difference that it bears.[25] Antigone's fate is not to regenerate and, thus, recirculate the blood of her House, but rather to die childless, having refused the terms imposed on the life of her city by both the curse placed on her family and by a tyrant whose acts sought to vanquish that curse and conquer the gods who pronounced it. Her actions break the endlessly repetitive cycle of Theban crimes and in doing so transform her from *genos* to *xenos*, a known stranger (if not, quite, a foreigner) on familiar territory.

What Valerie Hartouni calls "Antigone's Dilemma"[26] is precisely that—a situation where action and inaction alike harbor the consequence of noninnocence, where neither the womanliness of inaction advised by Ismene and demanded by Creon, nor the "unwomanliness" of public action offer any means of escape from tragedy. If Antigone cannot survive her own acts, her death returns to Thebans not the opportunity to begin yet again, but rather the opportunity to begin anew by continuing on different terms. What is generated by Antigone's dispute with Creon is the possibility not for a repetition of the past but for the clearing of a space we might call the political present, which appears "as if for the first time, in its profound difficulties and divisions . . . ripe with possibilities once foreclosed."[27]

A Different "Past"?

Rereading Sophocles' *Antigone* is a valuable enterprise for contemporary feminist political thinkers precisely because its heroine shows us how we may innovate from within a tradition; how we may speak through a set of languages handed down to us by disciplinary conventions that may not comfortably accommodate feminist politics; how we may employ those languages in ways that do not simply reiterate our own exclusion from those traditions, but instead remake them for the present. In doing so, we use the past not to legitimate our speech, not to establish it as our own, as an ontological foundation from which we may speak and act as feminists, but rather to establish our present as different from the past, to put an end to past inegalitarian, exclusionary doctrines and practices that make feminism appear impossible.

What, then, could treating the past as a relation of difference mean? As I have tried to suggest through my own reading of *Antigone*, feminist critics who must work within a canon of texts and textual practices may produce the critical present as distinct from its past(s) by looking to those moments, those texts, those "historical accidents" where difference emerges in ways that are at once irreducibly complex and yet also fully within the tradition(s) in which they reside. Surely *Antigone* in this regard is but one example of many. Feminist political thinkers may not—indeed, *do* not—share the same relationship to the "languages of the political theory fathers" as do our brothers, and yet we may nonetheless speak them *to produce a difference*, a countercurrent, in the very place where disciplinary practices may seem to ensure the continuity of the same. In this sense, we might view both Antigone and the disciplinary canon in which she resides as a "past from which we may spring rather than that from which we seem to have derived," to borrow an expression from Nietzsche.[28]

The past is a powerful and suggestive place, a place that we can neither fully escape nor strategically reinstate. It shows us that the present can be other than what it is or appears to be, and it can provide us with many of the tools and the terms we need to imagine something radically different from our present. But if in turning to the past we embrace it as the key to the political present, if we seek to reestablish its terms *as* our political present *in* our political present, we run the risk of normalizing the past and thus we rob it of its difference(s)—and in doing so we deprive ourselves of the very insights that we might draw from it.

In very different ways, Elshtain, Dietz, and Zerilli each look to some aspect of a past, and with those pasts to Antigone, to locate a space and a stance that contemporary feminists may reclaim as the ground of feminist political speech and action. As Hannah Arendt knew, however, the space in which politics takes place does not precede political action; it is brought into being by it.[29] In this sense, the ground of feminist politics need not—indeed, *cannot*—be settled on in advance.

If we look to Antigone for a link that might connect us with a prepatriarchal or preauthoritarian past, what Sophocles' heroine shows us is the necessity of suspending that linkage, of learning how to engage the past—and how to *value* the past—as a relation of difference lest we, like the people of Thebes, collapse temporal distinctions and by doing so lose ourselves as well as our capacity to judge and to act. Indeed, Antigone's turn to the past embodied in her articulation of a familiar Theban language brings that past to its long overdue terminus, to a conclusion that recalls past riddles and past experiences even as it reformulates them. The artistry of Antigone's response to the crises of her House and her city consists in her ability to find within her tradition the means by which she can effect a "minute deviation" from it, and thus cultivate a difference in the very place where difference was once most impossible in terms of the very language that makes it most necessary.

"What seems to have been forgotten," as Wolin reminded us nearly three decades ago, "is that one reads past theories, not because they are familiar and therefore confirmative, but because they are strange and therefore provocative."[30] If, in reading past texts, feminists look only for moments that help us assimilate the past to our present, we are bound to uncover only what we already have in common with those texts, and we engage only what is already most familiar to us. In doing so, we disregard—indeed, we obliterate—important opportunities to discover and to engage the play of difference, of sexual difference, within those texts and within that past. Like Oedipus conducting his inquiry into the murder of King Laius, we learn only what we already knew, we encounter only what we already recognize as our own, and we derive from the past a ground for feminist politics that confirms only what is already given. Feminist political theory so conceived is only then *truly* impossible because it is a politics deprived of vision, neglecting the challenge of *each* of its constitutive terms: feminism, politics, theory.

Notes

1. Sheldon S. Wolin, "Political Theory as a Vocation," *American Political Science Review*, vol. 63 (1969), p. 1082.

2. Sheldon S. Wolin, *Politics and Vision: Continuity and Innovation in Political Thought* (Boston: Little Brown, 1960), p. 26.

3. Jean Bethke Elshtain, "Antigone's Daughters," *Democracy*, vol. 2 (1982), p. 46. Hereafter, Elshtain references are given parenthetically within the text.

4. See Jean Bethke Elshtain, "Antigone's Daughters Reconsidered: Continuing Reflections on Women, Politics, and Power," in *Life-World and Politics: Between Modernity and Postmodernity*, ed. Stephen K. White (Notre Dame, IN: University of Notre Dame Press, 1989), pp. 229, 231–233.

5. Mary G. Dietz, "Citizenship with a Feminist Face: The Problem with Maternal Thinking," *Political Theory*, vol. 13 (1985), p. 25. Hereafter, Dietz references are given parenthetically within the text.

6. Linda M. G. Zerilli, "Machiavelli's Sisters: Women and 'the Conversation' of Political Theory," *Political Theory*, vol. 19 (1991), p. 257. Hereafter, Zerilli references are given parenthetically within the text.

7. Importantly, although Dietz marshals the past in her effort to reconstruct citizenship "with a feminist face," her understanding of the relationship between the state and a patriarchal order is significantly different than that posed by her interlocutors. Whereas Elshtain and Zerilli see central state and patriarchal authority as different expressions of the same phenomenon, for Dietz the rise of the state may coincide with, but is not intrinsically linked to, patriarchy.

8. See, for example, Adrienne Rich, *Of Woman Born: Motherhood as Experience and Institution* (New York: Norton, 1986); Gerda Lerner, *The Creation of Patriarchy* (New York: Oxford University Press, 1986); and Mary O'Brien, *Reproducing the World: Essays in Feminist Theory* (Boulder: Westview, 1989). On nationalism, see Homi Bhabha, *Nation and Narration* (New York: Routledge, 1990); Benedict Anderson, *Imagined Communities: Reflections on the Origin and Spread of Nationalism* (New York: Verso, 1991); and Geraldine Heng and Janadas Devan, "State Fatherhood: The Politics of Nationalism, Sexuality, and Race in Singapore," in *Nationalisms and Sexualities*, ed. Andrew Parker, Mary Russo, Doris Summer, and Patricia Yaeger (New York: Routledge, 1992).

9. Friedrich Nietzsche, *Untimely Meditations*, trans. R. J. Hollingdale (Cambridge, UK: Cambridge University Press, 1983), p. 60.

10. Froma I. Zeitlin, "Thebes: Theater of Self and Society in Athenian Drama," in *Nothing to Do with Dionysos? Athenian Drama in Its Social Context*, ed. John J. Winkler and Froma I. Zeitlin (Princeton, NJ: Princeton University Press, 1990). Hereafter, Zeitlin references are given parenthetically within the text.

11. According to the Theban myth of origins, the city was established when Cadmus slew the dragon of Ares and sowed his teeth like seeds in the ground. From those seeds grew the Spartoi, who were torn by infighting; the five who survived became Thebes' first inhabitants, grown from the earth on the very spot where the city stood.

12. Page duBois, *Sappho Is Burning* (Chicago: University of Chicago Press, 1995), pp. 20–21; Eric Dodds, *The Greeks and the Irrational* (Berkeley: University of California Press, 1951).

13. J. Peter Euben, *The Tragedy of Political Theory: The Road Not Taken* (Princeton, NJ: Princeton University Press, 1990), p. 113.

14. Ibid., p. 103.

15. Sophocles, *Antigone*, trans. Hugh Lloyd-Jones (Cambridge, MA: Harvard University Press, 1994), p. 19. All references to the play are from this translation if nothing else is noted. Hereafter, *Antigone* references are given parenthetically within the text.

16. J. Peter Euben, *Corrupting Youth: Political Education, Democratic Culture, and Political Theory* (Princeton, NJ: Princeton University Press, 1997), p. 166.

17. Sophocles, *Antigone*, trans. Richard Claverhouse Jebb (New York: Bentham Books, 1982), p. 128.

18. According to Greek mythology, Niobe was the daughter of Tantalus, King of Sipylus. After having boasted about her superior progenitive capacities, Apollo and Artemis punished her, killing her children. As legend has it, her sorrow turned her to rock on Mount Sipylus, which continues to weep when snow melts.

19. I take issue here with Martha Nussbaum's conclusions that Antigone's actions are solitary and without public effect (Martha C. Nussbaum, *The Fragility of Goodness: Luck and Ethics in Greek Tragedy and Philosophy* [Cambridge, UK: Cambridge University Press, 1986]), although in Nussbaum's estimation this is not particularly damning.

Insofar as Antigone acts alone, Nussbaum suggests, unlike Creon she harms no one: "she may be strangely remote from the world; but she does no violence to it" (66). By contrast, *if* Antigone's actions can be said to be solitary ones (although Antigone herself contests this characterization when she claims that Thebans are sympathetic to her cause), their effects are neither private nor individual.

20. Michel Foucault, "Nietzsche, Genealogy, History," in *The Foucault Reader*, ed. Paul Rabinow (New York: Pantheon, 1984), p. 81.

21. Euben, *Corrupting Youth*, p. 166.

22. Ironically, Antigone's "success" lies in the fact that she does not "win" her dispute with Creon. Had events worked out differently, had Antigone persuaded Creon to allow her to bury her brother, had Antigone not been imprisoned and thus led to commit suicide, we have little reason to believe that the course of Theban time would have been altered at all. On the contrary, Antigone's marriage to her cousin Haemon would have introduced her family and her city into yet another cycle of Theban time, and a new generation into Thebes' endless cycle of beginnings.

23. Technically, Antigone is not "the last" of her family because her sister Ismene survives her. Insofar as Ismene has already capitulated to Creon's reorganization of power and kinship, however, she has arguably divorced herself from this strange family and thus normalized herself as, in the words of Slavoj Žižek, "the figure with which we can [most readily] identify" (Slavoj Žižek, *The Sublime Object of Ideology* [London: Verso, 1989], p. 117). For a discussion of Ismene's survival in ancient myth and in twentieth-century theater, see George Steiner, *Antigones* (New Haven, CT: Yale University Press, 1996), p. 148.

24. Seth Benardete, "A Reading of Sophocles' *Antigone*: I," *Interpretation*, vol. 4 (1975), pp. 156–157.

25. Arlene Saxonhouse, *Fear of Diversity: The Birth of Political Science in Ancient Greek Thought* (Chicago: University of Chicago Press, 1992), p. 69. Interestingly, Zeitlin reads this only as an (inevitable) repetition of the fate of Thebes, and as evidence of "Antigone's . . . overvaluation" of death (152). Saxonhouse, on the other hand, reads it as evidence of Antigone's refusal of gender, an attempt to "neuter herself" in her refusal to marry and give birth to a new generation of young Thebans (69).

26. Valerie Hartouni, "Antigone's Dilemma: A Problem in Political Membership," *Hypatia*, vol. 1 (1986), pp. 3–20.

27. George Shulman, "American Political Culture, Prophetic Narration, and Toni Morrison's *Beloved*," *Political Theory*, vol. 24 (1996), p. 312.

28. Friedrich Nietzsche, *The Use and Abuse of History*, trans. Adrian Collins (Indianapolis, IN: Bobbs-Merrill, 1949), p. 24.

29. Hannah Arendt, *The Human Condition* (Chicago: University of Chicago Press, 1958), pp. 199–207.

30. Wolin, "Political Theory as a Vocation," p. 1077. (Ed. note: At the publication of this volume, it has been *four* decades since Wolin's text was published).

2

On the Body of Antigone

Adriana Cavarero

In *Antigone* human corporeality and female identity cohere within a single—dreadful and apolitical—concept. Within the drama's contingency, the body that the city excludes and expels outside its walls is first, the dead body of Polyneices, and then the body of Antigone, buried alive. But its symbolic value is that of pure body: the unnerving realm of womanly power inscribed in raw life and in the fundamental code of blood. The conflict involves, on the one hand, the city built by men and, on the other, a body rooted in the female. The plot unwinds in an uncontrollable contest between violent expulsions and terrifying returns.

In its very founding categories, the political order of classical Greece clearly excludes a corporeality judged to be mere material support for the human capacity for language and thought, at the same time excluding women, insofar as they are "naturally" rooted in matters of the body. Sophocles' *Antigone* might then simply fit within the codes and symbolic framework of the age. Regarding these codes, however, the tragedy seems to evoke a series of ambiguous *contrapassi* and unresolved tensions. A body at the drama's center, expelled from the polis, comes back to invade the palace in large-scale slaughter, raising doubts about where, between the polis itself and the ancient law of blood, the true site of the uncanny (*deinon*) lies. The play crucially recounts the story of a body, a body that, both in its exclusion from the city and its return to it, takes on the ghastly guise of a corpse, both victorious and vanquished. This body disorders and disrupts through the foul dissolution of its flesh, which was evoked at the play's outset by the haunting figure of the unburied Polyneices.

A longer version of this chapter was originally published as chapter 1 of *Corpo in Figure* (Milan, Italy: Giangiacomo Feltrinelli Editoro, 1995), and in English translation in *Stately Bodies: Literature, Philosophy, and the Question of Gender,* trans. Robert de Lucca and Deanna Shemek (Ann Arbor: University of Michigan Press, 2002). This modified version has been approved by the author. Reprinted with permission of the publisher.

The clash between the polis and the body is here also a clash between order and disorder. This clash takes place in a tragic framework where the body plays the part of the prelogical and the dreadful, both cadaverous nausea and incestuous sexuality, blurring even into a myth concerning our animal origin. In a dramatic fiction in which the polis exhibits that which it has had to repudiate and fight against in order to arise, the body is vindicated by the figural emphasis it acquires through its own expulsion. Clearly, the body, here associated with the murky, carnal recesses of female power, is radically *distinct* from the polis, its tragic antithesis and exact opposite. No macrocosm encompasses the body and the polis in a superior embrace, nor does any image of one or the other weave analogies between them.

The irreconcilability of opposites, the extreme that constitutes opposites as *the* problem, is typical of tragedy. Thus between the polis and the body we find no reconciliation here. Rather, we see the radicalization of a conflict that squares off its two opponents against each other on a field of mutual incompatibility. And yet, precisely as tragedy and indeed perhaps to a degree greater than in any other tragedy, *Antigone* is wildly eccentric regarding the Greek vision of the "whole" that inscribes the nature of each thing within the cosmic order. This vision often links the body and the polis on the philosophical plane through various figurative correspondences and inaugurates, among other things, the long relationship between the corporeal figure and political metaphor. For these reasons the anomalous details of Sophocles' *Antigone* seem all the more numerous and significant. On the one hand, the tragedy represents the polis' mythical expulsion of a body that is uncanny by birth and that returns in the form of a corpse. On the other hand, the polis is denied that reclaiming of the body that would turn the corpus into a tamed, metaphorical figure of its order. This raises the question of whether tradition and *Antigone* are telling us two versions of the strange story that, over thousands of years, has linked the body with politics. It is an ancient tale, perhaps forgotten by the body-politic metaphor in the progressive fading of myth, but which Sophocles' text continues to illuminate with its significant and unorthodox irregularities.

An Absent Soul

A body is at the center of *Antigone*, that which is declared from the start as the object of the tragic contest: Polyneices' corpse. A dead body, or cadaver (*nekus*), but also a body (*soma*) that once belonged to a living man.[1] Strikingly absent on this threshold that leads to the dwelling of the departed, in this scene conjuring merciful burial, however, is the soul, the psyche. That man by the name of Polyneices who was once a living body is now *entirely* there, in his unburied body by the Theban walls.

In this tragic sequence hinged on the theme of burial, the absence of allusion to the psyche of the dead man seems exceedingly strange. It is so strange, indeed, that we must justify the word *entirely* (an equivocal and allusive term) when we adopt it in connection with Polyneices. We must confess that this word is merely a verbal expedient to avoid the category of the *individual,* or, in other words, of subjective *identity.* Both the term and the idea are indeed too modern to inhabit the ancient world without difficulty. Nonetheless, they are so alluring that we hazard using them, even at the price of continually tripping over them. Certainly, there is no reason why the critic cannot attempt a study of Greek foreshadowings of a theory of individuality, what we might call a dim etiology of the ego or even the tragic affirmation of the self in its individualization. Indeed a predictable appeal to the celebrated Hegelian reading of the text seems hardly out of place: the figure of Antigone is the emblem of the law of the family, whose sole rationale is the "individual as such." Here we see the particular individuality of the subject that has not yet "passed" into the political sphere. Precisely this recognition of the individual subject, especially as agent and as responsible source of its actions, constitutes the crux of Greek tragedy. So for the moment, linguistic caution allows us to say provisionally that Polyneices' individuality consists entirely of his unburied body.

Indeed, the decisive problem here seems to be the body that each of us *is* more than the body that each of us *has.* For enigmatically in this tragedy, a consanguine body verges on overstepping its own boundaries, on merging with the *genos* in a symbiotic union. On the hermeneutic plane of evidence, *Antigone* seems to express this problem in a strikingly absent psyche, thus in an unusually central body that, given the psyche's absence, can function onstage as absolute symbol. The radical opposition between Creon's and Antigone's reasoning appears most poignant in the emphasis Sophocles' tragic vision placed on this absolute corporeality. Their antithetical arguments concern what should be done with Polyneices' body, but the word *psyche* is never pronounced by either of them in their dialogic conflict over the dead man. As if the topic were merely a body to be buried, the conflict only over a body; as if the burial of a corpse, denied or permitted, would not irresistibly evoke in the Greek spectator the image of a psyche either departing toward a fated dwelling or lingering by the corpse.

The entire tradition concerning funeral rites in diverse forms from Homer to the Platonic myths and beyond tells of the soul's final voyage. The Sophoclean anomaly stands out all the more surprisingly, then, as a kind of reminder of the centrality of the body, here made forcibly explicit, and of its unrivaled figural power. The sister who wishes to grant burial to Polyneices, and Creon who forbids it, are in fact competing, with equal determination, for the fate of a dead body that seems to possess no psyche at all: neither in the sense of the Homeric duplicate image, nor as seat of that spiritual identity Plato and

Euripides recognized. Thus it appears that the centrality of the body in *Antigone*, precisely because of its surplus of meaning with respect to tradition, is meant to be the fulcrum of Sophocles' text. Indeed it is not hard to see how that central positioning of the body brings the rivals together. The symbolic power of the body, inasmuch as it is the substance of the individual and aside from the fact that it is now the corpse of a dead man, becomes the nontranscendable horizon of their struggle.

In the opposing positions of Antigone and Creon is a common and nearly obsessive regard for Polyneices' body, rendered all the more unusual and set in sharp perspective by the ostentatious silence concerning his soul. Largely as a result of this corporeal centrality, the gaze of the two opponents translates into the irreconcilability of two contrary visions, tragically acted out by Creon and Antigone. If it is true that the matter here is *only* the body, it is equally only over the body that the two gazes contend. Antigone's is a consanguineous way of seeing from an extremely close horizon already corporeally oriented and hinged on incest. While, in contrast, Creon's is a way of seeing from afar, a seeing through the impenetrable walls of the polis that has perhaps severed corporeal ties, or tamed their call.

The Incestuous Body

Antigone and Creon, the family and the state: these are the categories that (in Hegel's reading) the tragedy proposes, although the modern notion of the state does not well convey the sense of the Theban polis Creon ruled. The word *family*, which should describe a consanguineous principle of incestuous kinship, is also problematic.

Once we have abandoned the term *state* because of its inappropriateness, however, we must then make sure to distinguish between the ancient Theban polis as represented onstage, and the polis in the fifth century BCE when the play was presented. Sophocles' theater, in fact, arises within the context of the decisive democratic order of the classical city that chose Athens as its model. This is the familiar political structure that identifies itself with a limited group of free men and that has definitively expelled women from its androcentric sphere. This exclusion is precisely what is played out on stage and what constitutes one of the play's most genuinely tragic dimensions.[2] Another equally important feature is that the body is symbolically expelled from the polis along with the women. In that invaluable ideological manifesto of the city known as the funeral oration, the Athenian citizen in his political guise does not, in fact, have a body: "The *soma* was a gift of the city and the soldier's death clears the debt."[3] This body is, in any case, no longer living flesh in all its physicality, but pure abstraction. All the more, then, must we attend to the unusual emphasis in *Antigone* linking the theme of the body with the excesses of a feminine mask. That irregularity must be seen in the logic of an already liquidated past (which may be authentic or presumed, but is in any case active in the collective imaginary). The fearful reality of that past is now placed onstage to legitimate its definitive defeat.

Still more complicated is our recourse to the word *family*, a single term we use to translate two Greek nouns (*domos* and *oikos*) characterized by semantic slippage. At first they denote the social group connected by extended kinship and occupying the same "house." But they soon assume the meaning of "building" or the habitat shared by the master's family and his slaves.[4] This semantic shift, in which a genealogical term is absorbed by a nomenclature of territorial division, deals precisely with the emergence of the polis. The polis places itself squarely against the genealogical model of the extended family and upsets its configuration. Antigone finds herself at the beginning of this process, and Creon at the threshold of its end.

Saying that Antigone represents the initial stage of this movement is not enough, however. In the figure of Antigone, in fact, the family, although it is indicated sometimes with the term *domos*, is rooted in the notions of *genos* or *philia*, or rather in the concept of that consanguineous chain linking those who belong by birth to a common breed and who therefore share not only the same house, but also the same blood inscribed in *generation*. Even this, however, does not say enough because the degree of blood kinship upheld by the ancient exogamous model of marriage between cousins is radicalized in *Antigone* by the endogamous model of a generation whose sole source is maternal incest. Thus, in the skillful weaving of Sophocles' text, another more audacious anomaly disrupts the scene. Within the centrality of the body that has already emerged with absolute symbolic power, the play inscribes a consanguineous principle that stakes the extreme limits of the symbol on incest.

Put another way, Antigone and the principle of common blood ties that she (literally) incarnates take the already crucial theme of the body and develop it to its utmost symbolic capacity. This is done through an absolute representation of corporeality that in the end is revealed as the appropriate base for a family model centered on the Theban myth's closed and radical endogamy of incest. Nothing in this symbolic framework stays quietly in place, and nothing lets itself be docilely inscribed within the parameters of tradition. On the contrary, the anomalous and the dreadful invade a stage on which every element linked to the body seems to be blown out of proportion and highlighted as carnal excess, whether on the plane of birth or that of death.

Polyneices' dead body dominates the scene, but it is blood generated by the mother that polarizes the tragic action and creates its antithesis. The sister wishes to grant burial precisely to the "dead man born of my mother."[5] It is thus the power of blood that moves Antigone. This maternal identification forces her to self-sacrifice in order to carry out *her mother's desire* incarnated in the dead Polyneices.[6]

Ordinarily we point to the father, blinded by his own hand, and we invoke the race of Oedipus.[7] The necessarily masculine name of the family is the one known to the Theban polis. Within the family itself, however, and from Antigone's point of view, it can only be Jocasta, the mother, who initiates the blood lineage: so much a mother, in fact, that she is mother not only of her ill-starred last four children, but also of their father. Thus, from the daughter's point of view, as represented by Antigone, the father-brother Oedipus is overpowered by the common mother, Jocasta: for Oedipus, a mother-wife (53) who generates his sons-brothers and daughters-sisters. Indeed, the endogamic module complicates kinship down to its very terminology.[8] But the consanguineous principle invoked here still indicates its criterion with incisive efficacy. The incest of the son with the mother allows us to attribute to the same generative woman the sons and daughters, like successive bodily offshoots of one flesh.

The centrality of the body makes in *Antigone* for a scene in which self-generating unions (*koimemata autogenneta*) dominate. These spring from the bed of a sole mother (862–865), confusing and exceeding the individual identities of Jocasta's children. Each of them feels pulsating in his or her body not a specific individual identity, but the life of blood kin, symbiotically becoming one substance with them.

A carnal implosion marks this symbiosis, and it significantly influences Antigone's language in Sophocles' tragedy. It permeates her syntactical and grammatical forms and couches her speech in an obsessive style in which she appeals again and again to the *same blood*, or in other words to a common birth, from the same father and shared mother. Hence we must return to the celebrated and untranslatable line that opens the tragedy: "*o koinon autadelfon Ismenes kara.*"[9] These words Antigone addresses to her sister's head, twice invoked for its quality of being "common" (*koinon*) and "of the same sisterhood" (*autadelfon*). The impossibility of translating this line is due to the density of meanings woven in the very form of the language, easily observable in the line's odd construction. Here Ismene's individuality lies entirely in her given name, which appears, however, only to designate the possessor of the "head" as privileged part of the body. This precise recourse to the archaic notion of an individuality conceived as body and of a corporeality conceived as head inscribes itself easily within the horizon of symbiotic attraction already signified by the line's beginning with the terms *koinon* and *autadelfon*.[10] The meaning of "common" for the word *koinon* also carries the possible shading of "related by blood," while the term *autadelfon*, through its intensifying form, emphasizes that *adelphos* which originally signified a co-uterine sister/brotherhood of explicit maternal origin.

To this whirlpool, which plunges individuality into symbiotic substance, we may also add Sophocles' use of the Greek dual, that is, the reflexive verbal form that designates a double agent. Antigone uses this form in the first lines of the tragedy and then changes to the first-person singular after Ismene refuses to act along with her sister. Indeed the first-person singular grows to be an ego crying out in uprooted solitude.

The symbolic scheme that links this ego of Antigone, who is forced to act alone, and the horizon of "antiegoic" blood kinship on which the action unfolds, is ambiguous. That Sophocles' play would represent the glorification of the individual against the polis, as has often been claimed in readings that take their cue from the chorus' appellation of Antigone as *autonomos* (821), is therefore improbable.[11] Rather we encounter here an ego in the final stage of violent separation from its symbiotic niche, which announces with a painful, nearly sacrificial gesture the birth of a self. That self is concerned with the paradox of an act bound to the antiegocentric law of maternal symbiosis.

The ego of Antigone, in fact, persists in seeking its law within the impersonal roots of the self: bodily, incestuous, and consanguineous roots, which are the sources of the tragic trajectory within which the girl both moves and is moved. As if the play aimed to compare Ismene's ego, which has already abandoned those roots to move within the polis in obedience to the masculine laws of the mightiest, with the ego of Antigone who, in her immovable loyalty to consanguineous kinship, suffers in total solitude.

At the drama's center, and beyond the differences among the Sophoclean masks, lies a "pre-egoic" blood tie. That is, a story of flesh narrated through maternal generation, on which singularity is based and into which it is submerged. Here, the corporeal bloodline is transcendental, but it is also the immanent, blooming again in each of its offspring. The closed circle of the familial *philia*, which Antigone takes as her rule, can only allude to a bare life that has its end in itself and in the conservational incarnation of identical blood.

Constitutive for Antigone are her roles as daughter and sister, and not those of wife and mother. She is a daughter who gets her bearings from the fact of being a daughter and thus from her status as sister of those born of her mother. Daughter and sister: these names are not frequent among tragic heroines, who are usually embodied, in observance of a very ancient, enduring, and familiar social code, in the figures of brides and mothers who act under the cloud of a steady misogyny.[12] In *Antigone*, maternal blood commands the action: the figure of the mother intrudes on the stage with the enormous power of her attraction. She summons the daughter to recognize herself in the law of procreative blood and thus to take the side of the body and the fleshly bonds sprung from uterine generation. Thus, the lesson of Sophocles is a symbolic composition in which the body, the woman, and the mother are combined in a single figural knot. Through a therapy of excess and a centripetal endogamy underscored for the occasion, the fearful bond succeeds completely in evoking the full range of pity and terror that the female figure can inspire.[13] It is no coincidence that this feeling of terror is rooted in the corporeal materiality of existence. Existence, here, is utterly rooted not only in the fact of a death that ruins the corpse and that no immortal psyche seems able to redeem, but also in the fact of a birth that links each body to the carnal, internal, and bloody recesses of the female womb.

One is born of a woman's body, of a maternal blood that generates and encloses: a terrifying and uncanny fact from the perspective of the polis' virile logocentrism. The carnal site of a human origin, its speakability seems to be the standard against which the language of this tragedy measures itself, seeking to give theatrical, cathartic expression to "the intellect of man wandering among the unthinkable."[14]

A Dreadful Meal

The story of a body made of flesh and bone is that of a body born of another body, of its blood pulsing in another body. Bodies are born, live for a time, and die, succumbing to the organic dissolution in which they vanish. Seen from the perspective of flesh and blood, death does not appear as the sudden instant of separation. It is a threshold in the process of metamorphosis toward the realm of the inorganic. He who was body is still body. He who was born in the body dies in the body. And yet he is *disfigured*: By the long sojourn in the earth, or by the dreadful prospect of being torn by animal fangs that transform human flesh into the food of beasts, shredding that precise figuration that renders it a unique body, a body of a man, articulated into myriad limbs and functions that, however, possess *figural unity*, and thus a proper name. This originary identity—one that relies on the particular shape of the body—is undone by death.

Obsessive protagonists in this tragedy of an unburied body are the dogs and birds who feed on the corpse. The malicious fury of their cries as they partake of their dreadful meal is evoked again and again. They crowd hungrily around Polyneices, *outside* the Theban walls, outside that polis that has built its order "on essential delimitations between the human and the animal spheres."[15] And these essential boundaries are precisely those narrated by the chorus in *Antigone*, in lines whose critical importance for interpreters has come to equal that of the incestuous figure's fate. The chorus' famous first line, "*polla ta deina*" ("the many dreadful things" of which mankind is the most dreadful, *deinoteron*) (332–333) already announces its own crucial weight, telling how the extraordinary creature that is man "taught himself the word and the thought, rapid as wind, and civil customs" (353). Man acquired these specifically human traits, however, and acquired human specificity (the "rational" and the "political") at the cost of separation from the natural order. The separation therefore takes place as a domination and subjection of cosmic forces through intellect and technology.

The contents of the Sophoclean chorus, then, seem to refer to the traditional definition of a technological and political specificity of man, founded on his separation from the immediacy of the natural world, and on his ability to tame it, which Hesiod had already amply described. Yet Sophocles extraordinarily defines mankind as *deinoteron*—an untranslatable term pondered philosophically by exceptional interpreters such as Friedrich Hölderlin and Martin Heidegger, and roughly meaning "dreadful," "monstrous," and "uncanny."[16] The latter word perhaps seems particularly apt to suggest that bewilderment linked to the estrangement of mankind—burdened with violence and plagued by the awareness of death—from primitive immersion in the pure order of life. It is a sort of sign and destiny of one whose essence is this tearing *away from* and *against* the natural world in a boundless will to dominate and in anguish over his own death.

As this lacerating action occurs, the crucial link with bestiality is also forged. The tie is severed, yet it remains as the memory of a dangerous relation for the displaced creature. Thus man cannot renounce the repetitive compulsion to tell the story of that constitutive separation. Just as he begins to detach himself from the animal state and establish what he considers an unbridgeable distance, the resemblances seem to reappear, urged on by the very pulsing of the body. It is as if the ancient story of man's continuity with the animal were conserved within the biological memory of the *soma*, a history that he either does not recall or is afraid to narrate, except through rites of initiation that confirm and mimic the separation. In the distancing through which the logos, to the detriment of the *soma*, signals the immense leap of human difference, the *soma* shows that it is capable of maintaining myth on its side of the gap. It is as if the juxtaposition between the noetic soul and the animal body were unsatisfying; as if the body, in all its uncompromising bestiality, were still claiming its place of origin.[17]

The awful contest between man and animal would, however, be unequal if man, who is utterly lacking in the natural gifts of the predator, were not aided by the "fraudulent trick" (346–347) of technology (*techne*). By means of this trick, man makes up for his deficiency as the "not yet fixed" animal,[18] or rather as animal whose specialized survival instincts are by now lacking, and shows his ability to capture wild animals through cunning. This capacity does not, however, automatically cancel the terrible law that makes his own body appetizing prey for dogs, birds, and other beasts. The family or the polis must grant burial to the dead body, thus underlining through the culture of last rites the difference between humans and beasts.

It is precisely this culture, with all its terrifying prehistory, that forms the background of *Antigone*. For contrary emotive reasons, the cadaver arouses similar alimentary anguish in the minds of Antigone and Creon. The sister wishes to pluck the sweet treasure of Polyneices' corpse from the "birds who gaze at it, hungry for a meal" (29–30), while the tyrant desires that "the dogs and birds devour the unrecognizable pile of limbs" (205–206). In this specular opposition we find a perfect image of alimentary anxiety, in negative and positive.

The dreadful meal as symbolic emblem of the inhuman as extrapolitical applies, however, to Creon alone. Only for the tyrant does a distance exist between men and animals based on the anthropological foundation of the polis, whereas for Antigone, who is by definition *apolis*, the political sphere certainly cannot form that boundary. The dreadful feasting on the body of Polyneices is inhuman for her, but the intolerableness of this spectacle marks for her neither the coincidence of the animal and the inhuman, nor a coincidence between the human and the political. We could even say that animality is as close to the corporeal universe represented by Antigone as it is far from the political order represented by Creon.

In this tragedy where, we recall, the chorus earlier compared the warrior Polyneices to an eagle (112), we find further evidence for the human-animal association in the "distinctly feminine tonality" of the names Sophocles gives to the birds cited in the chorus.[19] But we see it most of all in the metaphor used when Antigone, at the sight of her brother's body, "laments with the strident voice of an anguished bird at seeing the empty nest that has been robbed of its young" (423–425). The comparison is crucial in many ways. It evokes the nest with the word *lechos* (bed), thus establishing a paradoxical correspondence between the pain of a mother/bird who sees the nest emptied of its young and the pain of a woman/sister who sees no void, but rather the exposed body of her brother. She gains an *empty* marriage bed, without children, because of her decision to bury that body.

In the relationship of Antigone to the animal world, therefore, exists a complex ambivalence that seems to push the system of bodily imagery to its profoundest depths. Here, indeed, carnivorous diet, incest, and cannibalism pile up in a swift allusive series. A distant, animal origin becomes human prehistory, while a woman's body once again conveys the terror of that past. At the same time, the complex image challenges that limit (so often represented in literature) at which "the possibility of metamorphosis is located."[20] Within Antigone's language the animal is extraordinarily present, especially in the image of birds, which conveys the twin stories of a desperate maternal cry and the dreadful meal of fraternal flesh.

The dramatic absoluteness of a body that evokes female generative potency thus broadens through the allusion to animal origins implied by that potency. *Antigone* is an *archaic* tragedy in the literal sense: a tragedy of the *arche*. It is a tragedy that speaks of the origin of man, in his quality of separateness from the other animal species. The drama's narrative depends on two equally frightening hypotheses. The first alludes to the dreadful aspects of the female, a naked life, a wild corporeity and carnal profundity that prevents the self from becoming the singular destiny and conscious aim of its own existence. The second, instead, contemplates the dreadful aspects of the male and the separation from and command of the animal by means of intelligence and technology; in this hypothesis the individual remains controlled by the consciousness and anticipation of death (360–362). Thus if the female, in orienting herself toward birth, risks entrapping her potential subjectivity within the fetters of a paralyzing maternal figure, the male, in looking toward mortality, founds his sense of self upon death itself.

Between technological pride and the uncertain nostalgia for an absolute elsewhere, the human species in *Antigone* ponders itself on the crucial threshold between the animal and the human: no longer animal, yet no more than animal. Not that Sophocles hesitates in figuring the missing link between man and beast in terms of the feminine and the corporeal. Still, the ancient text is inclined, even from its already logocentric perspective, to question its own political foundation and to recount all its political obsessions. Alien, indeed antithetical, to the political order of men, Antigone is also, in the isolated suffering that reveals her uniqueness, alien to that symbiotic order of the maternal body from which she is now torn. Her mask, more enigmatic than any other in this tragedy that bears her name, finally oscillates between the maternal demand for self-sacrifice and the retreat of the gods on a stage where the birth of the self is experienced as an unmourned sacrifice.

The Enemy Body

Creon and Polyneices (at least while the latter is alive) are on the same side of that symbolic patriarchal order that assigns a domestic domain to women and a higher and more humanly progressive, political sphere to men. When the already dead Polyneices invades the scene only as a body emblematically kept offstage, Creon, above all, most embodies the union between male identity and political identity *against* the apolitical nature of the other sex. The misogynist notes in his speeches are frequent and obvious, especially if compared with Antigone's position. Antigone, for her part, does not seem at all concerned with proclaiming her sexual identity, almost as if it were already inscribed naturally within that consanguineous horizon of maternal origin, which strengthens her resolve.

She is, of course, not unaware that she was *born* a woman because, aside from her sexing as a female, which is read within the social order as the determination of her subordinate role, her action arises precisely from the fact that she was born of a mother's womb. For her, in fact, the significance of being born a woman and that of being born *of* a woman are linked by the symbolic code of the generative female body.[21] These facts also link her with ties stronger than blood to that brother she buries precisely because they share the same mother. She acts in spite of the polis and outside the preestablished representation of a womanhood whose foundation she locates elsewhere and that needs no further public confirmation.

On the other hand, Creon's emphasis on male identity is obsessive and insistent.[22] At the attempted burial of Polyneices he exclaims, "Who among men (*andron*) has dared do this?" (248). To Creon, transgression of his orders is possible only by a male and must be interpreted as a political act. In direct conflict with Antigone, however, the tyrant's words begin to dwell insistently on the political basis of male identity. He repeats over and over his speech concerning sexual difference in which the roles are as rigidly opposed as they are prone to frightening reversals: "If she can thus flout authority unpunished, I am a woman, she the man. . . . No woman will be master while I live" (484–485, 525). His speeches are markedly misogynistic as he warns his son, Haemon, of the corrupt pleasure that comes from a woman and from the cold embraces of an evil woman, invoking with monotonous regularity the dishonor of letting oneself be overcome by a woman, of submitting to a woman, and so on. A single refrain runs throughout his diatribes: a man who submits to a woman is ignoble (746) because he abandons the human dignity of his superior, and thus political, male sex. Haemon, however, parries this paternal accusation that he is "fighting for a woman" by saying: "If you are a woman, yes—since my concern is all for you" (741; translation altered). The conflict between father and son—which can also be read politically as a conflict between tyranny and democracy—takes as its rhetorical figure the reciprocal accusation of behaving like a woman. It thus betrays a sort of male fear of becoming female, the anguish of doubtful virility. That virility is hence constrained to affirm itself obsessively against its tendency toward the feminine.[23] The greater the feeling of risk, the more the political citadel on which masculine identity is founded must be reinvigorated with the vital tonic of misogyny.

Additionally, none of the classic fundamentals of the conceptual horizon of the polis seem to be lacking. The political distinction between *friend* and *enemy*, crucial to Creon, is especially present. Eteocles is a friend and Polyneices an enemy. This discrimination is something that transcends the time and place of the Theban battle, concretizing itself in the two corpses and consigning them to opposite destinies. With the binomial friend/enemy, we are, in fact, as Carl Schmitt points out, in the presence of the political sphere par excellence. In this sphere, however, the opposition between friend and enemy is only apparent because the binomial is completely weighted toward the enemy and, in great part, toward the real possibility of war that the opposition presupposes.[24] Nothing makes the foundational role of war more apparent than the centrality of the idea of the enemy.

The history of the political may also be told through the history of the notion of the enemy: a notion that every age elaborates and expresses according to its own particular perspectives. If epistemologically framing the term *politics* around war is characteristic of the ancient world, the term *enemy* and the semantic field surrounding it may also be shown to be equally representative. As Schmitt explains, in Greece we find in fact a distinction between the term *echthros* and *polemios*, conserved in Latin in the words *inimicus* and *hostis*, which modern languages have lost. Those ancient tongues entrusted to two separate words the distinction between internal and external enemy on which Plato expounds in detail in a celebrated passage of the *Republic*.[25] The argumentative context within the dialogue is importantly the burial reserved for soldiers fallen in battle. This becomes an excellent occasion for Socrates to ponder the notion of "enemy" through an examination of the terminology for denoting hostility. He does this after advising that the city bury its dead with honors and allow the burial of the enemy without any plunder of their corpses. The Socratic discourse distinguishes between two types of conflict to which correspond the two meanings of the word *enemy*: the internal fight or civil war (*stasis*), in which the enemy takes the name of *echthros*, and the external conflict (*polemos*), in which the enemy is instead called *polemios*. The lexical pair *stasis*/*echthros*, therefore, points to the meaning of an internal conflict between men of the same community, whereas the pair *polemos*/*polemios* indicates war against strangers and foreigners.[26]

Socrates' philological precision functions above all as a condemnation of the internal struggles and hostilities between fellow citizens. The distinction between *echthros* and *polemios* does not, however, translate into different attitudes toward the corpses left on the battlefield. It would thus appear that Socrates takes Antigone's side against Creon. This is a bit more than simple literary fancy: Socrates' speech concerning the burial of the bodies of the enemy, in fact, fits so perfectly with our reading of *Antigone* that it seems to be a specific commentary. It is curious, to say the least, that when Socrates refers to the "plunder of the corpses and the placing of obstacles to the burial of the enemy," he declares, "To consider the corpse of the enemy *polemios* is worthy only of a woman or those with wretched natures, because the *echthros* has by now left it. That with which the *echthros* fought is all that remains."[27]

In this page of the *Republic* the possible allusions to *Antigone* are recognizable in two strange turns of argument. The first has to do with the fact that Socrates calls defining the body (instead of the soul) as enemy an attitude "worthy of a woman." From this it would logically follow that to deny burial to the enemy's corpse would be a piece of female obstinacy, since tradition has it that this atrocious custom is typically male. In fact women are not infrequently represented as *supplicants* for the honor of burial to the dead. So that, leaving aside the plausible hypothesis that "worthy of a woman" has value simply as a generic term denoting stupidity, the reversal of traditionally masculine and feminine attributes may allude here to the accusation of "behaving like a woman" that Creon and Haemon make to each other in *Antigone*. The indictment seems to especially upset Creon, the man who denies the enemy burial.

The second oddity in Socrates' analysis is even more intriguing. He suggests that, contrary to what women think, it is not the body that is inimical (*echthros*) but the enemy (*polemios*), whose hostility is totally substantiated in his soul and whose body is only an instrument for fighting. Once again, an implicit allusion to *Antigone* is plausible. In fact, Creon reserves for Polyneices the term *echthros*, even when Polyneices is already a stinking corpse. The term fits perfectly with Plato's philology because the *echthros* is nothing other than a friend, of one's same group (*sungenes*) and familiar (*oikeion*) by nature, who subsequently transforms into an enemy. This is just what happens to Polyneices. He is indeed *oikeion* and *sungenes* to Creon, being of the same blood, because he is the son of Creon's sister Jocasta. All the more reason for the name of *echthros*: An internal enemy, extreme symbol of an internecine struggle played out in the fratricide of a common, incestuous blood.

Even if all these possible allusions were unintentional, Plato's text would remain a sort of perfect and synthetic definition of the criterion guiding Creon's actions. This criterion judges the dead *body* to be the *enemy*, considering it not as a mere envelope of muscle and flesh by means of which the enemy fought while alive, but as possessing a nontranscendable corporeal individuality to which the definition of "enemy" clings utterly, whether the body is dead or alive. "An enemy can never be a friend, not even when he is dead," the tyrant exclaims (522; translation altered). For Creon, being an enemy to the polis has little to do with the one who fought by means of the body and who by now has gone elsewhere, leaving on the battlefield only his lifeless and apolitical corpse, as Socrates would have it. The body itself is the enemy, insofar as it substantiates all of the enemy's reality.

Our recourse to Platonic philology has been valuable. We can now see how a body that already commands the stage also comes to contaminate Creon's political language, forcing onto it a carnal theme. This is rendered possible by the absence of a psyche separate from the body, or rather of a psyche that, according to a tradition already established in Sophocles' time, laid claim to being the true seat of a subjectivity that could be labeled enemy. Within that tradition, the body figured as a mere material envelope, devoid of any political quality whatsoever—neither friend nor enemy. The Platonic distinction between the psyche and the *soma* means, for all intents and purposes, just this: that only the soul may be the principle of action. Of that which may properly be defined as political action for or against someone, the body is a mere instrument. The Sophoclean horizon, in contrast, remarkably lacks this distinction and impels Creon to regard the body itself as the active protagonist thus to attribute to it those political qualities that even the corpse, as individual body, preserves. Both in theory and in fact, the enemy appears as pure body: a body that takes sides against the bodies of cocitizens, a warring body, a body that kills and is killed: *body politic* in a direct, rather than metaphorical, sense.

If in Antigone's case the ambiguity of the tragic depends on an affirmation of the self whose action is necessitated by symbiotic flesh, in Creon's instance ambiguities multiply around a body that carries a double connotation. It is apolitical, even antipolitical in its mythical, symbolic suction into a prelogical abyss of animal and female potencies. It is political, however, insofar as it is the sole, true locus of the notion of the enemy. Thus the body not only throws the scene out of kilter when it reappears before Creon in the form of a consanguineous corpse, but it also saturates the political lexicon, including its founding category of enemy, with its bloody substance. The politics that banishes the body from within its walls speaks indeed, from beginning to end, only in the grammar of the body.

Antigone pits the *philos* against the *echthros*, rendering only the former term absolute. In so doing, she severs the political binomial *philos/echthros*: "My nature is for mutual love (*sunphilein*), not hate (*sunechthein*)" (523). This celebrated statement splits the single, bipolar concept friend/enemy (which had been, moreover, weighted on the side of the enemy), while at the same time affirming *philia* as a symbiotic union that knows no opposite. Friendship "according to nature" and based on ties of kinship is for Plato unnaturally disrupted by the emergence of the internal enemy. It is radicalized in *Antigone* by means of an incestuous consanguinity whose cohesive power is so strong that it allows no reversal. Precisely this is the female principle of Sophocles' play: an apolitical *philia* inscribed within maternal generation, which neither contemplates nor recognizes its contrary. It is the principle of an absolute and unconditional bond in which brothers, because they are loved by the sister out of love for the mother, exist only as objects and not subjects of the *philein*: of the same blood, the same mother and father, brothers who kill each other as enemies by the Theban walls. This death observes the political criterion of *philos/echthros* for which no better figuration exists than simultaneous and mutual fratricide.

Conclusion

Sophocles' text weaves a dense cloth of mythical legend, setting squarely in the present a series of problems that increase the weight of the undecidable and awaken distress about it. One of these problems occurs in identifying the mask of Antigone with a free, responsible agent. This same mask must also announce the birth of a self still held back within a symbiotic, maternal body, a self that suffers its very formation as a sort of unbearable rending. It is, in fact, remarkable that such a painful declaration of individuality should choose to speak with the voice of a young woman. In this way, it alludes to the relation between mother and daughter in which the latter ambiguously wavers between an all-encompassing maternal bond and a detachment that results in complete solitude. It also points, however, to a link between the generative body and the generation of a self: the riddle of all life that issues from woman.

The body as life, as pure existence of living beings, prior even to the soul's claim to reign therein, is in fact evoked by the tragedy in two ways. The first way points to the body in its role of closest origin for which each of us is a body of flesh and blood born of a mother and soon to die in the dreadful feast of the corpse. The second way points to the body as the distant origin of the human species in its supraindividual substance. And here the body is a chasm, opening onto prelogical bestiality and onto the uncanny that provokes fear in the long night of the mothers, persisting in both the nostalgia for a vital immediacy that has been irrecoverably lost and a fear that the animal in us will again take control. Finally, an analogous story seems to narrate the body as death in two versions. There is the death of someone with a specific name who ceases to dwell among the living and disappears into the darkness of the elsewhere, and the anguish of the corpse, which reminds the meat-eater of his "natural" role in the food chain common to beasts and men.

The figural weave is intricate; it makes the most of the ambiguity characteristic of tragedy, while at the same time it lends a dramatic order to this polysemy. The polysemy of the body is heaped onto the mask of Antigone, which is contrasted by the political mask of Creon. We know that the political order in Greece is founded on a series of exclusions that are at once drastic and destined to endure in history. In this context, *Antigone* tells a story whose reassuring outcome the public already knows and whose symbolism is already familiar.

Yet the expulsion of the body and of the women from the city, so emphatically heightened by the monstrous aspect of what is banished, does not constitute the only feature of the narrative. The expulsion also points to all the problems inherent in a seductive alterity that the excluded themselves still seem capable of evoking. Nor is the narrative silent about an androcentric guilt that the polis, or at least its mythical tyrant, calls upon himself. Creon, arrogant, misogynist, and vulgar, "monarch of the desert and slayer of sons," is in fact nothing in the end. His crime consists in having wished to keep the enemy body of a man outside the city and turn it into food for wild beasts. But it also consists of having banished the live body of a woman so that the guilt of her atrocious and wicked burial would not fall on the polis.

Notes

1. Both words appear significantly in line 410. As is well known, the term *soma*, which in the Homeric texts denotes only the corpse, comes later to signify the body in general, whether alive or dead.

2. Jean-Pierre Vernant and Pierre Vidal-Naquet, *Mito e tragedia nella Grecia antica*, vol. 2 (Turin, Italy: Einaudi, 1976), p. 94. First published as *Mythe et tragédie en Grèce ancienne* (Paris: Éditions La Découverte, 1972), and in English as *Myth and Tragedy in Ancient Greece*, trans. Janet Lloyd (Cambridge, MA: Zone Books, 1990).

3. Nicole Loraux, *Il femminile e l'uomo greco* (Bari, Italy: Laterza, 1991), p. 84. First published as *Les expériences de Tirésias: Le feminin et l'homme grec* (Paris: Gallimard, 1989).

4. Émile Benveniste, *Il vocabulario delle Istituzioni indo-europee*, trans. Mariantonia Liborio (Turin, Italy: Einaudi, 1976), pp. 226–246. First published as *Le vocabulaire des institutions indo-européenes* (Paris: Minuit, 1969).

5. Sophocles, *Antigone; Oedipus the King; Electra*, trans. H. D. F. Kitto (Oxford, UK: Oxford University Press, 1994), lines 466–467. Hereafter references are given parenthetically within the text.

6. Luce Irigaray, *Speculum: L'altra donna* (Milan, Italy: Feltrinelli, 1989), p. 203. First published as *Speculum de l'autre femme* (Paris: Minuit, 1974), and in English as *Speculum of the Other Woman*, trans. Gillian C. Gill (Ithaca, NY: Cornell University Press, 1985). In Irigaray's work Sophocles' *Antigone* receives constant critical attention and passes through various interpretive phases (on this score, see Luisa Muraro, "Female Genealogies," in *Engaging with Irigaray: Feminist Philosophy and Modern European Thought*, ed. Carolyn Burke, Naomi Schor, and Margaret Whitford [New York: Columbia University Press, 1994]). In her *Speculum* essay, Irigaray examines Hegel's reading through a double hermeneutical filter that criticizes the patriarchal horizon at work in both Sophocles and Hegel. In this context, Antigone's identification with her mother is linked to her nullification of self within a maternal desire turned prevalently toward the son.

7. Interestingly, in Sophocles, Creon and the chorus underscore Antigone's and her brothers' descent from Oedipus (see 193, 471, 600, 856, and 1018; in the last two, Tiresias is the speaker). The speeches assigned to Antigone, however, always allude to the maternal origins of the family (see 513, 862–866, 911).

8. Elisa Avezzù, "I figli di Edipo e la revoca di paternità," in *Koinon aima: Antropologia e lessico della parentela greca*, ed. Elisa Avezzù and Oddone Longo (Bari, Italy: Adriatica, 1991), pp. 128ff.

9. The literal translation of this line is, more or less, "Common, of the same sisterhood, of Ismene the head." On the numerous interpretations of this verse, see, for example, the bibliographical note of Antonio Sestili in his edition of *Antigone* (Editrice Dante Alighieri, "Traditio," Serie greca, vol. 68, pp. 126–127); and George Steiner, *Antigones* (Oxford, UK: Oxford University Press, 1984), pp. 85–86.

10. Hölderlin's celebrated translation of *Antigone* condenses the two terms into the unpronounceable *Gemeinsamschwesterliches* (Friedrich Hölderlin, *Sämtliche Werke* [Stuttgart, Germany: Kohlhammer, 1952], p. 205).

11. I agree that Antigone's character is one of "non-instrumental relationality," as stressed by Giulia Paola Di Nicola in *Antigone: Figura femminile della trasgressione* (Pescara, Italy: Edizioni Tracce, 1991), but I stress the corporeal quality of that relational nature. The model is loaded with obsessive carnal symbolism, which is represented as absolute. This system does not easily transfer to any other context of "values."

12. For the strong misogynistic values of the tragic horizon, see Eva Cantarella, *L'ambiguo malanno: Condizione e immagine della donna nell'anticità greca e romana*

(Rome: Editori Riuniti, 1981), pp. 84ff.; and Eva C. Keuls, *The Reign of the Phallus: Sexual Politics in Ancient Athens* (New York: Harper and Row, 1985).

13. Aristotle, *Poetics*, trans. George Whalley (Montreal, Canada: McGill-Queen's University Press, 1997), p. 1149b.

14. Friedrich Hölderlin, "Note all'Antigone," in *Sul tragico*, trans. Pasquinelli G. Editore, ed. Remo Bodei (Milan, Italy: Feltrinelli, 1989), p. 103. For Hölderlin that intellect, however, locates the unthinkable in the chaos of natural forces to which man returns upon death. See, in this connection, Remo Bodei, "Hölderlin: La filosofia e il tragico," introduction to *Sul tragico*. I tend to think that birth, and not death, is the backdrop for *Antigone*, and thus a corporeality that harbors the natural, inscrutable, and panic-causing powers of the origin.

15. Steiner, *Antigones*, p. 227.

16. Ibid., pp. 174–177. The history of the interpretation of *deinon* is very rich: Richard Bodéüs gives a brief bibliographical survey in "L'habile et le juste de l'Antigone de Sophocle au Protagoras de Platon," *Mnemosyne*, vol. 37 (1984), pp. 271–290, linking its meaning to the Promethean myth of civilization narrated in the *Protagoras* of Plato (320c–322d), and to the positive evaluation of the *deinotes*, as technical ability, which Aristotle theorized in the *Nicomachean Ethics* (1144a23–28). What seems certain is that the Sophoclean verse is among those representations that Greek culture of the fifth century BCE devotes to the theme of human progress as a civilizing process that works through technological and political action (cf. Christian Meier, *La nascita della categoria del politico in Grecia* [Bologna, Italy: Il Mulino, 1988], pp. 457ff. First published as *Die Enstehung des Politischen bei den Griechen* [Frankfurt am Main, Germany: Suhrkamp, 1983]).

17. Umberto Galimberti, *Il corpo* (Milan, Italy: Feltrinelli, 1987), p. 86.

18. This famous expression (in German "das noch nicht fest-gestellte Tier") derives from Friedrich Nietzsche, in *Beyond Good and Evil*. It is developed, however, for anthropological philosophy by Arnold Gehlen in *Der Mensch, seine Natur und seine Stellung in der Welt* (Wiesbaden, Germany: Aula-Verlag, 1950), as part of an interesting revaluation of the importance of corporeality in human evolution. For a summary of research in this field, see Bruno Accarino's excellent essay "Tra liberta e decisione: Alle origini dell'antropologia filosofica," in *Ratio Imaginis: Uomo e mondo nell'antropologia filosofica*, ed. Bruno Accarino (Florence, Italy: Ponte delle Grazie, 1991), pp. 7–63.

19. Steiner, *Antigones*, p. 226.

20. Jacques Lacan, *Le Séminaire, Livre VII: L'éthique de la psychanalyse* (Paris: Seuil, 1986), p. 308. For Lacan the deep meaning of Antigone is found, however, in her incarnation of the death wish, a thesis with which I disagree.

21. For Sarah B. Pomeroy, Antigone is the model of a masculine heroine (see *Donne in Atene e Roma* [Turin, Italy: Einaudi, 1975], pp. 106ff. First published as *Goddesses, Whores, Wives, and Slaves: Women in Classical Antiquity* [New York: Schocken, 1975]). For a confutation of this theory, see S. Wiersma, "Women in Sophocles," *Mnemosyne*, vol. 37 (1984), pp. 25–55.

22. Diego Lanza, *Il tiranno e il suo pubblico* (Turin, Italy: Einaudi, 1977), p. 52.

23. Loraux, *Il femminile*, vii ff.

24. Carl Schmitt, *Le categorie del politico* (Bologna, Italy: Il Molino, 1972), pp. 101–165. First published as *Begriff des Politischen* (Hamburg, Germany: Hanseatische Verlagsanstalt, 1933).

25. Plato, *Republic*, trans. Robin Waterfield (Oxford, UK: Oxford University Press, 1993), 469d–471a.

26. Ibid., 470b. See Schmitt, *Le categorie del politico*, pp. 111ff.; and Jean-Pierre Vernant, *Mito e società nela Grecia antica* (Turin, Italy: Einaudi, 1981), pp. 24–25 (first published as *Mythe et société en Grèce ancienne* [Paris: Maspero, 1974]). In addition to Plato's pages, on the conceptual horizon of the age the four terms in question belong to semantic fields that are not separated, but rather overlapping (Meier, *La nascita della categoria del politico*, p. 215, n. 180). The relationship between friend and enemy characterizes, however, an archaic behavioral model within the same clan (pp. 145, 215–216). In this sense, one could hypothesize that the *echthros* in *Antigone* directly refers to the primeval female root of the clan itself.

27. Plato, *Republic*, 469d–469e.

3

Impossible Mourning

Sophocles Reversed

Fanny Söderbäck

> Anyone who reads [Sophocles] with clear eyes and from the point of view of [his] own time will appreciate how highly Aristotle valued the genius of his art, and will realize that everything he says was virtually the opposite of what modern times have been pleased to make of it.
>
> — Johann Gottfried Herder

At its very core, Greek tragedy relies on oppositions and confrontations—between humans and gods, freedom and necessity, culture and nature, state and family, the living and the dead. G. W. F. Hegel emphasizes that the particularity of dramatic poetry in relation to other art forms is that "action has to encounter hindrances from other agents and fall into complications and oppositions where both sides struggle for success and control."[1] Tragedy is commonly understood as emerging in response to a moment of transition from a mythological past, associated with divine law (and women), to a political present, represented by human law (and men).[2] It is seen as a medium through which the Greek audience could make sense of their experiences of the "new" society.[3] Many have argued that we find the most compelling example of this in *Antigone*, where a seemingly unbridgeable gap and irresolvable opposition is raised between human and divine law.[4] But while most interlocutors of this classic drama associate its heroine with divine law and the private realm and see Creon as a representative of human law and politics, I trace what I call a *Sophoclean reversal* at the heart of the play, suggesting, with Herder, that things are "virtually the opposite" of what they seem to be.[5] Focusing on the way in which sexual difference is articulated in *Antigone*, I offer a reading that negates the dialectic most commonly ascribed to the play. Everything must be reversed: through a series of "contaminations" we arrive at a reversal of the oppositions with which we started, and this should bring our attention not only to the complex relationship between the private and public realms—one that I explore through the work of Hannah Arendt—but also to the ambivalent and perplexing position of woman within the field of politics—a theme that remains underdeveloped in Arendt's own thinking and that I wish to elucidate through my reading of *Antigone*.

A Sophoclean Reversal: Arendt and the Division between Home and State

In *The Human Condition*, Arendt turns to the Greek polis to uncover the conditions of possibility for political action.[6] In ancient Greece, she finds a model that clearly distinguishes between the *oikia* (home or household) and the *polis* (the public realm). The tragedy of our times, for Arendt, is that we have lost the world in which politics can take place, the public realm where human beings could act and speak in concert. With the emergence of the social realm, the distinction between private and public has collapsed: our modern nation-states are run as gigantic households. Arendt's work could thus be seen as an obituary of sorts: she mourns the loss of the political and regrets the disappearance of the public realm. In this sense, she picks up where Antigone ended her work of mourning.

The Arendtian characterization of Greek society as founded on a sharp distinction between the private and public realms has been criticized and challenged. Many have argued that family and state were, in fact, closely interconnected in ancient Greece and that matters such as kinship and religion were not confined to the intimate realm of the household, but were rather an integral aspect of political life.[7] I will, nevertheless, follow the Arendtian description of the Greek public sphere as distinctly separate from the private realm because this allows us to read *Antigone* in a way that it has not traditionally been read and because this subsequently helps me to think about the structural problems that follow from this very distinction.

Being political, according to Arendt, is to act and speak in concert. Plurality is the ontological condition of politics. Action, as distinguished from both labor and work, "is never possible in isolation; to be isolated is to be deprived of the capacity to act" (188). Action "always establishes relationships and therefore has an inherent tendency to force open all limitations and cut across all boundaries" (190). Action is transgressive in nature, yet this by no means makes it a merely destructive activity because it has the capacity to be a founding moment, a moment of creation or, as Arendt so often puts it, a new beginning.

Readers of *Antigone*, as we have noted, traditionally see Creon as a representative of the polis. Although most interpreters before me have noted that he acts like a tyrant, and although much evidence in the text leads us to believe that this is the case, he is nevertheless associated with the political realm. From the point of view of democratic Greece, this is a contradiction in terms. Following Arendt, we know that the very distinction between ruler and ruled belongs to the private realm, in the household. In *The Human Condition* she writes: "The whole concept of rule and being ruled, of government and power in the sense in which we understand them as well as the regulated order attending them, was felt to be prepolitical and to belong in the private rather than the public sphere" (32). This relationship between ruler and ruled, Arendt contends, "precluded all possibility of action" (224). And for Arendt, of course, a public without action is no public at all.

Creon rules over Thebes as a father rules over his family. His name, *kreion*, means exactly ruler or lord, derived from *kratos*, which means power or strength. One of the interesting consequences of Arendt's emphasis on our fundamental plurality is the concept of power that it leads to. Power, for Arendt, is always "a power potential and not an unchangeable, measurable, and reliable entity like force or strength . . . power springs up between men when they act together and vanishes the moment they disperse" (200).[8] Creon's name indicates that his power is different from the Arendtian understanding thereof. It is based on *strength* rather than *plurality*. It is not the empowering power of many, but the force or strength of one. Tiresias condemns Creon's actions as violent in nature.[9] "To be political, to live in a *polis*, meant that everything was decided through words and persuasion and not through force and violence," Arendt explains (26). And the latter, she notes in *On Violence*, can only result in impotence; its end is the "destruction of all power."[10] Haemon tells his father that he would "rule a desert beautifully alone" (739). This statement echoes all the way to the last scene of the tragedy, where Creon stands as the lonely warrior in a battlefield surrounded by the corpses of his loved ones.[11]

Arendt writes about nonviolent resistance that it is "one of the most active and efficient ways of action ever devised, because it cannot be countered by fighting, where there may be defeat or victory, but only by mass slaughter in which even the victor is defeated, cheated of his prize, since nobody can rule over dead men" (201). Creon literally attempts to rule over the dead. And just like Oedipus (who acted in blindness) was punished by being blinded, Creon (who attempts to govern the dead) is granted a kingdom of corpses. The only way he can stop Antigone is to kill her. And her death is just the first in a series of deaths: violence can, in Arendtian fashion, only lead to more violence.

In her analysis of action, Arendt points out that both Greek and Latin originally had two verbs with the meaning "to act." One of them meant "to begin" (*archein/agere*) and the other "to carry out" (*prattein/gerere*). While the second term has continued to signify action, the first has come to mean "to rule" or "to lead." Margaret Canovan has pointed out that Arendt makes this point in order "to insist that no leader, however heroic, can act by himself, and that those who carry through initiatives need not be merely passive subjects of rule, but can themselves be participants in action, and must in any case join in responsibility for what they carry out."[12] Creon's action is not only authoritarian, thus separating *archein* from *prattein* the way we moderns do; in it he also tries to escape the *responsibility* inherent in action. In carrying out the punishment, he decides to bury Antigone alive instead of actually killing her, leaving open the possibility that she might survive so that he can "clear the city from the guilt of death" (776). Creon is fierce in punishing Antigone, but he does not want to take responsibility for her death. Avoiding the risk of guilt, he lets her choose whether she prefers to die or live inside a tomb: "There let her choose," he says to the chorus, "death, or a buried life. / No stain of guilt upon us in this case, / but she is exiled from our life on earth" (888–890). Creon, moreover, not only escapes responsibility, but he also turns a public event into a hidden one. Originally he had informed the citizens that whoever buried the dead body would be punished by public stoning. He subsequently threatens to kill Antigone while forcing Haemon to watch: "she shall die / full in his sight," he announces (759–760). Instead, he ultimately decides to take her "where the foot of man comes not," hiding her in a cave where no one will see or hear her (773). Creon does not dare to inhabit the Arendtian space of appearance that would turn his deeds into true action.

As Luce Irigaray and others have emphasized, Creon, moreover, has gained his kingship by virtue of kinship—that is to say that his power is based on familial bonds of blood rather than on speech and deeds.[13] "I hold all the power and the royal throne," he admits, "through close connection with the perished men" (173–174). Creon, the king, who has inherited power through kinship, cannot simply be equated with the Greek polis as we know it. He rather belongs to a prepolitical sphere, to the time of the warlike deeds of the Homeric kings. "A public realm," Arendt explains, "had never come into being between the members of a family" because "these were known to be non-political and even anti-political" (54).[14]

The act that most clearly seems to situate Creon within the public realm, however, is his legislative power. But Arendt would, again, raise concerns here: she explains that the Greeks "did not count legislating among political activities. In their opinion, the lawmaker was like the builder of the city wall, someone who had to do and finish his work before political activity could begin" (194). As Plato and Aristotle will later do (on Arendt's account), Creon makes the mistake of substituting making for acting, thus treating the state as a well-ordered household rather than a space where politics can take place. Creon "fabricates" laws instead of initiating political action, and this "fabrication"—insofar as it is masked as political action—makes his power violent in nature.

This is where I take the Herder quotation that we started with quite literally: only when we "realize that everything [Sophocles] says was virtually the opposite of what modern times have been pleased to make of it," can we really make sense of the play. The events unfolding within it take place in Thebes, a city that was ruled by kings and hence differed from the democratic Athens for whose citizens it was meant to be performed. Froma I. Zeitlin has argued that the city of Thebes, in ancient drama, was understood as an anti-Athens, a place marked by otherness: "If we say that theater in general functions as an 'other scene' where the city puts itself and its values into question by projecting itself upon the stage to confront the present with the past through its ancient myths, then Thebes, I suggest, is the 'other scene' of the 'other scene' that is the theater itself."[15] Radicalizing Zeitlin's characterization of the role of Thebes in Greek tragedy, we should read *Antigone* with this double negation in mind. If theater as such is that scene where the (political) present is confronted with its (mythical) past, then the other of this scene would not, as Zeitlin suggests, be "the mirror *opposite* of Athens,"[16] but rather a mirror image of Athens in its current state.

Antigone takes place exactly at the point of transition from a mythological past where kings ruled like fathers rule a house, to a political present characterized by speech and action in the public sphere, and the events of the play reflect the turmoil of this very transition. We should not equate the figure of Antigone, however, with the past (divine law and household politics), nor should we continue to see Creon as representing the new order (human law and a democratic polis). The Sophoclean reversal—and the negation of negation that I understand it to represent—structures the entire play, and it forces us to reconsider the roles of the two characters and the subsequent relation between the sexes.

Antigone: Action and Narration in the Public Sphere

What I have suggested so far allows us to see Antigone, instead of Creon, as a representative of the new order. She acts like the hero Arendt associates with the public sphere. She marks the beginning of something new—nothing less, in fact, than the political understood in democratic terms—an argument I elaborate in what follows. She seemingly does so by protecting that which belongs in the past: the family and divine law. In protecting divine law, however, Antigone simply draws a clear distinction between the private and the public realms—a distinction that would come to lie at the very foundation of the democratic polis as Arendt characterizes it. Antigone refuses to let the ruler interfere with private matters such as grief and mourning.[17] And she simultaneously refuses to let the city be run as a (patriarchal) household. By transgressing the law she sets a new standard for lawmaking. She introduces a new model of the political, a model based on speech and action rather than tyrannical rule.

There are several ways in which we can describe Antigone as a political agent in the Arendtian sense of the term. We saw that Creon failed to take responsibility for his deed and that he acted in secret. Antigone, conversely, takes full responsibility for her actions, even if she knows that it will lead to certain death. Her sister, Ismene, suggests early on that she keep her action secret. But Antigone despises the very thought of secrecy: "Dear God! Denounce me. I shall hate you more / if silent, not proclaiming this to all," she responds (86–87). And when she has been caught, faced with the king's outrage, she confesses her crime without hesitation: "I say I did it and I don't deny it" (443). For Antigone, as for Arendt, action and speech go hand in hand, and they demand courage.[18] If Arendt associated action with the extraordinary, with miracles and revolutions, Antigone must be the example par excellence of an actor.[19] Ismene tells her that she craves "what can't be done," that she chases "what cannot be" (90, 92). Antigone wills and does the impossible, the extraordinary. She buries Polyneices against all odds.

Her own death is a *kalos thanatos*, a beautiful death, a heroic death. This, as Cecilia Sjöholm has pointed out, usually refers to the honorable death of a warrior and is intimately connected with manliness.[20] Antigone's death is an act of courage (generally speaking an impossibility for a woman in ancient Greece), and courage is "one of the most elemental political attitudes" according to Arendt (35). A political hero worthy of that name must dare to risk his or her life: "To leave the household . . . demanded courage because only in the household was one primarily concerned with one's own life and survival" (36).[21] Antigone herself characterizes her actions as courageous, when she announces her plan to bury Polyneices, at the very end of Aeschylus' *Seven against Thebes*: "Courage! I shall find the means to act," she exclaims.[22] Sjöholm argues that Antigone, both through her deed and through her death, challenges the very conception of masculinity and femininity.[23] And she importantly observes the mutuality of this reversal: "It has often been pointed out that Antigone does not act like a woman. It has less often been observed that Creon does not act like a man."[24] At the end of the play, the roles have been reversed: the wailing Creon is alone in his grief, and neither his sister (Jocasta) nor his wife (Eurydice) are there to carry out the work of mourning traditionally ascribed to them as women. The sole survivor of his family, Creon will have to shoulder the burden of the burial rites Antigone once took on despite his decree. *He* is the weeping woman now and comes to represent the household sphere whose logic and power structure he had defended all along (albeit in the name of the state). *Her* heroic death simultaneously makes her a man, and she becomes the founding principle of a political order where action is carried out by the many and no longer appropriated by the king alone.

But if politics, as Arendt claims, "is never for the sake of life" (37), what then is its relationship to death and to the dead? The care for the dead is undoubtedly the central theme of the play, and we must try to situate it in our discussion here. Following Zeitlin we should take note of the fact that the very relationship between life and death is subject to an important reversal: Creon, Zeitlin suggests, "proves to confound the most significant difference of all—that between life and death—when he entombs Antigone alive and keeps the dead unburied above the earth."[25] Many interlocutors have depicted Antigone as an "impure heroine," who transgresses and destabilizes rigid boundaries,[26] and these are, indeed, characteristics typically ascribed to women. We should note, however, that it is Creon who disrespects and reverses categories and distinctions, and who stands out as "excessive" insofar as he tries to reach beyond the realm of power mandated to him as king: he wants to control not only the state, but the household realm, too, and even the underworld of the dead.

Antigone's act, as we know, is to bury her brother, to commemorate him, and to publicly mourn him. Her transgressive deed is preceded by another—one that has taken place prior to the events of the play, but that nevertheless frames and conditions it: Polyneices and Eteocles, Antigone's two brothers, have killed each other in war. Although this, too, is a significant political event, it can only be perceived as such insofar as it brings about a *narrative*. Political action, we might say following Arendt, unfolds in three steps: first in an action, then in the witnessing of this action, and finally in the memory and commemoration of it. Heroic deeds only attain full significance if they are witnessed by spectators who are willing to remember and recount them. Or, as Julia Kristeva puts it in her book on Arendt:

> We must acknowledge that the actor himself, no matter how heroic his exploits themselves may be, cannot constitute wonderful action. Action is wonderful only if it is memorable. And where should we search for memory? The spectators are the ones who "accomplish" history, thanks to a thought that follows the act. This accomplishment takes place through recollection, without which there is simply nothing to recount. It is not the actors but the spectators . . . who make the polis a productive place to organize memory and/or history and stories.[27]

Memory is thus crucial for the survival of political life. "Without remembrance and without the reification which remembrance needs for its own fulfillment,"

Arendt writes, "the living activities of action, speech, and thought would lose their reality at the end of each process and disappear as though they never had been" (95).

What Antigone defends in insisting on burying her brother (twice!) is not only her right as a sister to honor the memory of her brother: Her insistence on carrying out the burial rites more importantly marks the inauguration of a public realm that functions, in Arendtian terms, as "a remedy for the futility of action and speech," which is to say that it renders action "immortal," prevents it from being forgotten, makes the deeds and stories of fellow citizens "imperishable," thus creating a kind of "organized remembrance," which is exactly what the polis was meant to provide (197–198). Antigone interestingly inhabits both of the roles on which the new order depends: by burying Polyneices, she both commemorates *his* story and as an extension comes to be the protagonist of yet another story, a story carrying *her* name, one that we continue to recount and draw inspiration from time and again.[28] She is a spectator and an actor at once.

But just as the city within the new order, as we learn from Haemon, cannot possibly be "possessed by one man only" (737), actors within this new order are not the authors of their own stories. Rather, they depend on spectators to commemorate them and narrate their stories. Here we find what might be articulated as the *tragic* aspect of Arendt's own thinking: because action is unpredictable and irreversible and because we depend on others to narrate our story, all actors are doers and sufferers at once. In a passage that gets to the heart of the destiny awaiting all tragic heroes, Arendt contends that to do and to suffer "are like opposite sides of the same coin, and the story that an act starts is composed of its consequent deeds and sufferings" (190). That the doer must suffer and the sufferer must do is, according to R. P. Winnington-Ingram, "the very formula for tragedy."[29] While Greek tragedy—with its profound rootedness in destiny and necessity—would seem like a strange place to turn to in search of Arendtian political action grounded in freedom (Arendt describes freedom as the raison d'être of the political in the sense of the polis),[30] we might say that tragedy highlights an important aspect of the notion of freedom that Arendt herself has developed in her work: Because the actor "appears much more the victim and the sufferer than the author and doer of what he has done" and because, therefore, "neither in labor, subject to the necessities of life, nor in fabrication, dependent upon given material, does man appear to be less free than in those capacities whose very essence is freedom [in other words, in action]" (234), we are forced to rethink freedom altogether. If freedom traditionally has been aligned with sovereignty and autonomy, on Arendt's account it is and must be mutually exclusive with sovereignty. The latter, she argues, "is contradictory to the very condition of plurality" (234), which, as we know, is the condition of possibility for politics. If we identify freedom with sovereignty, "the simultaneous presence of freedom and non-sovereignty, of being able to begin something new and of not being able to control or even foretell its consequences, seems almost to force us to the conclusion that human existence is absurd" (235).[31] Antigone does not teach us that human existence is absurd. What she does teach us, however, goes beyond the Arendtian insight that the actor is a doer and sufferer at once. Antigone reveals yet another perplexing aspect of political action, one that Arendt herself never quite thematized. We now turn to this perplexity.

Impossible Action: The Blind Spot of Sexual Difference

An important fact that we have not addressed is that it is not only Creon who acts alone, but Antigone as well. She invites her sister to bury their brother, but Ismene refuses, afraid of Creon's power. The people of Thebes, we are told, mutter and talk behind their ruler's back, but no one—with Haemon as the sole exception—does anything in her defense. The Thebans, like Ismene, are afraid of breaking the law: Antigone and Haemon, alone, dare to stand up against the king.[32] Antigone complains about this loneliness and isolation: she notes that no one is mourning for her, that she is "unwept," "unfriended," and destined to die alone (878). And yet we know that the condition of possibility for action, on Arendt's account, is *plurality*. We act and speak *in concert*. Why, then, is Antigone alone? Why does she have no followers? Why is nobody there to witness and support *her* transgressive act?

At this juncture we have to address the question of sexual difference in greater detail. One of the fundamental conditions of the polis Arendt praises is that of free citizenry. To belong to the polis meant neither to rule nor to be ruled. Arendt explains: "The polis was distinguished from the household in that it knew only 'equals,' whereas the household was the center of the strictest inequality" (32). The Greek public space was a space shared by equals—it was a space of freedom. The necessities of life and survival were left behind, in the intimate sphere of the home.[33] What Arendt (problematically) does not sufficiently address, however, is that the household included men, women, and slaves, whereas the polis only allowed free *men*. This should shed new light on the impossibility of Antigone's deed. She not only transgresses the royal law, but *she also enters into—even founds—a sphere, which exists solely through her very exclusion from it*—because Antigone is, of course, no man. Honorable death and transgressive action notwithstanding, she is viewed and treated as a woman and is repeatedly reminded that she must respect the limitations imposed on her due to her gender—despite the fact that she herself never evinces her gender.

Antigone is an anomaly. "She is not a human," Judith Butler writes in *Antigone's Claim*, "but she speaks in [human] language. Prohibited from action, she nevertheless acts."[34] As a woman, in the time and place of the staging of the play that bears her name, she simply cannot be equal. Therefore, she must act alone. Ismene steps back at the very thought of carrying out the deed with her: "We must remember that we two are women / so not to fight with men," she says (61–62). I think this is the key to the many scattered comments about sexual difference in the text. They do not, as has commonly been suggested, simply point to the well-known tension between an old (matriarchal) society and a new (patriarchal) one.[35] They point, rather, to something paradoxical about the new society as such. At its very foundation is a feminine subject who is its condition of possibility—indeed its very creator—and yet, who ultimately must be excluded in order for it to exist at all. In acting as one who has no right to act, Antigone, in Butler's words, "speaks within the language of entitlement from which she is excluded."[36] She is, indeed, an "everlasting irony" or an "internal enemy," as Hegel says.[37] She figures as someone who cannot be contained within the boundaries of the polis. Creon describes her as excessive: "There is too much of you," he exclaims in a moment of despair (573).

In this sense my reading of the play addresses a blind spot at the very heart of Arendt's thinking. What does one do with an anomaly such as Antigone? How does one account for the feminine aspects of political life?[38] Judith Butler has argued that what Arendt failed to give an account of in *The Human Condition* is "precisely the way in which the boundaries of the public and the political spheres were secured through the production of a constitutive outside."[39] Woman is this outside. But as a constitutive outside she simultaneously finds herself at the very heart of what is inside. *The polis would not exist without her. Yet the polis can only exist without her.* And Antigone—this paradoxical figure on the limit between life and death—establishes the very boundary that distinguishes private from public, but at the same time she is excluded from the political sphere that is founded in such a way. She inaugurates the very order that will exclude and destroy her.

In her commentary on Hegel's reading of *Antigone*, Sjöholm has argued that what Antigone ultimately shows is that "an order of justice with a claim for universality can be instituted only at the cost of a loss that will continue to haunt the development of consciousness: a tragic remainder that will put the universal claim into question."[40] She goes on to claim that woman "laughs at the public order to which she will never have access. She not only will in some way always remain outside of the community, but she will threaten to dissolve it in her perversion of it."[41] What I have tried to show, however, is that Antigone not only threatens to *dissolve* the community (this is how she is commonly understood), but that she—as the *instigator* of the new order—is, in fact, the *creator* of the very community that she, as a woman, is bound to be subsequently excluded from. Creation and destruction take place through one and the same figure.

This figure, Antigone—doer and sufferer at once—makes visible the self-destructive structure of a society that can only maintain itself by the establishment of a constitutive outside, a repressed other: woman. And yet she does so, paradoxically, precisely by defending and establishing the very strict division between family and state that would place her as a woman outside of the political realm that she herself founds (in refusing to let Creon interfere with private businesses such as mourning and burial rites). Antigone is thus situated in a precarious and double-edged position: she creates the very order that will exclude her by insisting on the very division (private/public) that will place her and women like her on the outside of politics. Structurally speaking, we might want to say that this makes her a rather typical tragic hero(ine). Think, for example, of Oedipus, whose very attempt to escape destiny and claim agency over his own life is what throws him back into the relentless web of destiny. The (self-) destructive outcome of what was intended as constructive agency lies at the very core of tragedy. What makes Antigone unique, however, is the profoundly political consequences that her tragic action implies.

My views here come close to a line of thought that appears in Roger Just's study of the role of women in ancient Greece (although our larger arguments differ on several counts). In an attempt at making more complex his own account of how men came to represent the ordered life of the polis while women were confined to the natural-irrational realm of the family sphere, he offers a reading of Aeschylus' *Seven against Thebes*—a play whose dramatic content precedes that of *Antigone*, as it narrates the story of how Eteocles and Polyneices, her two brothers, kill each other in war. Just recounts how Eteocles—the brother who is subsequently celebrated by Creon and who as a character to some extent mirrors Creon—attacks the chorus, whose exclusively female members beg him to avoid war to save the city: "As Eteokles exits, the chorus sings of the fate of the fallen city, and it is through the voices of women that Aischylos can convey the full meaning of that event: the total destruction of a community."[42] At this point Just speaks of a reversal: "Whereas with Eteokles the women are represented as in allegiance with the destructive forces that lie outside the boundaries of the *polis*, now it seems that the women represent the very values of the *polis* in danger of being destroyed."[43] We might add that if Eteocles mirrors Creon, who later will come to his defense, Polyneices, whom Antigone will honor, shares her precarious position within the structure of the play: he, like his sister, is an internal enemy, a Theban who nevertheless attacks Thebes, someone who is integral to the very founding of the city (as a member of its royal family), yet who will nevertheless bring about its downfall.

My claim is that *Antigone* is a play about the inherent impossibility of the ancient Greek polis and, more generally, of societies founded on that same structure of exclusion. They, like Thebes, will fall: the very repression that constitutes them is bound to tear them apart. The polis, as represented in the play, carries within it the seed of its own downfall. *Antigone embodies the condition of impossibility of the society she founds.* In this sense we might say that she truly is a death-seeking creature. Her self-negation goes far beyond suicide or personal death. It represents the enigmatic role of women at large—that of being the constitutive ground of a political order that proceeds to expel them. In the case of Antigone, the question is not—as for one of our modern tragic heroes—whether she should be or not be. What is at stake, for her, is the possibility of belonging or not belonging—to be one of them or not be one of them (as Marcel Proust has put it). And insofar as she does not belong, insofar as she is not one of them, she cannot be at all.

The characterization of the Greek polis as a self-destructive project should remind us of the Arendtian criticism of modern society. She describes our modern world as one in which "both despair and triumph are inherent in the same event" (262). The epigraph of the last chapter of *The Human Condition* comes from Franz Kafka: "He found the Archimedean point, but he used it against himself; it seems that he was permitted to find it only under this condition" (248). Galileo Galilei, Martin Luther, and the great seafarers are the characters that in Arendt's view embody the conditions of impossibility of our own modern world. The latter "submitted to the call of the distant," but instead "abolished distance"; they wanted "to enlarge the earth," but ended up shrinking her "into a ball" (250). I see Antigone as embodying this paradoxical position. At the limit of the Greek polis she is both its beginning, or founding principle, and its inherent end. As her name implies, she is an *anti-seed*: creative and destructive at once.[44]

Conclusion: New Beginnings

Is Antigone merely an impossible figure then? Is her action bound to fail, just as she herself was bound to die? If she establishes the very order and private/public distinction that will come to exclude women altogether, why should we see her as a feminist heroine, as a figure to which feminist readers ought to return?

One can, of course, view her death as nullifying her act; one can claim that she initiates something only to subsequently bring it to a dead end. Antigone is commonly (and most obviously) seen as a character married to death. Her desire is a desire to die, and the dark tomb is described as her bridal chamber.[45] She is placed at the end of generations: an antigenerative force, childless, perverted, an incestuous offspring. The emphasis on death would contradict the kind of "new beginning" Arendt praises. But as is made abundantly clear by the many Antigones that figure in performances around the world—2,500 years after she first appeared on the Greek stage—our heroine continues to be reborn: fueling stories and narratives across the globe, she rises from the dead, time and again, and appears in times of oppression and injustice wherever the need arises for dissidence and resistance.[46]

The contours of yet another reversal take shape: her desire for death begins to look more like a desire for life. Antigone's death immortalizes her by making her actions memorable. Antigone has been described as the first anarchist, the first feminist, the founder of civil disobedience. And no one, as the title of George Steiner's book *Antigones* suggests, has initiated and given birth to so many new stories. The Arendtian notion of starting something anew, of new beginnings, new narratives, is, in fact, perfectly embodied in the impossible yet stubbornly resurrected figure of Antigone; just as she fought to commemorate her brother's deed, her own actions have not only survived in various stories for generations to come, but also continue to inspire and make possible subsequent acts of resistance. If we, following Arendt, experience a "second birth" each time that we appear in public (176), then Antigone, who has been viewed as a figure of death, appears before us instead as a character marked by incessant birth.

As viewers and readers of *Antigone*, we witness what Haemon once called her "glorious acts" (695), and we are compelled to be courageous and outspoken like her, moved to fight injustice the way she once did, and perhaps to rethink politics yet again, in more inclusive terms. If she as an actor were wrapped up in the contradictions of her own actions (action, Arendt reminds us, is unpredictable and irreversible, and actors lack the "disinterested distance" that it takes to see the implications of their own actions),[47] then we as spectators—if attentive to the reversals at play in the play—might grasp the implications of these very reversals (and of the contradictions the figure of Antigone makes visible) and make political judgments accordingly. As readers and viewers of *Antigone*, we are spectators indeed, and as spectators we enter the political space Arendt described. In *The Human Condition* she characterizes theater as "the political art par excellence" because "only there is the political sphere of human life transposed into art" (188). In her later work, she would again bring attention to the relationship between art and politics, and while she did not live to write her volume on judgment, her lectures on the topic provide clues as to why we cannot reduce the story of Antigone to a mere story about failed or futile action: *Antigone*—the story of a woman who dares to transgress the law and who unhesitatingly appears before us—allows us to establish what Arendt, following Immanuel Kant, would come to call a world community of spectators.[48] And if Arendt is right that taste "decides not only how the world is to look, but also who belongs together in it,"[49] then the many oppressed around the world who return to and appreciate *Antigone* time and again may find the inspiration and courage to instigate new political spaces in which they themselves will be included at last.

Notes

Author's note: This chapter is the result of my thinking about the figure of Antigone as it has developed over the last few years. I have presented several earlier versions of it in seminars and at conferences: *Tragedy and Philosophy* (graduate seminar at the New School for Social Research, New York, 2005), *Women in Philosophy* (works-in-progress seminar at the New School for Social Research, New York, 2006), *Canadian Society for Continental Philosophy* (University of Montreal, Canada, 2008), *philoSOPHIA Conference for Continental Feminist Philosophy* (Decatur, GA, 2008), and *The Hannah Arendt Circle* (Emory University, 2008). I am grateful to those who have raised productive questions along the way. I would especially like to thank J. M. Bernstein, whose reading of *Antigone* continues to inspire, and Rocío Zambrana, whose insightful comments on several drafts have been invaluable.

1. G. W. F. Hegel, *Aesthetics: Lectures on Fine Art*, trans. T. M. Knox, vol. II (Oxford, UK: Clarendon Press, 1988), p. 1162.

2. See Jean-Pierre Vernant, "Myth and Tragedy," trans. J. Lloyd, in *Essays on Aristotle's* Poetics, ed. Amélie Oksenberg Rorty (Princeton, NJ: Princeton University Press, 1992), pp. 33ff.

3. In this sense, the Greeks and the moderns have much in common. The Greek tragedians and their audience, much like the nineteenth-century modern German philosophers who became so obsessed with tragedy in general and with the figure of Antigone in particular, were experiencing the death of God and the void of meaning that followed as a consequence. Friedrich Nietzsche was not the first to kill God and put Man in his place. The Greeks had done it before, and tragedy inhabited and embodied this crisis.

4. Hegel is, as we might expect, full of praise for the play: "Of all the masterpieces of the classical and the modern world," he declares, "*Antigone* seems to me to be the most magnificent and satisfying work of art of this kind" (*Aesthetics*, p. 1218). In her dissertation on Hegel's concept of love, Laura Werner notes that it is "not hard to see why Sophocles' play appealed to Hegel. Like each chapter of *Phenomenology of Spirit*, it too could be read as presenting two seemingly irreconcilable positions, and then showing how each of these in themselves, taken as isolated or singular, prove to be one-sided" (Laura Werner, *"The Restless Love of Thinking": The Concept of Liebe in G. W. F. Hegel's Philosophy* [Helsinki, Finland: Helsinki University Press, 2007], p. 117).

5. Johann Gottfried Herder, "Shakespeare," trans. Joyce P. Crick, in *German Aesthetic and Literary Criticism: Winkelmann, Lessing, Hamann, Herder, Schiller, Goethe*, ed. H. B. Nisbet (Cambridge, UK: Cambridge University Press, 1985), p. 164.

6. Hannah Arendt, *The Human Condition* (Chicago: University of Chicago Press, 1998). Henceforth references to this book are given parenthetically within the text.

7. See Roger Just, *Women in Athenian Law and Life* (New York: Routledge, 1989), p. 20. Just grants, however, that Greek democracy "accentuated a major disparity between the lives of men and women . . . which can be seen in terms of *the continual contrast between public and private which runs throughout Athenian thought*" (23, emphasis added).

8. This is a characteristic of power that Arendt never abandoned. In a later text, *On Violence*, she writes that power "is never the property of an individual; it belongs to a group and remains in existence only so long as the group keeps together. . . . The

moment the group, from which the power originated to begin with . . . disappears, 'his power' also vanishes" (Hannah Arendt, *On Violence* [New York: Harcourt Brace, 1970], p. 44).

9. Sophocles, *Antigone*, in *Sophocles I: The Complete Greek Tragedies*, trans. David Grene, ed. David Grene and Richmond Lattimore (Chicago: University of Chicago Press, 1991), l. 1074. I use this translation throughout the chapter. Henceforth references to the play are given parenthetically within the text by line number.

10. Arendt, *On Violence*, p. 54.

11. In *The Human Condition* Arendt turns to Montesquieu (who she describes as "the last political thinker to concern himself seriously with the problem of forms of government") as she addresses the relationship between tyranny, loneliness, and power: "Montesquieu realized that the outstanding characteristic of tyranny was that it rested on isolation—on the isolation of the tyrant from his subjects and the isolation of the subjects from each other through mutual fear and suspicion—and hence that tyranny was not one form of government among others but contradicted the essential human condition of plurality, the acting and speaking together, which is the condition of all forms of political organization. Tyranny prevents the development of power, not only in a particular segment of the public realm but also in its entirety; it generates, in other words, impotence as naturally as other bodies politic generate power" (202). As a consequence, Arendt concludes, tyranny "develops the germ of its own destruction the moment it comes into existence" (203). Creon is, in other words, bound to exit the scene as a lonely warrior among corpses. As we will see, however, my own reading of the play will suggest that Greek democracy—whose space of appearance and a community of "equals" constitutively depends on the exclusion of women and slaves—similarly carries within it the seed of its own downfall. If Creon is the embodiment of the impossibility of tyranny, Antigone embodies the impossibility of the very democratic polis Arendt celebrated (one defined by an opposition between private and public).

12. Margaret Canovan, *Hannah Arendt: A Reinterpretation of Her Political Thought* (Cambridge, UK: Cambridge University Press, 1992), p. 141.

13. Luce Irigaray, "The Eternal Irony of the Community," in *Speculum of the Other Woman*, trans. Gillian C. Gill (Ithaca, NY: Cornell University Press, 1985), pp. 214–226. The work is also republished in this volume.

14. Arendt assures us that it was "a simple historical fact that the foundation of the *polis* was preceded by the destruction of all organized units resting on kinship, such as the *phratria* and the *phylé*" (24).

15. Froma I. Zeitlin, "Thebes: Theater of Self and Society in Athenian Drama," in *Nothing to Do with Dionysos? Athenian Drama in Its Social Context*, ed. John J. Winkler and Froma I. Zeitlin (Princeton, NJ: Princeton University Press, 1990), p. 144.

16. Ibid., p. 144, emphasis added.

17. Just points to a legal document ascribed to Solon, which was meant to ensure that funerals remained discreetly private affairs. The law, interestingly, limits the participation of women in funerals. Just suggests that the document "constitutes a clear recognition that what could transform a private funeral into an emotionally fraught and hence potentially dangerous public demonstration was precisely the uninhibited conduct of women" (Just, *Women in Athenian Law and Life*, p. 198). Solon apparently worries that the wailing and crying of women will disrupt the order of the polis. We are reminded

of Antigone, whose burial rites are accompanied by "the shrill cry / of an embittered bird" (424–425). Insofar as Creon has attempted to make funeral rites a public matter, Antigone will, indeed, publicly perform her grief and mourning, and in so doing, will bring our attention to the fatal disorder this confusion of boundaries leads to.

18. Arendt writes: "The connotation of courage, which we now feel to be an indispensable quality of the hero, is in fact already present in a willingness to act and speak at all, to insert one's self into the world and begin a story of one's own" (186).

19. Arendt, again: "The fact that man is capable of action means that the unexpected can be expected from him, that he is able to perform what is infinitely improbable" (178).

20. Cecilia Sjöholm, *The Antigone Complex: Ethics and the Invention of Feminine Desire* (Stanford, CA: Stanford University Press, 2004), p. 44. In a footnote, Sjöholm refers to Nicole Loraux, who has given a lengthy account of the gendered nature of the beautiful death in *The Experience of Tiresias: The Feminine and the Greek Man* (trans. Paula Wissing [Princeton, NJ: Princeton University Press, 1997]), showing that it constitutes a figure of masculinity (Sjöholm, *The Antigone Complex*, p. 165, n. 33).

21. The political realm in ancient Greece, Arendt explains, is one "from which everything merely necessary or useful is strictly excluded" (25). "No activity that served only the purpose of making a living, of sustaining only the life process, was permitted to enter the political realm" (37).

22. Aeschylus, *Seven against Thebes*, trans. H. Weir Smyth, Loeb Classical Library (London: Heinemann, 1922), l. 1047.

23. In the passage just quoted from *Seven against Thebes*, Antigone frames her claim to courage with a disclaimer: "Even if I am a woman . . ." (1044). In *Oedipus at Colonus*, Oedipus actually suggests that Antigone and her sister are more manly than their brothers by being loyal to their miserable father. He says to Polyneices: "I might have lived or died for all your interest. / But they [Antigone and Ismene] have saved me, they are my support, / And are not girls, but men, in faithfulness. / As for you two, you are no sons of mine!" (Sophocles, *Oedipus at Colonus*, in *The Complete Greek Tragedies*, 1366–1369). Steiner, too, emphasizes Antigone's masculinity, contrasting her with Ismene, who he thinks represents pure womanliness. Among other things, he points to the use of syntax at line 464, at the moment of Antigone's sovereign acquiescence in death, when she refers to herself in the masculine gender: "how shall he not be glad to gain his death?" Steiner, however, argues that as the play unfolds Antigone's femininity is deepened and affirmed: "Made victim, Antigone grows into essential womanhood" because she mourns the children she will never have. She laments "the crowning conditions of a woman's existence" (Steiner, *Antigones*, p. 241).

24. Sjöholm, *The Antigone Complex*, p. 44.

25. Zeitlin, "Thebes: Theater of Self and Society," p. 151.

26. For examples of this approach, see Irigaray, "The Eternal Irony of the Community"; Judith Butler, *Antigone's Claim: Kinship between Life and Death* (New York: Columbia University Press, 2000); and Werner, *The Restless Love of Thinking*.

27. Julia Kristeva, *Hannah Arendt*, vol. 1 of *Female Genius: Life, Madness, Words*, trans. Ross Guberman (New York: Columbia University Press, 2001), p. 72.

28. For Arendt, narration is thus a constitutive aspect of political life. For examples of how the model of politics as narration has been used and developed by feminist thinkers, see Lisa J. Disch, *Hannah Arendt and the Limits of Philosophy* (Ithaca, NY:

Cornell University Press, 1994); Adriana Cavarero, *Relating Narratives: Storytelling and Selfhood*, trans. Paul A. Kottman (London: Routledge, 2000); and Judith Butler, *Giving an Account of Oneself* (New York: Fordham University Press, 2005).

29. R. P. Winnington-Ingram, *Sophocles: An Interpretation* (Cambridge, UK: Cambridge University Press, 1980), p. 264.

30. Hannah Arendt, "What Is Freedom?" in *Between Past and Future* (New York: Penguin Books, 1993), p. 154.

31. For further elaboration of Arendt's conception of freedom, see "What Is Freedom?" In this essay, Arendt likens the Greek polis "with a kind of theater where freedom could appear" (154). The parallels pointed to here are by no means meant to suggest that Arendt's notion of freedom is reducible to a Greek notion of destiny or necessity—such a gesture would be absurd. I am merely underlining the fact that freedom for Arendt is irreconcilable with a Christian notion of free will and that her emphasis is instead on the unpredictability of action and the interdependence that we as humans experience in the political sphere—an interdependence that is the sine qua non for politics and therefore not something that we should even try to overcome.

32. This should bring our attention to another important and stark antagonism within the play, namely that between generations. When we speak of age rather than gender, it is more straightforwardly obvious that Antigone and Haemon represent the new order, while Creon stands for the past and tradition.

33. Arendt contests that "all Greek philosophers, no matter how opposed to *polis* life, took for granted . . . that freedom is exclusively located in the political realm, that necessity is primarily a prepolitical phenomenon, characteristic of the private household organization, and that force and violence are justified in this sphere because they are the only means to master necessity—for instance, by ruling over slaves—and to become free" (31).

35. Butler, *Antigone's Claim*, p. 82. This part of her book is included in this volume.

35. See, for example, Irigaray, who describes "the work of Sophocles" as marking "the historical bridge between matriarchy and patriarchy" (Irigaray, "The Eternal Irony of the Community," p. 217).

36. Butler, *Antigone's Claim*, p. 82.

37. G. W. F. Hegel, *Phenomenology of Spirit*, trans. A. V. Miller (Oxford, UK: Oxford University Press, 1977), p. 288.

38. My main concern here is not to develop a detailed critique of this aspect of Arendt's work—this has been done elsewhere—but rather to shed light on how this blind spot in Arendt's thinking complicates—while at the same time helping us understand—the story of Antigone and the perplexing situation in which this figure finds herself. Extensive feminist literature exists on the private/public distinction in Arendt's thinking. For some representative examples, see Adrienne Rich, *On Lies, Secrets and Silence: Selected Prose, 1966–1978* (New York: Norton, 1979); Mary O'Brien, *The Politics of Reproduction* (Boston: Routledge and Kegan Paul, 1981); Anne Philips, *Engendering Democracy* (Cambridge, UK: Polity Press, 1991); Joan B. Landes, "Jürgen Habermas, *The Structural Transformation of the Public Sphere*: A Feminist Inquiry," *Praxis International*, vol. 12, no. 1 (April 1992), pp. 106–127; Seyla Benhabib, "Feminist Theory and Hannah Arendt's Concept of Public Space," *History of the Human Sciences*, vol. 6, no. 2 (1993), pp. 97–114; and Benhabib, "Models of Public Space: Hannah Arendt,

the Liberal Tradition, and Jürgen Habermas," in *Feminism: The Public and The Private Realm*, ed. Joan B. Landes (Oxford, UK: Oxford University Press, 1998). For several interesting essays as well as an annotated bibliography of feminist engagements with Arendt, see Bonnie Honig, ed., *Feminist Interpretations of Hannah Arendt* (University Park: Penn State University Press, 1995).

39. Butler, *Antigone's Claim*, p. 82.

40. Sjöholm, *The Antigone Complex*, p. 49.

41. Ibid., p. 49.

42. Just, *Women in Athenian Law and Life*, p. 200.

43. Ibid., p. 201.

44. Insofar as woman is a constitutive outside, she will always embody this double-edged logic. As Just suggests, women "become in their 'domesticated' state the representatives and symbols of society's *continuity*, embodying quite literally the natural processes on which that continuity rested," while, at the same time, and as outsiders, they come to *threaten* "the structure of a society which, though it might have had ultimate need of them, nevertheless tried to separate itself off from them" (Just, *Women in Athenian Law and Life*, p. 213, emphasis added).

45. For an emphasis on this aspect of the figure of Antigone, see Jacques Lacan, *The Ethics of Psychoanalysis 1959–1960*, book 7, trans. Dennis Porter, ed. Jacques-Alain Miller (New York:. Norton, 1988).

46. For concrete examples, see Tina Chanter's chapter in this volume—which treats a specific South African example—and Moira Fradinger's prologue, which follows the (uncanny) journey of the more than seventy Antigones that have appeared on theatrical stages around the world in the past sixty years or so.

47. Action, moreover, "almost never achieves its purpose" according to Arendt (184). What it accomplishes, however, is that "it 'produces' stories with or without intention as naturally as fabrication produces tangible things" (184). What matters, again, is that a story is being produced, not that action follows the exact course that we had hoped for it to take.

48. Arendt's last philosophical work was an intended three-part project entitled *The Life of the Mind*. She lived to complete only the first two parts, "Thinking" and "Willing" (Hannah Arendt, *The Life of the Mind* [New York: Harcourt, 1971]), writing only the title page of the third part, "Judging." Her (incomplete) trilogy was written in the wake of Immanuel Kant's three *Critiques*, and while the *Critique of Practical Reason* has most commonly been viewed as Kant's political corpus, Arendt instead sees the seed for a radically different political philosophy in his *Critique of the Power of Judgment*, a book more commonly viewed as his treatise on aesthetics. Her claim hinges on the idea that aesthetic judgment, and the *sensus communis* that it involves, help us to understand politics in terms of public appearance and spectatorship. While she did not live to develop her thoughts in this matter, her lectures on the topic, delivered at the New School for Social Research in 1970, have been published as *Lectures on Kant's Political Philosophy*, ed. Ronald Beiner (Chicago: University of Chicago Press, 1992), and offer her most sustained meditation on the central role of judgment in and for political life.

49. Hannah Arendt, "The Crisis in Culture: Its Social and Its Political Significance," in *Between Past and Future*, p. 223.

4

The Performative Politics and Rebirth of Antigone in Ancient Greece and Modern South Africa

Tina Chanter

If the death of tragedy can be asserted with confidence from the perspective of Friedrich Nietzsche, not everybody was invited to the funeral: Antigone, for instance. As many times as she dies, she comes alive, reborn time and again, born anew each time she enters the theatrical stage, inserting herself into a new political history, providing a commentary on the history of a people, embodying the hopes for the rebirth of a nation. What accounts for this incessant rebirth of Antigone in widely divergent, international, political contexts?

Perhaps Antigone's excessive character—her excess of love for her brother and her refusal to be circumscribed by Creon's law—subsists less in the appeal her character makes to unchanging, timeless, eternal laws, and still less in an Hegelian invocation of her sublimity—a gesture that succumbs to his taming of the terrifying visage of Antigone's extremity, surrendering her spirit to the ostensibly reasonable demands of the state—than in her strategic political reemergence at times of political crises, which tells a different story. If so, then the contingency of the lines demarcating Antigone's exclusion precisely marks out her story, a contingency that becomes all the more pronounced with each rebirth of the play, as each new political context continues to plot out a history of the unstable content of excluded yet constitutive others, a history that proves to be variegated over time and across cultures. If there is a sense in which Antigone exceeds any attempt to reduce her to the politics and ideology of the classical era, in which it would have been enough to be a woman to suffer a politics of exclusion, I also want to resist the abstract gesture that is content to construe Antigone as a figure of excess, as if she merely marked the limits of the articulate, serving as a placeholder to designate that which is outside discourse as if her multiple dramatic rebirths did not themselves etch out a political genealogy of multiple occupancy, a continual renaissance of that which is said to be excessive for each new political staging of Antigone's rebirth. The sense in which Antigone would constitute a figure of excess for a given interpretation informs us about that which a given political culture finds intolerable in its self-understanding, that which it finds impossible to represent without either embracing self-contradiction or resorting to fetishization.

While the tropes of the uncanny (Martin Heidegger) and the monstrous (Jacques Lacan) have tended to posit Antigone as a prepolitical figure, I build on more recent work, including that of Judith Butler, J. Peter Euben, Luce Irigaray, Warren and Ann Lane, Mary Beth Mader, and Patchen Markell, to argue against a Lacanian and Žižekian tendency to fetishize the figure of Antigone, in favor of a political reading of Antigone that understands her excess as symptomatic of a society that cannot tolerate integrating her into its sanctioned self-representations.[1] Unlike the Hegelian, the fetishist has no trouble at all in simultaneously sustaining positions that, if cashed out logically, would yield contradiction. The fetishization of Antigone oscillates between glorifying her as an enigmatic savior and denigrating her as unnatural or uncanny without compromising the integrity of either position. I read the figure of Antigone as making an intervention into the reifying and stabilizing logic of fetishistic disavowal, as drawing attention to the politics of its excluded but constitutive other.[2] One of the ways in which this plays out is in the political imperative stipulating the performative conditions of Greek tragedy in fifth century BCE Athens, which dictated that male actors perform female roles to an all male audience. This exclusion is accomplished in fifth century BCE Athens by means of a porous boundary, which operates to include the representation of women in a limited, controlled, and very specific way, even as it prohibits their bodily presence.

Critics such as Euben argue that tragedy calls into question the silencing of women, and others such as David Halperin point out that the silencing of actual women in Greek political life was the necessary corollary of the volubility of fictional women in tragic drama.[3] Yet little attention has been paid to the peculiar relationship obtaining between the political imperatives informing the performative conditions of ancient Greek tragedy—as opposed to the performative conditions of modern appropriations of the tragic—and the resulting constraints on how tragic drama might impact the idea that a citizenry has of itself. Where dramatic performances were sanctioned by the state, where the attendance of a male citizenry was mandated, and where women were excluded from the political processes of self-representation and self-reflection afforded by such performances, this relationship would have played out with largely predictable results.

By contrast, in *The Island*, a South African play within a play, which reinvents *Antigone* in the political context of the racial oppression of colonialism and apartheid, a context in which (depending on the color of one's skin and the township in which one lived) to perform a play was to risk arrest—the results are far from predictable. In *The Island*, by Athol Fugard, John Kani, and Winston Ntshona, two Robben Island prison inmates perform a version of *Antigone* in which the prisoner playing the role of Antigone, who is obliged to dress as a woman, becomes an object of ridicule.[4] The play thus destabilizes the cross-dressing of Greek drama that Kirk Ormond has argued would have operated neither as "drag" nor "as a kind of flirting with an alternate gender identity," but rather in terms of a strategy of containment.[5] This destabilization occurs in the wider context of political resistance to a system that legitimates racial inequality. The legitimated sexual inequality of ancient Greece that constituted the background of tragic drama is transposed into a political legal system that uses racial identity to legislate inferiority. Yet this transposition leaves a residue.

While Irigaray and Butler have argued in different ways that questions of sexuality are central to Antigone's legacy, the logic of Antigone extends beyond these questions. Not only does it lend itself to commentary on racial issues of postcolonial identity, but it also points out how exclusionary logics reiterate themselves. My point here is not to suggest that race—rather than gender or sexuality—is the real abject, but rather to explore the complex interrelation between race and sexuality, whereby sexuality comes to be abjected in a racially fraught context in a play that nonetheless acknowledges at another level how gender and race operate as metaphors for one another. *The Island* both explores and protests an unjust racial politic and draws attention to the performative constraints dictated by apartheid South Africa. It does so in a way that reconfigures the exclusionary conditions pertaining to the performance of Greek tragedy in Athens, transposing the logic of exclusion into one that can be thematized within the theatrics of the performance itself and serving to interrogate the exclusionary politic that dictates apartheid. If in one way it usurps Antigone's outsider status for its own ends in a literature of resistance that reinvents the gendered exclusionary terms that others have contested in Antigone's name, in another way it thereby spells out the procedure by which the logic of the excluded other replicates itself, even within progressively political texts.

In articulating the politics of *Antigone* with reference to the historical legacy of political performances of the play, I do not simply want to overturn the construction of Antigone as representing the family in opposition to Creon's representation of the state. Butler is correct to insist not only on the sense in which Antigone throws into productive crises the categories of the familial and the political, but also the sense in which Antigone could represent any institution in an uncomplicated way. Antigone brings into question the narrowly authoritarian terms in which Creon construes the interests of the polis, interrogating the vision of the political that such a view presupposes and the naturalized hierarchies that support it. If Antigone can be reread as figuring the political, she must be read as calling for a renewal of the political itself. In Athens/Thebes Antigone contests Creon's claim of absolute power, which proceeds from a king who demands total loyalty from those subjects whose contribution to the well-being of the state he recognizes as worthy, while refusing recognition to other, subordinated members of the polity. In one sense Antigone is exemplary of those whose contributions, while vital to the continuation of the state, do not merit recognition as such, those who are not seen as worthy of political representation. In another sense, the fate under which she labors exempts her from making any political contribution, and precisely the way in which she takes up this exemption alters her position of subjugation at the same time that it reveals the pretension of Creon's absolute claims. Equally, Antigone points to the chimerical quality of sovereignty in the modern polity. Ostensibly an expression of the will and self-governance of the people, the apparent sovereignty and harmony of the state is exposed as having been purchased for *some* at the expense of those to whom it systematically denies effective representation.

The political renews itself in Antigone's reconstitution of *philia* as central to the polis in such a way as to confirm the need to oversee the lines of inheritance, even as she contests the very definition of the political as masculine. Where Oedipus had mingled eros with *philia*, making of Jocasta a loved one in two divergent and incompatible respects (as both mother and wife) thereby redoubling the bonds of *philia*, Antigone "disambiguates" *philia* from eros, putting not only her blood relationship with Polyneices before her erotic bond with Haemon, but in doing so specifying and delimiting the sense in which Polyneices is a loved one, *philos*.[6] Unlike Creon, Antigone neither wants order for the sake of order, nor does she act in such a way as to merely confirm or disrupt the prevailing conventions of femininity. If she works to reinstate distinctions that are vital to both familial and political life, this work neither merely eliminates the disorder that women's association with eros was conventionally taken to embody, nor does it merely introduce disorder into the political order. Instead, it opens up to interrogation that which Creon tries to define as civil order by decree.

As the brother of Jocasta, according to the laws of inheritance of ancient Greece, Creon has a legitimate claim to be heir to the throne.[7] As the brother of Oedipus' mother (rather than the brother of his wife), Creon would have no such claim. Symbolically, then, in denying Antigone the right to bury Polyneices, Creon is undercutting his own claim to the throne because if Mader is right in her essay "Antigone's Line," in burying her brother, Antigone both clarifies that Polyneices is her brother—and *only* her brother (rather than her nephew or her uncle)—and at the same time confers on Oedipus the symbolic status of father—*and nothing else* (not also the brother that Oedipus' marriage to his mother had made of him to Antigone). In failing to recognize that Antigone's act symbolically affirms his right to be king, Creon would thus seem to be unwittingly undermining his own claim to kingship by persevering in his absolute prohibition against the burial of Polyneices. Were it not for the fact that Creon is the brother of Jocasta, and as such the brother of the king's wife, he would have no claim to the throne. That is, the very relationship that Antigone seeks to honor, namely the familial relation of a brother to a sister, is the one on which Creon's claim rests. In this sense, Antigone's attempt to clarify kinship roles, to establish their integrity, and to insist on their mutual exclusion from one another, legitimates Creon's claim to be next in line as king.

Instead of appreciating Antigone's attempts to repair the lines of kinship that ensure his claim to kingship, Creon inadvertently destroys the continuation of his own *oikos*. Creon's insistence on putting Antigone to death results in his bringing his *oikos* to an end without any male issue to continue his familial line. Antigone's death is also the cause of Haemon's death, which in turn is the cause of Jocasta's death, while Creon's other son has already died in battle. No son will be born, therefore, who can inherit either Creon's property or his royal lineage.[8] In his failure to recognize Antigone's attempt to distinguish between the familial positions of her immediate kin, rectifying the conflation that Oedipus had effected, Creon brings his own family line to an abrupt end.

If Antigone acknowledges Creon's claim to kingship in terms of the formal kinship laws that recognize his filiation to Jocasta, she contests Creon in two other important respects. First, as a woman she presumes to speak on an equal footing with him, and in doing so she contests the unwritten kinship laws that specify that only the male line of filiation legitimates a claim to sovereignty. Even as Antigone observes Creon's rightful claim according to the laws of kinship she seeks to restore, she disrupts his claim according to another claim that those laws do not respect, namely the rights of women; that is, she refuses to accept her second-class status as a woman. Second, she contests the content of the proclamation Creon issues when he prohibits the burial of Polyneices. In doing so, she consecrates in general Creon's particular claim to the throne, while contesting the particularity of the configuration of these specific kinship laws. Insisting on the burial of Polyneices is then, paradoxically, a way of upholding Creon's claim to kingship in one way, even as it undercuts his authority in two other ways. On the one hand Antigone refuses Creon's claim to absolute authority by violating his edict, but on the other hand, in doing so she shows herself to be more cognizant of the mutual implication of kinship and state than Creon himself. At the same time she does so as a woman, and in this respect she contests the particular way in which the kinship lines are construed, such that they sanction the claims of male kin to kingship, while excluding any claim that female kin might have as part of the royal line.

For Lacan, whose influential reading of the play is determinative to some extent of the scope of Butler's investigation, the symbolic as a structure of intelligibility is inseparable from the prohibition against incest. The very possibility of meaningful discourse is bound up with acknowledging that different subject positions exist and that these subject positions are symbolic of certain familial kinship structures. Insofar as the symbolic constitutes the condition for any particular normative kinship system to be meaningful, rather than being equated with a specific kinship system, Lacan insists on specifying that the symbolic, in and of itself, does not imply or endorse any particular set of kinship laws. Even if Lacan's account of the symbolic purports to admit of contingency, Butler points out that it nonetheless tends to operate as an ultimate authority and that it does so precisely insofar as Lacan maintains its status as formal and independent of social configurations. Butler takes issue with the claim that the symbolic operates in a purely formal register, questioning the idea that it can in principle be entirely free of those injunctions that operate at the normative level. In doing so, she casts doubt on the possibility of the symbolic remaining independent of the heteronormative order.[9]

In reflecting on the issues raised in *The Island*, I want to introduce a set of different but related considerations. Let us grant, for now, the plausibility of Lacan's assumption that the very possibility of linguistic communities is bound up with the prohibition of incest and that therefore any meaningful exchange—including the exchange of marriage vows—must take place in a context that presupposes the inauguration of the symbolic order. Even on its own terms, Lacan's account of the symbolic could be rewritten to take account of the sense in which not only sexual but also racial categories might be infused into the very possibilities of recognition it facilitates. If there is a sense in which the kind of recognition at stake in kinship laws presupposes a prior recognition of an other as human (rather than nonhuman), and if there are some cases in which the humanity of some racialized group is rendered dubious in advance by some feature that would seem to mark it out as less than human, would this more primordial sense of recognition not operate at a level that is even more fundamental than—or at least as fundamental as—kinship?[10] When certain groups, classified according to the color of their skin, are denied basic human rights, when laws are erected to prevent them from enjoying the protection of those laws from which other racially classified groups benefit due to the color of their skin, this deprivation of human rights signals a failure to recognize those groups as equally deserving of legal rights. Racial taboos that rest on neglecting to concede that certain individuals qualify as properly human, taboos that acquire legal authority under certain conditions, such as apartheid, do not afford those individuals the protection under the law that other groups can assume, including the right to marry regardless of skin color. If certain humans' humanity is in question, humans who do not unequivocally qualify as human, and if their failure to qualify as unambiguously human puts them off limits as sexual or marriage partners, this appears to prescribe that only those whose humanity is not in question are acceptable sexual partners. If skin color becomes a mark of race, and race becomes a way of distinguishing between those who qualify unproblematically as human, and those who barely qualify as human, then racial taboos would seem to function as inarticulate conditions, invisibly built into the incest prohibition.[11] Not only are members of one's immediate family put out of bounds as potential marriage partners, but so too are members of certain races.

In *The Island*, Antigone is used as a vehicle to speak out against apartheid laws, including those prohibiting marriage between whites and blacks. Of particular interest here is the way in which homophobic and gendered anxiety serves as a metaphor to explore the racial divisions of apartheid. The play compares the intensity of the bond that has developed between John and Winston to that of a marriage, a comparison that is evoked because they spend so much time together that they might as well be husband and wife and because they are so often handcuffed to one another.[12] The forced proximity of prisoners sharing a cell with one another develops into a mutual dependency that is threatened when John unexpectedly hears that his sentence has been reduced from ten to three years as a result of an appeal filed by his lawyer on his behalf. Winston must confront the fact that in three months time he will be left in prison while his cellmate is set free. He will have to learn to share his days with new cellmates, to develop new strategies for survival, to let go of the old habits that he and John devised to get through their days—recalling the plots of favorite movies, imagining phone calls to mutual friends on the outside, remembering happier times in days gone by.

At John's instigation, Winston has agreed to take part in an abbreviated version of *Antigone* in a performance that will constitute the finale of the annual prison concert. As *The Island* begins, the performance is scheduled to take place in six days time, and John wants to rehearse Winston on the details of the plot. Having been subjected by the prison guard Hodoshe—a character named after and based on a notorious guard at Robben Island—to the grueling, "back-breaking" (47), dehumanizing, and futile labor of shoveling sand from one pile to another, Winston is exhausted and has trouble remembering that Antigone is not the mother, but the sister of Polyneices (51), and that it was not Eteocles, but Polyneices whom she buried against Creon's orders (52).[13] When it comes to whether Antigone pleads guilty or not guilty, Winston cannot make sense of why Antigone would plead guilty. John tries to reason with him:

> JOHN: Now look, Winston, we're not going to argue. Between me and you, in this cell, we know she's Not Guilty. But in the play she pleads Guilty.
>
> WINSTON: No, man, John! Antigone is Not Guilty. . . .
>
> JOHN: In the play. . . .
>
> WINSTON [*losing his temper*]: To hell with the play! Antigone had every right to bury her brother. (52–53)

While John insists on Winston getting the plot right, he agrees with Winston that Antigone had every right to bury Polyneices; this is precisely why the dispute between Antigone and Creon resonates with him and why he insists on staging an abbreviated version of *Antigone.* In the words of Winston—the final words of the play—like Antigone, he too "honoured those things to which honour belongs" (77). We learn the reason Winston is in prison, condemned to a life sentence, is because of his involvement in a protest in which he burned his passbook in front of a police station (63). According to Errol Durbach, the "pass-law system [gave] the state the right to control the movement of Blacks in South Africa, which [could] compel them to work in a specific area under penalty of being deported to one of the Bantustans, which ha[d] the effect of enslaving the worker to his permit, destroying families, and depriving the Black man [*sic*] of mobility, self-determination, and freedom."[14] In the gloss that John provides, Winston put his "head on the block for others" (72). He stood up for the rights that were being systematically denied to some South Africans on the basis of their skin color under the system of apartheid. Winston honored his race, a thing to which honor belongs, in the face of the dishonor accorded it by apartheid.

While Winston concentrates on memorizing the plot of *Antigone*, John schemes to find ways of improvising costumes for Creon and Antigone and discovers a way to fabricate a wig and false "titties" for Antigone. When Winston tries them on with only one more day to go before the performance, John teases him mercilessly, circling him in mock admiration, fondling Antigone's breasts, and removing his own trousers, implying that he finds the figure that Winston cuts, dressed up as Antigone, sexually irresistible. John's relentless laughter and sexual innuendo finally proves too much for Winston, who rips off the costume, and tells John, "Take your Antigone and shove it up your arse! . . . I'm *not* doing Antigone. . . . I'm a man, not a bloody woman" (56–60). When John's laughter subsides and he tries to backtrack, not wanting to lose Winston's commitment to playing the role of Antigone, Winston only reiterates his refusal. "I am not doing your Antigone! I would rather run the whole day of Hodoshe. At least

I know where I stand with him. All *he* wants is to make me a 'boy' . . . not a bloody woman" (60). Winston's claim to prefer the treatment he suffers at the hands of the prison guard rather than performing Antigone is a striking one. We have witnessed the acute humiliation, including physical abuse, to which Hodoshe has subjected Winston. We know that it enrages him, and yet he professes to prefer such treatment to the ridicule to which his cellmate subjects him. Such a profession is a measure of how unnerved Winston is by John's sexual taunting. The terms in which Winston expresses his preference are indicative of his anxiety about his sexual identity. He would rather tolerate Hodoshe because the prison guard only wants to make Winston into a "boy," not into a "woman." Winston would rather be infantilized, he attests; he would rather suffer a retardation of his manhood than be made into a woman by his cellmate, becoming the butt of John's sexual jokes.

Toward the beginning of the play, John had affirmed to Winston, "I'm a man, brother, A man!" (49), but confesses that if Hodoshe had kept them to the "back-breaking and grotesquely futile labour" (47) for "five minutes longer," he would have become a "baby" (49). "I nearly cried," says Winston (49). The stage directions at the beginning of the play clearly recall Oedipus and the riddle of the Sphinx, as John and Winston are shackled together and forced to run to their cell "three-legged" (47), but they fail to run fast enough to avoid being beaten by Hodoshe, whose offstage presence is figured as the curse under which the Oedipal family labors. The beatings John and Winston sustain, which recall the routine beating slaves received in fifth century BCE Athens, as much as they do the treatment of black South Africans under apartheid, leave Winston with "a bad blow to the eye" and John with a sprained ankle (47). Both of them are reduced to crawling across the cell—John because of his injured foot and Winston because he is "blind with rage and pain" (47). Crawling on all fours, running "three-legged," asserting their manhood in trying to stand on their own two feet, sustaining foot and eye injuries, Winston and John embody the various stages of man that Oedipus deciphers in the Sphinx's riddle. At the same time they reflect the injury inflicted on Oedipus as an infant that resulted in his name, and the injury he inflicts on himself, when he blinds himself, casting out his eyes. If at the beginning and end of the play—when Winston and John resume their three-legged run (77)—the Sphinx's riddle is recalled, in the middle of the play the feminization Oedipus suffers at the hands of the Sphinx is also explored.[15] At John's hands, not only Winston's sex, but also his sexuality, is questioned. Winston can apparently abide being made into an immature male—treated as a boy—by the prison guard, but he cannot put up with having his sexual identity questioned by his cellmate. He cannot tolerate having his sexuality challenged. He is, he insists, a man, not a woman. But what makes him capable of abiding the treatment to which Hodoshe subjects him is precisely the intimate relationship that he maintains with John, a relationship that the play figures in myriad ways in terms of a symbolic marriage.

Despite his vociferous protests, Winston ends up playing the role of Antigone after all. In this sense his repudiation of being "made into a woman" is recuperated. Yet at what cost is this recuperation effected? Friendship is elevated above Winston's anxiety about his sexual identity, but in the process, is an appeal to a universal humanism that transcends all differences invoked? Is such an appeal not precisely that which Butler's performative understanding of norms questions? The audience is not privy to Winston's change of heart, but we gather that his friendship and loyalty to John, with whom he has learned his time is finite given the reduction of John's sentence, trumps his disinclination to risk the ridicule of his cellmates. Winston's commitment to John overcomes his distaste at being made into the butt of John's sexual jokes. When, in the final scene, Winston appears as Antigone, standing up for her rights against Creon, there is no hint of ridicule. So, too, when the performance that inspired *The Island* actually took place in the prison at Robben Island, there was no sign of the laughter that Winston fears.[16]

What, then, do we make of Winston's reluctance to deal with John's ridicule of him? And what is the significance of the fact that he manages to overcome his aversion to playing Antigone? Clearly the fact that as cellmates Winston and John must, of necessity, deal with the pressure of each other's constant company needs to be taken into account. Winston's sensitivity to John's sexual innuendos is due in no small part to the constraints of a situation in which the two men are required to be one another's companions day in and day out. Privacy is nonexistent. They clean each other's wounds; tell one another stories; they work, sleep, eat, and wash together in the same confined space. When John makes fun of Winston's attire, his laughter might well be a means of relieving the pressure that builds up in such a situation. It might also be a defense, a means of distancing himself from any sexual tension that has built up between the two of them. To act as if he is enamored of Winston, but to do so in such a way as to induce humor, both allows John to express sexual feelings toward his cellmate and yet at the same time to deny them. To understand the complexity of this situation is to understand both that John is availing himself of a generic cultural ethos of homophobia—taking advantage of the available social text of homophobia—while at the same time manipulating the situation to render it safe for him to express a sexually charged desire for Winston that is tightly circumscribed within the bounds of humor. When Winston aggressively deflects John's sexual reaction to him in the guise of Antigone, his response must also be read against the intense relationship that has been established between the two cellmates.

When John, in a desperate attempt to convince Winston to agree to wear the makeshift costume of Antigone after all, adorns himself with the wig and false breasts, inviting Winston to laugh at him, the appeal he makes to Winston appears to be simple and direct: "behind all this rubbish is me, and you know it's me" (62). Just as Winston can see beyond the façade of his costume to John, so the other prisoners will see through the costume; they will know that the person underneath is really Winston. At the same time, Sophocles' Antigone shares something in common with Winston, which makes it so hard for John and ultimately for Winston too, to give up the idea of performing a version of *Antigone*: They are both being punished for what they know to be right. Neither of them is prepared to compromise the principle in which they believe. In this sense, John's suggestion takes on another, more profound meaning. The prisoners will know that Winston has an affinity with Antigone that is deeper than any hilarity his costume might occasion. They will recognize his refusal to give up his conviction that he is right to honor "those things to which honour belongs" (77). The boundaries of sexual dimorphism are safely reinstalled after their temporary destabilization, as are those of the heteronormative order. John's assurance to Winston that his audience will know it is really him rings true because the heteronormative order and the demarcation between female and male are back in place. Any deviation is just that, and we can all rest easy. While *The Island* effects a partial recuperation of the abject figuring of homosexuality, then, insofar as Winston takes on the risk of playing Antigone, an implicit appeal also exists to abstract humanist values, which tend to be modeled on the idealized features of specific citizens. We are all fundamentally the same, we all deserve equal rights. Some are just more equal than others, and rights discourse tends to proceed by requiring those to which equality is formally extended to resemble those who enjoy rights by fiat—and what this tends to mean is that recognition of otherness in fact proceeds according to the capacity of others to be represented as if they were not in fact other, but rather the same.

This chapter, then, is part of an attempt to outline the political logic according to which Antigone lends herself to myriad political struggles by figuring the excluded yet constitutive ground of a polity. If in some cases this logic is reiterated at one register, even as it is questioned at another, in other cases the mythological reiteration of Antigone throughout various epochs, becomes a theme for investigation within the play itself.[17] Antigone illuminates the processes according to which any contingent fact (not just gender or sexuality, but also race, class, nationality, religion, or some other contingency) can become a ground for an exclusionary politics. In this sense, it is not a question of Antigone acting as a woman—or in any other specifically gendered way. Rather it is a question of her acting in such a way as to rewrite or transform the grounds on which her exclusion from the system is written off as unintelligible to it. Whether Antigone is rendered intelligible only at the cost of rendering some newly othered group unintelligible is a question that must be negotiated by each new rendering of *Antigone*. Antigone calls herself into intelligibility by challenging the grounds on which the polity writes her as unintelligible, unreadable, and unsignifiable within its terms. Were her exclusion to have become capable of representation within the set of significations that requires it, then that system itself must have undergone transformation. Antigone calls for a redrawing of the lines of the polity so that it is no longer able to cast her out as its excluded outside—that is, to refuse her "proper" representation—while simultaneously drawing on her resources for its own purposes. In this sense Antigone calls into being a future polity that does not rely on the political exclusion of some of its members, while legislating that exclusion as unthinkable or rendering it nonnegotiable. She draws attention to political gestures that rely on casting as unintelligible those on whom it depends materially and psychically, but whom it systematically excludes from legitimate, symbolic representation. Antigone becomes a site for the reworking of the distinction between the improper and proper, between that which is cast outside a system of intelligibility as impermissible within its current configuration and that according to which something is cast out as unacceptable: She calls into question the very terms that render an order proper by designating something other than it as improper.

The incessant, theatrical rebirth of Antigone in diverse political contexts opens up the possibility of interrogating conventions that have consolidated themselves as political necessities, which might take shape as enshrining the need for apartheid, and the dangers of dismantling it—or might require numerous other boundaries of containment. By interrogating not only the specificity of the excluded other that Antigone comes to represent in each new appropriation of her tragedy, but also the particular political configurations that demand such exclusions, whether these comprise a limited democracy such as that of ancient Athens or an exclusionary racial politic such as apartheid in South Africa, I have begun to delineate the political logic according to which the tragedy of *Antigone* can participate in a regeneration of the political. I have pointed not only to the contingency of Antigone's position as excluded, but also to the contingency of a political system of domination that excludes her. The extent to which a polity affords its excluded others the possibility of self-representation, and the precise ways in which it sanctions or prohibits such representation, constitute the sites of negotiation between the tragedy of *Antigone* and politics of its interpretation. If tragedy is not what it used to be, this is in part because the political function of theater has changed: modern appropriations of the tragic tend not to be officially legitimated, which was the case for the Greeks. If in the guise of *Antigone* the tragic has come to embody a means of resisting oppression in the name of restoring, for example, a democracy that has been violated, the different logics according to which this resistance takes place and how these logics are specified by and implicated in the relationship between politics and the art forms that tragedy becomes can be parsed out. These logics will be reiterated in ways that sometimes replicate the logic of constitutive exclusion in more or less self-conscious ways, and this logic will sometimes be interrogated even by texts that use it. Each new iteration of *Antigone* helps to specify the history of these multiple and multiplying Antigones, and in so doing, she is reinvented in ways that both resemble Sophocles' Antigone and depart from her. Each new departure contributes to the replication of Antigone, taking its place in a mimetic history that refigures Sophocles' Antigone, reenacting her drama in new ways, making of her something new, addressing a new set of political constraints.

If tragedy attests, in the words of Timothy Reiss, to a certain "absence of significance" or "meaninglessness," and does so precisely in calling for a discursive shift if it arises at moments of "epistemic change," flowering in a particularly virulent form in fifth century BCE Athens and again in sixteenth- and seventeenth-century Europe, perhaps its resurgence at moments of crisis signals the attempt to render visible suffering that is in danger of remaining invisible or insignificant.[18] Thus Antigone demands the attention of Jean Anouilh (1951) and Bertolt Brecht (1947) in Nazi-torn Europe; of Seamus Heaney (2004); Aidan Mathews and Marianne McDonald (2005), Tom Paulin (1985), and Brendan Kennelly (1996) in the time of the troubles in Ireland; Janusz Glowacki (1997) in the context of homelessness in New York; Fugard, Kani, and Ntshona (1974) under apartheid in South Africa; and Fémi Òsófisan (1999) under European imperialism in Nigeria.[19] Perhaps these instances of turning to Antigone signal in their own way a call for an epistemic shift by registering the meaninglessness of suffering under prevailing regimes of representation and thereby rendering it meaningful, calling for its alleviation. In such instances, a performance of *Antigone* articulates the failure of dominant regimes to make visible, or acknowledge suffering, a failure that occurs even as the continued existence of such regimes as dominant requires that others suffer. Suffering is both constitutive of hegemony and refused representation by it. In this sense, the rebirth of *Antigone* effects a critique of the conditions that perpetuate such systematic blindness—calling for a future that does not allow suffering to continue as the unabated and unacknowledged condition of prevailing regimes of representation.

Notes

1. Martin Heidegger, *An Introduction to Metaphysics*, trans. Ralph Manheim (New Haven, CT: Yale University Press, 1959); Jacques Lacan, *The Ethics of Psychoanalysis 1959–1960: The Seminar of Jacques Lacan*, book VII, trans. Dennis Porter, ed. Jacques-Alain Miller (New York: Routledge, 1992); Judith Butler, *Antigone's Claim: Kinship between Life and Death* (New York: Columbia University Press, 2000); J. Peter

Euben, introduction to *Greek Tragedy and Political Theory* (Berkeley: University of California Press, 1986); Luce Irigaray, *Speculum of the Other Woman*, trans. Gillian C. Gill (Ithaca, NY: Cornell University Press, 1985); Warren J. Lane and Ann M. Lane, "The Politics of Antigone," in *Greek Tragedy and Political Theory*, ed. J. Peter Euben (Berkeley: University of California Press, 1986), pp. 162–182; Mary Beth Mader, "Antigone's Line," *Bulletin de la société Américaine de philosophie de langue Française*, vol. 14, no. 2 (2005), pp. 18–40; Patchen Markell, *Bound by Recognition* (Princeton, NJ: Princeton University Press, 2003); and Slavoj Žižek, "From Antigone to Joan of Arc," *Helios*, vol. 31, no. 1–2 (2004), pp. 51–62.

2. Freud attributes a lack to women, based on their failure to live up to the expectation that women, like men, have penises, a mythical castration that provokes castration anxiety. Fetishism is a defense against the threat that women thereby represent. Symbolically, the role of the fetish is always and only to represent a penis that never existed. Or rather, it only ever exists as conforming to the *expectation* fostered in the masculine imaginary that organizes Freudian and Lacanian psychoanalysis, namely that women *should* have a penis. The fetish is produced in an attempt to ward off the threat that this difference presents and to rein in its significance not by canceling it out, but by allowing it to coexist: I know that women are castrated, but by producing a fetish I can deny it. See Sigmund Freud, "Fetishism," in *The Standard Edition of the Complete Psychological Works*, ed. and trans. James Strachey, vol. 21 (London: Hogarth Press, 1953), pp. 152–159.

3. J. Peter Euben, *Greek Tragedy and Political Theory*, p. 37; David M. Halperin, "Why Is Diotima a Woman? Platonic Eros and the Figuration of Gender," in *Before Sexuality: The Construction of Erotic Experience in the Ancient Greek World*, ed. David M. Halperin, John J. Winkler, and Froma I. Zeitlin (Princeton, NJ: Princeton University Press, 1990), pp. 257–308.

4. Athol Fugard, John Kani, and Winston Ntshona, "The Island," in *Statements: Two Workshop Productions. Sizwe Bansi Is Dead, and The Island; and a New Play, Statements after an Arrest under the Immorality Act* (New York: Theatre Communications Group, 1986), pp. 45–77.

5. Kirk Ormond, "Oedipus the Queen: Cross-Gendering without Drag," *Theatre Journal*, no. 55 (2003), pp. 1–28.

6. Mader sets out to explain Antigone's enigmatic claim that "she would not have deliberately violated Creon's command, would not have intentionally broken his law or edict, had this edict barred her from burying a child or a husband of hers" (Mader, "Antigone's Line," p. 18). By emphasizing that Antigone's claim relates not to all brothers, but to Polyneices, the son of an incestuous union, Mader shows that commentators go astray when they fail to understand Antigone's claim to relate to this very specific case. Here is the principle according to which Antigone acts, as Mader sees it: "she is establishing (or attempting to establish) her brother as *only* her brother by symbolically refusing a family precedent, namely that of *generating one's own sibling*" (28). The law according to which Antigone acts, in Mader's view, is "recognize your parents as they who can generate those who you can, though must not, generate. The crucial causal corollary is: it is precisely by this recognition that such beings as parents, children, and siblings are made as such in this particular kinship order" (35).

7. See Roger Just, *Women in Athenian Law and Life* (London: Routledge, 1989), p. 87.

8. This would not prevent, however, the possibility of Creon adopting a son, a practice that was fairly prevalent in fifth century BCE Athens.

9. Lacan acknowledges that the symbolic position of the father might, in principle, be filled by anyone. Yet Butler insists on asking whether it makes a difference who fills this position. If two gay parents perform the function of parenting, for example, that function does not remain the same. These positions do not function as neutral categories, empty of any content, but rather tend to carry with them implicit, normative features (see Butler, *Antigone's Claim*, pp. 69–71). Whatever sense of universality the symbolic claims for itself, if its universality is used to shore up its own authority as unassailable and intractable, it appears to remain immune from any changes in actual social relations. "If the Oedipus complex is not universal in one way, but remains in another, does it finally matter which way it is universal if the effect is the same?" (45).

10. That recognition is something that must occur between two humans, rather than something that can proceed from inanimate objects, is one of the lessons of the master-slave dialectic. Markell's discussion of the master-slave relationship in this regard is illuminating. See Markell, *Bound by Recognition*. The importance of this dialectic for Lacan is well established.

11. A play such as Fémi Òsófisan's *Tègònni: An African Antigone* (Ibadan, Nigeria: Kenbim Press, 1999) treats racial taboos against miscegenation explicitly.

12. Fugard et al., "The Island," p. 65. Hereafter references to this text are given parenthetically within the text.

13. *Hodoshe,* a Xhosa word meaning carrion-fly, was the nickname of the prison guard—a name that has peculiar resonance for Sophocles' *Antigone*, in which the corpse of Polyneices was exposed to the birds. The guard, then, hovered over his prisoners, who endured a living death, and whose incarceration refigured Antigone's premature entombment by Creon in an underground cave. The guard in question was renowned for his attempt to break the spirits of the prisoners on Robben Island.

14. Errol Durbach, "Sophocles in South Africa: Athol Fugard's *The Island*," in *Drama and the Classical Heritage: Comparative and Critical Essays*, ed. Clifford Davidson, Rand Johnson, and John H. Stroupe (New York: AMS Press, 1993), p. 248.

15. Olga Taxidou suggests that Oedipus internalizes the Sphinx and is thereby feminized in *Tragedy, Modernity and Mourning* (Edinburgh, Scotland: Edinburgh University Press, 2004), pp. 47, 54, 69.

16. Athol Fugard, "*Antigone* in Africa," in *Amid Our Troubles: Irish Versions of Greek Tragedy*, ed. Marianne McDonald and J. Michael Walton (London: Methuen, 2002), p. 134.

17. See Òsófisan, *Tègònni.*

18. Timothy J. Reiss, *Tragedy and Truth: Studies in the Development of a Renaissance and Neoclassical Discourse* (New Haven, CT: Yale University Press, 1980), pp. 2–3.

19. Jean Anouilh, *Antigone: A Tragedy by Jean Anouilh*, trans. Lewis Galantière (London: Methuen, 1951); Bertolt Brecht, *Sophocles' Antigone*, trans. Judith Malina (New York: Applause Theatre, 1990); Seamus Heaney, *The Burial at Thebes: A Version*

of Sophocles' Antigone (New York: Farrar, Straus and Giroux, 2004); Aidan Mathews, *Antigone: Gone Anti* (unpublished manuscript, undated, courtesy of the author); Marianne McDonald, *Antigone by Sophocles* (London: Nick Hern Books, 2005); Tom Paulin, *The Riot Act: A Version of Sophocles'* Antigone (London: Faber and Faber, 1985); Brendan Kennelly, *Sophocles' Antigone* (Tarset, UK: Bloodaxe Books, 1996); Janusz Glowacki, *Antigone in New York*, trans. Janusz Glowacki and Joan Torres (New York: Samuel French, 1997), and Fémi Òsófisan, *Tègònni: An African Antigone* (Ibadan, Nigeria: Kenbim Press, 1999). (Ed. note: For further examples of the resurrection of Antigone around the world, see Moira Fradinger's prologue in this volume.)

5

The Eternal Irony of the Community

Luce Irigaray

> On the one hand, the uterus in the male is reduced to a mere gland, while on the other, the male testicle in the female remains enclosed within the ovary, fails to emerge into opposition, and does not become an independent and active cerebrality. The clitoris moreover, is inactive feeling in general; in the male on the other hand, it has its counterpart in active sensibility, the swelling vital, the effusion of blood into the corpora cavernosa and the meshes of the spongy tissue of the urethra. The female counterpart of this effusion of blood in the male consists of the menstrual discharges. Thus, the simple retention of the conception in the uterus, is differentiated in the male into productive cerebrality and the external vital. On account of this difference therefore, the male is the active principle; as the female remains in her undeveloped unity, she constitutes the principle of conception.
>
> "In the case of the eye," says *Sömmerring*, "it seems that the arteries are continued in finer branches, which no longer contain red blood. These branches pass initially into a similar vein, but finally into veinlets carrying red blood."
>
> —Hegel[1]

The purpose that moves blood relatives to action is the care of the *bloodless.* Their inherent duty is to ensure *burial for the dead,* thus changing a natural

This chapter was originally published in *Speculum de l'autre femme* (Paris: Les Editions de Minuit, 1974), and in English translation in *Speculum of the Other Woman,* trans. Gillian C. Gill (Ithaca, NY: Cornell University Press, 1985). Reprinted with permission of the publisher.

phenomenon into a spiritual act. One more step (into negation) and we see that the task of womankind, guardian of the blood tie, to gather man into his final figuration, beyond the turmoil of contingent life and the scattered moments of his Being-there. Man is thereby raised into the peace of simple universality. In essence, woman has to take it upon herself over and over again, regardless of circumstances, to bury this corpse that man becomes in his pure state. She has to enable man to sublate a universality that smacks too much of the natural, or so it would seem, by affirming—for this is pure truth restored—that death is merely the peace of/and universality of the conscious essence of self. Man is still subject to (natural) death, of course, but what matters is to make a movement of the mind out of this accident that befalls the single individual and, in its raw state, drives consciousness out of its own country, cutting off that return into the self which allows it to become self-consciousness. Just as man must strive to turn this negativeness into an ethical action by sacrificing his life for the city—in war for example—so woman must be that external and effective mediation that reconciles the dead man with himself *by taking upon herself the operation of destruction* that the becoming of mind cannot manage without. Thus woman takes this dead being into her own place on his return into the self—a being that is universal, admittedly, but also singularly drained of strength, empty and yielded passively up to others. She must protect him both from all base and irrational individuality and from the forces of abstract matter, which are now more powerful than he. Shielding him from the dishonoring operation of unconscious desires and natural negativeness—*preserving him from her desire, perhaps?*—she places this kinsman back in *the womb of the earth* and thus reunites him with an undying, elemental individuality. To do this is also to reassociate him with a—religious—community that controls the violent acts of singular matter and the base urges which, unleashed upon the dead man, might yet destroy him. This supreme duty constitutes the divine law, or *positive* ethical action, as it relates to the individual.

Yet, on the other hand, human law places a negative meaning upon this individualism. In fact each member of the city has a right both to a living and to Being-for-itself, wherein the mind finds its reality and its Being-there. But the mind is at the same time the strength of the whole, and hence it gathers *these individual parts* into *one negative entity*. The mind reminds the parts that they are dependent upon this totality and that they owe their *life* to it entirely. Thus any associations—such as families—that one assumes have been founded primarily to serve individual ends, whether the acquisition of personal wealth or the search for sexual pleasures, invite a war that may disrupt their intimate life and violate their independence since these threaten to shatter the whole. All those who persist in following the dictates of individualism must be taught by the government to fear a master: death. They must be prevented from sinking into the neutral Being-there, from regressing into the inner world of the senses, from ecstatically entering a world beyond, lacking all predicates that can be appropriated by the self of consciousness. *The cult of the dead and the cult of death* would thus be the point where divine law and human law join. And also that point where, at least on the higher ethical level, the relationship between man and woman is possible.

This unsullied relationship takes place only *between brother and sister*. They are the same blood, but in them blood is at rest and in balance. Thus they do not desire each other, they have neither given nor received this Being-for-the-self from each other, they are free individualities vis-à-vis each other. What is it, then, that impels them to unite so that finally one passes into the other? What meaning does each have for the other that draws them thus into this exchange? Is it recognition of *blood*? Of their common allegiance to the power of the *same blood*? Could it be their complicity in the permanence, the continuance of blood that a matriarchal type of lineage ensures in its purest and most universal being? In this sense the family of Oedipus would be quite exemplary because the mother of the husband is also his wife, thus re-marking the blood tie between the children of that union—including Polyneices and Antigone. Furthermore, the uncle—the mother's brother—will in this family be the representative of an already patriarchal power. Or is it rather that brother and sister share in the *same sperm,* thus giving consanguineity an (other) equilibrium, ridding it of its own magic passion but counterbalancing it with another? In fact, however, the sperm does not join with the blood (though it was long thought to do so) but with the ovum: had this copulation been given its full weight and "effectiveness," it would already have irremediably shattered the unity of mind and ethical substance. Moreover, copulation takes place only in the impure mingling of the marriage of husband and wife. Are we then to seek this pact between sister and brother in a *common name*, in the notion that their co-uterine attraction is matched by their submission—represented by the patronymic—to symbolic rules that might be supposed to carry the potency of blood one step further and already to raise the family community to the types of laws in force in the city?

Thus, for one instant, brother and sister would recognize each other in their single self, each able to affirm a right that is achieved through the power each has when balanced in/by the other; the power of red blood and of its reabsorption, its sublation into a process of denominating—that is, of semblance. An ideal distribution would hypothetically occur in which the (ethical) substance of matriarchy and of patriarchy would coexist, contributing their own subsistence to each other, in a peace without alloy, a relationship without desire. The war of the sexes would not take place here. But this moment is mythical, of course, and the *Hegelian dream* outlined above is already the effect of a dialectic produced by the discourse of patriarchy. It is a consoling fancy, a truce in the struggle between uneven foes, a denial of the guilt already weighing heavily upon the development of the subject; it is the delusion of a *bisexuality* assured for each in the connection and passage, one into the other, of each sex. Yet both sexes, male and female, have already yielded to a destiny that is different for each. This is so even if rape, murder, breaking and entering, and injury were still, in appearance at least, in general at least, suspended between brother and sister. But in fact such is not the case, as Hegel admits when he affirms that the brother is for the sister that possibility of recognition of which she is deprived as mother and wife, but does not state that the situation is reciprocal. This means that the brother has already been invested with a value for the sister that she cannot offer in return, except by devoting herself to his cult after death.

Certainly, in the work of Sophocles, which marks the historical bridge between matriarchy and patriarchy, things are not yet that clear. No decision has yet been made about what has more value. On the one hand, *blood is no longer pure* in Sophocles: the father, at least for a time, was king; the king thereby affirms his rights as father, as well as the complicity between family (patriarchal) power and that of the State. And tragedy enacts the punishment that is incurred by a taste for blood. On the other hand, *the privilege of the proper name is not yet pure*: the power of the father's name, had its right already been in force, should have prevented Oedipus from committing murder and incest. But this is not what happens. Moreover, the fact that each sister and brother has a double also indicates that this is still a transition in which the extremes—which will later be defined as being more masculine or more feminine: that is, Eteocles and Ismene—seem almost like caricatures. Now, whereas Ismene is termed a sister because she shares *the same blood* as Antigone, and whereas Polyneices is termed a brother because he was born of *the same mother*, Eteocles is brother because he is the son of *the same father and the same mother*.

These things can be stated in other ways. *Ismene* seems indisputably a "woman" in her weakness, her fear, her submissive obedience, her tears, madness, hysteria—all of which in fact are met with condescending scorn on the part of the king. Ismene is subsequently shut up, as a punishment, in the palace, the house, with the other women, who are all thus deprived of their freedom of action for fear that they may sap the courage of the most valiant warriors. For *Antigone* things are less simple, and the king himself fears she may usurp his manhood—"Better be beaten, if need be, by a man, than let a woman get the better of us"—if she does not pay for her insolence with death.[2] Antigone does not yield to the law of the city, of its sovereign, of the man of the family: Creon. And she will choose to die a virgin, unwedded to any man, rather than sacrifice the ties of blood, rather than abandon her mother's son to the dogs and vultures, leaving his double to roam in eternal torment. Better to die than to refuse service to the divine law and to the attraction she feels for the gods below. There her jouissance finds easier recognition, no doubt, her allegiance to them frees her from the inventions of men. She defies them all by/in her relationship to Hades. In her nocturnal passion she acts with a perversity that has nothing in common with the wretched crimes that men stoop to in their love for money—or so the king says. Indeed she boasts of this, stating publicly that she would rather die than give up such practices. And that, moreover, *between her and the king, nothing can be said.* She alone among the Cadmeans, *the literates,* reasons thus. At least out loud. In this way, she becomes the voice, the accomplice of the people, the slaves, those who only whisper their revolt against their masters secretly. Without friends, without husband, without tears, she is led along that *forgotten path* and there is *walled up* alive in *a hole* in the rock, shut off forever from the light of the sun. Alone in her crypt, her cave, her den, her womb, she is given just enough food by those who hold power to ensure that the city is not soiled and shamed by her decay. She is alone in confronting the underground god in order to see—again—if she will survive that solitary ritual.[3] But love, for her, has far too many fatal representations for her desire to recover from such punishments. However guiltless, she feels she bears the burden of her mother's fatal marriage, feels guilty for being born of such terrible embraces. Thus she is damned, and by consenting to a punishment she has not merited and yet cannot escape, at the least she accepts on her own account the death knell of her jouissance—*or is mourning itself her jouissance?*—by killing herself. Does she thus anticipate the decree of death formulated by those in power? Does she duplicate it? Has she given in? Or is she still in revolt? She repeats, in any case, upon herself the murderous, but not bloody, deed of her mother. Whatever her current arguments with the laws of the city may have been, another law is still drawing her along her path: identification with her mother. *But how are mother and wife to be distinguished?* This is the dreadful paradigm of a mother who is both wife and mother to her husband. Thus the sister will strangle herself in order to save at least the mother's son. She will cut off her breath—her voice, her air, blood, life—with the veil of her belt, returning into the shadow (of a) tomb, the night (of) death, so that her brother, *her mother's desire,* may have eternal life. She never becomes a woman. But she is not as masculine as she might seem if seen from an exclusively phallic viewpoint—for it is tenderness and pity that have motivated her. Rather, she is a captive of a desire whose path has reached a dead end, has never been blazed. And did she seek the relationship with the mother in *Polyneices* because he was the more feminine of the brothers? The younger? Or at any rate the weaker, the one who is rejected. The more irritable and impulsive one, who in his anger will seek to open the veins of his blood again. He who is armed for/by the love of a woman, married, unlike his siblings, and through that foreign match condemning his sister to die buried alive. At least in his passion for blood he has annulled the right of his brother—*Eteocles*—to command, has destroyed his brother's—his elder's?—relation to power, reason, property, the paternal succession. And has, with the same blow, killed himself.

Yet the government's mode of action remains unchanged. Another man was ready to take up the challenge: *Creon*. He also is alone—like Antigone—but he has the instrument of the law. Desperate he is, no doubt, but he yet claims that all power is his alone. Although he has brought son and wife to utter destruction, he climbs back onto the throne, without love, and the scepter remains in his hands. Death-stricken he is, and/but regulating his practice rigidly. Inflexible in his severity. Implacable in his reasons. His fragile strength, as apt to be broken as to break, demands that he fear pleasure, domination by women, the passion of youth represented by his son, the plots of the people, the slaves' revolt, even the gods (who are still controlled and divided by desires), soothsayers, therefore, and finally the "elders." He defends his privilege of being the sole safeguard of speech, truth, intelligence, reason—the fairest of all possessions—although at the same time he raves a little wildly in his relations with the gods and with women, for example. And in this mass grave of all the members of his family—Ismene is set aside in a golden prison which a change of ruler in fact risks transforming into a simple private home—in this general outflowing of blood, he thus (thereby) remains *one*. But nonetheless, he is *broken* between a self-sureness that is now only misfortune—is he not a superfluous man, weighed down by an unbearable destiny, for whom everything and everybody has become equally contingent?—and the rigid sovereignty of a Being-for-the-self empty of content (of the substance of blood), an omnipotence alien to itself. A man who receives his personal power only by exercising a right that has resolved all (blood) ties between individuals into abstract universality. Soon a God, but a god without any desire but that of submitting everyone to the law of blood congealed in the status of semblance: the Ego.

This is a necessary moment in the development of the mind, but Hegel expresses almost melancholic regret of/in this passage, and the dream of going back to that attraction to the/his sister, which is unmingled (by blood). Back to the time when the species and genus had, it seems, not yet come into being, and when that unity, that individuality, *that still living, blood subject* simply took place. And in the nostalgia aroused by this return into the past. Hegel reveals his desire for a relationship that is certainly sexuate but does not need to pass through the realization of sexual desire. Desire intervenes to break the harmony unified in its blood cycle, in which brother and sister are theoretically between the phases—still relatively undifferentiated in their animality—of blood's circulation: inspiration/expiration, fluidity/hardening, apprehension/resorption of an outside. Thus one (male or female) would breathe out while the other would begin to breathe in, he/she would be becoming red blood while the other would return to self in his/her veins, he/she would affirm atomic individuality as cell(s) while the other would remain lymph, he/she would return to the earth in the form of carbon at the very moment when the other is rousing from torpor and taking fire, and so forth. But perhaps they are already irremediably separated throughout that process called *digestion*. For if the female one can recognize herself in the male one, who has therefore supposedly assimilated her, the reverse is not necessarily true. And if Antigone gives proof of a bravery, a tenderness, and an anger that free her energies and motivate her to resist that *outside* which the city represents for her, this is certainly because she had digested the masculine. At least partially, at least for a moment. But perhaps this will have been possible only at the time when she is mourning for her brother, just long enough to give him back the manhood he had lost in death and to feed his soul therewith. And to die in the act.

Already, then, the balance of blood has been upset, changed, dissolved. And the unadulterated happiness that is to be had from digesting one's own substance, from giving oneself fluidity, from breaking into one's own movement, from giving birth to oneself, is not shared equally between male and female, brother and sister. But, as long as the sister goes on in her living unity she can be the self-representative basis of that substance—the blood—that the brother assimilates in order to return to the self. She can guarantee that the son develops for himself (*pour soi*), independently of the couple that made him: she is *the living mirror*, the source reflecting the growing autonomy of the self-same. She is the privileged place in which red blood and its semblance harmoniously (con)fuse with each other, although she herself has no right to benefit from this process. And the different recognition that the city pays to their autospeculation, the one in the other, has always already perverted their union, although sometimes a public remark is needed to make it obvious that the one must eliminate the other.

Thus male and female will be split further and further apart. The wife-mother will henceforward become more and more associated with nourishing and liquefying *lymph*, almost *white* while she loses her blood in cyclic hemorrhages, *neuter and passive* enough in her matter for various members and organs of society to incorporate her and use her for their own subsistence. The man (father) will persevere in developing his individualization by *assimilating* the external other into and for the self, thus reenforcing his vitality, his irritability, and his activity; a particular triumph is experienced when man absorbs the other into himself in his intestine. The Father-king will repeat the rupture of (living) exchange between man and woman by sublating it into his discourse. Blood is burned to cinders in the writing of the text of law whereby man produces (himself) at the same time (as) the double—differently in him, in his son, and in his wife—and the color of blood fades as more and more semblances are produced, more atoms of individual egos, all bloodless in different ways. In this process some substance is lost: blood in its constitution of a living, autonomous subjectivity.

At the heart of the dialectic is hypochondria, melancholia. It can be linked to a clot of blood, cruor, reminiscent of the bloody calvary that set it on high, or else to the last froth left by an in(de)finite liquid which opens up the cup of its chalice even in Absolute Mind. Such clots and lymph, had they been able to close up wounds without weeping fluids, would have left the mind (only) to stony solitude and innocence. Assuming that the stone referred to serves to close off and mark the space in which femininity dies.

Thus we must go back to the decisive ethical moment which saw the blow struck producing a wound that no discourse has closed simply. The harmonious relationship of brother and sister involved a (so-called) equal recognition and nonviolent copenetration of two essences, in which femininity and masculinity achieve universality in human and divine law. But this mutual agreement was possible only for as long as *adolescence* lasted and neither was impelled to act. A prolongation of childhood, a kind of Eden shielded from war and blessed by the household gods. But these idyllic and/because *immaculate* loves of childhood could not last. And each will soon realize that his or her equal is also his or her worst enemy, negation, and death. For the rule of law is impossible in a situation of mutual sharing in which one has as much value as the other, is equitably the same. In such circumstances consciousness could not recognize its simplicity or that wholeness which is the pathos of its duty. It must therefore make up its mind to act in accordance with that part of the ethical essence which has become apparent to it—that is, to the part which would correspond to its natural allegiance to one sex. Thus, without realizing it, consciousness finds itself embroiled willy-nilly in the rape of the other, who is henceforward injured by the partial character of such an operation. It is immediately clear, however, that the particular individual is not guilty or at fault. He is but the ineffective shadow acting on behalf of a universal self. And in fact, whatever his lack of personal responsibility, he will pay for his crime by finding that, subsequently, he is cut off from/in himself. In any event, he becomes conscious of that scission whereby the other side is now revealed to him in opposition and enmity. A dark potentiality that has always been on the watch comes suddenly into play when the deed is done: it catches the consciousness of self in the act—the act of also being, or having, that *unconsciousness* that remains alien to it but yet plays a major role in the decision consciousness makes. Thus the public offender who has been killed turns out to be the father, and the queen who has been wedded is the mother. But the purest fault is that committed by the ethical consciousness, which knew in advance what law and power it was disobeying—that is to say, necessarily, the fault committed by femininity. For if the ethical essence in its divine, unconscious, feminine side remains obscure, then its prescriptions on the human, masculine, communal side are exposed to full light. *And nothing here can excuse the crime, or minimize the punishment.* And in its burial, in its decline into ineffectiveness and pure pathos, the feminine must recognize the full measure of its guilt.

What an amazing vicious circle in a single syllogistic system. Whereby the unconscious, while remaining unconscious, is yet supposed to know the laws of a consciousness—which is permitted to remain ignorant of it—and will become even more repressed as a result of failing to respect those laws. But the stratification, on top/underneath the two ethical laws, the two Beings-there of sexual difference—which in fact have to disappear as such after the death of brother and sister—comes from Self, of itself. The movement by which the mind ceaselessly sublates necessity, climbing to the top of its pyramid more easily if the other is thrust deeper down into the well. Thus the male one copulates the other so as to draw new strength from her, a new form, whereas the other sinks further and further into a ground that harbors a substance that expends itself without the mark of any individualism. And it is by no means sure that the rape to which she continues to be subjected is visible in broad daylight, for the rape may equally well result in her retreating down into a crypt where she is sealed off. Or else in the resurgence of an "essence" so different, so other, that even to expect it to "work on the outside" reduces it to sameness, to an unconscious that has never been anything but the unconscious of someone conscious of human law alone. Which is as much as to say that the crime can easily occur unnoticed and that the operation may never be translated into a fact. Unless each of these/its terms is doubled so radically that *a single dialectic is no longer sufficient to articulate their copulation.* For if it is asserted that the one character and the other are split into a conscious and an unconscious, with each character itself giving rise to that opposition, then the question remains of how it will be possible to *translate* the laws of the unconscious into those of the conscious, the so-called laws of God into the laws of philosophy, the laws of the female into those of the male. What will be the passage of their *difference* in the subsequent movement of the mind? Or rather, how will that difference be resolved? How does the mind acquire in a variation of deferred action (*après-coup*) the right to make laws and official statements about (the) matter, when a certain process of statement has already excluded difference in its desire to return to sameness? This problem can be approached in another way: the masculine will be able to retrace the path of his discursive law, but it is also the role of the masculine to prescribe the law for the female because she can have no knowledge (of it) for herself. And the fact that, ideally, each is both unconscious and conscious does not in practice prevent the conscious from being identified as masculine, whereas the unconscious remains fixed on the female side, repressed as a result of the impossibility of differentiating the maternal. This implies that masculinity—in man and possibly in woman—will to some extent be able to dialecticize its relationships and identificatory allegiance to the maternal, including a negativization of female singularity, but this would not be true for femininity, which is aware of no difference between itself and the maternal, or even the masculine, except one that is mediated by the abstract immediacy of *the* being (as) or by the rejection of *one* (as) being. The female lacks the operation of affirming its singular and universalizable link to one as self.

Woman has no gaze, no discourse for her specific specularization that would allow her to identify with herself (as same)—to return into the self—or to break free of the natural specular process that now holds her—to get out of the self. Hence, woman does not take an active part in the development of history because she is never anything but the still undifferentiated opaqueness of sensible matter, the store (of) substance for the sublation of self, or being as what is, or what he is (or was), here and now. There is a doubling of a present of utterance in which present is already no more, has already passed into the universal, when woman appears in that *quasi-subjectivity* that is supposedly hers. And that cannot be possessed as consciousness of self. In her case "I" never equals "I," and she is only that individual will that the master takes possession of, that resisting remainder of a corporeality to which his passion for sameness is still sensitive, or again his double, the lining of his coat. Being as she is, she does not achieve the enunciatory process of the discourse of History, but remains its servant, deprived of self (as same), alienated in this system of discourse as in her master and finding some hint of her own self, her own ego, only in another, a You—or a He—who speaks. Her own will is shattered so afraid is she of the master, so aware of her inner nothingness. And her work in the service of another, of that male Other, ensures the ineffectiveness of any desire that is specifically hers.

But when woman renounces her claim to desire, external things are positively molded, their forms are determined by a self that is not remarked by any individual pathos or by any contingent arbitrariness, things in which the mind might intuit itself as objectal reality. This would be the final meaning of the obedience demanded of woman. She is merely the passage that serves to transform the inessential whims of a still sensible and material nature into universal will.

Woman is the guardian of the blood. But as both she and it have had to use their substance to nourish the universal consciousness of self, it is in the form of *bloodless shadows*—of unconscious fantasies—that they maintain an underground subsistence. Powerless on earth, she remains the very ground in which manifest mind secretly sets its roots and draws its strength. And self-certainty—in masculinity, in community, in government—owes the truth of its word and of the oath that binds men together to that substance common to all, repressed, unconscious, and dumb, washed in the waters of oblivion. This enables us to understand why femininity consists essentially in laying the dead man back in the womb of the earth, and giving him eternal life. For the *bloodless one is the mediation that she knows in her being*, whereby a being-there that has given up being as a self here passes from something living and singular and deeply buried to essence at its most general. Woman can, therefore, by remembering this intermediary moment, preserve at least the soul of man and of community from being lost and forgotten. *She ensures the* Erinnerung *of the consciousness of self by forgetting herself.*

But at times the forces of the world below become hostile because they have been denied the right to live in daylight. These forces rise up and threaten to lay waste to the community. To turn it upside down. Refusing to be that unconscious ground that nourishes nature, womanhood would then demand the right to pleasure, to jouissance, even to effective action, thus betraying her universal destiny. What is more, she would pervert the property/propriety of the State by making fun of the adult male who no longer thinks of anything but the universal, subjecting him to derision and to the scorn of a callow adolescence. In opposition to the adult male, she would set up the strength of youth possessed by the *son*, the *brother*, the *young man*, for in them, much more than in the power of government, she recognizes a *master*, an *equal*, a *lover*. The community can protect itself from such demands only by repressing them as elements of *corruption* that threaten to destroy the State. In fact these *seeds* of revolt, in principle, are quite powerless, are already reduced to nothing by being *separated from the universal goal* pursued by the citizens. Any community has a duty to transform these too immediately natural forces into its own defenders by inciting the young men—in whom the woman's desire takes pleasure—to make war upon each other and slaughter one another in bloody fights. It is through them that the still living substance of nature will sacrifice her last resources to a formal and empty universality, scattering her last drops of *blood* at such a multitude of points that it will no longer be possible to gather up in the intimacy of the familiar cave.

And if, in those *points*, the *sperm*, the *name*, the *whole individual* can find a representing basis that allows them to rise up again and recover, blood in its autonomous flow will never reunite again. But the eye—at least in the absolute—would have no need of blood to see with anymore, perhaps, than the Mind to think with.

Notes

1. Trans. note: The epigraphs are taken from Hegel's *Philosophy of Nature*, trans. and ed. Michael John Petry (London: Allen and Unwin, 1970), pp. 175 and 123, respectively. Hegel's discussion of Sophocles' *Antigone,* upon which much of this chapter is closely based, can most easily be found in English in *Hegel on Tragedy*, trans. J. B. Baillie, ed. Anne and Henry Paolucci (New York: Doubleday, 1962), pp. 260–273.

2. Trans. note: Sophocles, *Antigone*, in *The Theban Plays*, trans. E. F. Watling (New York: Penguin Classics, 1947), p. 144.

3. Trans. note: "I'll have her taken to a desert place / Where no man ever walked, and there walled up / Inside a cave alive, with food enough / To acquit ourselves of the blood guiltiness / That would else lie upon our commonwealth. / There she may pray to Death, the god she loves / And ask release from death or learn at last / What hope there is for those who worship death" (ibid., p. 147).

6

"the celestial Antigone, the most resplendent figure ever to have appeared on earth"

Hegel's Feminism

J. M. Bernstein

He loved her. Exorbitantly.

Hegel loved Antigone. In the *Phenomenology of Spirit* the upshot of this love is that Hegel makes Antigone the hero of the chapter on Spirit, its progressive movement terminating in a vindication of her defiant criminal transgression of Creon's law prohibiting the burial of her brother Polyneices. Her criminality, her transgressiveness, and her work of negation are for Hegel what, in their necessity and inevitability, require acknowledgement and legitimation. She is the force of the negative. It is Antigone's self-conscious law-breaking and her embrace of her guilt and doom that lead Hegel to find her nobler than Socrates and even, perhaps, more awesome than Jesus.[1] Not only is Antigone the hero of the *Phenomenology*, but Hegel identifies with her, modeling his philosophical work of memory on her ritual work of memorializing her brother, her love of the dead adumbrating and demanding the great forgiveness of history's slaughter-bench that makes his memory work possible.

Yet, despite Hegel's exorbitant love for Antigone, and despite the fact that his gender-structured reading of the play has set the terms for the work's reception both in the nineteenth century and in our own time, feminist critics have routinely interpreted Hegel's treatment of Antigone as at least androcentric if not downright misogynistic. His reading is said to faithfully mirror the traditional Western symbolic system in which male identity is realized in the political arena and female identity restricted to the family and domestic sphere; to support the myth of gender complementarity in which man is a figure of spiritual life while woman is a figure of nature (hence, sustaining the duality between spirit and nature, consigning women to perpetual naturalness); to support Creon over Antigone and hence by implication to decide in favor of the universal over the individual; and to make Antigone's knowing reductively intuitive as opposed to Creon's consciousness and light.[2] Each of these claims involve some version of the fallacy of blaming the messenger for the message (which is to acknowledge that some sentences in Hegel *do* supply grounds for these criticisms), effectively ripping Hegel's reading out of its argumentative context. For the sake of simplicity, I call the collection of androcentric ideas (and whatever views follow directly from them) that Hegel is presumed to have espoused "the social metaphysics of gender complementarity."[3] My opposing claim is that a central critical thesis in the discussion of *Antigone* in the *Phenomenology* is the logical incompatibility of the social metaphysics of gender complementarity with any possible self-conscious ethical life. Roughly, on Hegel's account, the emergence of subjectivity, of singular individuality and the agency necessary for it, requires the dismembering, the shredding of the social metaphysics of gender complementarity. That is the nub of Hegel's feminism, and it is the story I sketch in what follows.

From Kant to Greece: A Dream of Ethical Life

> Thus, for one instant, brother and sister would recognize each other in their single self, each able to affirm a right that is achieved through the power each has when balanced in/by the other. . . . An ideal distribution would hypothetically occur in which the (ethical) substance of matriarchy and of patriarchy would coexist, contributing their own subsistence to each other, in a peace without alloy, a relationship without desire. The war of the sexes would not take place here. But this moment is mythical, of course, and the *Hegelian dream* . . . is already the effect of a dialectic produced by the discourse of patriarchy.[4]

Assume, as Luce Irigaray is doing here, that the mutual recognition between sister and brother, between Antigone and Polyneices, is meant to exemplify and realize the ideal mutual recognition between man as citizen of the polis and woman as the keeper of the hearth, the representative of the family, then in the mutual recognition between them there is simultaneously an exquisite balancing of powers, a harmonizing of ends, a setting in place an ideal sexual division of spiritual labor. There is certainly a dream here, but it is not Hegel's.[5] His diagnosis of Greek ethical life is offered in two radically distinct parts: "a. The ethical world. Human and Divine Law: Man and Woman," and "b. Ethical action. Human and Divine knowledge. Guilt and Destiny."[6] What is the significance of the contrast between "ethical world" and "ethical action [*sittliche Handlung*]"? There is no evidence that the world/action distinction is of Greek provenance.[7] Rather, the ethical world is an abstract, idealized version of Greek ethical life, one unmoved and untested by the lives of actual individuals. Just this is implied when Hegel states at the commencement of "Ethical action" that "[*a*]*s yet, no deed* has been committed; but the deed is the *actual self.* It [the deed] disturbs the peaceful organization and movement of the ethical world" (§ 464; first emphasis added). In being a representation of ethical life prior to the deed, prior to what makes the lives of individuals actual, Hegel is claiming that the ethical world is a representation of ethical life in its ideal presentation, as, precisely, the dream or fantasy of ethical life.[8] The world/action opposition is what structures and orients Hegel's entire account; it is a contrast between ideality and actuality, between fantasy and reality, between a picturing of a world and its practical actuality, between a vision of harmony and an intrinsically contradictory reality, between a certain categorial social imaginary and its tragic impossibility.

But the notion of dream or fantasy is for Hegel particularly pertinent here. His account of Greek ethical life emerges as the phenomenological successor to and dialectical sublation of Kantian morality. What is the logic that makes ancient Greece come (logically or phenomenologically) after Kant? Hegel's critique of the moral law—the demand that a maxim of action be universalizable—is that in crucial cases both a maxim of action (for example, "I will steal as necessity requires") and its negation are equally universalizable. Stealing as necessary is wrong if one affirms a system of private property, but is morally consistent if one thinks private property is theft and one proposes another system for the distribution of necessary goods. Kantian universality is "empty" because it underdetermines moral necessity. The source of further determinacy can only come from society as a whole: "we" affirm the system of private property as superior to competitors, and as maximally harmonious with our values and other social institutions. This "we" then conditions the possibility of any "I's" moral deliberations. Hegel denominates this "we" Spirit: Spirit is a We that is an I, and an I that is a We.

To get beyond Kantian rationalism some notion of a social collective as the fundamental resource for individual ethical orientation and practice is necessary. Hegel's predecessors and contemporaries—from Lessing and Winckelmann, through Schiller, Hölderlin, Schelling, Schlegel, and Goethe—all perceived in Greek art, politics, and philosophy the kind of society in which a reconciliation of universality ("we") and individuality ("I") was accomplished. They also saw something more. Following Rousseau, post-Kantian idealists and romantics all claimed that rationalized reason, modern scientific reason, especially as it governs the impersonal economy and the mechanical state, generates a new and radical division of social labor that in turn leads to the fragmented and alienated modern subject. Idealist and romantic critics of modernity here too lodged their criticism from the perspective of the ideal form of life represented by classical Greek culture whose functional order and harmonious integration appeared to represent an unalienated, "happy" form of life—beautiful the way a work of art is beautiful.

In a profound sense, then, the perspective of Greek ethical life really was taken as the *rational successor* to Kant's moral law and the rationalized fate of the modern society it produced. This beautiful form of life as promoted first by Winckelmann, Goethe, Schiller, and then Hölderlin, and which prior to the writing of the *Phenomenology* Hegel too had espoused, was presented by these thinkers as the necessary and only viable alternative to the broken middle of alienated modernity.[9]

For Hegel this alternative was simultaneously an acknowledgement of the achievement of Greek ethical life and an *aesthetic* fantasy about it—Germany dreaming the Greek past. This is emphatic in Hegel's conclusion in which he claims that what is revealed in the downfall of Greek ethical life is "the contradiction and seed of destruction that the beautiful concord and tranquil equilibrium [*die schöne Einmütigkeit und das ruhige Gleichgewicht*] of the ethical spirit possess *precisely in their tranquility* [*Ruhe*] *and beauty*" (§ 476; emphasis added; translation modified). All the language of peace, tranquility, harmony, and beauty that saturate Hegel's account are intended as indices of the Greek ethical *world* being an aesthetic vision, an aestheticization of Greek ethical life sufficient for it to achieve its appointed task of being the successor to Kantian morality, but whose contradictory character resides precisely in what makes that beautiful appearing possible.

What makes it uniquely possible for Greek ethical life to appear *as* beautiful, as a self-sufficient world, is that in it the spiritual division of labor between universality and individuality, between polis and family, is organized through and mediated by the *natural* division and complementary relation between man and woman. The sexual division of spiritual labor in assigning man to human, civil law and woman to divine law entails that for both their spiritual orientation appears natural, given—given in the way an aesthetic totality's whole and parts in perfect harmony appears as given, as effortlessly and spontaneously necessary. Hegel begins the final paragraph of his account of the ethical world by first underlining its aesthetic perfection: "In this way the ethical realm in its subsistence is an immaculate world, unsoiled through internal discord. Similarly, its movement is a tranquil passage of one of its powers into the other, so that each contains the other and brings it forth" (§ 463; translation modified). Aesthetic language here is not rhetorical flourish, but a fundamental component of the conceptual blockage being interrogated. Hegel then elaborates this tranquil whole as bound together by the mutual recognition of man and woman.

> The union of man and woman constitutes the *active* middle term of the whole and the element which sunders itself into these extremes of divine and human law. It is equally their *immediate union* which converts those first two syllogisms into one and the same syllogism, and unites into one process the opposite movements [downward toward death and upward toward civil daylight]. (§ 463; emphasis added)

The romantic metaphysics that posits an "immediate union" of man and woman is introduced into the functional demands of family and state, divine and human law, to give them a naturalness, immediacy, and complementarity they would not otherwise possess. It is thus the presumptively natural complementarity between the sexes that sutures the competing political and religious regimes of law into a beautiful whole. This scheme constitutes what Hegel views as the idealist aesthetic construction of a Greek social metaphysics of gender complementarity, and this setup licenses Hegel's contention that the fall of this world derives in part from what makes it appear tranquil and beautiful.

The *idea* of the ethical *world* is thus to be understood as a radically idealized abstraction taken from Sophocles specifically and Greek tragedy generally that offers the optimum idealist/romantic case for interpreting Greek ethical life as the rightful critical successor to Kantian morality. Although overwrought, Hegel's treatment of the brother-sister relation (§§ 457–459) belongs to this same effort of aesthetically idealizing Greek ethical practices through the natural relation between the sexes. As Irigaray rightly implies, the brother-sister relation as "a relationship without desire" is a moment in the German dream of Greek ethical life. Because this moment belongs to a position Hegel is overturning, he has no particular stake in the ethical purity of the mutual recognition between brother and sister. Nonetheless, we may fairly ask why this exorbitant moment is there at all and if it is phenomenologically necessary. I understand these paragraphs to be a rational reconstruction of Antigone's agonizing speech in which she addresses Polyneices directly, proclaiming she would not have defied the people's will for husband or child, but only for him, her brother.[10] These lines have almost always been interpreted as Antigone confessing a personal motive for her act and thus revoking her constant claim that she was acting on the unshakeable ground of divine law. If that interpretive line held, then grand tragedy would devolve into personal pathology. In the context of proffering the German philosophical dream of Greek *Sittlichkeit* through *Antigone*, it becomes plausible that Hegel should seek to provide a rationalizing reconstruction of Antigone's speech—making the lemonade of pure recognition out of the lemon of sibling devotion. The effort is philosophically and textually misguided: the attempt to separate brother-sister recognition from that of husband-wife, mother-son, and so forth, *distorts* rather than clarifies the general account of gender complementarity in ethical life that must hold equally for all the male-female relations in question. Thus while the purifying effort makes sense against the reductive reading of Sophocles' lines, it deforms the overall aesthetic logic Hegel is attempting to elaborate. What Hegel no doubt interpretively sensed is that lacking the erotic intensity of a relation between husband and wife or the fierceness of maternal love, Antigone's devotion can strike the spectator as purer or nobler. But when Antigone makes her own case, the argument is brutally opposite: husbands and children are replaceable, and this heats up the brother-sister relation in a manner Hegel thought needed suppressing. His brother-sister thesis, however, does not work textually—Sophocles does mean for Antigone's speech to be a revelation of sibling love; but it is also misplaced—Antigone does not renege on her claim to act on the ground of divine law. One could further argue that Hegel, of all people, should not have found the two sides of Antigone's position a source of difficulty; as he later insists against the moral psychology of his idealist and romantic predecessors, private motives are irrelevant to the public meaning of acts (§ 665). But that thought makes it seem likely that even the original textual anxiety about Antigone's true motive derives from the idealist dream of Greek ethical life.[11]

The End of Beauty: Antigone's Deed

Hegel took the aesthetic Hellenism of Hölderlin and Schelling as the dominant philosophical program of his time and hence as what he most needed to overcome—both substantively and methodologically—and he needed to do so explicitly. In the Preface to the *Phenomenology*, Hegel situates his project in fierce opposition to that idealism and romantic holism that reifies substance into a prereflectively, immediately given whole in which no part possesses individual integrity. In explicating the necessity and nature through which the self-enclosed circle of beautiful substance comes apart, becomes subject, Hegel offers what in essence is a conceptual recasting of Antigone. So he states that what makes it possible for an accident as such to become detached from the whole inscribing it, for it to come to have a separate existence and a "separate freedom" of its own, "is the tremendous power of the negative; it is the energy of thought, of the pure 'I.' Death, if that is what we want to call this non-actuality, is of all things the most dreadful . . ." (§ 32). Hegel equates the force of the negative with the pure I, the power of the "I think" in its opposition/negation to anything given and equates both of these with death. The power of the negative, then, is the power of negating action (and thus Understanding—judgment, discrimination, analysis), which enables a part to become separated from the whole on which it nonetheless depends. Hence, negating action is both a condition for individuality—independence and subjectivity—and the essential power of the individual. Because the operation of negation involves separation and detachment of a part from its living context, then negation is also death and the authority of death.

In the next sentence, Hegel immediately opposes the force of the negative to romantic beauty: "Lacking strength, Beauty hates the Understanding for asking of her what it cannot do. But the life of Spirit is not the life that shrinks from death and keeps itself untouched by devastation, but rather the life that endures it and maintains itself in it" (§ 32). This beauty is the beauty of ethical life for the idealists. And all this—the beautiful whole without fully independent parts, the negation of the whole, the arising of the "I," tarrying with death—are the orienting elements of Hegel's reading of *Antigone*. Hegel's core philosophical vocabulary recapitulates in a conceptual mode what *Antigone* accomplishes in its phenomenological retelling. Antigone's self-conscious transgression of Creon's law is thus simultaneously the devastation of the beautiful whole of the idealist dream of ancient Greece and, with respect to our understanding of Greece as a form of Spirit, the first moment of our spiritual history because it is the first moment when the force of the negative is felt and the claim of subjectivity, the right of individuality, becomes manifest.

The second part of the account of ethical life, ethical action, must thus be seen as innovating this new conceptual terrain. Ethical action, then, is no more a direct interpretation of *Antigone* than was the account of the ethical world. Hegel's *Antigone*, in contrast to Sophocles',[12] seeks to demonstrate, using the resources provided by the play, *both* the possibility of the idealist dream of Greek ethical life, *and* that the reading that makes a certain Hellenism the paradigm of post-Kantian thought is false, false to the Greek world itself (that world is tragic, not happy), and philosophically false (no actual reconciliation of individuality and universality can occur in that form of world).

As we have already seen, Hegel claims in the first paragraph of "Ethical action" that "self-consciousness has not yet come forth in its right as *singular* [*einzelne*] *individuality*" because as yet no deed has been done, "yet the deed is the *actual self*" (§ 464; translation modified). Hegel does not mean here that he has not yet considered the question of action and individuality with respect to Greek ethical life, but rather that the entire *picture* of Greek ethical life as presented in the previous section itself leaves no space, practically or conceptually, for either singular individuality or significant action, the deeds through which a self becomes actual. The absences are ontological, not analytic. Hegel intends his account to demonstrate that Antigone's transgression retrospectively reveals itself to be both the birth of significant action and the birth of subjectivity. This raises an obvious question: On what grounds can Hegel claim that in the actual ethical world prior to Antigone—or, more properly, prior to *Antigone*—there were truly no subjects, no singular individualities, and no one ever acted?

Hegel understands Sophocles to be depicting a traditional society in which an individual's relation to himself or herself and to society is determined by his or her social role. Social roles give individuals social identities, identities that determine how they are recognized and valued by others, how they can understand themselves, and the body of rights and duties that provide the practical script for their participation in society. In this type of world, Hegel contends, roles determine and exhaust individuals' self-relation, and hence they leave no room for singular individuality: "Self-consciousness descends within the people from the universal only as far as particularity, not as far as singular individuality that posits in its conduct an excluding self, an actuality that is negative toward itself" (§ 468; translation modified). What this entails is that no space exists between the self and the role she inhabits. But this is equally part of the ethical beauty of this world: because there is no space separating self from role, then individuals experience their ethical obligations as absolute and immediate: "As ethical consciousness, self-consciousness is the simple, pure orientation to . . . duty. In it there is no arbitrariness, nor even struggle, nor indecision for the [Kantian] giving and testing of laws has been given up" (§ 465; translation modified). These two sentences demonstrate how aesthetic ideals come to structure philosophical ethical ideals.

Creon, as king, in possessing legislative authority, has a certain individuality built into his social role. Antigone instigates and installs negation and individuality far more radically according to Hegel. The privilege of Antigone's position for Hegel's conceptuality, why it is she and not Creon who innovates individuality, emerges directly through his consideration of the meaning of Antigone burying Polyneices twice. In burying Polyneices the first time—at night and leaving no sign—Antigone is, above all, fulfilling her ritual obligation; in burying him a second time, in blazing daylight, Antigone is both honoring the dead and affirming that her ritual work negates Creon's civil law. Her first effort of burial is primarily duty-satisfying, her second effort is distinctly law-breaking (although of course both acts in fact have both significations); her second act, we might say, lays claim to the first act and takes on the burden of the transgression it commits by repeating it. In acting again, Antigone takes full responsibility for her act: she owns it.

Sophocles, lacking the categories of subjectivity, singular individuality, conscience, conscientious objection, civil disobedience, and the like, must find practical, *dramatic* means to begin to insinuate what will later be articulated through this body of concepts. Sophocles appears to be seeking to generate, internal to his conceptual scheme, something like what we understand through the language of conscience. In order to accomplish this he must isolate and singularize Antigone and then make her ethically reflective—all through dramatic rather than conceptual means. His first strategy is to radically dissociate Antigone from Ismene, thus isolating/singularizing her, while simultaneously demonstrating that her relation to the law is different than, even opposed to, her sister's relation to that same law (Creon's law by itself destroys the immediacy and purity of *both* Antigone's *and* Ismene's relation to divine law; yet initially both respond as if what is law was still immediate: only their responses are opposed). Sophocles' second move is to have Antigone commit her transgressive deed twice. Practically, the repetition insures that there be no uncertainty regarding the identity of the individual who did the first act of burial: not one of the sentries, not a hired scoundrel, not nature, not the gods. Formally, however, the repetition gives the act a reflective aspect, repeating as reflective choosing. Third, then, is Antigone's individual confrontation with Creon. Her first words to Creon are unequivocal: "I did it. I don't deny a thing" (443). It is with this "I did it" that Antigone must be seen—certainly by us—as taking a stand on her action, staking who she is on what she has done, and done in a sense utterly different from a scripted, role-bound doing. Antigone's "I did it" places her in radical opposition to Creon and the laws of the city he represents in the very space of those laws—directly facing Creon. Through taking a stand on her action—"Here I stand. I can do no other"—and thereby determining herself as the one who broke the law representing the whole of which she is a part, Antigone isolates herself from that whole, from the city, becomes *apolis*, standing radically alone: a singular individual. She can only hold firm to her doing by accepting that it *is* simultaneously a negation; hence she *must* take a stand on unwritten law because its doing *is* a negation of written law. It is the position she must take. Thus through her retrospective taking responsibility for her action as also having the full weight of a negation of Creon's law and thereby discounting it, Antigone's action takes on the character of being her own, and because uniquely her own, she emerges as a self for herself; a reflective self-relation forced on her by circumstances, her cold defiance step-by-step hollowing out a domain of wrenching inwardness.[13] Hegel states this core thesis as follows:

> Just because self-consciousness is a self to itself, and advances to the deed, it raises itself out of *simple immediacy* and posits the *division* itself. Through this deed it surrenders the determinateness of ethical life, gives up being the simple certainty of immediate truth, and posits the separation of its own self into itself (as agent) and in what stands opposite to it an actuality that is negative for it. (§ 468; TT)

I am claiming that in acting again and claiming her act Antigone advances to the deed and hence departs from "simple immediacy." In surrendering the determinateness of ethical life, that world comes to appear to her as no longer fully hers, and she is no longer unproblematically a simple part of the whole.

H. S. Harris entitles the sections on ethical world and ethical action "The Eden of Spirit" and "The Expulsion from the Garden" respectively, signifying that the Antigone story is Hegel's origins story, with her transgressive disobedience being his wholly secular, wholly human replacement for the idea of original sin.[14] Two theses are connected here: First, in locating the emergence of significant action and singular individuality in transgression, Hegel means to demonstrate that the "mineness" of any action is made possible by the power of negation. Second, the idea of there being a social whole *for* consciousness depends on consciousness separating from that whole, emerging out of it by coming to have a negative relation toward it. In order then for an ethical Eden to appear it must be lost; hence it is always lost, and it exists only as a lost and impossible origin, as a beautiful dream. This is the final way in which the ethical world is necessarily a fantasy. It is not the Greek world itself which is a fantasy, but Greek ethical life as "true spirit" (the title of this section as a whole) that is a dream.

The final section of the chapter on Spirit is entitled "Conscience, the Beautiful Soul, Evil and its Forgiveness." The core of this final dialectical moment is a struggle between "acting consciousness" and "judging consciousness," which are two aspects or sides of conscience. For reasons I have detailed elsewhere,[15] these two forms of conscience are best interpreted as modern, autonomous versions of Antigone (acting consciousness) and Creon (judging consciousness—who becomes, of course, "the beautiful soul"). What is pertinent for present purposes is the fundamental stakes at issue in this final battle for recognition. Hegel comes to regard conscientious action as paradigmatic because he comes to view transgressive action, action that opposes existing norms of action, as paradigmatic of significant action generally.

Although Hegel's argument for this thesis is complex, the core of it is that only in a closed society in which individuals are immediate functions of the roles they inhabit would it be possible for there to be a complete table of all normatively acceptable actions. While the ideal of a perfectly closed social order is always a fantasy, in a modern complex society that has already come to value freedom and autonomy, and the right of subjectivity, no such table is either conceivable or desirable. But from this it follows that a modern society will be forced to routinely handle actions that *initially* appear as transgressive since they do, in fact, depart from existing shared norms. But this is as much to say that free action, autonomous action, conscientious action, creative action, and transgressive action, under standard circumstances, will necessarily overlap or converge with one another. Transgressive, negating action is just action twisting free of tradition, habit, routine, and agreed upon norms. Transgressive action is also the kind of action that can be expressive of the singular individual doing it. Because modern autonomous action cannot avoid becoming transgressive, cannot avoid being taken as evil from the standpoint of the existing community (the truth of judging consciousness), forgiveness must emerge as the medium of recognition among conscientious selves. For this reason Hegel comes to the view that the understanding of the meaning of an action is necessarily retrospective; and, since the self is actual only in its deeds, then mutual recognition too is fundamentally retrospective and transient, always ready to be lost and require renewal.[16] In fine, *the chapter on Spirit concludes with a systematic vindication of Antigone's transgressiveness as the paradigm of autonomous action.*[17] Greek ethical life neither had room for singular individuality nor for transgressive action—the unavoidability of the latter entailing the necessity of the former. Antigone's transgressive action, in destroying the beautiful whole, in revealing the tragedy of ethical life as such, sets the task for Spirit generally: to generate a reconciliation between singular individuality and universality that acknowledges the exemplary character of Antigone's transgressive action. Spirit is nothing but the story of how Antigone would finally be allowed to choose life rather than death.

The End of the Social Metaphysics of Gender Complementarity

It follows from Irigaray's claim that the glue creating the illusion of a perfectly integral society in which human and divine laws, universal and particular, can be harmoniously united is the gender complementarity between man and woman (leaving aside the brother/sister red herring), that this very complementarity is itself the ultimate cause for the collapse of that ideal world. This is a judgment Hegel unequivocally and emphatically shares. In the continuation of the passage in which he links the possibility of significant action with transgression, guilt, and crime—all in opposition to Ismene's guiltless, role-bound doings—Hegel states that "ethical action has the moment of crime in it, *because* it does not sublate the *natural* distribution of the two laws to the two sexes" (§ 468; TT; first emphasis added). Notice that, for Hegel, what is at stake is not whether there is a fundamental conflict between human law and divine law—since those bodies of law are mutually dependent they could not logically conflict—rather, it is the distribution of those necessarily mutually dependent laws to the two sexes that is the difficulty. That sexual distribution causes the one-sidedness: "[R]ather, being an univocal orientation towards the law, [ethical action] remains within natural immediacy, and, qua action, turns this one-sidedness into guilt by seizing on only one side of the essence, and adopting a negative attitude towards the other, that is, violating it" (§ 468; translation modified). Hegel does not claim that the *content* of either Antigone's or Creon's action is internally conditioned by sexual identity. How could he, given that he takes the actual content of those laws as specifying the meaning of universality and individuality in that ethical life to be legitimate? Rather, his emphatic complaint is that *access* to spiritual meaning in being determined by sexual identity becomes dualistic and one-sided, a one-sidedness that takes on all the arbitrariness of nature.

But even that says too little. If the spiritual role I am to inhabit is naturally determined, determined outside anything I might say or do, then there can be no "me" in that role, hence no individuality. If my relation to Spirit is determined by nature, then it is not spiritual or "mine" at all. The consequence of this is that the sexual stamping of spiritual placement by barring each sex from direct access to the other's spiritual domain makes what should be, indeed must be, the complementary duality of universal and individual, city and family, into an antagonistic dualism; and, further, reduces the individual to the role he or she inhabits. It is not social roles as such that are the problem here. It is, rather, as Hegel said earlier, that those roles in traditional societies only reach as far down as the particular, which entails not only that the roles are not chosen, but that there is no space between self and role through which that relation may be elaborated, criticized, or repudiated: No voice, no exit.

Hegel is here doubtlessly assuming that sexual difference is natural and hence immediate. He is not contesting what he considers natural fact; rather, on the contrary, he is arguing that the very fact that sexual difference is immediate and natural makes it logically unsuitable for orienting a relation to Spirit because it will necessarily generate a dualism of lawfulness that makes social belonging necessarily contradictory. The tragedy of Antigone is the tragedy of that world caused by its rigid sexual distribution of spiritual labor. That Hegel regards this as the fundamental issue here is underlined by the way in which he begins the final paragraph of the section:

> This ruin of the ethical Substance and its passage into another form is thus determined by the fact that the ethical consciousness is directed on to the law in a way that is essentially *immediate*. This determination of immediacy means that Nature as such enters into the activity of ethical life . . . (§ 476; translation modified)

The social metaphysics of gender complementarity is necessarily disastrous because in making one's spiritual fate depend directly, immediately, on one's sexual identity it allows nature to enter directly into ethical life, which is to say, it makes ethical life not ethical but natural. If this is right, then exploding the social metaphysics of gender complementarity is central to Hegel's entire critique of ethical life. Because the idealist dream of ethical life transformed gender complementarity from a romantic ideal into a social metaphysics, then conversely, the destruction of ethical life requires the sublation of gender complementarity, requires that access to the law, that is, the possibility of having a social identity in general, not be determined by sexual identity. And this is exactly how Hegel commences the very next paragraph in which he announces how the Roman idea of right sublates Greek ethical life. If the problem of Greek ethical life was that it was a community without individuals, Rome is a conglomeration of individuals without community. Nonetheless, Rome makes good on the deficit in ethical life by making individuality a *wholly* formal, legal matter, whereby one is recognized as an ethical person: "This dead spirit, the universal—the universal split up into the atoms of absolutely many individuals—is an *equality* in which *everyone* counts as *each* one, that is, as *persons*" (§ 477; TT). For some, say Irigaray, this way of sublating sexual difference might be thought to entail a worse repression and a deeper androcentrism than the social metaphysics of gender complementarity; but that Hegel is here confirming the barring of sexual identity from having a determining role in spiritual life there can be no doubt. If there is an affirmative feminine principle at work in Spirit, it will appear elsewhere.

This sexual stamping argument explains the end of beauty analysis without being the cause of the contradiction determining it. Again, the core contradiction in ethical life is between ethical world and ethical action, that is, between a conception of an internally integrated and functionally harmonious whole, and the need of that whole for singular individual agents, a need that is in principle unsatisfiable in ethical life *because* it is true ethical life, that is, immediate and natural—via gender complementarity. The sexual stamping of ethical identity, in essence, *naturalizes* a spiritual scheme, and in naturalizing it reduces the individuals who are the bearers of roles to the roles they bear.[18] Hegel's critique of the social metaphysics of gender complementarity is not, of course, an ethical critique of patriarchy, but a phenomenological/metaphysical critique of the representation of Spirit as an ethical whole, or substance, existing independently of the individual agents who are its members, and the ethical naturalism of the sexual division of spiritual labor that holds that representational scheme in place and makes it possible. There could not be a givenness of substance unless an organizing element of substance was itself given; sexual difference plays that role in ethical life. It is because Hegel's critique is not ethical but metaphysical that it has critical depth: Any sexual division of spiritual labor must necessarily undermine the categorial requirements of individuality for any possible self-consciously self-determining community.

What then is to be made of the infamous passage in which Hegel makes of womankind the eternal irony of the community that transforms the universal purpose of government into a private purpose through intrigue—a passage routinely taken as the decisive evidence of Hegel's misogyny? All the critical accounts of this passage I know take it out of context. Worse, given that in the *Phenomenology* Antigone's agency and individuality are consequential for the argument as a whole, it is hardly plausible to think that Hegel intends to direct the offending passage at her.

The passage occurs in the long (two-plus pages) penultimate paragraph on Greek ethical life; in it Hegel provides a compressed account of the essential dialectic of ethical life as a whole, demonstrating how its own internal structure leads to its downfall and the consequent uprising of a new form of life "whose life principle is the *singular* individual as singular" (§ 475; TT). In brief, this paragraph is again making a case for the right of individuality, a right that is insufficiently acknowledged in Greek ethical life. Hegel summarizes the core dialectic that yields this conclusion thus:

> The community can maintain itself, however, only through the oppression of this spirit of singularity, and, because that spirit is an essential moment, the community really engenders it as well. In fact, by its oppressive attitude toward the spirit of singularity, it engenders it as a hostile principle. (§ 475; TT)

The spirit of singularity, a spirit, indeed an actuality that the community needs, is produced as a hostile principle by its repression. Singularity's appearance *as a hostile principle* is a consequence of its repression. Again, what is repressed is the very item, an individual's singularity, that Hegel demonstrates throughout as necessary for the possibility of spiritual life. If this is right, then what Hegel is doing in this paragraph is *explaining and diagnosing* the hostile appearance of woman in Greek tragedy generally and in *Antigone* in particular because woman is the bearer of repressed singularity. He is *not* supporting that charge. The very idea of womankind as the irony of the community is a product of the oppression of the spirit of singularity by the community; the conflict between Creon and Antigone is a product of the ethical world repression of individuality—but those two thoughts state, exactly, how the end of beauty and end of gender complementarity arguments fit together.

What then of the offending passage itself? Notice, first, that it is immediately followed by a reference to the *Bacchae* and the absurd figures of Cadmus and Tiresias in their Dionysian dress. Hegel is evidently posing a consonant if contrasting Greek view about singularity and the woman principle, this time indicating how universality when insulated against the claims of singularity, "to pleasures and enjoyments, as well as to any active role," becomes a laughingstock and object of contempt. This suggests that the previous statement about womankind is also of Greek origin, most plausibly, given the setting, from *Antigone.* There is, I think, little doubt that the womankind passage is meant as a *prose précis* of Creon's first long speech to Haemon (640–680). The core of that speech, and everything that follows in the dialogue between them, turns on the contrast between womankind as representing disorder through individualism and man as representing order through collectivism and obedience. This is consistent with Creon's double litany throughout the play that the order of the state is threatened by money-seekers and women. What money-seekers and women share for Creon is their privileging of the claims of the individual (family) over those of the community. There may indeed be "gender panic"[19] in Creon's responses to Antigone, but his argument, as consistently acknowledged by the chorus, is that there is an incompatibility between the demands for order as represented by the state, and the desires of individuality as represented by women and money-seekers. This thought reaches fever pitch in Creon's contrast between anarchy, which "destroys cities, rips up houses, breaks the ranks of spearmen into headlong rout," and those who "owe their lives to discipline" (756). Creon then turns the anarchy/order contrast directly into one between woman and man: "Therefore we must defend the men who live by law, / never let some woman triumph over us" (756–757). *In fine*, Creon perceives the issue as between womankind and the claims of the state. Hegel reports Creon's ideas with perfect accuracy; there is, however, no evidence in the *Phenomenology* that he supports those views. To suppose he does would make the entire section on ethical life unreadable.

"I am Antigone" (Hegel on Loving the Dead)

Care for the dead, Hegel argues, is the one ineliminable ethical function carried out by the family in ethical life. Since we have already seen in Hegel's Preface that the life of Spirit, for him, is not one that shrinks from death, but rather "the life that endures it and maintains itself in it" (§ 32), we know already that an emphatic conceptual connection exists between Antigone's reverence for the dead and Hegel's philosophical practice.

Consistent with his guiding argument, Hegel makes action and individuality the core issues concerning the burial of the dead. Strikingly, Hegel argues that the demand for the recognition of individuality first emerges in ethical life with the requirement for burial of the dead. This thought is worked twice-over. First, generally, Hegel claims that the only ethical action that embraces "the whole existence of the blood-kinsman" as the single one who belongs to the family can concern the dead rather than the living because as a living individual he is "dispersed" into his many actions (§ 451; TT). Singular individuality can come to the self only when its many actions are complete because Greek ethical life lacked both a conception of a self independent of its roles, and the idea of the self expressing a singularizing "who" through its actions; thus, only the whole of a life, fully gathered, could be singular.

Second, making the first claim more concrete, as citizen an individual is valued primarily not as a singular one but solely as citizen (§ 451). Death, Hegel argues, "is the fulfillment and highest labor that the individual as such undertakes for the community" (§ 452; TT); to sacrifice one's life for the sake of the community, to sacrifice one's individuality to the universality of the state, is to acknowledge the authority of the state. Sacrifice to the universal is the truth of citizenship; hence the truth of citizenship is death. But if taking on the status role as citizen is one's universal purpose, then one's value as an individual is obliterated by the very institution that gives it value. Because the state's ultimate action in lifting and fitting individuals to the standpoint of the universal is to sacrifice them, the state must depend on the family, must, that is, depend on the production and valuing of selves as individuals that is the work of the family.

Hegel is thus arguing that the death of men in war makes manifest and fully actual the relation between each of those men and the state that holds generally in Greek ethical life. This is why he takes the action of *Antigone* to be representative. The absence of recognized individuality becomes obvious, pressing, and urgent with war dead.[20] Furthermore, in taking on the activity of destruction the family member transforms "what has happened" into a "work instead, with the result that being, the ultimate, is something willed" (§ 462; TT)—again a movement of substance becoming subject. Thus in the same way in which the claims of singular individuality become pressing with the war dead, so exactly in the case of those dead does the necessity of action become manifest, absolute: burial of the dead makes death something culturally done rather than only naturally undergone.

This patently is the key to Hegel's reading of *Antigone*, how the drama itself enacts the transition from world to action. It is the attempt to perform the ritual action of providing Polyneices with the burial that would be the recognition of him as a singular individual that forces Antigone to act transgressively; in her action of taking on the burden of Polyneices' singular individuality, she herself becomes a singular individual. Antigone can only protect Polyneices' right of individuality through the negating action that individuates her; she must perform the act of lodging a claim of individuality for herself to satisfy her obligation to him.

Antigone's action makes Polyneices a "companion" of the "community" of Thebes (§ 452; translation modified). An individual's singularity is saved not simply for himself or herself, but for each of them as a member of the community; burial rites ensure continued membership, they connect the "I" to the "We." By ensuring the membership of the dead in the community, burial rites simultaneously extend the community beyond the present, beyond the recent past and near future, beyond the living. A nation without extension beyond the lives of those living in it would be equivalent to a gang, a mutual protection racket, an instrument for those in it to pursue their private ends—something thus not unlike what social contract theorists imagine the state to be. Hegel's entire tragic argument for singular individuality and agency could not even begin if community meant only the community of the living because, again, for him it is the war dead who first press the claim for the recognition of their singular individuality against the universalities of nature and community. For Hegel, a community of the living only would be a literally soulless community, and hence, ironically, a dead community.

Generational bonding is the manifestation of the female principle beyond the sexual division of spiritual labor, beyond gender complementarity. Nothing else explains why Hegel locates generational bonding in the family and not in religion, why he makes religion fundamentally an expression of family connectedness. In making family and not religion the bearer of generational bonding, Hegel is underlining that the stakes here are wholly immanent and secular, that the unwritten law is not peculiarly "religious," not about any beyond. The claims of the dead to recognition are claims immanent to the possibility of ethical life in general, claims any community capable of successfully reproducing itself as a spiritual totality must be capable of honoring. *We are necessarily a community of the living and the dead.*[21]

In forging this claim Antigone's example is peculiarly salient. Creon, in pressing his demand that Eteocles should be honored and Polyneices dishonored, depends on a norm central to rational morality, namely, that justice requires that unlike cases be treated unlike; to treat the evil man and the morally noble man the same is to commit an injustice to nobility. To this claim Antigone replies, "No matter—Death longs for the same rites for all" (519). Creon responds by saying that even in death an enemy is not a friend; Fagles, anticipating Creon's reply, translates Antigone's next line "I was born to join in love, not hate—that is my nature" (523); at which Creon snaps back, "Go down below and love, / if love you must—love the dead" (524).[22] To see in Creon's defense only blindness and hubris is a mistake; it is not just an ethic of friends versus enemies he is propounding, but a fundamental postulate of moral rationality, indeed of rationality generally (like cases should be treated alike, and unlike cases unlike). As Creon affirms, Antigone's claim exceeds the bounds of rationality and morality; to be born to love is to be born to recognize claims to recognition that exceed the bounds of rational morality.

The claim of love here must, in other words, connect with the demand for recognition of the dead with respect to the categories of action and individuality. The issue here is: On what grounds can the doer of evil be counted as having the same claim as the doer of good? On what grounds and how can evil possibly be set aside? To reply that there is divine law is not much help. Until this question is answered, Antigone's transgressive action and claim against Creon remains a matter of religious dogmatism (that the conservative Sophocles backs her defense of religion is hardly a sufficient defense; it is just the truth of his support that is in question). But, as I suggested above, Hegel does vindicate Antigone, finally, in the section on conscience in which transgressive action becomes the paradigm of free action; in which conscientious action in a community of conscientious agents becomes the means through which the expression of singular individuality finally becomes possible; in which the "mineness" of action is finally understood as requiring retrospection; and in which, in order for all these claims to stand, we must adopt the standpoint of "forgiveness" as the routine medium of mutual recognition since negating, "evil," action is an unavoidable element in communal life. Antigone's love of the dead is thus the adumbration of modern forgiveness in its categorical generality, but only Hegel's wholly secular, wholly immanent, wholly modern conceptual framework fully vindicates Antigone's claim. Furthermore, Antigone *intuits* that the *claim* to recognition, as a claim, will always exceed the positive terms, always exceed the written law, always exceed present consciousness, hence always exceed the means through which it is realized at any given time. Whatever system of recognition we might possess, however elaborately couched, the *demand* for recognition will remain more than that, unwritten and unwritable, its authority only manifest after the effects of its transgression again ruin our complacent present. The demand for recognition is beyond good and evil. This urges a final thought.

In her love of the dead, in going beyond good and evil, in reclaiming Polyneices for the community, in her assertion that we are a community of the living and the dead in which honoring the dead, remembering them, is the condition for us being who we are, Antigone models and anticipates the work of phenomenological memory. The love of the dead's adumbration of forgiveness is central here because, as H. S. Harris rightly remarks, "Spirit is forgiveness."[23] Spirit is love of the dead because the standpoint of Spirit through which we come to know who we are through the memory-work charting the developmental path to conscience presupposes the standpoint of forgiveness, presupposes a loving of the dead.

Ethical forgiveness is the logical presupposition of what is involved in understanding human actions "objectively," in what they have contributed to the comprehension of human knowledge. The rightness and wrongness of actions must be sublated into the wider scheme of Spirit's development, a development that routinely plunges forward through terror and bloodshed. When, at the beginning of his book, Hegel invites us to adopt the phenomenological method of observing forms of consciousness in their own self-posited terms, we were, unknowingly, adopting an ethic of forgiveness, we were learning to love the dead, learning a more comprehensive, less judgmental mode of understanding. The implicit must become explicit. The demand for loving the dead, the demand for what becomes the standpoint of Hegelian philosophy, emphatically enters Hegel's narrative only with the account of Antigone, only with Antigone defiantly breaking Creon's law as she washes Polyneices' corpse and covers it with dust, wailing in the blazing light.

Notes

Author's note: For immensely helpful criticisms and suggestions I am grateful to Sara Beardsworth; to Adam Gies for reminding me of night and day in the burial scene; and to Fanny Söderbäck for her uncanny editorial judgment.

1. For a brief discussion, see George Steiner, *Antigones* (Oxford, UK: Oxford University Press, 1986), pp. 40–41.

2. Apart from the works mentioned in the following, I have been most challenged and inspired by: Seyla Benhabib, "On Hegel, Women and Irony," in *Feminist Interpretations of G. W. F. Hegel*, ed. Patricia Jagentowicz Mills (University Park: Penn State Press, 1996), pp. 25–44; Judith Butler, *Antigone's Claim* (New York: Columbia University Press, 2000); Adriana Cavarero, *Stately Bodies: Literature, Philosophy, and the Question of Gender*, trans. Robert de Lucca and Deanna Shemek (Ann Arbor: University of Michigan Press, 2002); Tina Chanter, *Ethics of Eros: Irigaray's Rewriting of the Philosophers* (London: Routledge, 1995); Kimberly Hutchings, *Hegel and Feminist Philosophy* (Cambridge, UK: Polity Press, 2003)—chap. 4 presents a fine critical engagement with the readings of Irigaray, Butler, and Mills; Patricia Jagentowicz Mills, "Hegel's *Antigone*," in *Feminist Interpretations of G. W. F. Hegel*, pp. 59–88—an essay I have used for teaching since its first publication in 1986; Martha C. Nussbaum, "Sophocles' *Antigone*: conflict, vision, and simplification," chap. 3 in *The Fragility of Goodness: Luck and Ethics in Greek Tragedy and Philosophy* (New York: Cambridge University Press, 1986); Heidi M. Ravven, "Has Hegel Anything to Say to Feminists?" in *Feminist Interpretations of G. W. F. Hegel*; and Cecilia Sjöholm, *The Antigone Complex: Ethics and the Invention of Feminine Desire* (Stanford: Stanford University Press, 2004).

3. Broadly speaking, I take this to be the social metaphysical scheme whose categorial structuring, history and social reproduction is analyzed in Simone de Beauvoir's *The Second Sex*, trans. H. M. Parshley (New York: Knopf, 1954). For what it is worth, I also take Beauvoir's feminism to provide the essentials of a Hegelian feminism.

4. Luce Irigaray, *Speculum of the Other Woman*, trans. Gillian C. Gill (Ithaca, NY: Cornell University Press, 1985), pp. 216–217, emphasis in the original.

5. Any more, for example, than the very opening of the *Phenomenology* in "sense-certainty," which the account of ethical life in its "immediacy" is meant to echo, is Hegel's dream; amongst other things, the *Phenomenology* is an encyclopedia of philosophical dreams.

6. G. W. F. Hegel, *Phenomenology of Spirit*, trans. A.V. Miller (Oxford, UK: Clarendon Press, 1977), §§ 446, 464. Hereafter all references to the *Phenomenology* refer to this edition; they will be placed in parentheses in the text, with the paragraph (§) number from Miller's edition. I have also made use of G. W. F. Hegel, *Spirit: Chapter Six of Hegel's* Phenomenology of Spirit, trans. Hegel Translation Group (Indianapolis, IN: Hackett Publishing, 2001), which if sometimes less elegant is for the most part more accurate. A paragraph number followed by TT marks those places where I have followed the Toronto translation fully. Some translations are my own.

7. I am here disagreeing with Joseph C. Flay, *Hegel's Question for Certainty* (Albany, NY: SUNY Press, 1984), pp. 164–167; for a fine structuring of these sections see Terry Pinkard, *Hegel's* Phenomenology*: The Sociality of Reason* (New York: Cambridge University Press, 1994), pp. 134–145.

8. Hence, in Hegelian terms, the movement from ethical world to ethical action is approximately a move from seeing ethical life from the perspective of consciousness, picturing it, to seeing it from the perspective of self-consciousness. The movement from "observation" to "action" also structures the chapter on Reason.

9. For the pervasive role of the Greek ideal in Hegel's early thought, see H. S. Harris, *Hegel's Development: Toward the Sunlight 1770–1801* (Oxford, UK: Clarendon Press, 1972).

10. Sophocles, *Antigone*, in *The Three Theban Plays*, trans. Robert Fagles (New York: Penguin Books, 1984), lines 891–929. All references in the text are to the line numbers in the Greek text, which appear at the top of the page in Fagles' translation.

11. My preferred interpretation of these lines is offered by Bernard M. W. Knox in *The Heroic Temper: Studies in Sophoclean Tragedy* (Berkeley: University of California Press, 1983), pp. 103–107. This reading is compatible with Mary Beth Mader's compelling "Antigone's Line," included in this volume.

12. For strong readings of the play see Knox, "Antigone 1" and "Antigone 2," chaps. 3–4 in *The Heroic Temper*; and Charles Segal, "*Antigone*: Death and Love, Hades and Dionysus," chap. 6 in *Tragedy and Civilization: An Interpretation of Sophocles* (Norman: University of Oklahoma Press, 1999).

13. It is that emergent inwardness that I think reveals itself in the famous brother-sister speech. For a fine handling of the retrospection issue, see Allen Speight, "Tragedy and Retrospectivity: Hegel's *Antigone*," chap. 2 in *Hegel, Literature and the Problem of Agency* (New York: Cambridge University Press, 2001). For an analogous handling of how Antigone models the possibility of singular individuality, see Christoph Menke, *Tragödie im Sittlichen: Gerechtigkeit und Freiheit nach Hegel* (Frankfurt am Main: Suhrkamp, 1996). See also Jeffrey A. Gauthier, "Historically Emergent Agency: Antigone and Creon," chap. 1 in *Hegel and Feminist Social Criticism: Justice, Recognition and the Feminine* (Albany, NY: SUNY Press, 1997).

14. H. S. Harris, *Hegel's Ladder II: The Odyssey of Spirit* (Indianapolis, IN: Hackett Publishing, 1997), p. 214. Harris' account provides a compelling documenting of how thoroughly Hegel is tracking his Greek sources. My reading is throughout indebted to his.

15. J. M. Bernstein, "Conscience and Transgression: The Exemplarity of Tragic Action," in *Hegel's* Phenomenology of Spirit*: A Reappraisal*, ed. Gary K. Browning (Boston: Kluwer Academic Publishers, 1997), pp. 79–88.

16. I am here agreeing with Patchen Markell, *Bound by Recognition* (Princeton, NJ: Princeton University Press, 2003), p. 94.

17. I defend this thesis in detail in J. M. Bernstein, "Evil and Forgiveness: Hegel's Poetics of Action," in *Beyond Representation*, ed. Richard Eldridge (Cambridge, UK: Cambridge University Press, 1995), pp. 34–65.

18. Markell, *Bound by Recognition*, pp. 99–102.

19. Ibid., p. 113.

20. As it still can. In my household everything comes to a halt each night when the evening news on PBS gives the name and a picture of the U.S. war dead from Iraq. I note that no other war dead from Iraq are there named; they have yet to find their Antigone.

21. The absence in Hegel's argument just here is patent: he provides no sufficient account of birth and maternity.

22. Hugh Lloyd-Jones, in the Loeb edition, *Sophocles II* (Cambridge, MA: Harvard University Press, 1994), thinks the line should literally be translated: "I have no enemies by birth, but I have friends by birth." Fagles' translation must be capturing the intended sense however, given how Creon replies to Antigone.

23. Harris, *Hegel's Ladder II*, p. 498.

Part II

Incestuous Desire

Sexuality, Kinship, and Psychoanalytical Approaches

7

Promiscuous Obedience

Judith Butler

In George Steiner's study of the historical appropriations of *Antigone*, he poses a controversial question that he does not pursue: What would happen if psychoanalysis were to have taken Antigone rather than Oedipus as its point of departure?[1] Oedipus clearly has his own tragic fate, but Antigone's fate is decidedly post-Oedipal. Although her brothers are explicitly cursed by her father, does the curse also work on her and, if so, through what furtive and implicit means? The chorus remarks that something of Oedipus' fate is surely working through her own, but what burden of history does she bear? Oedipus comes to know who his mother and father are but finds that his mother is also his wife. Antigone's father is her brother because they share a mother in Jocasta, and her brothers are her nephews, sons of her brother-father, Oedipus. The terms of kinship become irreversibly equivocal. Is this part of her tragedy? Does this equivocity of kinship lead to fatality?

Antigone is caught in a web of relations that produce no coherent position within kinship. She is not, strictly speaking, outside kinship or, indeed, unintelligible. Her situation can be understood, but only with a certain amount of horror. Kinship is not simply a situation she is in but a set of practices that she also performs, relations that are reinstituted in time precisely through the practice of their repetition. When she buries her brother, it is not simply that she acts *from* kinship, as if kinship furnishes a principle for action. Her action is rather the action *of* kinship, the performative repetition that reinstates kinship as a public scandal. Kinship is what she repeats through her action; to redeploy a formulation from David Schneider, it is not a form of being but a form of

This chapter was originally published as chap. 3 of *Antigone's Claim: Kinship between Life and Death* (New York: Columbia University Press, 2000). Reprinted with permission of the publisher.

doing.[2] And her action implicates her in an aberrant repetition of a norm, a custom, a convention, not a formal law but a lawlike regulation of culture that operates with its own contingency.

If we recall that for Jacques Lacan the symbolic, that set of rules that govern the accession of speech and speakability within culture, is motivated by the father's words, then the father's words are surely upon Antigone; they are, as it were, the medium within which she acts and in whose voice she defends her act. She transmits those words in aberrant form, transmitting them loyally, and yet betraying them by sending them in directions they were never intended to travel. The words are repeated, and their repeatability relies on the deviation that the repetition performs. The aberration that is her speech and her act facilitates such transmissions. Indeed, she is transmitting more than one discourse at once, for the demands that are upon her come from more than one source: her brother also petitions her to give him a decent burial, a demand that in some ways conflicts with the curse that Oedipus has laid on his son—to die in battle and be received by the underworld. These two demands converge and produce a certain interference in the transmitting of the paternal word. After all, if the father is the brother, then what finally is the difference between them? And what is to elevate the demand of Oedipus over the demand of Polyneices?

The words are upon her, but what does that mean? How does a curse come to inform the action that fulfills the prophecy inherent in the curse? What is the temporality of the curse such that the actions that she takes create an equivocation between the words that are upon her, that she suffers, and the act that she herself performs? How are we to understand the strange *nomos* of the act itself? How does the word of the Other become one's own deed, and what is the temporality of this repetition in which the deed that is produced as a result of the curse is also in some ways an aberrant repetition, one that affirms that the curse produces unanticipated consequences?

Oedipus, of course, unknowingly sleeps with his mother, slays his father, and is driven into the wilderness accompanied by Antigone. In *Oedipus at Colonus* the two of them, along with a small party of followers, are given shelter by Theseus in a land governed by Athens. Oedipus learns that his sons have explicitly forbidden his return to Thebes and also learns that they have turned against one another in a bitter battle for the throne. Toward the end of that play, the second of the trilogy, Polyneices visits Oedipus and calls upon him to return. Oedipus not only refuses but levels a curse against Polyneices, that "you shall never conquer in war your native land . . . but shall perish by your brother's hand and kill him who drove you out!"[3]

Antigone stands by, importuning her father to show benevolence toward Polyneices, and fails. And it remains unclear whether the brother whose act will kill him is Eteocles who delivers the fatal blow, or Oedipus, whose curse both predicts and mandates the blow itself. Polyneices, despite Antigone's protest, decides nevertheless to go into battle with Eteocles, and Antigone is left, crying out, "My heart is broken!" She then speaks a line that prefigures her own knowing approach to her own fate: "Brother, how can anyone / *not* mourn, seeing you set out / to death so clear before you?"[4] Indeed, Antigone will and—given the chronology of the plays—"already has" undergone precisely the fate she predicts for her brother, to enter death knowingly.

Antigone not only loses her brother to her father's curse, words that quite literally yield the force of annihilation, but she then loses her father to death by the curse that is upon him. Words and deeds become fatally entangled in the familial scene. The acts of Polyneices and Eteocles seem to fulfill and enact the father's words, but his words—and his deeds—are also compelled by a curse upon him, the curse of Laius. Antigone worries over their fate even as she embarks upon her own course of action for which death is a necessary conclusion. Her desire to save her brothers from their fate is overwhelmed, it seems, by her desire to join them in their fate.

Before he dies, Oedipus makes several utterances that assume the status of a curse. He condemns her, but the force of the condemnation is to bind her to him. His words culminate in her own permanent lovelessness, one that is mandated by Oedipus' demand for loyalty, a demand that verges on incestuous possessiveness: "For from none did you have love more than from this man, without whom you will now spend the remainder of your lives" (1617–1619). His words exert a force in time that exceeds the temporality of their enunciation: they demand that for all time she have no man except for the man who is dead, and although this is a demand, a curse, made *by* Oedipus, who positions himself as her only one, it is clear that she both honors and disobeys this curse as she displaces her love for her father onto her brother. Indeed, she takes her brother to be her only one—she would risk defying the official edict for no kin but Polyneices. Thus she betrays Oedipus even as she fulfills the terms of his curse. She will only love a man who is dead, and hence she will love no man. She obeys his demand, but promiscuously, for he is clearly not the only dead man she loves and, indeed, not the ultimate one. Is the love for the one dissociable from the love for the other? And when it is her "most precious brother" for whom she commits her criminal and honorable act, is it clear that this brother is Polyneices, or could it be Oedipus?

Knowing that he is dying, Oedipus asks, "Will they even shroud my body in Theban soil?" (406), and he learns that his crime makes that impossible. He is thus buried by Theseus out of everyone else's sight, including Antigone's. Then, Antigone, in the play by that name, mimes the act of the strong and true Theseus and buries her brother out of sight, making sure that Polyneices' shade is composed of Theban dust. Antigone's assertive burial, which she performs twice, might be understood to be for both, a burial that at once reflects and institutes the equivocation of brother and father. They are, after all, already interchangeable for her, and yet her act reinstitutes and reelaborates that interchangeability.

Although Sophocles wrote *Antigone* several years before *Oedipus at Colonus,* the action that takes place in the former *follows* the action of the latter. What is the significance of this belatedness? Are the words that goad the action understandable only in retrospect? Can the implications of the curse, understood as extended action, be understood only retrospectively? The action the curse predicted for the future turns out to be an action that has been happening all along, such that the forward movement of time is precisely what is inverted through the temporality of the curse. The curse establishes a temporality for the action it ordains that predates the curse itself. The words bring into the future what has always already been happening.

Antigone is to love no man except the man who is dead, but in some sense she is also a man. And this is also the title that Oedipus bestows upon her, a gift or reward for her loyalty. When Oedipus is banished, Antigone cares for him, and in her loyalty, is referred to as a "man" (*aner*). Indeed, she follows him loyally into the wilderness, but at some point that following imperceptibly turns into a scene in which *she* leads *him*: "Follow, follow me this way with your unseeing steps, father, where I lead you!" (183–184).

Indeed, she is at once cursed with a loyalty to a dead man, a loyalty that makes her manly, and compels her to acquire the attribute that carries his approbation such that desire and identification are acutely confounded in a melancholic bind. Oedipus clearly understands gender as something of a curse itself, since one of the ways in which he condemns his sons is by leveling his accusation through the trope of an orientalizing gender inversion:

> Those two conform altogether to the customs that prevail in Egypt in their nature and the nurture of their lives! For there the males sit in their houses working at the loom, and their consorts provide the necessities of life out of doors. And in your case, my children, those who ought to perform this labour sit at home and keep the house like maidens, and you two *in their place* bear the burdens of your unhappy father's sorrows. (337–344, emphasis added)

Later, Oedipus maintains that Ismene and Antigone have quite literally taken the place of their brothers, acquiring masculine gender along the way. Addressing his sons, he says:

> And if I had not begotten these daughters to attend, me, I would not be living, for all you did for me. But as it is they preserve me, they are my nurses, they are men, not women, when it comes to working for me; but you are sons of some other, and no sons of mine. (1360–1364)

His daughters thus become his sons, but these same children (Antigone and Ismene), he maintains earlier, are also his "sisters" (330). And so we've arrived at something like kinship trouble at the heart of Sophocles.[5] Antigone has, then, already taken the place of her brother; when she breaks with Ismene, it mirrors the break that Polyneices has made with Eteocles, thus acting, we might say, as brothers do. By the time this drama is done, she has thus taken the place of nearly every man in her family. Is this an effect of the words that are upon her?

Indeed, words exercise a certain power here that is not immediately clear. They act, they exercise performative force of a certain kind, and sometimes they are clearly violent in their consequences, as words that either constitute or beget violence. Indeed, sometimes it seems that the words act in illocutionary ways, enacting the very deed that they name in the very moment of the naming. For Friedrich Hölderlin, this constitutes something of the murderous force of the word in Sophocles. Consider this moment in which the chorus in *Oedipus at Colonus* reminds Oedipus of his crime, a verbal narration *of* the deed that becomes the violent punishment *for* the deed. They not only narrate the events but also deliver the accusation, compel his acknowledgment, and inflict a punishment through their interrogatory address:

> CHORUS: Unhappy one, what then? You murdered . . . your father?
>
> OEDIPUS: Woe! You have struck me a second blow, anguish upon anguish!
>
> CHORUS: You killed him. . . . (540–545)

Thus Oedipus is verbally struck by the chorus for having struck and slain his father; the accusation verbally repeats the crime, strikes again where Oedipus is already hurt and where he is thus hurt again. He says, "You strike again," and they strike again, strike with words, repeating, "You killed him"; and the chorus who speaks is ambiguously addressed as "God in heaven," speaking with the force that divine words do. Such scenes no doubt prompted Hölderlin to remark upon the fatality of words in his "Anmerkungen zur Antigone": "The word becomes mediately factic in that it grasps the sensuous body. The tragic Greek word is fatally factic [*tödlichfaktisch*], because it actually seizes the body that murders."[6]

It is not just that the words kill Oedipus in some linguistic and psychic sense but those words, the ones composing the prior curse of Laius upon him, move him toward incest and murder. In murdering, he fulfills or completes the words that were upon him; his action becomes indissociable from the spoken act, a condition we might say of both the curse that dramatic action reflects and the structure of dramatic action itself. These are words that one transmits, but they are not autonomously generated or maintained by the one who speaks them. They emerge from, in Hölderlin's terms, an inspired or possessed mouth (*aus begeistertem Munde*) and seize the body that murders. They are spoken to Oedipus, but he also restages his trauma, as it were, as his words seize and kill his sons, seize them and make them murderous, and as his words also seize and gender as manly the body of his daughter, Antigone. And they do this precisely by becoming words that act in time, words whose temporality exceeds the scene of their utterance, becoming the desire of those they name, repetitious and conjuring, conferring only retrospectively the sense of a necessary and persistent past that is confirmed by the utterance that predicts it, where prediction becomes the speech act by which an already operative necessity is confirmed.

The relation between word and deed becomes hopelessly entangled in the familial scene, every word transmutes into event or, indeed, "fatal fact," in Hölderlin's phrase. Every deed is the apparent temporal effect of some prior word, instituting the temporality of tragic belatedness, that all that happens has already happened, will come to appear as the always already happening, a word and a deed entangled and extended through time through the force of repetition. Its fatality is, in a sense, to be found in the dynamic of its temporality and its perpetual exile into non-being that marks its distance from any sense of home.[7] According to Hölderlin, this prodigious performativity of the word is tragic both in the sense of fatal and theatrical. Within the theater, the word is acted, the word as deed takes on a specific meaning; the acute performativity of words in this play has everything to do with the words taking place within a play, as acted, as acted out.

There are, of course, other contexts in which words become indissociable from deeds, such as department meetings or family gatherings. The particular force of the word as deed within the family or, more generally, as it circuits within kinship, is enforced as law (*nomos*). But this enforcement does not happen without a reiteration—a wayward, temporal echo—that also puts the law at risk of going off its course.

And if we were to return to psychoanalysis through the figure of Antigone, how might our consideration of this play and this character lay out the possibility of an aberrant future for psychoanalysis, as that mode of analysis becomes appropriated in contexts that could not be anticipated? Psychoanalysis traces the wayward history of such utterances and makes its own lawlike pronouncements along the way. Psychoanalysis might be one mode of interpreting the curse, the apparently predictive force of the word as it bears a psychic history that cannot fully enter narrative form. The encrypted word that carries an irrecoverable history, a history that, by virtue of its very irrecoverability and its enigmatic afterlife in words, bears a force whose origin and end cannot be fully determined.

That the play *Antigone* predates its prehistory, is written decades before *Oedipus at Colonus*, indicates how the curse operates within an uncertain temporality. Uttered before the events, its force is only known retroactively; its force precedes its utterance, as if the utterance paradoxically inaugurates the necessity of its prehistory and of what will come to appear as always already true.

But how surefire is a curse? Is there a way to break it? Or is there, rather, a way in which its own vulnerability might be exposed and exploited? The one who within the present recites the curse or finds oneself in the midst of the word's historical effectivity does not precisely ventriloquize words that are received from a prior source. The words are reiterated, and their force is reenforced. The agency that performs this reiteration knows the curse but misunderstands the moment in which she participates in its transmission.

To what extent is this notion of the curse operating in the conception of a symbolic discourse that is transmitted in certain but unpredictable forms by the speaking subject? And to the extent that the symbolic reiterates a "structural" necessity of kinship, does it relay or perform the curse of kinship itself? In other words, does the structuralist law report on the curse that is upon kinship or does it deliver that curse? Is structuralist kinship the curse that is upon contemporary critical theory as it tries to approach the question of sexual normativity, sociality, and the status of law? And, moreover, if we are seized by this inheritance, is there a way to transmit that curse in aberrant form, exposing its fragility and fracture in the repetition and reinstitution of its terms? Is this breaking from the law that takes place in the reinstituting of the law the condition for articulating a future kinship that exceeds structuralist totality, a poststructuralism of kinship?[8]

The Antigonean revision of psychoanalytic theory might put into question the assumption that the incest taboo legitimates and normalizes kinship based in biological reproduction and the heterosexualization of the family. Although psychoanalysis has often insisted that normalization is invariably disrupted and foiled by what cannot be ordered by regulatory norms, it has rarely addressed the question of how new forms of kinship can and do arise on the basis of the incest taboo. From the presumption that one cannot—or ought not to—choose one's closest family members as one's lovers and marital partners, it does not follow that the bonds of kinship that *are* possible assume any particular form.

To the extent that the incest taboo contains its infraction within itself, it does not simply prohibit incest but rather sustains and cultivates incest as a necessary specter of social dissolution, a specter without which social bonds cannot emerge. Thus the prohibition against incest in the play *Antigone* requires a rethinking of prohibition itself, not merely as a negative or privative operation of power but as one that works precisely through proliferating through displacement the very crime that it bars. The taboo—and its threatening figuration of incest—delineates lines of kinship that harbor incest as their ownmost possibility, establishing "aberration" at the heart of the norm. Indeed, my question is whether it can also become the basis for a socially survivable aberration of kinship in which the norms that govern legitimate and illegitimate modes of kin association might be more radically redrawn.

Antigone says "brother," but does she mean "father"? She asserts her public right to grieve her kin, but how many of her kin does she leave ungrieved? Considering how many are dead in her family, is it possible that mother and father and repudiated sister and other brother are condensed there at the site of the irreproducible brother? What kind of psychoanalytic approach to Antigone's act would foreclose in advance any consideration of overdetermination at the level of the object? This equivocation at the site of the kinship term signals a decidedly post-Oedipal dilemma, one in which kin positions tend to slide into one another, in which Antigone is the brother, the brother is the father, and in which psychically, linguistically, this is true regardless of whether they are dead or alive; for anyone living in this slide of identifications, their fate will be an uncertain one, living within death, dying within life.

One might simply say in a psychoanalytic spirit that Antigone represents a *perversion* of the law and conclude that the law requires perversion and that, in some dialectical sense, the law is, therefore, perverse. But to establish the structural necessity of perversion to the law is to posit a static relation between the two in which each entails the other and, in that sense, is nothing without the other. This form of negative dialectics produces the satisfaction that the law is *invested* in perversion and that the law is not what it seems to be. It does not help to make possible, however, other forms of social life, inadvertent possibilities produced by the prohibition that come to undermine the conclusion that an invariant social organization of sexuality follows of necessity from the prohibitive law. What happens when the perverse or the impossible emerges in the language of the law and makes its claim precisely there in the sphere of legitimate kinship that depends on its exclusion or pathologization?[9]

In Slavoj Žižek's brief account of Antigone in *Enjoy Your Symptom!*, he suggests that her "No!" to Creon is a feminine and destructive act, one whose negativity leads to her own death. The masculine act is apparently more affirmative for him, the act by which a new order is founded.[10] By saying "No" to the sovereign, she excludes herself from the community and dooms herself to an unsurvivable exile. Yet it seems that masculine reparation and building are an effort to cover over that "traumatic rupture" caused by feminine negation. Here it seems that Antigone is once again elevated to a feminine position (unproblematically) and then understood to have constituted the founding negation for the polis, the site of its own traumatic dissolution that the subsequent polity seeks to cover over. But does Antigone simply say "No"? Surely negations riddle her speech, but she also approximates the stubborn will of Creon and her negation circumscribes a rival autonomy. Later, Žižek will make clear that Antigone counters Creon not with reasons but with a tautology that is nothing other than her brother's name: "The 'law' in the name of which Antigone insists upon Polyneices' right to burial is this law of the 'pure' signifier. . . . It is the Law of the name that fixes our identity."[11] But does Antigone call her brother by his name, or does she, at the moment in which she seeks to give him precedence, call him by a kinship term that is, in fact and in principle, interchangeable? Will her brother ever have one name?

What is the contemporary voice that enters into the language of the law to disrupt its univocal workings? Consider that in the situation of blended families, a child says "mother" and might expect more than one individual to respond to the call. Or that, in the case of adoption, a child might say "father" and might mean both the absent phantasm she never knew as well as the one who assumes that place in living memory. The child might mean that at once, or sequentially, or in ways that are not always clearly disarticulated from one another. Or when a young girl comes to be fond of her stepbrother, what dilemma of kinship is she in? For a woman who is a single mother and has her child without a man, is the father still there, a spectral "position" or "place" that remains unfilled, or is there no such "place" or "position"? Is the father absent, or does this child have no father, no position, and no inhabitant? Is this a loss that assumes the unfulfilled norm, or is it another configuration of primary attachment whose primary loss is not to have a language in which to articulate its terms? And when two men or two women parent, are we to assume that some primary division of gendered roles organizes their psychic places within the scene so that the empirical contingency of two same-gendered parents is nevertheless straightened out by the presocial psychic place of the Mother and Father into which they enter? Does it make sense on these occasions to insist that there are symbolic positions of Mother and Father that every psyche must accept regardless of the social form that kinship takes? Or is that a way of reinstating a heterosexual organization of parenting at the psychic level that can accommodate all manner of gender variation at the social level? Here it seems that the very division between the psychic or symbolic, on the one hand, and the social, on the other, occasions this preemptory normalization of the social field.

I write this, of course, against the background of a substantial legacy of feminist theory that has taken the Lévi-Straussian analytic of kinship as the basis for its own version of structuralist and poststructuralist psychoanalysis and the theorization of a primary sexual difference. It is, of course, one function of the incest taboo to prohibit sexual exchange among kin relations or, rather, to establish kin relations precisely on the basis of those taboos. The question, however, is whether the incest taboo has also been mobilized to *establish* certain forms of kinship as the only intelligible and livable ones. Thus one hears, for instance, the legacy of this tradition in psychoanalysis invoked by psychoanalysts in Paris in recent months against the prospect of "contracts of alliance," construed by conservatives as a bid for gay marriage.[12] Although the rights of gay people to adopt children were not included in the proposed contracts, those who opposed the proposal fear that such contracts might lead to that eventuality and argue that any children raised in a gay family would run the immanent threat of psychosis, as if some structure, necessarily named "Mother" and necessarily named "Father" and established at the level of the symbolic, was a necessary psychic support against an engorgement by the Real. Similarly, Jacques-Alain Miller argued that whereas he was clear that homosexual relations deserve recognition, they should not qualify for marriage because two men together, deprived of the feminine presence, would not be able to bring fidelity to the relationship (a wonderful claim made against the backdrop of our presidential evidence of the binding power of marriage on heterosexual fidelity[13]). Yet other Lacanian practitioners who trace the sources of autism in the "paternal gap" or "absence" similarly predict psychotic consequences for children with lesbian parents.

These views commonly maintain that alternative kinship arrangements attempt to revise psychic structures in ways that lead to tragedy again, figured incessantly as the tragedy of and for the child. No matter what one ultimately thinks of the political value of gay marriage, and I myself am a skeptic here for political reasons I outline elsewhere,[14] the public debate on its legitimacy becomes the occasion for a set of homophobic discourses that must be resisted on independent grounds. Consider that the horror of incest, the moral revulsion it compels in some, is not that far afield from the same horror and revulsion felt toward lesbian and gay sex, and is not unrelated to the intense moral condemnation of voluntary single parenting, or gay parenting, or parenting arrangements with more than two adults involved (practices that can be used as evidence to support a claim to remove a child from the custody of the parent in several states in the United States). These various modes in which the Oedipal mandate fails to produce normative family all risk entering into the metonymy of that moralized sexual horror that is perhaps most fundamentally associated with incest.

The abiding assumption of the symbolic, that stable kinship norms support our abiding sense of culture's intelligibility, can be found, of course, outside of the Lacanian discourse. It is invoked in popular culture by psychiatric "experts" and policy makers to thwart the legal demands of a social movement that threatens to expose the aberration at the heart of the heterosexual norm. It is quite possible to argue in a Lacanian vein that the symbolic place of the mother can be multiply occupied, that it is never identified or identifiable with an individual, and that this is what distinguishes it as symbolic. But why is the symbolic place singular and its inhabitants multiple? Or consider the liberal gesture in which one maintains that the place of the father and the place of the mother are necessary, but hey, anyone of any gender can fill them. The structure is purely formal, its defenders say, but note how its very formalism secures the structure against critical challenge. What are we to make of an inhabitant of the form that brings the form to crisis? If the relation between the inhabitant and the form is arbitrary, it is still structured, and its structure works to domesticate in advance any radical reformulation of kinship.[15]

The figure of Antigone, however, may well compel a reading that challenges that structure, for she does not conform to the symbolic law and she does not prefigure a final restitution of the law. Though entangled in the terms of kinship, she is at the same time outside those norms. Her crime is confounded by the fact that the kinship line from which she descends, and which she transmits, is derived from a paternal position that is already confounded by the manifestly incestuous act that is the condition of her own existence, which makes her brother her father, which begins a narrative in which she occupies, linguistically, every kin position *except* "mother" and occupies them at the expense of the coherence of kinship and gender.

Although not quite a queer heroine, Antigone does emblematize a certain heterosexual fatality that remains to be read. Whereas some might conclude that the tragic fate she suffers is the tragic fate of any and all who would transgress the lines of kinship that confer intelligibility on culture, her example, as it were, gives rise to a contrary sort of critical intervention: What in her act is fatal for heterosexuality in its normative sense? And to what other ways of organizing sexuality might a consideration of that fatality give rise?

Following schools of cultural anthropology inflected by Marxian analysis and Friedrich Engels' famous study of the origin of the family, a school of feminist anthropologists have taken distance from the Lévi-Straussian model—a critique exemplified perhaps most powerfully by Gayle Rubin,[16] Sylvia Junko Yanagisako, Jane Fishburne Collier, Michelle Rosaldo,[17] and David Schneider.[18] The critique of the structuralist account, however, is not the end of kinship itself. Understood as a socially alterable set of arrangements that has no cross-cultural structural features that might be fully extracted from its social operations, kinship signifies any number of social arrangements that organize the reproduction of material life, that can include the ritualization of birth and death, that provide bonds of intimate alliance both enduring and breakable, and that regulate sexuality through sanction and taboo. In the 1970s socialist feminists sought to make use of the unwaveringly social analysis of kinship to show that there is no ultimate basis for the normative heterosexual monogamous family structure in nature, and we might now add that it has no similar basis in language. Various utopian projects to revamp or eliminate family structure have become important components of the feminist movement and, to some extent, have survived in contemporary queer movements as well, the support for gay marriage notwithstanding.

Consider, for instance, Carol Stack's *All Our Kin,* which shows that despite governmental efforts to label fatherless families as dysfunctional, those black urban kinship arrangements constituted by mothers, grandmothers, aunts, sisters, and friends who work together to raise children and reproduce the material conditions of life are extremely functional and would be seriously misdescribed if measured against an Anglo-American standard of familial normalcy.[19] The struggle to legitimate African-American kinship dates back to slavery, of course. And Orlando Patterson's book *Slavery and Social Death* makes the significant point that one of the institutions that slavery annihilated for African-Americans was kinship.[20] The slave-master invariably owned slave families, operating as a patriarch who could rape and coerce the women of the family and effeminize the men; women within slave families were unprotected by their own men, and men were unable to exercise their role in protecting and governing women and children. Although Patterson sometimes makes it seem that the primary offense against kinship was the eradication of paternal rights to women and children within slave families, he nevertheless offers us the important concept of "social death" to describe this aspect of slavery in which slaves are treated as dying within life.

"Social death" is the term Patterson gives to the status of being a living being radically deprived of all rights that are supposed to be accorded to any and all living human beings. What remains uninterrogated in his view, and that I believe resurfaces in his contemporary views on family politics, is precisely his objection to slave men being deprived by slavery of an ostensibly "natural" patriarchal position within the family. Indeed, his use of G. W. F. Hegel supports this point. Angela Davis made a radically different point in *The Black Scholar* several years ago when she underscored the vulnerability of black women to rape both within the institution of slavery and its aftermath, and argued that the family has not served as an adequate protection against sexualized racial violence.[21] Moreover, one can see in the work of Claude Lévi-Strauss the implicit slide between his discussion of kinship groups, referred to as clans, and his subsequent writing on race and history in which the laws that govern the reproduction of a "race" become indissociable from the reproduction of the nation. In these latter writings he implies that cultures maintain an internal coherence precisely through rules that guarantee their reproduction, and though he does not consider the prohibition of miscegenation, it seems to be presupposed in his description of self-replicating cultures.[22]

The critique of kinship within anthropology has centered on the fiction of bloodlines that work as a presupposition for kinship studies throughout the past century. And yet, the dissolution of kinship studies as an interesting or legitimate field of anthropology does not have to lead to a dismissal of kinship altogether. Kath Weston makes this clear in her book *Families We Choose,* where she replaces the blood tie as the basis for kinship with consensual affiliation.[23] We might see new kinship in other forms as well, ones where consent is less salient than the social organization of need: something like the buddy system that the Gay Men's Health Clinic in New York has established for caring for those who live with HIV and AIDS would similarly qualify as kinship, despite the enormous struggle to gain recognition by legal and medical institutions for the kin status of those relations, manifested for instance by the inability to assume medical responsibility for one another or, indeed, to be permitted to receive and bury the dead.

This perspective of radical kinship, which sought to extend legitimacy to a variety of kinship forms, and which, in fact, refused the reduction of kinship to family, came under criticism by some feminists in the aftermath of the 1960s "sexual revolution," producing, I would suggest, a theoretical conservatism that is currently in tension with contemporary radical sexual politics. It is why, for instance, it would be difficult to find a fruitful engagement at the present time between the new Lacanian formalisms and the radical queer politics of, for example, Michael Warner and friends. The former insists on fundamental notions of sexual difference, which are based on rules that prohibit and regulate sexual exchange, rules we can break only to find ourselves ordered by them anew. The latter calls into question forms of sexual foundationalism that cast viable forms of queer sexual alliance as illegitimate or, indeed, impossible and unlivable. At its extreme, the radical sexual politics turns against psychoanalysis or, rather, its implicit normativity, and the neo-formalists turn against queer studies as a "tragically" utopian enterprise.

I remember hearing stories about how radical socialists who refused monogamy and family structure at the beginning of the 1970s ended that decade by filing into psychoanalytic offices and throwing themselves in pain on the analytic couch. And it seems to me that the turn to psychoanalysis and, in particular, to Lacanian theory was prompted in part by the realization by some of those socialists that there were some constraints on sexual practice that were necessary for psychic survival and that the utopian effort to nullify prohibitions often culminated in excruciating scenes of psychic pain. The subsequent turn to Lacan seemed to be a turn away from a highly constructivist and malleable account of social law informing matters of sexual regulation to one that posits a presocial law, what Juliet Mitchell once called a "primordial law" (something she no longer does), the law of the Father, which sets limits upon the variability of social forms and which, in its most conservative form, mandates an exogamic, heterosexual conclusion to the Oedipal drama. That this constraint is understood to be beyond social alteration, indeed, to constitute the condition and limit of all social alterations, indicates something of the theological status it has assumed. And though this position often is quick to claim that although there is a normative conclusion for the Oedipal drama, the norm cannot exist without perversion, and only through perversion can the norm be established. We are all supposed to be satisfied with this apparently generous gesture by which the perverse is announced to be essential to the norm. The problem as I see it is that the perverse remains entombed precisely there, as the essential and negative feature of the norm, and the relation between the two remains static, giving way to no rearticulation of the norm itself.

In this light, then, it is perhaps interesting to note that Antigone, who concludes the Oedipal drama, fails to produce heterosexual closure for that drama, and that this may intimate the direction for a psychoanalytic theory that takes Antigone as its point of departure. Certainly, she does not achieve another sexuality, one that is *not* heterosexuality, but she does seem to de-institute heterosexuality by refusing to do what is necessary to stay alive for Haemon, by refusing to become a mother and a wife, by scandalizing the public with her wavering gender, by embracing death as her bridal chamber and identifying her tomb as a "deep dug home" (*kataskaphes oikesis*). If the love toward which she moves as she moves toward death is a love for her brother and thus, ambiguously, her father, it is also a love that can only be consummated by its obliteration, which is no consummation at all. As the bridal chamber is refused in life and pursued in death, it takes on a metaphorical status and, as metaphor, its conventional meaning is transmuted into a decidedly unconventional one. If the tomb is the bridal chamber, and the tomb is chosen over marriage, then the tomb stands for the very destruction of marriage, and the term "bridal chamber" (*numpheion*) represents precisely the negation of its own possibility. The word destroys its object. In referring to the institution it names, the word performs the destruction of the institution. Is this not the operation of ambivalence in language that calls into question Antigone's sovereign control of her actions?

Although Hegel claims that Antigone acts with no unconscious, perhaps hers is an unconscious that leaves its trace in a different form, indeed that becomes readable precisely in her travails of referentiality. Her naming practice, for instance, ends up undoing its own ostensible aims. When she claims that she acts according to a law that gives her most precious brother precedence, and she appears to mean "Polyneices" by that description, she means more than she intends because that brother could be Oedipus and it could be Eteocles, and there is nothing in the nomenclature of kinship that can successfully restrict its scope of referentiality to the single person, Polyneices. The chorus at one point seeks to remind her that she has more than one brother, but she continues to insist on the singularity and nonreproducibility of this term of kinship. In effect, she seeks to restrict the reproducibility of the word "brother" and to link it exclusively to the person of Polyneices, but she can do this only by displaying incoherence and inconsistency.[24] The term continues to refer to those others she would exclude from its sphere of application, and she cannot reduce the nomenclature of kinship to nominalism. Her own language exceeds and defeats her stated desire, thereby manifesting something of what is beyond her intention, of what belongs to the particular fate that desire suffers in language. Thus she is unable to capture the radical singularity of her brother through a term that, by definition, must be transposable and reproducible in order to signify at all. Language thus disperses the desire she seeks to bind to him, cursing her, as it were, with a promiscuity she cannot contain.

In this way Antigone does not achieve the effect of sovereignty she apparently seeks, and her action is not fully conscious. She is propelled by the words that are upon her, words of her father's that condemn the children of Oedipus to a life that ought not to have been lived. Between life and death, she is already living in the tomb prior to any banishment there. Her punishment precedes her crime, and her crime becomes the occasion for its literalization.

How do we understand this strange place of being between life and death, of speaking precisely from that vacillating boundary? If she is dead in some sense and yet speaks, she is precisely the one with no place who nevertheless seeks to claim one within speech, the unintelligible as it emerges within the intelligible, a position within kinship that is no position.

Although Antigone tries to capture kinship through a language that defies the transposability of the terms of kinship, her language loses its consistency—but the force of her claim is not therefore lost. The incest taboo did not work to foreclose the love that it should have between Oedipus and Jocasta, and it is arguably faltering again for Antigone. The condemnation follows Oedipus' act and his recognition, but for Antigone, the condemnation works as foreclosure, ruling out from the start any life and love she might have had.

When the incest taboo works *in this sense* to foreclose a love that is not incestuous, what is produced is a shadowy realm of love, a love that persists in spite of its foreclosure in an ontologically suspended mode. What emerges is a melancholia that attends living and loving outside the livable and outside the field of love, where the lack of institutional sanction forces language into perpetual catachresis, showing not only how a term can continue to signify outside its conventional constraints, but also how that shadowy form of signification takes its toll on a life by depriving it of its sense of ontological certainty and durability within a publicly constituted political sphere.

To accept those norms as coextensive with cultural intelligibility is to accept a doctrine that becomes the very instrument by which this melancholia is produced and reproduced at a cultural level. And it is overcome, in part, precisely through the repeated scandal by which the unspeakable nevertheless makes itself heard through borrowing and exploiting the very terms that are meant to enforce its silence.

Do we say that families that do not approximate the norm but mirror the norm in some apparently derivative way are poor copies, or do we accept that the ideality of the norm is undone precisely through the complexity of its instantiation? For those relations that are denied legitimacy, or that demand new terms of legitimation, are neither dead nor alive, figuring the nonhuman at the border of the human. And it is not simply that these are relations that cannot be honored, cannot be openly acknowledged, and cannot therefore be publicly grieved, but that these relations involve persons who are also restricted in the very act of grieving, who are denied the power to confer legitimacy on loss. In this play, at least, Antigone's kin are condemned prior to her crime, and the condemnation she receives repeats and amplifies the condemnation that animates her actions. How does one grieve from within the presumption of criminality, from within the presumption that one's acts are invariably and fatally criminal? Consider that Antigone is trying to grieve, to grieve openly, publicly, under conditions in which grief is explicitly prohibited by an edict, an edict that assumes the criminality of grieving Polyneices and names as criminal anyone who would call the authority of that edict into question. She is one for whom open grieving is itself a crime. But is she guilty only because of the words that are upon her, words that come from elsewhere, or has she also sought to destroy and repudiate the very bonds of kinship that she now claims entitlement to grieve? She is grieving her brother, but part of what remains unspoken in that grief is the grief she has for her father and, indeed, her other brother. Her mother remains almost fully unspeakable, and there is hardly a trace of grief for her sister, Ismene, whom she has explicitly repudiated. The "brother" is no singular place for her, though it may well be that all her brothers (Oedipus, Polyneices, and Eteocles) are condensed at the exposed body of Polyneices, an exposure she seeks to cover, a nakedness she would rather not see or have seen. The edict demands that the dead body remain exposed and ungrieved, and though Antigone seeks to overcome the edict, what she grieves over or whether the public act she performs can be the site of its resolution is not entirely clear at all. She calls her loss her brother, Polyneices, and insists on his singularity, but that very insistence is suspect. Thus her insistence on the singularity of her brother, his radical irreproducibility, is belied by the mourning she fails to perform for her two other brothers, the ones she fails to reproduce publicly for us. Here it appears that the prohibition against mourning is not simply imposed upon her but is enjoined independently without direct pressure by public law.

Her melancholia, if we can call it that, seems to consist in this refusal to grieve that is accomplished through the very public terms by which she insists on her right to grieve. Her claim to entitlement may well be the sign of a melancholia at work in her speech. Her loud proclamations of grief presuppose a domain of the ungrievable. The insistence on public grieving is what moves her away from feminine gender into hubris, into that distinctively manly excess that makes the guards, the chorus, and Creon wonder: Who is the man here? There seem to be some spectral men here, ones that Antigone herself inhabits, the brothers whose place she has taken and whose place she transforms in the taking. The melancholic, Freud tells us, registers his or her "plaint," levels a juridical claim, where the language becomes the event of the grievance, where, emerging from the unspeakable, language carries a violence that brings it to the limits of speakability.

We might ask what remains unspeakable here, not in order to produce speech that will fill the gap but to ask about the convergence of social prohibition and melancholia, how the condemnations under which one lives turn into repudiations that one performs, and how the grievances that emerge against the public law also constitute conflicted efforts to overcome the muted rage of one's own repudiations. In confronting the unspeakable in *Antigone*, are we confronting a socially instituted foreclosure of the intelligible, a socially instituted melancholia in which the unintelligible life that emerges in language as a living body might be interred into a tomb?

Indeed, Giorgio Agamben has remarked that we live increasingly in a time in which populations without full citizenship exist within states; their ontological status as legal subjects is suspended. These are not lives that are being genocidally destroyed, but neither are they being entered into the life of the legitimate community in which standards of recognition permit for an attainment of humanness.[25] How are we to understand this realm, what Hannah Arendt described as the "shadowy realm," which haunts the public sphere, which is precluded from the public constitution of the human, but which is human in an apparently catachrestic sense of that term?[26] Indeed, how are we to grasp this dilemma of language that emerges when "human" takes on that double sense, the normative one based on radical exclusion and the one that emerges in the sphere of the excluded, not negated, not dead, perhaps slowly dying, yes, surely dying from a lack of recognition, dying, indeed, from the premature circumscription of the norms by which recognition as human can be conferred, a recognition without which the human cannot come into being but must remain on the far side of being, as what does not quite qualify as that which is and can be? Is this not a melancholy of the public sphere?

Arendt, of course, problematically distinguished the public and the private, arguing that in classical Greece the former alone was the sphere of the political, that the latter was mute, violent, and based on the despotic power of the patriarch. Of course, she did not explain how there might be a prepolitical despotism, or how the "political" must be expanded to describe the status of a population of the less than human, those who were not permitted into the interlocutory scene of the public sphere where the human is constituted through words and deeds and most forcefully constituted when its word becomes its deed. What she failed to read in *The Human Condition* was precisely the way in which the boundaries of the public and political sphere were secured through the production of a constitutive outside. And what she did not explain was the mediating link that kinship provided between the public and private spheres. The slaves, women, and children, all those who were not property-holding males were not permitted into the public sphere in which the human was constituted through its linguistic deeds. Kinship and slavery thus condition the public sphere of the human and remain outside its terms. But is that the end of the story?

Who then is Antigone within such a scene, and what are we to make of her words, words that become dramatic events, performative acts? She is not of the human but speaks in its language. Prohibited from action, she nevertheless acts, and her act is hardly a simple assimilation to an existing norm. And in acting, as one who has no right to act, she upsets the vocabulary of kinship that is a precondition of the human, implicitly raising the question for us of what those preconditions really must be. She speaks within the language of entitlement from which she is excluded, participating in the language of the claim with which no final identification is possible. If she is human, then the human has entered into catachresis: we no longer know its proper usage. And to the extent that she occupies the language that can never belong to her, she functions as a chiasm within the vocabulary of political norms. If kinship is the precondition of the human, then Antigone is the occasion for a new field of the human, achieved through political catachresis, the one that happens when the less than human speaks as human, when gender is displaced, and kinship founders on its own founding laws. She acts, she speaks, she becomes one for whom the speech act is a fatal crime, but this fatality exceeds her life and enters the discourse of intelligibility as its own promising fatality, the social form of its aberrant, unprecedented future.

Notes

1. George Steiner, *Antigones* (New Haven, CT: Yale University Press, 1996), p. 18.

2. David Schneider, *A Critique of the Study of Kinship* (Ann Arbor: University of Michigan Press, 1984), p. 131.

3. Sophocles, *Oedipus at Colonus*, lines 1385–1388. If nothing else is noted, all translations from Sophocles' plays are from the Hugh Lloyd-Jones edition, published in the Loeb Library Series (Cambridge, MA: Harvard University Press, 1994). Hereafter references to this text are given parenthetically within the text.

4. Sophocles, *Oedipus at Colonus*, in *Sophocles I: Oedipus the King, Oedipus at Colonus, Antigone*, trans. David Grene, ed. David Grene and Richard Lattimore (Chicago: University of Chicago Press, 1991), lines 1338–1340.

5. Ed. note: This "kinship trouble" is further emphasized in the same edition when, later on, the chorus asks, "So to you they are daughters and also. . . ." Oedipus provides the information that the chorus dares not pronounce: "Yes, sisters to their father!" (Sophocles, *Oedipus at Colonus*, lines 534–535).

6. "Das Wort mittelbarer faktisch wird, indem es den sinnlicheren Körper ergreift. Das griechischtragische Wort ist tödlichfaktisch, weil der Leib, den es ergreift, wirklich tötet." (Friedrich Hölderlin, "Anmerkungen zur Antigone," in *Friedrich Hölderlin, Werke in einem Band* [Munich, Germany: Hanser Verlag, 1990], p. 64). All English citations are from "Remarks on Antigone," *Friedrich Hölderlin: Essays and Letters,* trans. and ed. Thomas Pfau (Albany, NY: SUNY Press, 1977). See also Philippe

Lacoue-Labarthe, *Métaphrasis suivi de la théatre de Hölderlin* (Paris: Presses Universitaires de France, 1988), pp. 63–73.

7. Martin Heidegger offers a sustained meditation on Hölderlin's translation of *Antigone* (1803), as well as his "Remarks on Antigone" with respect to the various ways that Hölderlin brings forward Antigone's "uncanniness." The proximity to death underscored in the "Remarks on Antigone" corresponds in large measure to Heidegger's reading of Antigone as one whose exile from the hearth establishes her essential relation to a sense of being that is beyond human life. This participation in what is non-living turns out to be something like the condition of living itself. As in the reading supplied by Jacques Lacan, Heidegger also claims that "[Antigone] names being itself" (118), and that this proximity to being involves a necessary estrangement from living beings even as it is the ground of their very emergence. Similarly, Heidegger understands the "unwritten law" to which Antigone refers as a relationship to being and to death: "Antigone assumes as what is fitting that which is destined to her from the realm of whatever prevails beyond the higher gods (Zeus) and beyond the lower gods. . . . Yet this refers neither to the dead, nor to her blood-relationship with her brother. What determines Antigone is that which first bestows ground and necessity upon the distinction of the dead and the priority of blood. What that is, Antigone, and that also means the poet, leaves without a name. Death and human being, human being and embodied life (blood) in each case belong together. 'Death' and 'blood' in each case name different and extreme realms of human being" (Martin Heidegger, *Hölderlin's Hymn "The Ister,"* trans. William McNeill and Julia Davis [Bloomington: Indiana University Press, 1996], p. 117).

8. Several important works within anthropology in the last few decades have showed the limitations of structuralist paradigms for thinking the problem of kinship, including Marilyn Strathern, *Reproducing the Future: Essays on Anthropology, Kinship, and the New Reproductive Technologies* (New York: Routledge, 1992). In Jane Fishburne Collier and Sylvia Junko Yanagisako, eds., *Gender and Kinship: Essays toward a Unified Analysis* (Stanford, CA: Stanford University Press, 1987), the editors argue against a view of kinship that focuses exclusively on symbolic relations at the expense of social action. Perspectives in that volume that seek to elaborate the complex social conditions of kinship relations against both functionalist and purely structuralist accounts are to be found in the important contributions by John Comaroff, Rayna Rapp, Marilyn Strathern, and Maurice Bloch. See also Sylvia Junko Yanagisako, "The Analysis of Kinship Change," in *Transforming the Past: Tradition and Kinship among Japanese Americans* (Stanford, CA: Stanford University Press, 1985), where she faults both structuralist and functionalist accounts for failing to give a dynamic understanding of kin relations. David Schneider, in *A Critique of the Study of Kinship*, elaborates how the theoretical models of kinship elaborated by Meyer Fortes, Edmund Leach, and Claude Lévi-Strauss impose theoretical constraints on ethnographic perception, failing to account for societies that failed to approximate the theoretical norm and that, regardless of their claim not to take biological relations of reproduction as the point of departure of kinship study, still make that assumption operate as a fundamental premise of their work (see pp. 3–9, 133–177). In particular, the work of Pierre Clastres in France, clearly drawing in part on the prior work of Marshall Sahlins, argues dramatically and vociferously that the sphere of the social could not be reduced to the workings of kinship, and he cautions against any effort to treat kinship rules as supplying the principles of intelligibility for any social

order. He writes, for instance, that it is not possible to reduce relations of power to those of exchange: "Power relates . . . to the . . . essential structural levels of society: that is, it is at the very heart of the communicative universe" (37). In *Society against the State,* trans. Robert Hurley (New York: Zone, 1987), pp. 27–49, Clastres argues for relocating the "exchange of women" within relations of power. And in "Marxists and Their Anthropology," he offers a searing criticism of Maurice Godelier on the matter of kinship and the state. There he argues that the principle function of kinship is not to institute the incest taboo nor to exemplify relations of production, but to transmit and reproduce the "name" of the relative, and that "the function of nomination, inscribed in kinship, determines the entire sociopolitical being of primitive society. It is there that the tie between kinship and society is located." See Pierre Clastres, *Archaeology of Violence,* trans. Jeanine Herman (New York: Semiotext(e), 1994), p. 134. For a notion of kinship as embodied practice, see also Pierre Bourdieu, *The Logic of Practice*, trans. Richard Nice (Stanford, CA: Stanford University Press, 1990), pp. 34–35.

9. Here I am not suggesting that the perverse simply inhabits the norm as something that remains autonomous, but neither am I suggesting that it is dialectically assimilated into the norm itself. It might be understood to signal the impossibility of maintaining a sovereign lock on any claim to legitimacy, since the reiteration of the claim outside of its legitimated site of enunciation shows that the legitimate site is not the source of its effectivity. Here I am indebted to what I take to be Homi Bhabha's significant reformulation dispersed throughout his work of both speech act theory and the Foucauldian notion of discourse developed in the latter's *Archaeology of Knowledge.*

10. Slavoj Žižek, *Enjoy Your Symptom!* (New York: Routledge, 1992), p. 46.

11. Ibid., pp. 91–92.

12. Ed. note: A law intended to give legal recognition to homosexual couples was rejected in France in October 1998 (this essay was first delivered as a lecture that same year). The law was subsequently passed on November 15, 1999. The "contracts" Butler refers to here are known as PACS (*pacte civil de solidarité*). Gay marriage remains illegal in France to this day.

13. Ed. note: Butler is here referring to the scandalous extramarital relationship between President Bill Clinton and Monica Lewinsky revealed in January 2008.

14. See my contribution "Competing Universalities," in Judith Butler, Ernesto Laclau, and Slavoj Žižek, *Contingency, Hegemony, Universality: Contemporary Dialogues on the Left* (London: Verso, 2000), pp. 136–181.

15. One strategy here has been to argue that the incest taboo does not always produce the normative family, but it is perhaps more important to realize that the normative family that it does produce is not always what it seems. There is, for instance, clearly merit in the analysis Linda Alcoff and others offer that heterosexual incest within heterosexually normative families is an extension, rather than abrogation, of patriarchal prerogative within heterosexual normativity. Prohibition is not fully or exclusively privative, that is, just as prohibition requires *and produces* the specter of crime it bars. And for Alcoff, in an interesting Foucauldian move, the prohibition offers the cover that protects and abets the practice of incest. But is there any reason to check the productivity of the incest taboo here, at this dialectical inversion of its aim? See Linda Alcoff, "Survivor Discourse: Transgression or Recuperation?" *SIGNS,* vol. 18, no. 2 (Winter 1993), pp. 260–291. For a very interesting and brave Foucauldian discussion of the criminaliza-

tion of incest, see also Vikki Bell, *Interrogating Incest: Feminism, Foucault, and the Law* (London: Routledge, 1993).

16. Gayle Rubin, "The Traffic in Women: Notes on the 'Political Economy' of Sex," in *Toward an Anthropology of Women*, ed. Rayna R. Reiter, pp. 157–210 (New York: Monthly Review Press, 1975).

17. See Collier and Yanagisako, eds., *Gender and Kinship*. For an excellent critique of gender-based approaches to kinship, which shows how the uncritical presumption of marriage underwrites the anthropological approach to kinship, see John Borneman, "Until Death Do Us Part: Marriage/Death in Anthropological Discourse," *American Ethnologist*, vol. 23, no. 2 (1996), pp. 215–238.

18. David Schneider, *A Critique of the Study of Kinship; American Kinship* (Chicago: University of Chicago Press, 1980).

19. Carol Stack, *All Our Kin: Strategies for Survival in a Black Community* (New York: Harper and Row, 1974).

20. See, in particular, the very interesting use of Hegel in his discussion of the dehumanization in slavery in Orlando Patterson, *Slavery and Social Death: A Comparative Study* (Cambridge, MA: Harvard University Press, 1982), pp. 97–101. For Patterson's illuminating discussion of Antigone, see *Freedom*, vol. 1, *Freedom in the Making of Western Culture* (New York: Basic Books, 1991), pp. 106–132.

21. Angela Davis, "Rape, Racism, and the Myth of the Black Rapist," reprinted in *Women, Race, and Class* (New York: Random House, 1981), pp. 172–201.

22. Claude Lévi-Strauss, *Race et Histoire* (Paris: Denoël, 1987); *Structural Anthropology*, vol. 2, trans. Monique Layton (New York: Basic Books, 1974), pp. 323–362.

23. Kath Weston, *Families We Choose: Lesbians, Gays, Kinship* (New York: Columbia University Press, 1991).

24. Like Lacan, Jacques Derrida appears to accept the singularity of Antigone's relationship to her brother, one that Hegel describes as a relationship without desire. Although Derrida does not read the play, *Antigone*, in *Glas*, he does read the figure of Antigone in Hegel, working within the terms of that reading to show how Antigone comes to mark the radical outside to Hegel's own systematic thinking and Hegel's own "fascination by a figure inadmissable [*sic*] within the system" (Jacques Derrida, *Glas*, trans. John P. Leavey Jr. and Richard Rand [Lincoln: University of Nebraska, 1986], p. 151). Although I agree that neither the figure nor the play of Antigone can be readily assimilated into either the framework of *The Phenomenology of Spirit* or *The Philosophy of Right*, and is curiously applauded in the *Aesthetics* as "the most magnificent and appeasing work of art," it would be a mistake to take her persistent unreadability within the Hegelian perspective as a sign of her final or necessary unreadability.

25. Giorgio Agamben, *Homo Sacer: Sovereign Power and Bare Life*, trans. Daniel Heller-Roazen (Stanford, CA: Stanford University Press, 1998).

26. Hannah Arendt, *The Human Condition* (Chicago: University of Chicago Press, 1969).

8

Antigone's Line

Mary Beth Mader

Sophocles' *Antigone* has solicited many superlatives. Friedrich Hölderlin considered the play to be the most difficult, the most enigmatic, and the most essentially Greek of plays. This chapter treats a matter of enigma in the play, one that is crucial for understanding the central stakes of the drama. Its main purpose is to propose a novel account of this enigma and briefly contrast this account with two other readings of the play.

One passage in particular has prompted the view that the play is extremely enigmatic; it is a passage that has been read with astonishment by many commentators and taken to demand explanation. This is Antigone's defense speech at lines 905–914. Here, she famously provides what appear to her to be reasons for her burying her brother Polyneices against the explicit command of her king and uncle, Creon. Her claim is that she would not have deliberately violated Creon's command, would not have intentionally broken his law or edict, had this edict barred her from burying a child or a husband of hers. She states that if her husband or child had died "there might have been another." But since both her mother and father are dead, she reasons, "no brother could ever spring to light again."[1] Reasoning of this sort has a precedent in a tale found in Herodotus' *Histories*, and Aristotle cites it in *Rhetoric* as an example of giving an explanation for something that one's auditors may at first find incredible.[2] To Aristotle, then, Antigone's defense speech appears to have been "rhetorically satisfactory," as Bernard Knox says.[3] However, such a reception is rare among commentators.[4]

A slightly longer version of this chapter was originally published in *Bulletin de la Société Américaine de Philosophie de Langue Francaise,* vol. 14, no. 2 (2005), pp. 18–40. This modified version has been approved by the author. Reprinted with permission of the publisher.

Dramatic Implausibility

Indeed, commentators including Johann Wolfgang von Goethe and Jacques Lacan have considered this supposed reasoning a scandal and something closer to nonreasoning, something nearly inhuman. Goethe hoped that one day the passage would be shown to be interpolated.[5] Therese Ahern Augst writes that Antigone's valuing this particular brother uniquely means that she "approaches the limit of what is commonly understood to be human nature."[6] Others, such as Knox, find Antigone's thinking both distressing and contradictory. Knox argues that in this speech Antigone abandons the justification she had put forth throughout the play, namely, that of the priority of blood relations, especially over state commands or the laws of mortals or men. He alleges that:

> . . . her assertion that she would not have done for her children what she has done for Polynices is a spectacular betrayal of that fanatical loyalty to blood relationship which she urged on Ismene and defended against Creon, for there is no closer relationship imaginable than that between the mother and the children of her own body.[7]

It is, he argues, a "strange piece of reasoning" that Antigone marshals to justify the "disturbing statement" that she would not have committed her lawbreaking deed for a husband or child of hers. Knox realizes that the defense involves the irreplaceability of Polyneices. But his reading does not acknowledge that the questions which are the motor of the dramatic course and tragic problems of the play itself, as well as the answers which he takes for granted, are precisely what remain either unanswered or in play in the dramatic action of the work.

Attempted Solutions: "But you're in love with impossibility"

Knox interprets Antigone's true motive as betraying a general principle of devotion to blood relations. He holds that although she begins by defending herself in universal terms, with claims such as, "Hades longs for the same rites for all," she ultimately demonstrates that this is not the genuine motive for her prioritizing of her brother over a hypothetical husband or child in the defense speech.[8] He finds that in the end:

> . . . the driving force behind her action, the private, irrational imperative which was at the root of her championship of the rights of family and the dead against the demands of the state . . . is her fanatical devotion to one particular family, her own, the doomed,

> incestuous, accursed house of Oedipus and especially to its most unfortunate member, the brother whose corpse lay exposed to the birds and dogs.[9]

How does this relate to her championing of the divine law for Knox? He argues that this "purely personal" motive of devotion to her own family is the "determinant" for her allegiance to the divine law. He identifies Antigone as an instance of a Sophoclean hero whose determined actions and unyielding character are those of "human beings who refuse to recognize the limits imposed on the individual will by men and gods, and [who] go to death or triumph, magnificently defiant to the last."[10]

Others have regarded the passage as turning on a question of love, as either a rejection of the erotic, as in Martha Nussbaum's assessment, or as the incoherence of extreme passion, as in Elizabeth Wyckoff's account. Nussbaum writes:

> The best explanation for this coldly determined priority-ordering of duties is that Antigone is not animated by personal love at all, but by a stern determination to have a fixed set of ordered requirements that will dictate her actions without engendering conflict; her refusal of the erotic . . . is then sufficient to explain her choice of the brother.[11]

And Wyckoff offers the view that Antigone is "clinging to her irrational profundity of feeling for her lost and irreplaceable brother, devising legalistic arguments for her intellectual justification."[12]

These, then, are a few of the many reasons for which readers of the play have found this passage confounding, and several of the ways that they have sought to account for its oddity. Before a sketch of this chapter's proposed understanding of the enigma of the passage, a brief presentation of two inventive and important interpretations of the play follows: those of Lacan and Judith Butler. Each of these thinkers mines Sophocles' drama with relentless care for its philosophical yield. To clarify the details of this chapter's reading, their interpretations will be contrasted to it. The comparison focuses on the readings of the enigmatic passage at issue and points related specifically to it.

Jacques Lacan: The Tautology of Human Being

In *The Ethics of Psychoanalysis*, Lacan discusses Goethe's perplexity at Antigone's scandalous ranking of her brother over an eventual husband or child.[13] Although Goethe's shock at the passage includes the wish that it will one day be shown not to have been part of the original text, Lacan judges this hope unlikely; if it had been known to be so scandalous why would Aristotle have cited the passage as exemplary, a mere eighty or so years after its composition, despite that fact? One of Lacan's many aims in the seminar is to make sense of this apparently implausible passage.

According to Lacan, Antigone's elevation of her brother, her willingness—and will—to die for revering him, stems from her insistence on his very being, stripped of any of the contingencies of his individual history. This being, unadorned by a past of action, by inherited particularities—not caught in a knotted line of descent, or murderously counterpoised to a brother—is conceivable only thanks to the advent of language, according to Lacan. For her part, Antigone cites "the great unwritten, unshakeable traditions": if she disobeys Creon's royal command, it is to obey another law, and only to obey it.[14] Lacan argues that legality itself is of the structure of language and that even if Antigone's cherished laws are "unwritten," their nomological quality itself is conceivable only on the basis of the essence of language. The unique value of the brother's bare being, shorn of its lifetime of qualifiers, is a function of the individuating and reifying powers of signification. Signification alone permits the ontological isolation of the being of a being, abstracting it both from a Heraclitean flow of change and from its own causal history. Language freezes the frame on what passes as undifferentiated. In doing so, it reveals that which perdures in its tautological quiddity: it is what it is. Lacan explains:

> My brother is what he is, and it is because he is what he is, and because only he could be that, that I proceed towards this fatal limit. If it were any one else whosoever with whom I could have a human relation, my husband, my children, they are replaceable, they are relations, but this brother who is *athaptos*, who has this thing in common with me of being born of the same womb—the etymology of *adelphos* alludes to the womb—and of being tied to the same father, the criminal father whose criminal aftereffects Antigone is trying to cleanse—this brother is something unique, and it is this alone that moves me to oppose your edicts.[15]

The brother's value is held to be that of a unique being, the being named by a proper name. In fact, contrasting the human being with a dog, Lacan proposes that the text implies that the burial requirement itself flows from the nature of the being endowed with a proper name: "One cannot do away with his remains while forgetting that the register of the being of he who has been able to be situated by means of a name must be preserved by the act of the funeral."[16] But at the same time, Lacan holds that Polyneices is uniquely valuable because he *shares* a feature with Antigone, namely, being born of the same womb.

Although Lacan's interpretation is not entirely coherent, it is consistent in suggesting that uniqueness, and unique value, flow from signification. The proper name permits the ontological excision from the indistinction of constant change and the determination of any individual identity over time. But it would seem that Lacan's demonstration extends too broadly for it to be of specific use in his present argument. If true, it would be true of all of those other beings—husband, child, anyone (not born of the same womb?)—that the explanation is supposed to exclude from its scope.

The crux of Lacan's position with respect to the enigmatic passage is that there is a signifying void at the heart of Antigone's justification. This void is the radical break and the atemporality that paradoxically is inaugurated—that is, it occurs at a time—with the advent of the linguistic function of detaching pure being from everything else. Lacan writes, "This purity, this separation of the being from all the characteristics of the historical drama it has gone through, this exactly is the limit, the *ex nihilo* about which Antigone takes place."[17]

But perhaps Lacan is too hasty here. How does the brother's uniqueness stem both from "being born of the same womb" and from being radically detached from his "historic drama"? Is not "being born of the same womb" part of his "historic drama"? How "detached" from his history can he be if his very birth itself is consequential, that is, if his birth entails his uniqueness, or his uniqueness *to Antigone*? Is his birth prior to his history, displaced backward into an untimed, unthought, imagined zone so that he can exist purely as an ahistorically unique being?

One way of squaring Lacan's claims is to consider that Polyneices is unique because he is born of the same womb, as anyone who is also born of the same womb would be. This comes closer to expressing the heart of Antigone's thinking, in my view, but what remains to be investigated here is why Antigone might be particularly concerned with this. This chapter seeks to provide an answer to this question.

In the meantime, it would be helpful to note that when Lacan enumerates those for whom Antigone would allegedly not violate the royal prohibition, he writes "any one else whosoever with whom I could have a human relation, my husband, my children, they are replaceable, they are relations . . ."[18] Yet, this is a misleading characterization of Antigone's thought. In fact, she does not say that she would not break Creon's law for anyone else except her brother, or for anyone else except a brother, or, for that matter, for anyone else except someone "born of the same womb." She just says she would not break the royal edict for a dead husband or child. This is not the same as claiming she would do it for no one else besides her brother, or a brother, or a sibling.

Certainly, Antigone grants her invading brother a special status, even one that is special because he is born "of the same womb." The question the enigmatic passage raises, however, is a comparative one: why rank the brother *over* husband and child (and not, as Lacan implies, over anyone besides Polyneices)? Why not consider all *philous*, that is, all "friends" and "close relations,"[19] as equally worthy of risking death by violation of a royal decree prohibiting their burial? After all, why would husband or child not likewise each be what each is and each likewise be considerable and unique in his or her very being itself? If Lacan means that it is in his role as brother that Polyneices is what he is, then husband or child could likewise each be what each is in his or her role as husband or child.

Moreover, it is not simply that the brother is irreplaceable and an eventual husband or child is replaceable. As I hope to show below, there are two issues of replaceability: one is the issue of replaceability *per se,* and the other is the issue of replaceability *by Antigone*, that is, by her own effort or agency. Commentators have overlooked the second issue although its importance for the passage in question is great.

Were the first sort of replaceability solely what was at issue, this would imply that Polyneices would obtain his unique comparative value solely upon the death or infertility of his parents. For prior to either of those, he would be replaceable precisely in the sense that his parents could generate another son (assuming they could). That is, he would be replaceable in the very sense that Antigone proclaims her own future child to be; she could have another (child). Of course, it is odd to think that Antigone is dying to consecrate the special value of her brother as it emerged suddenly upon the death of her parents! We have reason to suspect that something else is operating to account for her reasoning.

Judith Butler: Normative Repetition and Radical Singularity

The scope of this chapter does not allow for an in-depth discussion of the far-ranging philosophical analysis offered in *Antigone's Claim*, Judith Butler's probing inquiry into Sophocles' *Antigone.*[20] The ultra-welcome critiques of G. W. F. Hegel and Lacan, the urgently clear questioning of a whole history of anthropological, feminist, and psychoanalytic thought on kinship, and the vitally topical formulations of conceptual problems confronting research on the philosophical issues that attend new, or apparently new, family forms and modes of kinship all light the way in particularly forbidding territory. They are equally courageous, politically stimulating, and insightful.

Butler is especially helpful in pointing out Antigone's profound kinship confusion, and the difficulty of locating Antigone in the drama either as a representative of any specific position on kinship or as a representative of any specific position within a kinship system. In addition, the book displays "the socially contingent character of kinship" (6) despite the fact that this contingency is repeatedly congealed into a static necessity in much critical assessment and theoretical use of the play. Perhaps most important for my present purposes, Butler's analysis presents the socially contingent nature of kinship in the play as a function of actions, and specifically of Antigone's claims about—and claiming of—her deeds. Her claims about her deeds are themselves likewise deeds that serve to create kinship as a repeated norm. For Butler, however, because a norm requires a repetition, and because no repetition can ever be "perfect," the possibility for the "aberrant repetition of a norm" (58) is itself a necessary feature of normativity. If the replication of a norm were guaranteed, were an inevitability, then of course there would be no obeying or disobeying it, no satisfying or failing to satisfy it. Were it impossible to disobey, it would be no norm. The norm has a function—or is what it is—only when it may fail to be met.

My view accords with this performative account of kinship on many points. However, it diverges distinctly from Butler's thought on the matter of when and where the aberrations in kinship occur in this tale. Without wishing to make of Antigone a regressive figure yearning to reinstate a stultifying family form, the account I propose locates the aberration fairly traditionally in Oedipus and Jocasta's offense and considers Antigone's struggle to be an essentially restorative or reparative effort. For Butler, Antigone's "incestuous love of her brother" (6) is a "deformation of kinship that she performs" (28). But certainly the play asserts that a deformation has already occurred in her parents' generation of her, Polyneices, Eteocles, and Ismene. This does not mean that she could not enact her own deformation of kinship, of course. However, although it is intense and unyielding, Antigone's love for her brother does not seem to be uniquely or extremely incestuous relative to other loves or professions of love in the play because Ismene and Haemon also express intense love that could be considered incestuous. Ismene professes her love for Antigone in tones that resemble Antigone's passionate pleas for her brother's priority. Of Polyneices, Antigone insists, "I will lie with the one I love and be loved by him" (63). But Ismene exclaims to Antigone, "What do I care for life, cut off from you?" (87). Pleading to die with Antigone, Ismene begs, "Oh no, my sister, don't reject me, please, / let me die beside you, consecrating / the dead together" (87). And finally, to Creon, she agonizes, "How can I live alone, without her?" (89).

For his part, Creon expects, or compels, his son Haemon to declare his unconditional love for him. Creon presses Haemon, "Are you coming now, raving against your father? / Or do you love me, no matter what I do?" Haemon replies, "Father, I'm your *son* . . . you in your wisdom / set my bearing for me—I obey you. / No marriage could ever mean more to me than you . . ." (93). Here, Haemon is pushed to profess his father's priority over any eventual wife—let alone over Antigone, his future bride—in his affections. Creon evidences no shame, in fact, in requiring of Haemon exactly what he just deplored in Antigone's defense of her actions: unconditional love. A mere eight pages prior to his demand on Haemon, Creon is outraged by Antigone's neglect of the condition that he believes renders Polyneices unmournable, namely, that he made himself an enemy of the city of Thebes.

Perhaps these two instances simply mean that these other characters express or desire intense loves that could be considered incestuous because, after all, they are all afflicted by the incestuous family history and are fatally repeating it. Even if this is so, however, these instances show that Antigone's intense devotion to Polyneices is simply not unique in the play. Indeed, that the brother-sister love is readily classed as incestuous by commentators while the love between sisters or the love between father and son is not, may simply express a preponderant anxiety about specifically heterosexual incest or perhaps reproductive incest. Of course, in some cases, this preponderance may actually be an incapacity to suspect incestuous potential in such relationships for the reason that same-sex relations have not registered as potentially amorous or erotic at all. But that any of these relations should be considered incestuous by the standards of the play is not at all clear. What is clear is that the reproductive mother-son incest of Jocasta and Oedipus is indeed considered a calamity and an offense.

Butler also argues that Antigone undermines her own pronouncements at several crucial junctures. She adopts Creon's language of sovereignty, deploying it to argue that she must violate the royal law in the interest of serving another law, the unwritten laws of the gods. And yet, Butler argues, this law is no true law, for its hyperbolic particularity means that it applies in only a single instance, to the case of the dead Polyneices. Butler construes Antigone's defense speech to mean that "she would risk defying the official edict for no kin but Polyneices" (60). Furthermore, Antigone seeks to express the "radical singularity of her brother" (77), but fails to achieve this singular reference due to the necessary multiplicity of language itself. Her use of the term "brother" will always be polyreferential and thus can never isolate her one love in a way that does justice to his uniqueness.

And this despite the fact, for Butler, that brother and father are hardly distinguishable by Antigone. "They are," Butler writes, "after all, already interchangeable for her, and yet her act reinstitutes and reelaborates that interchangeability" (61). Here, my view is nearly the contrary! It seems correct to say both that Antigone grapples with the question of who exactly are her brothers and that she attempts to refer only to her brother Polyneices in defenses of herself. But it seems that her efforts are motivated by the aim to disambiguate the multiple statuses of both Polyneices and Oedipus and that this aim precedes the staged events of the play. Furthermore, it does not seem that Antigone has claimed that she would perform the violative deed for no other kin. Perhaps, finally, an exposition of my understanding of the specific sense of the enigmatic defense speech will help to clarify my partially contrary reading.

Another Answer: Doom "extends to all the kin"

Although commentators are correct to stress the irreplaceability of Antigone's brother Polyneices, to consider her reasoning as concerning Polyneices as only *a* brother, that is, as *any* brother of *any* sister, is incorrect. In other words, many readers, like Hegel, extend the argument to apply to all brothers and sisters. This is an error for at least one crucial reason, and it is an error that almost all commentators on the play commit. Within the dramatic logic of the play, Antigone's family form itself is both singular and monstrous. In other words, most commentators have not taken seriously the very dramatic core that gives the play its tragic element: the horror that *is* the family and the very figures in the play, and especially the fact that the play treats this family as distinctly aberrational. To think that, in her defense speech, Antigone could be providing a universalizable or generally recommendable rationale for her action, then, is to ignore the exceptional nature of her family form and for any kinship relations within it (perhaps Sophocles' contemporaries did not make this error and thus perhaps did not experience the same baffled incredulity at her attempted explanation as have subsequent commentators). When Antigone argues for the irreplaceability of Polyneices, then, she should not automatically be taken to be arguing for the irreplaceability to a sister (or even to a sibling), of a brother (or even a sibling). This should not be done because her family form is singularly aberrant according to the play itself: the incestuous nature of her family *is* the source of her suffering, which the play repeatedly makes clear.

Accordingly, some readers tend to miss the profundity and meaning of Antigone's "family affection" for her brother. They also tend to ignore the importance of what she might wish *not* to do. Furthermore, the question of Antigone as agent, what she can do or effect and what she cannot or will not do or effect, is one of the play's great issues. This issue takes urgent shape in the questions: First, in particular, what exactly is a brother? Second, and more generally, how are family or kin relations created and maintained? *Antigone* is about the establishment, erosion, or reestablishment of a certain type of kin relation and the family constellation that preserves it.

Antigone is not simply honoring her brother because he is her brother; she is making a man be her brother by her treatment of him. Most importantly, she is establishing (or attempting to establish) her brother as *only* her brother by symbolically refusing a family precedent, namely that of *generating one's own siblings*. Antigone's devotion to her brother must be understood against the backdrop of her family story. Jocasta is both her mother and her grandmother.

That is, Jocasta is the parent of her own child Oedipus and of her own grandchildren; she is both the parent and the grandmother of her own children by Oedipus. Oedipus is both Antigone's father and her brother; she is both his sister and his daughter. Furthermore, taking into account Antigone's relation to Polyneices by way of her relations with other family members, Polyneices could also be said to be Antigone's uncle or her nephew. By way of Oedipus as Antigone's brother, Polyneices is the son of Antigone's brother, which makes him her nephew. But by way of Oedipus as Antigone's father, Polyneices is Antigone's uncle, since Polyneices is her father's brother. So, she is sister, aunt, and niece to Polyneices.

To understand Antigone's tragic efforts, consider two categories of kin relations:[21]

1. Relations that one cannot generate oneself. Of these, one cannot "get another" because one cannot get one *tout court*. According to the vocabulary of the normative form of kinship order from which the Oedipal family has departed, this category includes father and mother.[22]

2. Relations that one can generate oneself or help to generate oneself. Of these, one can "get another" in the sense that one plays a causal role in their coming to be. According to that same vocabulary of the normative form of kinship order from which the Oedipal family has departed, this category includes child, husband, and wife.

We can understand the question haunting Antigone as: Is "brother" of the first or the second sort of relation, is "brother" in category (1) or (2)? For when productive of a child, Oedipal incest amounts to putting the sibling relation or the brother relation in category (2). That is, Antigone *could* "get another" brother, were she to follow in her father's footsteps and generate a brother by him, her parent.[23] Against the background of Oedipal incest placing the sibling relation in category (2), we can read Antigone's violative deed as a passionate attempt to restore the sibling relation to category (1). Her burial of her brother is the making of a brother as something that "cannot" be made by oneself; it is an attempt to make a "can not" of an "ought not," to impart to a supposed social or moral necessity the strength of an ontological necessity. The point of the play is that we may not assume that this is given, but that brothers are *made* as brothers-who-are-not-also-uncles by a refusal of the Oedipal type of incest. In a sense then, if this refusal is a making, Antigone's insistence on performing the burial rites for her brother as brother consecrates not just a dead beloved sibling but a certain precarious version of siblinghood or brotherhood itself, and attempts to bring a lost generational order back to the family. It is precisely the precarious status of this generational order that is the source of the deep distress and anguish that fuels Antigone's determined course and the dramatic line of the play.

Given the uniqueness of her family genealogy, then, Antigone cannot be said to be fighting for parental, paternal, or maternal filiation or right per se. Her action, her violation of Creon's prohibition on burying her dead brother, is essentially both a necessary and an impossible attempt at restoration of her family's skewed genealogy. It is necessary because she must affirm the priority of the genealogically given, of those who were made, and made siblings, *by others* (than she), in this case, Polyneices. Note that she did perform "with my hands" burial rites for her dead brother Eteocles, as well (105). In some translations, Antigone clearly has already so honored her parents as well as Eteocles: "All three of you have known my hand in death."[24] In addition, in *Oedipus at Colonus*, a messenger reports that Ismene and Antigone prepared their father for burial: they "bathed him in holy water, decked his body out / in shining linen, the custom for the dead."[25]

So, given Antigone's family heritage, what can she do to try to restore or create a generational order that is not horrifying? In my view, she is adamantly affirming—with rites that are supposed to be for family members, and hence, especially mark them *as such*—family relations created not by her but by other family members. She is desperately trying to ratify these relations—not instituted or created by her—as, precisely, *beyond her creation*. This is the tragic paradox of having to *make* someone be a brother—and only a brother—through stressing that a brother is precisely what one ought not, though one can, *make*. Notice also that Antigone stresses that Polyneices is her brother (rather than her nephew or uncle) precisely by stressing that Oedipus is their father (rather than their brother). She is trying to disambiguate the dual status of brother-father in the case of Oedipus and the multiple status of brother-nephew-uncle in the case of Polyneices and of herself as sister-daughter relative to Oedipus and sister-niece-aunt relative to Polyneices. She is trying to insist on one of these positions—father for Oedipus and brother for Polyneices—in an essentially restorative effort, that is, an effort to reestablish a family tree with less horrifying articulations.

The obvious objection to these speculations is that, as Antigone herself says, her parents are both dead at this point in the tale. But perhaps we need to recall that Antigone interprets her suffering and that of her siblings as stemming from her father's wrongs.[26] And from this recollection, it is plausible that Antigone would be extremely vigilant about her family's criminal status and about her own potential for offense against the gods of the dead—even well prior to the period presented in the play. If her father's offense is "getting another brother" in part through his own agency, then Antigone could understandably be concerned to efface that offense and to bar its possible recurrence throughout the course of her life, even prior to her father's death. Hence, the elevation of the brother as "that which I cannot get for myself." Granted, here she implies that the only reason she cannot get one is because both of her parents are dead. The obvious interpretation of this is that *they* (that is, both Oedipus and Jocasta) are required to get her another brother and, being dead, cannot do so. Her insistence on her parents being the unique source of a brother is obviously significant in her task to efface the family crime. And it makes sense that she would be publicly proclaiming her realization of this unique source, in the form of an action known by the city as a whole, the burial of Polyneices.[27] But we can also easily imagine a knowing audience noting, with cruel humor perhaps, that of course, had Antigone's father *alone* been alive, she could have followed in his footsteps and procured for herself a brother by her parent.

Imagine, then, that the preoccupation with her confounding kinship precedes the burial prohibition, that awareness of her father's unwitting crime and its issue lays down for her the track of her tragic options. Imagine that well prior to her brothers' deaths by mutual slaughter, the shameful *ouroboros* in the branches of her family tree keeps her ever vigilant about precisely what acts constitute the family relations in question in her tale. Then consider her claim in the enigmatic passage to be: I cannot get myself another brother. Yes, the reason she provides is that her parents are required to give her a brother, and they are both dead. But the "I cannot" would be the constant, self-addressed, protective mantra whose more insistent sense is: "I must not." And this expression of "cannot–must not" is exactly what contains the unexpressed "law" she stresses but seems never to state explicitly. That law is: getting oneself a brother is the kind of action that one can perform though one must not, unlike getting oneself a husband or a child. In fact, children and husbands are constituted as only children and husbands—within the kinship order Antigone takes to be normative—in part precisely by constituting brothers as only brothers, or siblings as only siblings.

Of course, what a brother is, and what actions constitute a brother as only a brother, are strictly tied to the particular kinship order or orders operating in the play. Nowhere do I mean to imply the existence or validity of any universal, transtemporal or transcultural system, rule or order that would govern or express any constant content to the term "brother." Nor would I wish to attempt any kind of translation system for kinship, which is essentially what the work of Claude Lévi-Strauss and followers has sought. Rendering the terms of a different kinship order intelligible in one's own terms alone is the solipsistic goal of such approaches. The Hegelian reading of *Antigone* likewise imposes much too readily on the play Hegel's own assumptions about family relations, gender roles, and customs pertaining to death.

My attempt has been to remain as close as possible to the elements of kinship as they appear in the play and not to assume an easy continuity with kinship terms that operate in presently dominant Occidental kinship regimes. I do not mean to imply either that any coherent single perspective on kinship is evidenced in the play, aside from the fact that no voice in the drama expresses the view that the family crime in play is not a violation.

"No generation can free the next"

The subject of the play is the liberation of one generation by another. But in a family in which the generational order is, from within the play's own perspective on the matter of kinship, incestuously compressed, generatively overlapping, or relationally congested, the problem of one generation's freeing another is a problem latent in the very facts of human generation itself. That is, when it comes to Antigone's generation, one that is produced in violation of divine law, the effects of such generational violation spread through the very network they create; the poison is delivered throughout the system by and in the creation of the system. Hence, it has a kind of necessary means of propagation; the "curse" of the house of Oedipus is not most importantly the resounding power of a verbal malediction. It is rather the inescapability of existence as a violation, of being as being-wrong, or being-as-should-not-be.

Is it possible by one's living, in one's life, to reestablish or establish anew a limit when one's very life is a violation of that limit? Can Antigone establish a nonincestuous family? Tragically, the only way she can establish a nonincestuous family is by recognizing those family members that she did not bring about and, from within the predominating perspective of the drama, that she ought not bring about. For the incestuous violation in the play is due precisely to not recognizing a progenitor as a progenitor (or recognizing it too late) and, hence, not heeding a law that one ought to do all in one's power to heed; in other words, the limit must be imposed, it will not impose itself. The laws and gods of the family prescribe a limit, but the limit must be imposed by human beings, and the violation of it in this case actually *is* the children of Oedipus and their suffering. On this view, violating Creon's law should appear in itself to be a negligible offense in comparison with what is at stake in obeying it. Obeying Creon's law, for Antigone, means not recognizing her parents as parents, which is precisely Oedipus' failure, as well as the source of her very being.

So, prior to the tragic conflict of two unyielding wills, in the persons of Antigone and Creon, the deeper tragedy is the ever-ruined, imperfect set of options for restoring a less horrifyingly collapsed lineage. The deeper tragedy, then, is that the only minimal restoration of a cleansed lineage, for Antigone, can only be accomplished by way of honoring the very parents whose parentage is the ghastly violation. In order not to repeat her parents' offenses, she must affirm them as parents, which status is precisely the origin of their depravity.

Antigone, in a consuming orientation to purification or restoration of her family's debased state, views all possible actions as confined on all sides by actions that are awfully possible, yet deadly repetitions of her parents' accursed legacy. Why *must* she recognize and affirm them as parents, then? With all the weight of what she describes as a life of almost intolerable pain and sorrow pressing on her,[28] she is propelled by an overcompensatory vigilance and unconditional drive to fend off any possible repetition or hint of recurrence of the family's generative crime.

Perhaps, then, she endures a feared identification with her father. Oedipus' crime, after all, predominates in the tale as a whole, and this crime is essentially that of not recognizing both mother and father. By not recognizing his mother, he has created his children and their suffering. But Jocasta's crime is different; it is the crime of not recognizing her child, her son. So, by symbolically recognizing Polyneices as her brother, as not only irreplaceable in general but as irreplaceable by *her*, Antigone can affirm that her parents' generative power itself is irreplaceable, thus symbolically "avoiding" Oedipus' crime, since he supplanted his father in the couple that was his parents.[29] By "irreplaceable by *her*," I mean that Polyneices as a brother is not replaceable by her in contrast to the roles or relations of husband or child being replaceable by her own efforts. I might be charged with equivocating on the term "recognition" in this discussion, using it both to mean "to pay homage to" and "to identify by recollection." The double sense is not problematic for this reading, however, because I do mean to imply that the first sense includes the second one. So, in the case of Antigone's symbolic "recognition" of her brother as a brother only, "recognition" includes her reidentification of him as the brother Polyneices.

Antigone is particularly disturbed by her own understanding of her confused genealogy and especially by her relation with the hyperrelated Oedipus. It is clear that the entire tragic incestuous crime—that is, that such a thing is incestuous and criminal, *according to the play*—in fact depends on the importance of maternal filiation. If the blood tie went primarily through the father (as it clearly is legally determined to do at the end of Aeschylus' *Oresteia*), then Antigone's and Oedipus' relations would not be problematically mixed or would not be maximally so mixed. If paternal filiation were the rule, here, then Antigone and Oedipus, having different fathers, would not be both siblings *and* in a relation of descent—because they simply would not be siblings.[30] So the incestuous nature of Oedipus' procreation depends on the social logic in which parentage is importantly carried by maternity. In this family, the mother legates criminality with her very issue, or at least with the children of her second husband.

Endpoints

Plainly, despite some important commonalities, the proposed understanding of the enigmatic passage and of the play contrasts with the accounts Lacan and Butler offer on several points. To return to my discussion of Lacan's account, we can now see why Antigone might be so concerned with those who are "born of the same womb." On the proposed reading, Antigone's emphasis on those who are "born of the same womb" is not simply an emphasis on those who are irreplaceable per se. Yes, plainly, they are ranked more highly than others, but not just any or all others. The crucial comparative others at issue are those others who permissibly may be replaced by her own agency. The question is: Why is Antigone willing to die for this distinction between those whom one is permitted to generate and those who one is not permitted to generate? The answer is that violating that distinction was precisely the substance of the family crime. Antigone is willing to die to defend and consecrate the distinction between those who must be other-generated and those who can be self-generated. One tragic outcome of the play is that in her own case she must sacrifice the latter for the former.

For these reasons brother must be ranked over husband and child *in the case of this family*. And a weakness of Lacan's explanation is that it cannot account for the apparent necessity of this difference in treatment. It cannot do so because it does not construe Antigone's distinction properly as one between the illicitly autogenerated and the licitly heterogenerated.

On the reading proposed here, Butler's charge that Antigone appeals to a law that is no law at all receives no confirmation. For the proposed reading argues that Antigone appeals to a law whose application is not limited to Polyneices alone, and hence it is not disqualified from being a law by the paltry scope of its relevance. On this reading, the law would mean that siblings ought to receive special treatment as those whom one can, but ought not, create oneself. The law is: recognize your parents as they who can generate those who you can, though must not, generate. The crucial causal corollary is: it is precisely by this recognition that such beings as parents, children, and siblings are made as such in this particular kinship order. The law, then, is a form of incest prohibition, or more precisely the establishment of what counts as prohibited relations. Antigone's achingly retrospective affirmation of this law does not succeed in effacing the genealogical violation without eliminating its fruit: herself. The end of the play implies that she cannot undo that violation without undoing herself.

This is partially because of Creon's position on the priority of state and ruler over *philous*, kin and household. From the play's start, Sophocles presents Creon as the adamant defender of the priority of state and ruler over *philous*, kin and household. *Philous*, or friends and close relations, depend for their well-being on a stable, well-ordered state for Creon; the state makes possible strong and abiding friendships and close family relations.[31] Only at the dreadful unraveling of his own close family bonds at the play's end does Creon seem to realize that his iron governance has been no protection for his close relations. In exclamatory self-description, he cries: "Wailing wreck of a man, / whom to look to? Where to lean for support?"[32] That cradling ship of state he had earlier invoked is here no solace, no refuge.

In sum, the proposed view agrees with Butler's performative construal of the socially contingent nature of kinship, but takes the iterative character of the kinship norm in this case to indicate not Antigone's aberrant deformation of kinship, but rather her essentially reparative effort at re-formation of an unshamed and unashamed family constellation. Note that Antigone does not consider this restorative effort to be solely her own mission, either, at least not initially. The fact that she initially expects her sister Ismene to share her illicit initiative shows that on Antigone's view her sister is placed just as well to wish to carry out the burial duties as she is. More important, it demonstrates that the play cannot be about the incestuous desire of the individual figure Antigone, at least if the thought of Antigone should be counted in answering the question of her ultimate motivations. Surely, we have no reason to think that she was enjoining her sister to risk death for an incestuous desire they both shared for their ungrieved brother.

This chapter has argued that Antigone's aim is to undouble her overwritten kin, even those kin who are dead. How can anyone in her family free or honor the next—or the previous—generation when its generations are barely or tenuously individuated? If the reading sketched here has any plausibility, it indicates that fragile, confected kin relations can be approached by indirection as well as by targeted directness. If "doom extends to all the kin" precisely *as* the kin, if the helplessness of human beings in such netted bonds as families joins them by their choice and not, then Antigone's election of her brother Polyneices as the point at which to pluck at the generational tangle is likewise the choice to release all her kin from their family shame.

Butler is more right than her own claims indicate when she holds that Antigone "remains somewhat unthinkable" (22). For we must suspect that kinship itself is what is "unthinkable," still, after innumerable and continuing performances of the ancient Greek dramas of family passions. Otherwise how do we explain the seemingly automatic reversion to various "forms of idealized kinship" (28) that plainly have made the Oedipal family impervious to clear view and, particularly in the case of this enigmatic passage, have obscured the very nature of the horror that the play presents? Indeed, Knox's remonstration quoted above—"for there is no closer relationship imaginable than that between the mother and the children of her own body"—should sound like a joke when pronounced about the Oedipal family! "No closer"—is a little too close, in this case, no? That any one of us could read over the remark in seriousness is a demonstration of the persistent unthinkability of the everyday tangle of kinship.

Notes

1. *Antigone*, in *Sophocles: The Three Theban Plays*, introduction by Bernard Knox, trans. Robert Fagles (New York: Penguin Books, 1984), p. 105, lines 995–1005. The relevant passage is: "Never, I tell you / if I had been the mother of children / or if my husband died, exposed and rotting— / I'd never have taken this ordeal upon myself, / never defied our people's will. What law, / you ask, do I satisfy with what I say? / A husband dead, there might have been another. / A child by another too, if I had lost the first. / But mother and father both lost in the halls of Death, / no brother could ever spring to light again. / For this law alone I held you first in honor."

2. Aristotle, *The Rhetoric and Poetics of Aristotle*, trans. W. Rhys Roberts (New York: Modern Library, 1984), p. 209.

3. Knox in *The Three Theban Plays*, p. 47.

4. Dudley Fitts and Robert Fitzgerald excise the passage, regarding it as "dismal stuff," in *Sophocles: The Oedipus Cycle: An English Version*, trans. and ed. Dudley Fitts and Robert Fitzgerald (New York: Harcourt Brace Jovanovich, 1977), p. 240.

5. Knox in *The Three Theban Plays*, pp. 46–47.

6. Therese Ahearn Augst, "Difference becomes Antigone: Hölderlin and the Ethics of Translation," *seminar*, vol. 38, no. 2 (May 2002), p. 101.

7. Knox in *The Three Theban Plays*, pp. 45–46.

8. Ibid., pp. 44, 85. The quote in the title of this section is from ibid., p. 64.

9. Ibid., p. 49.

10. Ibid., p. 51.

11. Martha Nussbaum, *The Fragility of Goodness* (Cambridge, UK: Cambridge University Press, 1986), p. 440, n. 44. George Steiner advances this view as well, in *Antigones* (New Haven, CT: Yale University Press, 1996), p. 273.

12. See Tina Chanter, *Ethics of Eros: Irigaray's Rewriting of the Philosophers* (New York: Routledge, 1995), p. 290, n. 39.

13. Jacques Lacan, "L'Essence de la tragédie," in *Le Séminaire, Livre VII: L'Ethique de la psychanalyse* (Paris: Editions du Seuil, 1986), pp. 297–298. Translations are mine.

14. Sophocles, *The Three Theban Plays*, p. 82. The phrase Lacan discusses is: "the unwritten laws . . . of the gods." In *Antigone*, we read: "What law, / you ask, do I satisfy with what I say?" And: "For this law alone I held you first in honor" (*The Three Theban Plays*, pp. 105–106). References to the play will henceforth be given parenthetically within the text.

15. Lacan, *L'Ethique de la psychanalyse*, p. 324.

16. Ibid., p. 325.

17. Ibid., p. 325.

18. Ibid., p. 324.

19. See Fagles' notes to the translation in Sophocles, *The Three Theban Plays*, p. 395, n. 12, and p. 397, n. 213, for clarification of this Greek term.

20. Judith Butler, *Antigone's Claim: Kinship between Life and Death* (New York: Columbia University Press, 2000). Hereafter references to this text are given parenthetically within the text.

21. Note that the distinction between these two categories is not that between alliance and generation because the child relation is included in the same category as the husband and wife relation.

22. Plainly, I am leaving aside the cases of children selecting parents through adoption and analogous means.

23. Incidentally, because of Oedipus' incest with Jocasta, incest between Antigone and Oedipus would be father-daughter incest and/or brother-sister incest.

24. Sophocles, *The Complete Greek Tragedies: Sophocles I: Antigone*, ed. David Grene and Richmond Lattimore, trans. David Grene (New York: Washington Square Press, 1967), p. 194, line 900.

25. Sophocles, *The Three Theban Plays*, p. 379, lines 1816–1817; ibid., p. 152, lines 1602–1603. Here, however, Oedipus is not dead, and his grave will be kept secret from his daughters/sisters.

26. Antigone's first words include these: "dear sister, dear Ismene, / how many griefs our father Oedipus handed down!" (Sophocles, *The Three Theban Plays*, p. 59, line 2). Fitts and Fitzgerald render this line as: "You would think that we had already suffered enough / For the curse on Oedipus" (Sophocles, *The Oedipus Cycle*, p. 185).

27. Indeed, although the chorus seems not to understand the source of her inflexible drive to bury her brother, and at best is highly skeptical about the deed, this is not true of the city itself, according to Haemon's report to Creon. See Sophocles, *The Three Theban Plays*, pp. 84, 95, 97.

28. See ibid., p. 59, lines 6–9, and p. 82, lines 516–518.

29. Antigone does not appear to be as motivated to avoid her mother's crime as she is to avoid her father's. For the lines in her counterfactual imaginings that have so disturbed and surprised readers are an exact description of her mother's life. She says, "A husband dead, there might have been another. / A child by another too, if I had lost the first." Jocasta's first husband Laius was killed by Oedipus, who himself became "another" husband. Oedipus, Jocasta's first child, was lost to her by her own abandonment of him. And, of course, she had four more children by Oedipus. Despite this potential parallel, then, Antigone's driving anxiety seems focused on the danger of not recognizing one's parent, rather than on Jocasta's crime of not recognizing one's child. The play as a whole, though, plays down Jocasta's crime in contrast to Oedipus'.

30. Plainly, I ignore the question of the status of full- or half-siblings.

31. See Sophocles, *The Three Theban Plays*, p. 68.

32. Ibid., p. 127.

9

Beyond Pleasure

The Other History of Sexuality

Cecilia Sjöholm

You love the impossible, Ismene says to Antigone, your heart becomes warm as we talk of cold things. This reversal from hot to cold, from a heartbreaking tenderness to an incapacity to care for the living resounds throughout the tragedy of Sophocles. In *Antigone*, the protagonists embrace the dead and seek death for themselves in the name of love. Antigone's grave is her bridal chamber. She is cold, insensitive, dedicated only to the dead. Only when she enters the chamber of the grave is she transformed: her eyes beaming, her cheeks glowing. Toward the end of the play, when we find Haemon in the grave with Antigone's cold body in his arms, we see her own love for the impossible reflected in a cruel reversal. Even though she desires death, Haemon strives to possess her, she who has no love or tenderness to offer in return.

The chilling reversals of *Antigone* show us the face of eros as tragedy offers it to us. Eros is not reducible to physical desire. It is not a power or a force connected to philosophical love either, as Diotima taught us. The eros of tragedy can neither be interpreted as lust or pleasure, nor can it be associated with the philosophical love of truth, as Plato would formulate it later. Eros exposes man, taking us far beyond the kind of desires, pleasures, and sensations that we connect with the concept of eroticism. In fact, although the Freudian legacy has sexualized our view of Oedipus, there is no concept of sexuality in tragedy that is remotely close to a modern one. At the same time, imagining tragedy without eros is impossible. The two are intertwined. Eros, in tragedy, is the love of the impossible. It forces the kind of exposure that in the end produces both destruction and dignity. No individual in the web of tragedy remains unmarked by the destruction of eros. Eros floats through the protagonists, changing face and character, forcing fates and changing lives.

Rather than offering a premonition of a psychoanalytic notion of sexuality, for instance, or being linked to the technologies of the self Michel Foucault has analyzed, tragic eros, such as it has been traced in the readings of, for instance, Martin Heidegger and G. W. F. Hegel, is a specific form of the conditioning of human life. It depicts sexuality as a force that goes beyond the physical pleasure of the individual or even the borders of individual experience as such. Sexuality, when we look at it through the workings of eros in tragedy, is something that splits the individual subject, hitting it from the outside and tearing it apart. In tragedy, eros is not merely a divine agent with a specific goal in mind for the humans he is affecting. Eros is a *daimon*, situated between the human and the inhuman. He is also *deinon*, terrifying, because he is equally unpredictable in his powers and his force as death. To some extent he is even more terrifying than death because the agent of eros always appears to be human (although the workings of eros stretch far beyond the physical experience or the desires of an individual).

What is interesting, in this regard, is that the eros of tragedy gives witness to a form of sexuality that is closely linked to the feminine in ancient Greece. Most of the philosophical discussion concerning the sexual history of the Greeks has focused on the work of Foucault, who primarily was concerned with male sexuality. No mention is made, for instance, of Sappho in Foucault's work. Nor is an extended discussion of tragedy in its relation to sexual destiny to be found in the works of Aeschylus, Sophocles, or Euripides. Clearly, Sappho would have added a feminine perspective to Foucault's history. Had he looked closer at tragedy, the outcome could well have been the same. Tragedies, as we know, were written by men, but were concerned with women to an extent that had no equivalent in any other aspect of the cultural or political life of Athens, from which women were largely absent. As Froma I. Zeitlin, among others, has shown, the obsession with women in tragedy must be interpreted as a symptom. Zeitlin has argued that the mimicking of women in tragedy through male playwrights and actors was an attempt to domesticate and control the life of the other—the life of the women who were largely absent from the streets of Athens, but who therefore secretly and through their very invisibility posed a threat to the gendered order that was in place.[1] Elsewhere I have argued that the female characters of tragedy may have represented social, ethical, and political problems that male characters would not have been able to negotiate in the same manner; femininity as such offered a symbolic space for dealing with issues that were more contaminating and frightening than would have been appropriate for a male character to represent.[2]

The figure of Antigone has prompted some of the rare considerations of feminine desire in philosophy. Her story has inspired Hegel, Heidegger, and Jacques Lacan, among others, in their analysis of tragedy. The philosophical discussion of this tragedy has been obsessed with the enigmatic character of

Antigone, who is in love with "the impossible." In tragedy, however, the question of gender, and thereby of femininity, is not reducible to a marker determining the social, cultural, or biological identity of an individual. It is a category with a dramatic and relational function; when masculinity and femininity is mentioned, it is in relation to a tragic character and his or her place in the web of events. In tragedy, gender lines are crossed; Antigone acts like a man, her sister tells her, whereas the male characters become effeminized. When we look at tragedy, the force of eros may be connected to the question of desire and sexuality, and in the case of Antigone it may well pertain to feminine desire in particular, but femininity in tragedy is not merely a given social or biological identity.

The philosophical tradition, stretching from Hegel to Lacan, has failed to observe that femininity, and thereby also feminine desire and feminine sexuality, reaches beyond the limits established by the social roles of gender. Philosophical discussions have focused on the femininity of Antigone. But Creon, too, becomes an image of the feminine. You are like a woman, Creon says disdainfully to his son as Haemon is weeping over the dead Antigone. At the end of the tragedy, however, Creon stands like a woman himself, holding his dead son, transformed into a figure of maternal mourning, robbed of all the attributes that used to affirm his masculinity: power, property, and heirs. Femininity and masculinity, therefore, are floating concepts in the events of tragedy, capturing the relation between characters rather than social or sexual roles. In tragedy, femininity is a sign of neither weakness nor passivity. In the case of Creon, however, given that he has humiliated his son for being effeminate, his becoming woman is a sign of his downfall; he has turned into an image of his own disdain.

It is this aspect of tragedy that this chapter explores: What role does eros play in tragedy? How can we discuss it as a form of sexuality that offers an alternative, both to the Foucauldian history of the male subject and to the male view of femininity offered in the history of philosophy? Tragic eros is a form of sexuality that has more to do with weakness than virility, with exposure rather than active agency. It is observable not only through the figure of Antigone, or even through the figure of female characters alone, but also through the destiny of the characters as they are submitted to the transformations of fate. The work of Friedrich Schelling on tragedy offers a sideline to the other, more well-known philosophers. In Schelling's work we can discern a conception of tragic eros that offers a view of sexuality that differs from those wholly focused on the male subject. Tragedy shows us a face of sexuality, or perhaps rather a lack of face, that mostly seems to be set apart from the historical discussion of eros or eroticism among the Greeks. If we want to understand fully the Greek view of sexuality, however, tragedy offers us a perspective that must be taken into account: not only to create a balance between the history of masculinity and femininity, but also because it offers a view of sexuality in which it is no longer attached to the agency, or the actions, of a subject looking for pleasure. Instead, sexuality, or eros, becomes the force through which human destinies are intertwined to the degree that individuals become unable to control their fates or the outcome of their actions.

Greek tragedy is about transgression: patricide, matricide, incest. But the transgressor is never a perpetrator in any unequivocal sense. A tragic hero is not a criminal. He or she is never fully responsible for his or her actions. When Oedipus marries his mother and kills his father, he does it unknowingly. Ever since Aristotle such ignorance has been considered to enhance the dignity of the play. Psychoanalysis has attempted to respond to the riddles of tragedy in terms of drives and desires. However, in German Idealism we find the most sustained reflection on tragedy through a consideration of the dialectics of necessity and freedom. Schiller, Schelling, Hölderlin, and Hegel all try to answer the question of why the hero of tragedy falls into catastrophe without being evil. They all name this seeming paradox in different ways: the absolute, the sublime, the unbearable. As I will show, the issue of sexuality is present in Schelling's analysis of tragedy, although it is masked as an analysis of freedom. For Schelling, tragedy incarnates the issues of freedom and necessity with which he is concerned; it thereby allows us to comprehend a notion of the absolute that is impossible to encompass by argument alone. As we will see, however, the way tragedy represents these issues, according to Shelling, is through the fates the protagonists suffer in the name of desire and sexuality. What Schelling discusses in terms of freedom and necessity constitutes an analysis of tragic eros as well.

Foucault's Eroticism

Foucault's *History of Sexuality* contextualizes sexuality within a history of truths—in the end the commands concerning sexual conduct are connected to the words of the master as he is teaching the truth in Plato's dialogues. Sexuality may be a question of practice and conduct, but in the West the discourse of eros and desire is attached to a metaphysical understanding of truth. Admittedly, his own genealogy only claims to examine a limited aspect of the emergence of the discourse on sexuality. Given Foucault's suspicion of psychoanalysis, however, and given his attention to virility and his disinterest in the feminine, the outline of his genealogy is inspired by a tradition that takes little account of the Other, whether that Other be the unconscious or the feminine. For instance, there is no discussion of Sappho, or of tragedy.[3] The aspects of sexuality Foucault examines are primarily sexuality as conduct and the discourse of desire as attached to metaphysical questioning. Sexuality, in Foucault's genealogy, is always involved with the question of agency and experience, and in particular the becoming of the self through the virile mastery of the body. The question is: Is another view of sexuality available when we look at the tradition of the Greeks? And if so, what interest would such a view hold for us today?

The fact that the term "sexuality" was not established until the nineteenth century, Foucault writes, does not mean that tracing the emergence of the discourse of sexuality before that time is impossible.[4] The Greeks had no word for the various phenomena that we include under the concept of sexuality: *Ta aphrodisia* means "sexual relations" or "pleasures of love." Long before that time, Western man, Foucault argues, recognized himself as a subject of desire. Foucault's own inquiry, though pursued from the perspective of sexuality, begins with the question of the history of truth, or one might say of truths, because the truth emerging from the discourses informing the technologies of the self is radically different from the discourse informing metaphysical desire. The first kind of truth is examined in relation to a moral problem: How is it that people have come to problematize their lives through the linking of sexuality to issues of moral conduct? For Foucault, this connection is closely tied to "the arts of existence," the "techniques of the self," through which men were able to form themselves in ancient Greece.[5] His *History of Sexuality*, then, must be read in relation to the discussion offered in his work on the technologies of the self, rather than the hermeneutics of the self. The seminar entitled "Technologies of the Self" was published around the time of *The History of Sexuality* and focuses on different aspects of the discussion of how different modes of truth are being produced.[6] It is no coincidence that these techniques were later displaced by a Platonic discourse in which the question of truth, divorced from the experience of desire, replaced the conception of certain forms of sexual conduct as a sign of virility. In Foucault's analysis, sexuality in ancient Greece is to be considered a moral project, revealing man's relation to himself. The most important human practices are "technologies." These technologies of the self are the practices through which the individual molds his intellect, body, and emotions. Therefore, the technologies of the self have a particular place in Foucault's discursive analysis, representing a position through which the individual was able to formulate a productive conception of the self and a productive conception of truth before the systems of discourse that were regulative representatives of truth were set in place. From early Christianity onward, the discourses informing these techniques fell out of use.

Foucault thereby separates the technologies of the self, or the care of the self, from a hermeneutics of the self, which has been diffused throughout the West since early Christianity. The tradition of the technique of the self, linking the subject to truth, has been forgotten and obscured. The aim of the technique is not to discover the truth, as in the hermeneutics of the self, but rather to link the subject to a truth, one that is learned and progressively put into practice. To come to apprehend a relation to truth is to establish a relation to the external world. Foucault defines the self as a striving for knowledge and thereby also for the power associated with knowledge. The ancient technique of the self, or care of the self, in which philosophy and the truth-claims that belong to it participated could be described as an ethos rather than a science, a way of life in which body and soul take part on equal terms. The ethos of the care of the self aims toward achievements through which one becomes true to oneself. Foucault's point, then, is that the self is developed through different kinds of teaching, through experiences that allow and encourage the self to change, and through discursive technologies that influence the conception of the self. When new technologies develop, the care of the self also develops. In the end, however, the tradition of the technologies has been displaced for a hermeneutics and an important insight has been lost to Western philosophy; just as different ways of creating knowledge exist, different forms of the self also exist. When philosophy ceases to be a *poiesis* or a technology of becoming in which the care of the body is as important as the search for philosophical truth, when eros, in other words, ceases to be a part of philosophical life, then all those aspects of life that belong to the body are taken over by institutions, thereby becoming aspects of disciplinary technologies.

Foucault's history, tracing a different conception of truth than the one linked to hermeneutics, links sexuality to a certain conception of the self. Although his vision of the technologies of the self does indeed challenge the forms through which the West has come to define truth, knowledge, and the self—and above all the philosophical project through which the plurality of truths, knowledges, and selves has been lost—we have reason to remark on another challenge to such a reduction of plurality, a reduction that Foucault himself does not quite manage to analyze. The self Foucault describes is still gendered and relies on a view of masculinity in which social status and desire cohere. Sexuality becomes part of the very truth to which the masculine self is aspiring; a virile self is moderating his search for pleasure in such a way that his social status is preserved. Activity and passivity emerge as categories that distinguish between sexual activities: free men are viewed as active, while women, slaves, and children become seen as passive.[7] For the Greeks, sexual relations always involve a superior and a subordinate, a passive and an active part. The dividing line of gender was not set between masculine or feminine, homosexual or heterosexual, but between passive or active. Activity was defined as virile, passivity as feminine. A man could well be characterized as feminine when he proved incapable of containing his search for pleasures, whereas it was considered virile to exert self-control.[8] To be feminine, then, was to be passive in relation to pleasures. Immorality, for the Greeks, was a question of excess in relation to one's role—being active or passive. One might have thought that the question of morality would have been applicable to either mode, active or passive. But only the active function was valorized and taken as the proper site for morality.

Sexuality for the Greeks was not a question of the law, but of *techne*, a form of applicable knowledge. Plato's *The Laws* invokes a notion of spiritual combat in which one fights against desires, trying to take control of them. The difference between this agonistic fighting and that of Christianity is that in ancient Greece the attempt to take control was considered a fight against oneself, whereas the Christians considered excessive desires to stem from something foreign. In Greece, the ethical ideal was not abstinence from pleasures, but mastery over them. In classical Greek thought, "the 'ascetics' that enabled one to make oneself into an ethical subject was an integral part—down to its very form—of the practice of a virtuous life, which was also the life of a 'free' man in the full, positive and political sense of the word."[9] Freedom, for the Greeks, was a certain form of relation of the individual to himself. Freedom is the same as mastery of the self.

With Plato, the question of sexual desire is still posed, but it is displaced from any concern with the object of love. If the discourse of the technologies of the self puts the question of the object in ethical terms (What kind of object is one supposed to love?), then Plato instead puts it in metaphysical terms (What is the nature of love?). For Plato, this question can only be answered if one looks beyond the object. Eros, in the Platonic discourse, becomes a question of the relation to truth. Socrates does feel erotic love, but he knows the true object of that desire (knowledge). Not only does he control his own body, he is also a master of truth. The quest for knowledge and truth becomes unified with the quest for pleasure. Now the master of truth teaches wisdom to a pupil who can also become his object of pleasure. Foucault reads this move of Plato as a way of legitimizing the love for boys; whereas it used to be considered a problem that a boy, who was to be raised as an active man and sexual agent, had to play a passive, feminine part in the erotic relation with a man, he could now remain in that role of (sexual) passivity while developing his metaphysical desire for knowledge as an active agent. This would then ensure that the passive boy would not remain feminized on his path to becoming a man.

Foucault's own investigations, accordingly, are wholly focused on the role of the active man, his search for pleasure, and what might count as an excess or deficiency in this respect. Foucault examines the four great axes of experience: "the relation to one's body, the relation to one's wife, the relation to boys, and the relation to truth."[10] The use of pleasure bears witness to the modes of subjectivation of the virile man, but since sexuality and the use of pleasure are assumed to be equivalent discourses, there is no account of any sexuality beyond such an active pursuit and control of pleasure. Consequently, Foucault sees a search for truth take shape in Plato which pursues the idea of the truth-seeker as an active agent. The Foucauldian form of sexuality aspires to a certain relation to truth so that it can be connected to desire: the desire beyond the object is a quest for truth. Sexuality and the desire to know are part of the same movement:

the development of the individual, individuation, or a technology of the self in which the sensitivity of the body, social sensibility, and ethical sense all take part. In Foucault's genealogy, what is active, virile, and commanded by desire defines sexuality as well as the quest for knowledge. In other words, there is no discussion of any form of sexuality lying beyond such a definition; no place given to any passive form of sexuality that would be given over to exposure rather than knowledge, or associated with the "feminine" place in the genealogy. Again, Foucault has knowingly limited his material. We have reason, however, to look beyond that material decades after *The History of Sexuality* has come to occupy a central place in the academic discourse of the West.

The Other of Western Sexuality: Sappho

It is no coincidence that one of the few places where tragedy is mentioned in Foucault's genealogy is in the context of the moral codes examined concerning marriage and the specific situation of women in that regard.[11] As we know, one of the astounding aspects of tragedy is the prominent place it gives to women in spite of its being produced by men in a patriarchal society.

We have no reason to challenge Foucault or to criticize *The History of Sexuality* on the basis of his own material—on the contrary, his conception of sexuality as a question of gendered roles rather than sexual complementarity is useful in this context. However, looking at tragedy, another aspect of eros emerges that allows the question of sexuality to stretch well beyond the gendered categorizations of active/passive or excessive/deficient that Foucault analyzes. In tragedy, gender has to do with one's place in relation to fate. The protagonists risk becoming exposed, unable to attain agency, penetrated by forces more powerful than the virility associated with ethical conduct. Those subjected to fate are not looking for pleasure. Instead, they are subjected to sexuality and thus unable to sustain a virile form of morality, which, in Foucault's analysis, is that of moderation. They are not in control of themselves. Sexuality is not equivalent to pleasure—it is by nature something that exceeds control.

Interestingly, Sappho, the great poet from the seventh century BCE, offers a similar view of sexuality or eros. The Western literary tradition has taken up Sappho as one of the first poets to poeticize desire. She was a female poet, but her texts, like the tragedies, do not align with the gender roles that Foucault puts forth. As Page duBois has pointed out, Sappho offers a view of sexuality that has little to do with Foucault's because she is neither a wife (virtuous, mastered, and obedient, submissive to a master), nor is she driven by lust like a comic or tragic heroine. She is, rather, driven by memory, yearning, and a shared form of pleasure.[12] Moreover, duBois links Sappho to a form of desire, or a conception of the body, that has subsequently been forgotten following the legacy of

Plato. In the Platonic corpus, what is good is also beautiful, and what is good and beautiful is also loved. In the *Phaedrus*, physical desire is submitted to the metaphysical desire for love. Philosophy is love of wisdom and a quest for truth. For Sappho, however, what is beautiful cannot be determined universally; what is loved is also beautiful to each one who loves. But the Sapphic worship of eros, or Aphrodite, also has a political quality according to duBois. What we see emerging in the Sapphic poetry is an individual who shows himself or herself through his or her desire, but who resists the gendered hierarchies that recognize only one kind of subject. Sappho sings about the subject who loves the most, the individual who will later be connected to the democratic state. This is the individual who will compete with others and define himself or herself through his or her abilities and through his or her desire such as we have seen in the analysis of Foucault. In the cultural context of Sappho, Eros defines agency, and is thus a mark of social distinction, rather than moral weakness.

What is exceptional in the poetry of Sappho, duBois argues, is not only that she defines women as active agents of desire, but, more important, that she also does not create a hierarchy between the two genders. Instead, she shows what unites people in their difference: each one finds what is the most beautiful in the one they love. If one looks at the tradition of Sappho, then, one finds an alternative tradition of sexuality, eros, and the desire for truth than the one we associate with Plato. This is what makes her the Other of the European tradition, relevant also to discussions of philosophy. Jesper Svenbro goes even further, claiming that Sappho is the intertext that has to be overcome in Plato's own dialogues. She is not only *mentioned* in the *Phaedrus*—the dialogue, in fact, contains a long passage that reads like a fragment by her.[13] In the end of the dialogue, Sappho appears to have the weight of a pre-Socratic philosopher—she presents a philosophy of eros in which a conception of reflexive consciousness appears, and she does this prior to Socrates. The consciousness of one subject can never be known by another; it can only be transposed into language. It is the sustained celebration of eros that allows this conception to be formulated within the texts of Sappho; they bear witness not only to a reflection on the nature of love, but also on the nature of knowledge. The loss of most of Sappho's lyrics, therefore, is the loss of a pre-Socratic thinker who still looms in the background of Plato's own philosophy of eros and in its close connection with epistemology.[14]

We might also add another aspect of Sappho's poetry to this discussion. Whereas the Platonic dialogues struggle with the question of the body and how the corporeal senses and the search for pleasure relate to truth, Sappho's poetry indicates that knowledge can be found only through the senses and in one's own body—that there is no beyond, no transcendence, nothing higher to which we should aspire. The poetics of Sappho does not move toward the experience of something higher or a higher form of truth. Moreover, it shows a form of sensibility in which the conception of the self is not one of exerting power through eros, or at least that is not the only mode. In the famous "Hymn to Aphrodite," the only full lyric of Sappho's that remains, Aphrodite is introduced as a powerful but fearsome goddess, capable of crushing the human subject: "Shimmering-throned immortal Aphrodite, / Daughter of Zeus, Enchantress, I implore thee, / Spare me, O queen, this agony and anguish, / Crush not my spirit."[15] In one of the most quoted fragments, eros produces a feeling of exposure and suffering, immobility rather than pleasure, or at least a somatic experience that is difficult to define as sexuality, if by the latter we understand a search for pleasure:

I
Peer of the gods, the happiest man I seem
Sitting before thee, rapt at thy sight, hearing
Thy soft laughter and they voice most gentle,
Speaking so sweetly.

II
Then in my bosom my heart wildly flutters,
And, when on thee I gaze never so little,
Bereft am I of all power of utterance,
My tongue is useless.

III
There rushes at once through my flesh tingling fire,
My eyes are deprived of all power of vision,
My ears hear nothing by sounds of winds roaring,
And all is blackness.[16]

These lines have been considered outspokenly and scandalously erotic throughout the centuries of Sappho's reception, and more interestingly for our considerations, they have been subjected to endless discussions about agency. Who speaks in this poem? Who is the subject of jealousy? Do we hear the voice of a woman in love, or the voice of a man through the lines of a female poet? For the purposes of this chapter, however, the most interesting aspect of Sappho's lyric is not the gendered identity of the subject, but its depiction of a form of sexuality that goes beyond any kind of search for pleasure. For Sappho, love may well be a pleasure, but it is a pleasure that carries a weight that has to do with an alternative philosophy of eros: the pleasure of love proves the value of the body. To be moved is to be moved by what exists; in the physical sense, it is to experience a sensation that has no beyond and can only be experienced in the moment. Pleasure is one aspect of such a celebration of the body. Sappho offers us a philosophy of Aphrodite that does not take us beyond the experience of our bodies, but that sustains the sensibility of the body. As duBois has shown, the poem dedicated to Aphrodite may well make an appearance in the *Phaedrus*, but it is altered in such a way that the pain of the sufferer or lover is transformed into pleasure: "in Plato's hands the Sapphic model is appropriated and then disembodied, amputated. Sappho cannot remain in the philosophical text; even the disembodied Sappho, invoked allusively, like other women is exorcised from the Platonic dialogue."[17] In Plato's project—one that must overcome the heritage of Sappho in order to establish itself—pleasure is the beginning of the transcendence of the body. In Sappho's poetry, there is no transcendence and no clear hierarchy between pleasure and suffering in the sexual experience, in the same way that there is no hierarchy between active and passive components.

If Foucault's reading of the Greek history of sexuality offers us an "aesthetic of the self" that aims toward moderation and control of the use of pleasure, Sappho instead offers us an alternative that brings us back to the Greek term *aisthesis*. In Sappho's worldview, human existence is affirmed by being moved or affected, through corporeal sensibility, in the here and now of the moment in which Aphrodite makes her power felt. The tradition of Sappho sketches a form of "*aisthesis* of the self" that is wholly nonmetaphysical.

Such a philosophy of eros, or such an "*aisthesis* of the self," is not sustained by a search for pleasure that would confirm the philosophical quest for truth. The subject of the poem quoted above suffers and enjoys at the same time, losing all capacity to search for pleasure as an active agent, and yet, perhaps, enjoying eros all the more as she is exposed to the effects of an erotic sensation that she cannot control. The issue of gender here is less interesting than the fact that the intensity of the sexual sensation that is being produced depends on the full exposure of the subject. What Sappho shows us is a subject that cannot fit neatly into the categories of active or passive—what is at stake is no longer the question of penetration, or of who is in charge. What the poem depicts, rather, is the somatic experience of an erotic force over which one has no control, and the exposure to godly powers, beyond any kind of gendered hierarchy among men, to which the erotic subject must submit. Sappho depicts, then, a sexuality that has no agent or, rather, one in which agency is an undecidable factor. She is therefore describing a kind of sexuality that is opposed to the one Foucault describes, in which the question of agency, or of who is the active part, is the most important issue. The subject that is overcome with suffering and desire at the same time is both an active agent (as a spectator) and the passive sufferer of an ambivalent form of lovesickness. The undecidable position of the subject in Sappho's poetry, as well as the ambivalent character of the sexuality she describes, provides an opening for questions of sexuality that take us beyond the issues Foucault addresses, where sexuality remains a question of morality.

In Sappho, eros is something one both suffers and enjoys; the sensations of the body are equally important in both cases; they give proof of the kind of exposure to which the body is subjected. Sexuality, therefore, is not a mark of power, but rather an *aisthesis* of the self. Through the exposure to an outside, this *aisthesis* of the self affirms the self as a sensation of simultaneous enjoyment and suffering.

Sexuality as the Freedom of the Absolute: The Example of Schelling

In tragedy, as in Sappho's poetry, the manifestations of eros are far from the Foucauldian conception of sexuality and its account of subjectivity, agency, and experience. Instead, just as in Sappho's lyrics, sexuality is linked to the forms of negativity that manifest the limits of human agency and willpower. Incarnated by eros, a *daimon* creature between human and god, tragic sexuality challenges modern notions of lust and pleasure, and in fact the idea that sexuality is defined above all by corporeal experience. In tragedy, sexuality may well be embodied, but more than that, it has effects that bring the protagonists beyond themselves, out of their bodies, to fates that will finally bring about their destruction. Sexuality, in this sense, is not something you can practice as an individual choice—in this way, it takes you beyond the technologies of the self that are of interest to Foucault. In tragedy, sexuality hits you from the outside as part of a greater scheme of things, manifesting itself as a form of negativity in which an individual body is but a negligible element or contingency. Such a sexuality is represented as a destructive force, manifesting itself through the acts of an individual, its implications, however, stretch well beyond individual fates. The destructive power of such a sexuality is not limited to the consequences of isolated acts.

When Heidegger, in his reading of *Antigone*, remarks that death, for Dasein, is that *which he cannot escape*, he forgets the "Hymn to Eros." In tragedy, eros is even more terrifying than death. Antigone, Heidegger writes, is tragedy's "supreme uncanny."[18] That which is the most *heimlich*—that which appeared to revere family ties and the home, those things that appear the most understandable and natural to us—turns out to be the most *unheimlich*. Antigone challenges the naturalized representations of belonging. In doing so, she thereby discloses the lack of origin or exposure around which tragedy turns. Antigone points to the uncanny void that surrounds human existence. For Heidegger, this void is mediated through the "Hymn to Man," in which man is presented as the most *deinon* of creatures, since he challenges the limits of his own existence, thus bringing death unto himself. Antigone incarnates the "supreme uncanny" because through her death she lets us glimpse into the void. She exposes the uncanniness surrounding human existence. Heidegger shows Greek "being" to be violent and uncanny. He fails to mention, however, the intertwinement of eros and the tragic process as such. But if we follow Heidegger, while relating "Hymn to Man" to "Hymn to Eros," we nevertheless see a conception of tragic eros emerge that has not yet been fully explored in the philosophical discussion. As I have argued elsewhere, on Heidegger's reading feminine desire becomes a pure and naked figure for the kind of impossibility that is to be found at the heart of Dasein: a "striving" for something impossible. Feminine desire is but one aspect of what is at stake here. The other aspect is a tragic view of sexuality as such—because it is a striving after something that was laid out in the destiny of Dasein from the beginning, sexuality incarnates the supreme uncanny if we are to follow the consequences of Heidegger's reading of the tragedy. What the drama says is, in fact, not that death stands for the exposure of man, but rather that sexuality, or eros, is the underlying cause of such an exposure.[19]

The Heideggerian analysis of *Antigone* allows us to pursue an issue that has to do with more than the tragic uncanniness of Sophocles' play: In what way can we conceive of Greek eros as a form of sexuality that is more than pleasure? And in what way does it undermine our view of human freedom or autonomy and, therefore, our capacity to pursue a quest for truth?

The first Western philosopher to define sexuality in Greek tragedy as a specific force that must be considered to be deeply involved in the analysis of the human condition as such was Schelling, who wrote about tragedy as a poetics in *The Philosophy of Art*.[20] However, his most important writings on tragedy are to be found in the *Philosophical Inquiries into the Nature of Human Freedom*.[21] Although Schelling does not bring up the Platonic discussion of eros as a form of *daimon*, sexuality, to him, clearly has the status of being both internal and external to human subjectivity. The physical experience of lust or pleasure is secondary to the experience of freedom in its negative form that is manifested in tragedy by the protagonists.

To Schelling, what is most remarkable is that the hero is doomed to failure *out of necessity*. Freedom, as he explains in *Philosophy of Art*, cannot be represented in a positive manner, as an emotion or experience, or as freedom of choice. Instead, human freedom is manifested through the human tendency toward self-destruction. Schelling's concept of freedom has nothing to do with freedom as the manifestation of choice or free will. Freedom is negativity in both the temporal and spatial sense; it is a void that makes historical change possible. Such a notion of freedom is embodied in tragedy, through the hero. To Schelling, tragedy is defined by the fact that the hero is guilty of a crime *by necessity*. He compares Sophocles' *King Oedipus* to Euripides' *Hippolytus*, pointing to the fact that Phaedra, through falling in love with Hippolytus, her stepson, sets into motion the downfall of the house of kings and queens. One might observe, then, that human freedom, turned into necessity, is in fact equivalent to the sexual fate of the hero(ine).

Schelling is often bypassed and less often quoted on the poetics of tragedy than Hegel, Schiller, or the Schlegel brothers. He is, however, the first to create a philosophy of tragedy. In 1795 he wrote the *Philosophical Letters on Dogmatism and Criticism*.[22] Already in the first letter he declares the thread that is going to hold together an otherwise disparate project: the creation of a system of freedom. *Briefe* is addressed to a fictional friend to whom Schelling explains the motivations of his project. The last letter is the most remarkable. Freedom, Schelling writes, is the state where we "cease to be objects to ourselves," it is a state beyond reflection in which we become one with non-being, with destruction.[23] Absolute freedom is a state we cannot imagine through reason, but tragedy can depict the possibility of ". . . knowing with absolute certainty in your heart that there is an objective power that threatens to ruin our freedom, and to fight against that power, mobilizing all of your freedom and go under in that way."[24] Such a manifestation of freedom cannot take place in real life, but can only manifest itself in art through the "titans" of tragedy; the "great thought" of Greek art was the idea that we can freely choose to give up our freedom. This paradox is, however, not just the kernel of tragedy, where action is dissolved when "freedom fights itself" toward the end, as Schelling puts it in *Philosophical Inquiries into the Nature of Human Freedom*.[25] What Schelling tells us is that man, in life too, carries the tendency toward dissolution and disintegration within himself, in the name of freedom. His will or tendency to shake off every totalizing order is present also in his very way of thinking, even if the grand forms of tragedy are not immediately translatable into real life. These thoughts, presented in the last letter of *Briefe*, return later in *Philosophy of Art*, which should be read together with *Briefe*. When we put them together, we see that Schelling's analysis insists with astounding consistency that man manifests his freedom through the exposure to sexuality.

Oedipus' fight against his own destiny is also, in Schelling's view, what it releases. The root of evil does not begin with the transgression of the law of incest, but with Laius' decision to have a son against the will of the gods. Necessity is written from the moment the gods forbid Laius to have a son. From that moment forward, it is inscribed that Laius will challenge the gods, that he will go on to have a son, and that his son will kill him. Tragedy, as we well know, begins with a challenge against predestination. In the end, however, it turns out that man cannot liberate himself from destiny. What he can do, however, is to take it upon his own shoulders. Tragedy casts man outside of a divine order and allows him entrance into a human one. He can never return to a "natural" place established by the gods. Transgression is inscribed in the lawgiving itself. But it takes a human being to perform it. When Oedipus kills his father, it is the result of a will to avoid his destiny. That is why freedom, according to Schelling, fights against itself. Oedipus can only redeem himself if he acknowledges his own guilt. In doing so, he will also recuperate his dignity. This is accomplished when he pierces his eyes out, making himself blind. Certainly not by chance does Sigmund Freud refer to Schelling in his famous essay on the uncanny.[26] The kind of uncanniness that we associate with Freud's analysis of the castration complex or with the death drive, brings us, however, to another issue, namely the way in which the law inspires the death drive so that sexual desire can no longer be clearly separated from it.[27]

What is interesting to us in this context is the way in which freedom, in Schelling's negative sense, manifests itself through sexuality. What Schelling describes in terms of a fight between necessity and freedom could also be described as the performance of eros. The tragedy of *Antigone* makes clear that eros is *deinon*, terrifying, because the force of eros, like that of death, cannot be contained. Man, also, is *deinon*, terrifying in that he is striving toward what will inevitably ruin him. Schelling sees the same logic in his reading of *Oedipus*; he marries his mother, driven by his will to challenge his destiny, thereby following an eros that makes him *deinon*, marked by the gods and yet challenging them.

Schelling's reading of Euripides' *Hippolytus* accentuates the relation between sexuality and freedom as negativity. Aphrodite has cursed Hippolytus and his family because he refuses to honor her. Her curse says that Phaedra, the stepmother, will fall in love with him, and that his father will therefore kill her. Hippolytus himself is uninterested in women and is only interested in hunting, and this lack of interest sparks Aphrodite's wrath. Phaedra, in turn, is incapable of stopping the development of the events. She falls for Hippolytus and attempts to lure him to her. I have wondered, she says, how it is that "the lives of mortals have been ruined." She then goes on to reflect:

> I think that it is not owing to the nature of their wits that they fare badly, since many people possess good sense. Rather, one must look at it this way: what we know and understand to be noble we fail to carry out, some from laziness, others because they give precedence to some other pleasure than honor. Life's pleasures are many, long talks and leisure, a pleasant bane, and a modest restraint. Yet they are of two sorts, one pleasure being no bad thing, another a burden upon houses. If propriety were clear, there would not be two things designated by the same letter.[28]

She is driven toward the forbidden against her will, toward a pleasure that is but a burden and that will destroy her. She reveals her passion to her servant, who tells Hippolytus. His response is disgust.

Phaedra's problem, as she has described it herself, is that she has lost her honor through falling to the very destiny she had tried to avoid—falling in love with her own stepson. The only thing she can do to regain her own honor and her children is to kill herself. Why? Because the words of women are worth nothing, she says, since they always appear to draw shame on their families. She leaves a note by her bed blaming her stepson for having raped her. In this way, she hopes to escape the shame associated with suicide, thereby saving the reputation of her children. According to the patriarchal code, Phaedra is unable to take responsibility for her guilt, blaming Hippolytus instead. Her action will have consequences: when her husband returns home and finds the note, he attempts to kill his own son. By the time Hippolytus is able to persuade him of his innocence, it is too late. Phaedra's attempt to escape the curse of Aphrodite has resulted in the downfall of the family; it is crushed.

Schelling's comparison between the two tragedies places freedom at the center of the discussion. Both Oedipus and Phaedra are drawn toward a limit they cannot or should not cross; Phaedra's suicide, in accordance with the tragic logic, releases precisely the kind of catastrophes she has been trying to avoid, including her own elimination. Absolute freedom, the point where it is manifested through the battle against itself, is unleashed through her downfall. Like Oedipus, she makes herself into the cause of necessity. Through her suicide, she acknowledges that her transgression of the law has led nowhere but to the void in which she perishes. At the same time, she declares herself to be the agent of a sexual desire that she has been unable to control.

As we see, neither the act of Phaedra nor that of Oedipus can be isolated from the marks they have left on the history of the states and families to which they belong. Tragedy as freedom fighting against itself, and finally manifesting itself, is less about the sexual desire of a single person than about the negativity manifesting itself in the tragic action as such. Schelling's view is echoed in Nicole Loraux's analysis of female suicide in Greek tragedy; for the women of tragedy, suicide was often the only way to gain autonomy. This accounts for why so many women in Greek tragedy, Phadera and Antigone for instance, commit suicide. In Loraux's argument, such a death becomes the only possible manifestation of autonomy in a patriarchy where no other actions are possible for women.[29]

The unbearable expression of freedom exemplified through both Oedipus and Phaedra brings us close to the sublime. In *Philosophy of Art*, the sublime is described as *an excess of fate*; the tragic events being put into motion by an insurmountable fate in which the freedom of man lifts Phaedra up at the very moment that she is crushed.[30] The sublime is the acceptance of fate by people that have not committed a crime, but who are nevertheless still guilty. What interests Schelling is not catharsis. It is the idea that tragedy represents something to us that we cannot imagine, something unbearable that cannot be represented in any other way.

Schelling's thoughts on the sublime were inspired by Friedrich Schiller, for whom the sublime represents the human victory over nature. Whereas a tragic hero will perish, his autonomy will ensure that what is human will still persist. Nature is a much wider concept than a natural environment—it is everything that lies beyond reason, necessity, fate, weakness, and emotions. Freedom is the capacity to establish a limit between oneself and nature. A moral, rational culture places the tragic hero above the contingent forces of nature, assuring us that the human essence will persist. Tragedy, therefore, is set up as a conflict between what is unbearable and untouchable within us, which reason and our capacity for aesthetic judgment will uphold, and an outer world threatening to attack it. It is this outer world that we learn to detach ourselves from. The greatest of gestures in tragedy, giving proof to the persistence of human reason over chaotic nature, happen when the hero transforms what attacks him from arbitrary blows of fate into actions of his own.[31]

This gesture is what Schelling finds interesting. In his mind, however, it must be seen from the perspective of a system in which the difference between object and subject, nature and culture, which Schiller had wanted to enforce, breaks down. Schelling questions the lines of demarcation between reason and nature. Freedom is not reason, and man cannot identify himself with a reason through which he is to place himself outside of nature. What tragedy shows through the examples of sexual desire and the transgressions they bring about, is that man must integrate the causality of nature as part of himself and become the *cause of necessity*, as we have seen in *King Oedipus* and *Hippolytus*.

As we discussed earlier, the examples that Schelling gives are all tragedies in which the hero is overcome by eros, or sexual desire. In tragedy, overall, sexual desire is depicted as a dark force, not as pleasure. One could add the examples of Euripides' *Medea*, where Jason's decision to leave his wife for a lover will cause the death of his children, or Aeschylus' *Agamemnon*, where Clytemnestra kills Agamemnon for similar reasons. Just as in *Antigone*, eros is the force with the most tragic power in *Hippolytus*. What tragedy is most concerned with is the fact that eros, although it has the capacity to create pleasure, is the creator of a downfall that cannot be reversed. One could perhaps talk about it in terms of eros having a double face; creating lust and pleasure on the one hand, and death and disaster on the other. However, such a depiction must be discussed in terms that show the view of eros in tragedy to be much more than a question of dramatic detail. The tragic view of eros, rather, gives us a view of sexuality that is at odds with the analysis of sexuality as a question of pleasure, lust, sensation, and desire, and that of sexuality as dependent on the question of gender and necessarily coded through the categories that come with it. We may listen to the chorus in *Hippolytus*:

> Eros, eros, distilling liquid desire upon the eyes, bringing sweet pleasure to the soul of those you make war against, never may you show yourself to me for my hurt nor ever come but in harmony.

> For neither the shafts of fire nor of stars are more powerful than that of Aphrodite, which Eros, Zeus' son, hurls from his hand.[32]

What is interesting about such a tragic view of sexuality, as it has been analyzed through the sharp eyes of Schelling, is that *it undermines the demarcation line between culture and nature, active and passive, subject and object*. The question of human freedom, when looked at from the perspective of sexuality, is irreducible to these forms. What takes place in tragedy is determined not by the desire of a human agent searching for pleasure, but by fate. Eros is the godly incarnation of such a fate. When eros is involved, the bodies of the protagonists are submitted to sexual desire, unable to fight against it. The force of eros is not the striving of desire but the weakness of submission. The fate of eros is inscribed in the body. The body of the protagonist belongs to eros—coloring the cheeks of the virgin, as we are told by the chorus in *Antigone*. And yet, if we are to follow the argument of Schelling, the question of tragedy lies not in the issue of sexual desire as a particular aspect of human embodiment, but rather in the absolute submission under a condition from which man cannot escape.

Homeric man saw the world as a given. The gods were establishing the ways in which man falls in love, loves and dies, inspiring their actions as set on a great board of chess. In tragedy, however, the individual appears responsible for his own actions. To the philosophers of German Idealism—Hölderlin, Schelling, Schlegel, and Hegel—the actions of the individual are subordinated to another great plan; subjectivity in tragedy is not individual subjectivity but a representation of the conditions of a historical subject. This means that no free will can be tied to the individual subject. Instead, freedom is manifested as negativity. In Schelling this appears as chaos, as a sublime *lack of plan* in which fate appears meaningless.

Reading tragedy we perceive sexual destructivity as a threat to human possibilities: possibilities of choice, of desire, of agency, and so forth. As Schelling and Sappho show, however, the destruction that takes place in the name of sexuality is liberating at another level. The suffering subject of sexuality is neither a virile hero nor a helpless victim, neither an active, penetrating agent nor a passive object of penetration. If we transfer Schelling's ontological analysis of freedom to the domain of eros, we see a perspective on sexuality take shape, which belies, like the lyrics of Sappho, the idea that sexuality must be constrained through the terms of gender to activity or passivity. When fate and sexual desire become the same, when the pleasure of the body is inseparable from destruction, tragedy is no longer about the desire of the individual subject. Sexuality as a form of fate instigated beyond the logic of agency, releases not only suffering, destruction, and downfall, but also *the possibility of another freedom*. Rather than being reducible to activity and passivity, as a consequence of a social categorization of gender or transferred on to the metaphysical question of truth as in Platonic discourse, sexuality is the embodied force of human freedom. In this, sexuality has little to do with an individual choice or a search for pleasure. But it is precisely in the exposure to a passivity beyond choice, in identifying with a sexuality that one cannot escape, with the weakness and the void appearing past the actions guiding his fate, that man encounters freedom in the true sense of the word.

It is thus in the encounter with eros, rather than in the depiction of human agency as activity, that tragedy tells us that human freedom is emerging. It is not the human capacity to face the unexpected, but rather to accept the exposure to sexuality that demonstrates human freedom. In identifying eros as a force of freedom, Schelling observes a tradition in Greek thought that offers another view on sexuality than the one Foucault has studied, which as we have seen peaked with the writings of Plato. Together with the lyrics of Sappho, the tragedies of ancient Greece depict sexuality as a force that crosses the divides of gender: passivity and activity, object and subject, or nature and culture. We may then well return to Schelling, to the tragedies, and to Sappho to continue the work on sexuality, associating it with a freedom that takes us well beyond the categories of social domination.

When Ismene charges Antigone with a chilling kind of love, with an incapacity to care for the living, we are again reminded of a concept of eros irreducible to physical desire. As has been widely discussed, Antigone is the agent of an action that cannot easily be cast under categories of good or bad, destructive or constructive. She is rarely analyzed in categories of sexuality. She does what she does because she must, not because of lust. And yet her actions cannot be fully dissociated from lust or pleasure either. Antigone's eros is, just as in the case of Oedipus or Phaedra, an eros beyond eroticism, an eros exposing man to forces of sexuality that bring us well beyond a modern conception of what that would mean. When Antigone buries her brother, she does so because she must, not because she is manifesting an act of free will. In this way she is submitting to eros, who is forcing her to love the dead and the cold. Her act is not merely an act of choice or a manifestation to be considered in ethical and political terms, but it must be understood as an act of submission to a sexuality she cannot escape. The hidden sexual resonance of her act, forcing her death as suffering and enjoyment at the same time, that makes us return to Antigone again and again. Antigone can thus be added to the list of feminine figures who continuously force us to construct another history of sexuality.

Notes

1. Froma I. Zeitlin, *Playing the Other: Gender and Society in Classical Greek Literature* (Chicago: University of Chicago Press, 1996), pp. 341–375.

2. Cecilia Sjöholm, *The Antigone Complex: Ethics and the Invention of Feminine Desire* (Stanford, CA: Stanford University Press, 2004).

3. For an analysis that focuses on Foucault and tragedy see: Andrew Cutrofello, "Foucault on Tragedy," *Philosophy and Social Criticism*, vol. 31, no. 5–6 (2005), pp. 573–584. Cutrofello, however, looks at the issue from the perspective of Friedrich Nietzsche's philosophy of tragedy, which is not discussed in this chapter.

4. Michel Foucault, *The History of Sexuality: The Use of Pleasure*, vol. 2, trans. Robert Hurley (New York: Penguin, 1985), p. 35.

5. Ibid., p 11.

6. The second volume of Foucault's work on sexuality, *The Use of Pleasure* (which is the volume referred to in this discussion), was published in 1984 in France. The seminar entitled "Technologies of the Self" was given at the University of Vermont in 1982 and was published in 1988. See Michel Foucault, *Ethics*, vol. 1 of *Essential Works of Foucault 1954–1984*, trans. Robert Hurley, ed. Paul Rabinow (London: Penguin Books, 1994), pp. 223–253.

7. Foucault, *The Use of Pleasure*, p. 47.

8. Ibid., p. 85.

9. Ibid., p. 77.

10. Ibid., p. 32.

11. Ibid., p. 164.

12. Page duBois, *Sappho Is Burning* (Chicago: University of Chicago Press, 1995), p. 145.

13. Jesper Svenbro, "Försokratikern Sappho," in *Försokratikern Sappho och andra studier i antikt tänkande* (Gothenburg, Sweden: Glänta, 2007), pp. 35–38.

14. Ibid., p. 47.

15. Sappho, "Hymn to Aphrodite," fragment 1 in *The Poems of Sappho,* http://www.sacred-texts.com/cla/usappho/sph02.htm, trans. Edward Marion Cox, 1925.

16. Sappho, "That one seems to me the equal of gods, . . ." fragment 2 in *The Poems of Sappho,* http://www.sacred-texts.com/cla/usappho/sph03.htm, trans. Edward Marion Cox, 1925.

17. duBois, *Sappho Is Burning*, p. 67.

18. ". . . des Unheimlichsten das höchste Unheimliche" (Martin Heidegger, "Hölderlins Hymne 'Der Ister,' " in *Gesamtausgabe*, vol. 53 [Frankfurt, Germany: Vittorio Klostermann, 1942], p. 129; for an English translation, see *Hölderlin's Hymn "The Ister,"* trans. William McNeill and Julia Davis [Bloomington: Indiana University Press, 1996], p. 104).

19. See Sjöholm, *The Antigone Complex*, chap. 3.

20. F. W. J. Schelling, *The Philosophy of Art*, trans. and ed. Douglas W. Stott (Minneapolis: University of Minnesota Press, 1989), pp. 252–261.

21. F. W. J. Schelling, *Philosophical Inquiries into the Nature of Human Freedom*, trans. James Gutmann (La Salle, IL: Open Court, 1992).

22. F. W. J. Schelling, "Philosophical Letters on Dogmatism and Criticism," in *The Unconditional in Human Knowledge: Four Early Essays (1794–1796)*, trans. Fritz Marti (Cranbury, NJ: Associated University Presses, 1980).

23. F. W. J. Schelling, *Sämmtliche Werke*, div. 2, vol. 1 (Stuttgart, Germany: Joseph Cotta, 1856–1861), p. 324.

24. Ibid., p. 336.

25. Schelling, *Sämmtliche Werke*, div. 1, vol. 5, p. 969.

26. Sigmund Freud, "The Uncanny," in *The Standard Edition of the Complete Psychological Works of Sigmund Freud*, ed. and trans. James Strachey, vol. 17 (London: Hogarth Press, 1958), p. 224.

27. Whereas the early Freud places sexuality at the summit of psychic forces, in "Beyond the Pleasure Principle" he introduces his notion of the death drive. "The Uncanny," written just before "Beyond the Pleasure Principle," is considered to anticipate such a shift in view. See *The Standard Edition*, vol. 18, pp. 3–67.

28. Euripides, *Hippolytus*, trans. David Kovacs, Loeb Classical Library (Cambridge: Harvard University Press, 1995), lines 382–387. "Pleasure" in this text is a translation of the Greek word *hedonai*.

29. Nicole Loraux, *Tragic Ways of Killing a Woman*, trans. Anthony Forster (Cambridge, MA: Harvard University Press, 1991), p. 17.

30. Schelling, *The Philosophy of Art*, pp. 254–255.

31. Friedrich Schiller, "On the Sublime," in *Essays*, trans. Daniel O. Dahlstrom, ed. Walter Hinderer and Daniel O. Dahlstrom, The Germany Library, vol. 17 (New York: Continuum, 1993), p. 12.

32. Euripides, *Hippolytus*, lines 525–528.

10

Transgressing With-In-To the Feminine

Bracha L. Ettinger

Tiresias: The "Impossible" Knowledge of/from Feminine Sexuality

"A congress on feminine sexuality is not going to hold over us the threat of the fate of Tiresias," says Jacques Lacan, meaning by this that we are not in any way getting closer to understanding feminine sexuality.[1]

Tiresias is a mythological male figure transformed into a woman for seven years and then back into his original sex. As a man who had experienced female jouissance he could be seen as master of its knowledge. Tiresias is famous for replying to Zeus and Hera that if ten parts of love's ecstasy—or jouissance—were given to human beings, women took nine parts and men only one. Hera, furious that the secret of her sex was revealed, punished Tiresias with blindness, whereas Zeus endowed him with the gift of prophecy. Sigmund Freud associates the punishment of blindness with the idea of castration connected to man's fear of the feminine, and we can add that the gift of prophecy hints at the link between the feminine and the time of the future.[2]

Fourteen years after this brief reference to Tiresias, Lacan mentions Ovid's version of that myth again in order to say that we cannot incarnate such a figure. Knowledge of feminine sexuality is impossible because the structure of language itself, and the structure of the symbolic—and therefore of the unconscious—makes what would be a knowledge of heterogeneity impossible. This

A slightly longer version of this chapter was first published in *Leonardo's Glimlach,* ed. Claire Van Damme, Francisca Vandepitte, and Patrick van Rossem (Ghent, Belgium: Academia Press, 1999); then in *Women's Philosophy Review, Special Issue on Aesthetics,* no. 25 (2000), pp. 56–85; and finally in *Differential Aesthetics: Art Practices, Philosophy and Feminist Understandings,* ed. Penny Florence and Nicola Foster (London: Ashgate, 2000). This modified version has been approved by the author (the content has not been modified).

impossibility is what makes a woman "not all"/"not whole" whereas man is the prototype of "the same" and its reflections: of the *semblant*. He is "hommo-sexuated."[3] Lacan considers knowledge of femininity inaccessible to women no less than it is to men. For feminine sexuality bears an "impossible" *rapport*—a relation beyond human relationships:

> To say that a woman is *not-all*, it is this that the myth indicates for us, in that she is the unique whose *jouissance* passes beyond. . . . What one calls sex (indeed the second, when one is an idiot) is properly, in supporting itself by the *not-all*, the *Heteros* which cannot arrest itself up with a universe. . . . It is the logic of the *Heteros* which is to be made to depart . . . from the incompatibility of the One with Being.[4]

The *heteros*, Lacan continues, "erects the *man* in his status which is that of the *hommo*sexual," while the *not-all* cannot recognize herself in the parades of truth, seeming (*semblant*), enjoyment (*du jouir*), and excess (*d'un plus de*) in man's universe. In "the absence [*ab-sens*] of relation [*rapport*]" man is guided "toward his true bed [*couche*]" as he is "resituated by the return of the sublime phallus."[5]

We recognize here an earlier, and somewhat clearer claim, which carries a similar meaning but an opposite conclusion in the sense that for the late Lacan woman partly escapes the phallic structure, whereas for the early Lacan the libido is marked by the sign "male" while woman must assume it totally and recognize herself in man's universe; the only one symbolically available.[6]

Lacan considers knowledge of/from the feminine-beyond-the-phallus to be impossible, in agreement with Freud's conception of femininity as either derived from the masculine Oedipal complex and its mechanism of "castration," or a mysterious "dark continent" of which we know too little. In this Freudian-Lacanian account, a difference that is not structured via the couple phallus/castration is foreclosed from the symbolic. Such a difference would either be absent or present in fragments of nature, composing pure events of jouissance: The feminine is "pure absence" or "pure sensibility."[7] Lacking with regard to masculinity, or a surplus to it, she is the Other-Thing, an excess with no claim on subjectivizing desire. Woman here is a subject of course, but by virtue of her participation as an object in what I have termed the *phallic subjectivizing stratum*,[8]—which regulates sex difference, and where she can mark her resistance only by incarnating a masquerade,[9] while some obscure "femininity" still hovers behind it like a phantom—she remains forever enigmatic. Glimpses of/from such a *phantom of the subject* are considered mystical or crazy when appearing in the phallic domain.

Nonphallic psychical phenomena appear toward the end of Lacan's teaching in such terms as the topological sphere, the Moebius strip, the Klein bottle, or the cross-cap; and these terms join the feminine "heterogeneity," "not all"/ "not whole" and "no sexual *rapport*."

> It is the spherical topology of this object called (*a*) which is projected on the other of the composite, *heterogeneous*, that the *cross-cap* constitutes. . . . A Moebius strip, that is the putting in value of the a-sphere of the *not-all* (*not-whole*): It is what supports the impossible of the universe, that is, to take our formula, that which encounters the real. The universe is nowhere else than in the cause of desire, the universal no more. It is from there that proceeds [*sic*] the exclusion of the real . . . of this real: *that there is no sexual rapport.*[10]

With no proper symbolic apparatus to encompass and repress these inscriptions, with no process beyond-castration to in-form human desire, and with no passageway beyond metaphor and metonymy to deliver their potential meaning, they remain inaccessible to knowledge.

Whether a Woman-Other-Thing (in my terms), a product of the Real's non-sense or a radical Other; whether dangerously bordering on originary repression of the Thing, or equated with an elusive almost-nothing (*objet a*)—when described as "not all"/"not whole"—the concept of woman as defined in Lacanian psychoanalysis is always automatically reinforcing the phallic structure because "woman" is perceived as the holes in this structure; its scraps, rests, excess or surplus. If "there is no sexual *rapport*" and "a woman is *not-all*, there is always something of her that escapes discourse."[11] Her experience is in excess of the *phallic* jouissance a *supplementary* jouissance, but Lacan insists that she knows nothing about it.

From the woman's side, a sexual *rapport*—not organ, not essence, but some kind of relation—could have been elaborated into knowledge had such an elaboration been possible. But even a woman, says Lacan, cannot know anything of her own sex, and cannot report on a *rapport* that would have been feminine-Other if/where it does occur because, precisely, what could have been qualified as heterogeneity escapes the imaginary and the symbolic by definition, and what can be included inside these domains is already phallic. In this conception, Tiresias' position of both experiencing feminine different sexuality—*and* knowing it—is out of reach.

Yet in departing from elaboration of the *not-all* and *supplementary jouissance*, it is difficult to clarify feminine *heterogeneity* in a way that would be independent from the *all* to which it is related and from the experience to which it is *supplementary*. Only a departure that does not derive at all from the phallic structure would allow us to account for hybrid feminine instances "*between* center and absence" and their twilight zone.[12] I propose departing from a difference that is feminine from the onset, from a *rapport* of *borderlinking* in an originary psychical sphere that I have named "matrixial." In the matrixial sphere, *not-knowing* the feminine difference is impossible inasmuch as this difference in itself is a *co-naissance* (knowledge of being-born-together). A feminine in-between instance of "*rapport*" is a poietic process that carries in itself aesthetic knowing, a process I have named "metramorphosis." Metramorphosis is both action, perception, inscription, and memory of processes that I call "borderlinking" and "distancing-in-joining." A mental swerving-in-borderlinking with the other—opening a distance-in-proximity while separating-in-jointness with/from the other, or borderlinking while differentiating—is a feminine matrixial process.[13] My *encounters* in the Real with my others are swerved to register traces coming from me and from others concerning the *Thing* as a traumatic event.

These psychical traces witness and account for co-emergence or co-fading of several subjects, partial-subjects, partial-objects, and of their links with one another and with the traumatic *Thing-event.* A noncognitive mode of knowledge that reveals itself in such an ontogenetic witnessing-together, in *wit(h)nessing*, is what I call *co-poiesis*, where *trans-scription* occurs. It is here that, following an intimate encounter between several partners, which affects in different ways each *I* and *non-I*, traces of the affected encounter-events of my others are unknowingly inscribed in me and mine are inscribed in others, known or anonymous, in an asymmetrical exchange that creates and changes a trans-subjective matrixial alliance.

Such a trans-scription is a dispersed sub-symbolic and affective memory of event, paradoxically both forgotten and unforgettable, a memory charged with freight that a linear story cannot transmit, a memory that carries dispersed signifiers to be elaborated and affects as sense-carriers. It is not the story inscribed for reminiscences that I carry in place of a non-I. Rather, fragmented traces of the event's complexity carry fractured and diffracted memory, memory of oblivion itself and of what could not be inscribed in others, even though it "belongs" to a memory that is theirs, but only trans-scribed for/from them in me. Affected traces of a matrixial encounter echo in the present earlier matrixial encounters while modifying older traces and being modified by them. Traces of past metramorphic processes and matrixial events will in their turn modify the processing of further future encounters.

Under the matrixial light, the transgression in the figure of Tiresias between man and woman is not a transgression of a frontier between known maleness and unknown femaleness. Rather, because the matrixial *I* carries traces of experiences of the matrixial *non-I*, inasmuch as *I know in the other* and my other *knows in me*, nonknowledge of the feminine, in the matrixial borderspace, is impossible by virtue of the transgression itself. This cross-inscription is transmitted by matrixial effects such as empathy, awe, com-passion and compassion, languishing, horror, and maybe telepathy. *However, the transgression itself is a bridging and an accessing to the other already in the feminine.* It is inscribed in a psychical matrixial channel opened to begin with between a future-mother and a prenatal subject-to-be, where it is only by joining the maternal's psyche that the subject-to-be will achieve separation, and where through differentiating-in-coemergence the m/Other caringly knows her *non-I*. Such transgressions transform the frontiers themselves, so that even though *my non-I(s)* are never entirely cognized, they are not entirely cut away from me either. Transgressing with-in-to the feminine with-in borderlinking with-in-to the other is in itself a kind of knowledge transcribed.

Antigone: Beauty and the Impossible Knowledge of/from Death in Life

Before taking this idea of the matrixial feminine difference further and drawing out some of its aesthetic consequences, I would like to add to the picture the figure of Antigone from Lacan's seminar on *Ethics* in 1959–1960, an addition inspired by a strange allusion Lacan makes to her when he mentions Tiresias once more in 1972. There the impossible transgression of the frontiers between maleness and femaleness, and the impossibility of extracting knowledge of/from/on the feminine, are associated with another transgression and another impossibility: the transgression of the frontiers between life and death and the impossibility of knowing about death in life. Let us first make resonate together two passages where Lacan briefly and enigmatically links the tragic transgression to death both to the mystery of the feminine and to the aesthetic experience:

> You have satisfied me, little man. You have understood what was needed. Go on, from being stunned [*étourdit*] there is not too much, for it to return to you in the afternoon and after being half-said [*après midit*]. Thanks to the hand that will respond to Antigone who is called the child, you call it, the same that can tear you apart from what I—feminine and sphinx like—prophesy [*sphynge*] as my *not-all*, you will even be able toward evening to make yourself the equal of Tiresias, and like him, from having been made the Other, to divine what I have said to you.[14]

The second passage is introduced by Lacan's claim that "the question of the beautiful can only be found at this level as operating at a limit. Even in Immanuel Kant's time it is the form of the human body that is presented to us as the limit." Lacan then asks:

> . . . is it the same image that constitutes a barrier to the Other-thing that lies beyond? That which lies beyond is not simply the relationship to the second death. . . . There is also the libido . . . the only moment of jouissance that man knows occurs at the site where phantasms are produced, phantasms that represent to us the same barrier as far as access to jouissance is concerned, the barrier where everything is forgotten. I should like to introduce here, as a parallel to the function of the beautiful, another function . . . a sense of shame. The omission of this barrier, which prevents the direct experience of that which is to be found at the center of sexual union, seems to me to be at the origin of all kinds of questions that cannot be answered, including notably the matter of feminine sexuality.[15]

What associates Tiresias and Antigone together is a conjunction of beauty that blinds, the limits of feminine sexuality, the limits of death, and the impossibility of inscribing the transgressions of these limits as knowledge—an impossibility that in fact turns the death-drive itself into a feminine *not-all/not-whole* issue. Both figures have transgressed the frontiers of the laws of nature—transgressing the natural corporeal limit between the sexes in the case of Tiresias and choosing death over life in the case of Antigone. Thus, in associating such a transgression into death with the enigma of the feminine, Lacan reanimates a mythological relation that traverses cultures and centuries—the relation of death to the feminine—and locates the *aesthetic* effect of "the passage to the second death" in the domain of the feminine as the beautiful. This also qualifies the relationships that both "woman" and death are bearing witness to as "impossible."

The aesthetic dimension arises in *The Ethics of Psychoanalysis* via the question: What is the surface that allows the emergence of "images of passion"? The extraordinary passion that transports death into life and impels life toward death arises, says Lacan, from some contact with that which *is*, the unique, the irreducible, and irreplaceable, with that which has no substitute and cannot be exchanged. Beauty enters the picture through the idea of relations to the irreplaceable. A disappearance in appearance creates beauty's effect. The effect of beauty results from the *rapport* of the subject to the "horizon of life" from traversing to "the second death." From Antigone's point of view, life "can only be lived or thought about, from the place of that limit where her life is already lost, where she is already on the other side. But from that place she can see it and live it in the form of something already lost."[16] This limit, detached from historical time, is a source of creation ex nihilo.

If the surface of passion captures such a unique value to make an image of it, this image creates a barrier that blocks the subject from traversing to the other side, and "the effect of beauty is the effect of blindness"—blindness to the other side, blindness as a castrating schism. The function of the beautiful is precisely "to reveal to us the site of man's relationship to his own death, and to reveal it to us in a blinding flash only."[17] The beautiful is a limit of a sphere that we can only approach from the outside, a phenomenological limit that allows us to reflect on what is behind it. "Outrage" is the term that implies, according to Lacan, the crossing of some invisible line, which allows beauty to join with desire. "Outrage" whose meaning is "to go out or beyond [*aller outre, outrepasser*]," is the aesthetic effect of Antigone. This "most strange and most profound of effects" arises in the limit zone *in-between*-life-and-death, where "a fate" is enacted and a death is "lived by anticipation, a death that crosses over into the sphere of life, a life that moves into the realm of death. . . . The glow of beauty coincides with the moment of transgression." The aesthetic question engages the beauty-ideal, which operates at a limit materialized and represented in art by the human body. The human body, "the envelope of all possible phantasms of human desire" is that barrier which transports "a *rapport* of the human being with its second death," and in doing so blocks the passage to it.[18] Beauty, in the form and image of the human body, is the ultimate barrier in our movement toward the Other-thing "beyond"—to be understood not only as a "second death," but also as "supplementary femininity," because this barrier is also what keeps us from a direct apprehension of "sexual *rapport*," which, as we have seen, is feminine.

It is in the domain of aesthetics that the frontier that separates the human being from death converges with the frontier that separates the human being from the feminine. In the phallic structure the figure that transgresses them is sacrificed to death or blindness. From a matrixial angle we cannot speak, in the dimension of the feminine, of separation, but rather of separation-in-jointness whose risks and wonders are beyond the phallic scope in which the act of creation concerns the individual with its presence/absence, subject/object, and interior/exterior dichotomies. A matrixial transgression operates in a copoietic psychical borderspace shared with several others from the start. Thus, the human body with-in the feminine is not the last barrier between us and the Other-beyond, but is, rather, the passage to a matrixial other. Therefore, the question of sacrifice moves to the margins in the matrix to make place for the question of witnessing as withnessing: wit(h)nessing.

Antigone incarnates the death-drive, and Lacan adds that she incarnates the desire of the Other linked to the desire of the mother, which is the origin of every desire, "the founding desire," which in this case is also "a criminal desire" because it was incestuous. Transgression is thus fatally linked to and binding with the death-drive, incest, and the desire of the mother. Antigone's transgression is her fate in the sense that it is a result of "the crime," which should be understood as the infliction of death or incest by one's ancestors, by someone else on someone else, played at the horizon of the subject's existence and thus being a part of what allowed the subject's coming into life.

At the center of Lacan's argument lies his interpretation of Antigone's idea concerning "having been born in the same womb . . . and having been related to the same father," an interpretation that leads him to say that the heart of the matter is the uniqueness of the brother.[19] In so referring to Antigone's hinting at the maternal womb, Lacan is folding the womb into the phallus/castration stratum. Being born of the same womb is equated with being of the same father and leads to paying the price of the parental crimes of incest or killing by traversing beyond the human chain of exchange. The specificity of this conjunction results in Lacan's representation of the brother, for whose memory Antigone is willing to die, as an incarnation of the idea of the unexchangeable One. The matrixial prism conveys a different interpretation of Antigone's referring to the womb and a supplementary value to the figure of the brother. Transgression is still linked to the death-drive, incest, and the desire of the mother, but this linkage itself is transformed and with it the meaning of each of these concepts in the feminine. To elucidate this I will first elaborate further the matrixial sphere, which will subsequently allow me to locate another conjunction between Tiresias and Antigone in the *transgression with-in-to the feminine.*

The Impossibility of Not-Transgressing in the Matrixial Sphere

The matrix is an unconscious borderspace of simultaneous co-emergence and co-fading of the *I* and uncognized *non-I*—or partial-subjects or unknown others linked to me—neither fused nor rejected, which produces, shares, and transmits joint, hybrid, and diffracted objects via conductible borderlinks. The matrixial is modeled on a certain perception of feminine/prenatal borderlinking where the womb is conceived of as a *shared* psychical *borderspace* in which *differentiation-in-co-emergence, separation-in-jointness,* and *distance-in-proximity* are continuously reattuned by *metramorphosis* created by and further creating—together with matrixial affects—*relations-without-relating* on the borders of presence and absence, subject and object, among subjects and partial-subjects, between me and the stranger, and between partial-objects, partial-subjects, and relational objects/subjects up to the creation of shareable *transjects.* Co-emerging and co-fading *I(s)* and *non-I(s)* interlace their borderlinks in metramorphosis.

Metramorphosis is a process of intra-psychical and inter-psychical as well as trans-individual exchange, transformation, and affective "communication" between/with-in several matrixial entities. It is a passage through which the affected events, materials, and modes of becoming infiltrate and diversify onto nonconscious margins of the symbolic through/by subsymbolic webs. In a joint and "several" (not One, not multiple) marginal trans-subjective awareness, perceived boundaries dissolve to become new boundaries; forms are transgressed; borderlines surpassed and transformed to become thresholds; conductible borderlinks are conceived, transformed, and dissolved. Contingent transgressive borderlinks and a borderspace of swerve and encounter emerge as a feminine sex-difference and as a creative instance that engraves traces that are revealed/invented in wit(h)ness-in-differentiation. Relations-without-relating transform the uncognized other and me and turn both of us into partial-subjects—still uncognized but unthinkingly known to each other (prior to thought) and matrixially knowing each other—in subjectivity-as-encounter, where no other is an absolute separate Other.

Metramorphosis is a co-poietic activity in a web. It "remembers" swerves (originary differentiation in the realm of affects) and "rapports," bifurcations and relations. It remembers operations of borderlinking that inscribe the affective traces of jouissance and trauma that take place in encounters, and it transfers the knowledge of these events with-in-to the feminine. Via art's metramorphic activity, these traces are transmitted into culture and open its boundaries.

The matrixial designates a difference located, in its originary formation, in the linkage to invisible female corporeal specificity, to the archaic enveloping outside that is also an inside: the womb. However, by matrix I do not intend an "organ" or an "origin," but a complex apparatus modeled on this site of a female/prenatal *encounter* that puts in *rapport* any human becoming-subject-to-be, male or female, with female bodily specificity and the mother-to-be's encounter-events, trauma, jouissance, phantasy, and desire.

Through metramorphosis each matrixial encounter engenders its *jouissance*, traumas, pictograms, and phantasms on the affected psychic level, and channels death-drive oscillations, libidinal flow, and their affected traces in *several* partners, conjointly but differently, in com-passion. Traces circulate in a trans-subjective zone by matrixial affects and nonconscious strings and threads that disperse different aspects of traumatic events between the *I(s)* and *non-I(s)*. In the matrixial psychical sphere, "my" traces will be trans-scribed—pluri-scribed and cross-scribed—in others, thus my others will process these events for me. Thus, female bodily specificity is the site, physically, imaginatively, and symbolically, where a feminine difference emerges, where a "woman" is interlaced as a figure that is not confined to the one-body, but is the "webbing" of matrixial webs and metramorphic borderlinks between several subjects, who by virtue of such a webbing become partial. Metramorphosis, as a carrier of such originary difference and of its transforming potentiality, induces instances of coemergence and cofading *as* meaning and trans-scription as unforgettable memory of oblivion. In the matrixial borderspace a specific aesthetic field comes into light with metramorphosis as an aesthetic process with ethical implications.

The feminine/prenatal incest is here a necessary transgression, and it is not at all measured by, or compared to, perverse or genital-phallic Oedipal incest. The feminine/prenatal one is a primordial psychical field of trans-scription and of transgressions between trauma and jouissance, phantasy, and desire in severalty: between several partial-subjects—of trans-subjectivity and even *transjectivity*. Unlike the incest Lacan makes allusion to in Antigone's case (the Oedipal/paternal), in the matrixial sphere all mothers are *incestuous in a nonphallic and non-Oedipal sense*, inasmuch as the intrauterine relations between future mother and future subject are by definition incestuous. Because of the highly psychotic potentiality of this prebirth nonprohibited incest for the phallic subjectivizing processes, this m/Other-incest was deeply silenced, not even excluded from the symbolic (from which it could have returned as its repressed and produce an-other desire) but marginalized as unthought of and foreclosed. Whatever of the matrixial twilight zone that did get elaborated in the phallus was subjugated to its order, where it was regulated as a question of bringing children into a heterosexual framework where objects-women are exchanged in "the Name of the Father."

Julia Kristeva believes that giving birth must emerge as psychosis in culture.[20] I suggest that this is so only in a symbolic articulated within the phallic paradigm. Evocations and irruptions of the feminine/prenatal encounters are not psychotic. They only become psychotic when they have no symbolic access. Already before birth the subject-to-be aspires in phantasy and contacts "traumatically" a woman in whose trauma, phantasy, and desire he or she already participates.[21] The jouissance that spurts on the level of prebirth, nonprohibited incest, and the links between the trauma and phantasy of the becoming-subject-to-be (*I*), male or female, and the trauma, phantasy, and desire of the "woman" as its becoming-archaic-m/Other-to-be (*non-I*), both of them in their status of partial-subjects *and* partial-objects for each other, constitute a feminine cluster borderlinking *in-between several* participants while the link to the phallus is, however, always maintained through the woman's desire that is both phallic and matrixial, and where archaic traces of contact with the female body are inscribed as archaic trauma and jouissance, and are revealed in the phantasy of both participants of the encounter (males and females).

Female subjects have a double access to the matrixial sphere in the Real because they experience the womb both as an archaic out-side and past site, out of chronological time—which is true for males as well—*and* as an in-side and future site, whether or not they are mothers—that may (or may not) become present. While the out-and-past-side/site belongs both to the female and the male, the in-and-future-side/site belongs to the female alone. Male subjects are more radically split from this particular archaic time-and-space of inside and future because their *rapport* to it in the Real stays forever in the archaic *totally outside* and *too early* that is forever too late to access. *Women have some privileged access to a paradoxical time of future-past and a paradoxical space of outside-inside.* Men however are in contact with this time and space, as women are too, by compassionate matrixial jointing-in-difference with the m/Other, with others and with particular art presences—whether art-objects, art-actions, art-gestures, music—as transjects. That is: *As an aesthetic filter with its ethical perspective the matrixial apparatus serves both men and women.* Different nonconscious lanes that are opened toward and from femaleness are not limited to women only, although they do carry a special resonance for women when they treasure and screen their own bodily traces.

In "The Uncanny," Freud suggested that prenatal experience and womb phantasms participate in the aesthetic experience.[22] In "The Matrixial Gaze," I have isolated these phantasms and developed the idea of a matrixial complex as a specific nonphallic psychical apparatus.[23] Even though Freud himself did not fold the earlier phantasy inside the later, in psychoanalytic literature the phantasy of the maternal matrix is generally *excluded* from any particular considerations by *inclusion* within the "castration" complex, and it does not stand for any different psychical mechanism.[24] In my view, these two complexes ("matrixial" and "castration") constitute different psychical dimensions, heterogeneous to one another. In the matrixial dimension, feminine difference does not stem from masculine difference.

Matrixial awareness engenders a disturbing desire for jointness *with* a foreign world, with the unknown other, the uncognized, with a stranger who by definition is never a total stranger in the feminine when unthinkingly known in a nonconceptual way. Matrixial awareness channels the subject's desire toward the beauty and the pain, the phantasy and the trauma of others. My awareness cannot master you via your traces in my psyche; there is neither joining without separation nor separating without joining. The desire to join-in-difference and differentiate-in-co-emerging with the other does not promise any peace and harmony because joining is first of all joining with-in the other's trauma that echoes backward to my archaic traumas: joining the other matrixially is always joining the m/Other and risking a mental regression just until the maternal corpo-real matrix. A matrixial desire can generate dangerous encounters, it can become pathological, and it proposes no fixed settlement, no homogenous mixture but returning and hybridity, im-pureness, a continual contemplation and fear of unabolished difference in jointness. A matrixial love is care-full and com-passionate, yet painful because of the inevitable processing of the other's trauma and because of the inevitable participation in the transformation and opening of boundaries for transmission or reception, fragmentation, contracting and withdrawal, and of what I call "severalization": dispersal and sharing of the already joint-several yet partial and fragmented trans-subjective memory of oblivion. A matrixial loss by definitive cut is, in this psychical zone, a horror beyond its scope. This is the horror Antigone experienced in her reference to the womb that carried both herself and her brother: it is the matrixial prenatal incestuous co-emergence in a different time, beyond time, with the brother that is fatally traumatized. And this transitive encounter-event as a trauma has no common measure with the effects of the paternal incest.

Thus, putting this feminine difference beyond a schism and out of reach even for a masculine figure is an impossibility in the matrixial borderspace, and likewise, a total disjoining of living death by anticipation from the meaning of life itself is another kind of impossibility because life from the onset is linked to *nonlife*. This impossibility of not-transgressing *life and nonlife* in the matrixial sphere demands its price and originates its beauty; it has its solaces and moments of grace, but it is profoundly tragic. I therefore propose to locate Lacan's claim that we are far from approaching Tiresias' position in the phallic zone only. From a matrixial point of view, however, we have never been closer to such a position in the domain of aesthetics and ethics than we are today, inasmuch as we are carrying in this second half of the twentieth century enormous traumatic weight of/for the other in wit(h)nessing, and certain contemporary art practices are clearing the path to a better apprehension of the matrixial alliances that confront the limits of shareability in trauma and jouissance.

Meaning as a Transgression With-In-To the Trauma of the Other

We can now suggest understanding Tiresias as an evocation of the possibility of transgressing between male and female with-in a matrixial feminine dimension where Other and Outside are fatally engaged with *I* and inside, with no symbiosis nor foreclosure, where Other and Outside are knowable in/by *com-passing* between me and inside with others and outside—others of either sex; alive, not-yet in life, or dead. In other words, transgression between male and female is not a passage to the radical Other nor a transcending to the ultimately exterior, but a metramorphosing *with*-in-out of selves *with*-in-to the feminine that passes along the threads that turn the inside into the outside and the outside into the inside.

Transgression with-in-to the feminine is not a jump beyond a frontier but an access to the surplus beyond, and thus a transformation of the limits themselves with regard to my affective access to the question of the death of the other and the death of my other's Other. Metramorphosis opens the frontiers and turns them into thresholds. Transgression becomes an ontogenetic memory and meaning of sharing in distance-in-proximity with-in the trauma of the other. Meaning becomes a transgression with-in-to others via borderlinking. Both partial-subjects and transjects transform and are transformed by one another differently in a reciprocity without symmetry, creating joint compassionate and eroticized aerials to be further shaped by following the traces of their further affective irradiation.

We know about the crimes at the source of Antigone's desire, we know who their authors are, we know who suffers for them and who scarifies herself, but we do not know, in terms of the psyche, *whose trauma it is*. If we rethink

Antigone with the notion of trauma, and we ask the question of where its ineffaceable affected traces hide, the matrixial perspective takes us onto further new turns. What is at stake here is the psychic trauma of others with-in myself: by force of their matrixial alliance with the *I*, the *non-I(s)* are already, from the outset of any encounter, traumatic to the *I*. I am a wit(h)ness to traumas I did not witness, like that of the death of others I was not in direct contact with—a death that, however, has traumatized my *non-I(s)*. The beautiful, accessed via artwork in our era (and I emphasize again our era since we are living through massive effects of such a transitive trauma captivated by some artwork), carries and produces new possibilities for affective apprehending of such a proximity of a double-distance wit(h)nessing. We are experiencing the uncognized *non-I* by/in its difference as traumatized and traumatizing. I propose to understand Emmanuel Levinas' enigmatic claim that the Other in its vulnerability is traumatic to me in such a matrixial prism.[25] Therefore, the experience of reaching out to the affect-affectivity of the trauma of others in each encounter-event, while being aesthetic, therapeutic, and wounding is above all ethical. The aesthetic is therefore—while indirectly also ethical at the level of the proto-ethical—the experience of reaching out to the affect-activity of the trauma of others via artwork. The aesthetic is the trauma's transformed affectability in wit(h)nessing in/by art, beyond time, and in different sites and spaces, yet it has ethical and therapeutic consequences. Both the aesthetical and the ethical are therefore a healing potentiality offered by wit(h)nessing. The beautiful is that which offers whatever succeeds—as object, subject, or event—to suggest reaffectation-as-redistribution of traumatic traces of encounters with the *non-I* and of the trans-connected *non-I*.

Matrixial transgression of/by affect creates instances of aesthetic transjectivity with-in-to the feminine inasmuch as such transitivity is inseparable from its archaic form where originary prenatal incestuous encounter-Thing with-in the m/Other, that is noncriminally incestuous, is hidden. An archaic *wit(h)ness-Thing* is capsulated in this encounter. The archaic encounter, usually considered inaccessible to symbolic knowledge, is hereby considered the prototype of trans-subjective knowledge. Painting captures in producing or produces in capturing knowledge of a wit(h)ness-Thing. A possibility of ethically acknowledging the Real of the almost-other emerges in transferential wit(h)nessing, when someone else apprehends *with-in and with-out* the subject his or hers nonconscious matrixial sites by co-responding to them and joining in the circulating of their psychic traces.

Suddenly, in metramorphosing with the artwork, one might find oneself in proximity to a possible trauma, as if one had always been potentially sliding on its margins. One is threatened by its potential proximity yet also compelled by a mysterious "promise of happiness" (Friedrich Nietzsche's expression concerning beauty), a promise to re-find in jointness what faded away and was dispersed on condition of matrixially encountering the *non-I* because on the matrixial level one's own desire is the effect of others' trauma no less than of one's own. By such an effect of beauty, the feminine borderlinking does not qualify as dwelling beyond a barrier, a frontier. Rather, in-between pure absence and pure sensibility, it is a surplus of fragility embedded with-in co-affectation, and it makes sense as a transformation on the level of the limit. The artwork extricates the trauma of the matrixial other out of "pure absence" or "pure sensibility," out of its time-less-ness into lines of time; and the effect of beauty is to allow wit(h)nessing with non-visible events of encounter to emerge inside the field of vision and affect one.

Metramorphic beauty is coaffectation's obscure trail, skirting on sensation's edges and becoming visible when a passion based on marks of shareability becomes transgressive again and labors anew in com-passion. When a world, internal and external, from which the artist has to transfer and to which she has to transmit, is shared with-in-difference via artwork, this world is being brought into presence at the same instant that the work awakens its strange beauty and pain. A potentiality to make a difference with-in-for others becomes beauty when the artwork vibrates—and the spectator attracts to herself and transmits, back to it or onward to others—availability for co-affectation. No content, no form, and no image can guarantee that an event of co-affectation will take place via a particular artwork for particular viewers and that beauty will arise to attract a matrixial response. But when beauty arises, a matrixial co-affectability hides behind the form and the image, and we can think of it as sprouting, overflowing, and proceeding from shareable eroticized antennae of the psyche, acting all over the synaesthetic field and channeled by the scopic drive inside the field of vision.

The matrixial aesthetic effect attests that imprints are interwoven between several subjects, that something that branches off from others engraving traces in me and relinquishing me (or mentally unbearable to me) is yet accessing others, and that we are sharing erotic antennae but processing different re(a)sonating minimal sense from them. These erotic antennae register what returns from others as traces and transmit a centerless matrixial gaze.

The process of making art involves sensing a potential co-emergence and bringing into being objects or events that sustain it and transmit its inscription. Art evokes further instances of trans-subjectivity and makes almost impossible new borderlinking available, out of elements and links already available in part, but that need to be transformed in ways that cannot be thought of prior to the process of art itself. Trauma determines the trajectory of what is, out of art, a forever no-time. The beautiful links the time of too-early to the time of too-late, and plants it in historical time.[26] Metramorphosing a traumatic encounter is extracting times of too-early and too-late out of indifference on-to with-in-visibility with-in-difference, when new affects wake up archaic ones from beyond the walls of foreclosure. An aesthetic that is bending toward the ethical is the transform-ability of the no-time of an archaic encounter between several *I(s)* and *non-I(s)* in new co-emergence and co-fading.

The female body makes a sense based on knowledge of/from a body different to the male body. Lacan undoubtedly neglected this in-body difference as sub-knowledge when he claimed that knowledge of the "supplementary" femininity is out of reach for women just in the same way as it is inaccessible for men.

Even though the matrixial filter transgresses the boundaries of the body-in-identity as male and female and provides meaning to a variety of shifting traces with-in feminine borderlinking beyond gender identifications, and even though the matrixial alliance concerns any human being, the specific reference to the female body remains pertinent. The trail of co-affectivity transgresses the affective individual limits not to become another quality but as an access to others and through forms that will *follow* and will temporarily "capture" the excess, if a matrixial alliance will be in-formed.

The effect of beauty indicates for us, then, not only the place of relationships to one's own death, but also the *rapport* of the *I* to the matrixial partner before life and to the death of unknown others, a death that traumatized either my self or my others and for whom, through care-full com-passion, I am processing affective memory they cannot process alone, and I am digesting and transforming mental traces or inscriptions. When something that cannot be looked at, that blinds us, arises at the horizon of visibility, a form of death-drive is embodied in the phallic zone, so that any apparition of a point of emergence can only be represented as a "want-to-be." But we can discuss now, in this same experience, the representation of the point of emergence as a co-poietic birth as well, when with every metramorphosis, interconnected traces of the encounter with the archaic m/Other as a point of emergence are re-evoked-in-transformation, leading within the aesthetic field, through the *sharing of trauma and phantasy,* to the ethical position of *co-response-ability with-to* uncognized others. An *impossibility of not-sharing* comes forth in the transgression with-in-to the feminine in a way that holds some ethical implications: I have an alliance with others *even before* any full cognizing of difference is possible. In the feminine-matrixial *there is an Other of the other.*[27] But this other is an other-in-jointness. Antigone's brother who is the unique One in the phallic dimension is the partial-subject of a *unique jointness* in a matrixial transgression. This is attested to by the reference to the womb in the text.

The transgression with-in-to the feminine allows us to think the phenomenon of unconscious transmission between the sexes and between different generations and periods beyond life and presence in time and place.[28] The matrixial gaze conducts traces of events without witnesses and passes them on to witnesses who were not there, to what I have called wit(h)nesses with-out events.[30] The viewer, and this partially includes the artist in her unconscious viewer position, is the wit(h)ness with-out event par excellence. The viewer will take in traces of the event in continuing to weave metramorphic borderlinks to others, present and archaic, cognized and uncognized, future and past.

Borderlinking to the Other Sex by a Feminine-Matrixial Differential Potentiality

I can now draw further guidelines for reading-together the myth of Tiresias and the tragedy of Antigone. Both Tiresias and Antigone represent transgressing with-in-to the feminine. In the phallic stratum of subjectivization, if death and the feminine are the enigma of which we can know nothing, the transgression to the other side via the process of art has a particular aesthetic effect because the artist bears witness to a process otherwise inaccessible—to its "own disappearance from the signifying chain"—and she can articulate such "non-knowledge" of/in the Real as a "dynamic value."[30] In the matrixial stratum the artist positions herself on an-other's sides, joining-in-difference the others' traumas and webbing passages from this wit(h)nessing. We can now view the tragic quest of the figure trespassing into "second death" as fatally linked not only to the One and Unique brother, but also as having to bear an unbearable total subtraction from a joint matrixial configuration that cannot bear such a subtraction because it can only bear fading-out and fragmentations but not any total cuts. A subtraction (rather than contraction yet not just separation) of *non-I* from shareability, and an extinction of possible borderlinking to the other in a matrixial borderspace, must be paid in "your body"[31] as the body of the artist in which other bodies are cross-inscribed.

What in Antigone's argument is waiting to be heard and com-passioned is the suffering from the tearing apart of her principal partner-in-difference up until now separated-in-jointness from her into total separateness. If the almost-impossible knowledge of the thing-event concerns the originary feminine *rapport*, it is not death in itself that inflicts the horrible cut in the matrixial web, but the passage to a bestiality that threatens to blow up and explode this sphere all together into separate pieces. For life and death are constituted in the psyche as already human even when beyond reach of human-symbolic exchange or communication, even at the corpo-real level. Human body is not animal body. Nonhuman bestiality inflicted on my *non-I(s)* diminishes the metramorphic processes and can also abolish the capacity of the matrixial web for reabsorption of loss, for transference of memory, and for processing mourning. Antigone's private death is less a price for her to pay than living through an irremediable explosion of the matrixial borderspace. She literally acknowledges the corpo-real source of this psychical space—the shareable maternal womb.

Why is Tiresias related by the "feminine impossible *rapport*" to Antigone? What is waiting to be comprehended in Tiresias' story is that passing into the female and back again is not either imposing on her a male filter, mastering the experience by masculine knowledge, confusing it, or totally foreclosing a femaleness, but a specific kind of superposition-in-difference, or trans-position of maleness and femaleness. Such a superposition enables Tiresias to extract hidden sub-knowledge of the other-sex into shareable co-poietic meaning. Tiresias delivers a promise of a behind-appearance access to the other-sex body. We might tune-in-difference our body with-in the corporeal sub-knowledge of the other sex, in keeping to our own sex, with no relation to gender identification.

If feminine originary sex-difference is an enigma of which we can know something though the matrixial prism, and if this prism opens to us the contact with time-spaces of nonlife, the transgression with-in-to the feminine via the process of art has a particular aesthetic effect because in transmitting subknowledge from a site of transgression in a borderspace that contacts the surplus by borderlinking the artist can bear wit(h)ness and articulate subknowledge of/from the sex of the other. "The kind of Tiresias' fate" that is "impossible" for us in the phallic stratum is also a matrixial "promise of happiness" even if such a *beauty* is tragic. The artwork is a promise to deliver what, up to the appearance in a specific artwork of a particular encounter, was a nonknowledge concerning the transposition with the other. Tiresias reveals-while-hiding the other sex in a superposition only as long as distance-in-proximity is kept, difference is held in suspense within jointness, and the access to a surplus is captured for a while. But what I want to emphasize is that this kind of transgression between the sexes is a transgression with-in-to the feminine—in a matrixial borderspace—whatever its direction is.

Thus, the function of the beautiful is to reveal instances of co-birthing and co-fading and articulate their subknowledge when an-other surplus is suddenly distinguished out in the artist's matrixial borderspace. What is captured and given form at the end of such a trajectory with-in the time of "too late" as time of a traumatic encounter with-in the other and with the other's Other is no other than what has always been experienced as such in the time of the "too early," waiting for an almost-impossible articulation in a time of suspension-anticipation. Thus, a dynamic that indexes a difference in the Real is co-knowledged in with(h)nessing to become shareable again on some levels and for the first time on other levels, via the process of art.

Notes

1. Jacques Lacan, "Guiding Remarks for a Congress on Feminine Sexuality," in *Feminine Sexuality: Jacques Lacan and the* école freudienne, trans. Jacqueline Rose, ed.

Juliet Mitchell and Jacqueline Rose (New York: Norton, 1982), pp. 89–90. The original quote appears in Jacques Lacan, "Propos directives pour un congres sur la sexualité féminine," in *Écrits* (Paris: Seuil, 1966), p. 728.

2. Sigmund Freud, "The Uncanny," *The Standard Edition of the Complete Psychological Works of Sigmund Freud*, trans. and ed. James Strachey, vol. 17 (London: Hogarth Press, 1955), pp. 217–252. For Emmanuel Levinas, future time is feminine. See Bracha L. Ettinger and Emmanuel Levinas, *Time Is the Breath of the Spirit* (Oxford, UK: MOMA, 1993), and "The Feminine/Pre-Natal Weaving in the Matrixial Subjectivity-as-Encounter," *Psychoanalytic Dialogues*, vol. 7, no. 3 (1997).

3. A wordplay on the word *homme*—"man" in French.

4. Jacques Lacan, "L'Etourdit," *Silicet*, no. 4 (1973), p. 24. All references to this text are translated into English by Jack Stone.

5. Ibid., p. 24.

6. Lacan, "Propos directifs," p. 735. According to Lacan, women in their sexuated position vis-à-vis the phallic universal are situated between "pure absence and pure sensibility." Whereas men make of the phallic referent the universal supporting ground for their phantasm built to compensate for the deficiency of a primordial lack, a split from the Real, from the body, and from the Other, for women there is an extra-territory beyond the phallus.

7. Ibid., p. 733.

8. Thus reducing the domain of the phallus in the determination of the subject. See Ettinger, "Matrix and Metamorphosis," *differences*, vol. 3, no. 4 (1992).

9. Behind "the mask of womanliness," she is "either . . . castrated (lifeless, incapable of pleasure) or (as) wishing to castrate," said Joan Rivière. See "Womanliness as Masquerade," in *Formations of Fantasy*, ed. Victor Burgin, James Donald, and Cora Kaplan (London: Routledge, 1989), p. 54. Rivière's concept of "masquerade" concerns hiding female "factual" castration and her castrating wishes, and I therefore consider it to be a phallic concept.

10. Lacan, "L'Etourdit," p. 30.

11. Jacques Lacan, *Le Seminair, Livre XX: Encore* (Paris: Seuil, 1975), pp. 17, 35, and 34.

12. Jacques Lacan, *Ou pire*, unedited seminar, March 8, 1972. Lacan is quoting the poet Henri Michaux.

13. For more on this idea, see my "The With-In-Visible Screen," in *Inside the Visible: An Elliptical Traverse of 20th Century Art in, of and from the Feminine*, ed. Catherine de Zegher (Cambridge, MA: MIT Press, 1996), pp. 89–113.

14. Lacan, "L'Etourdit," p. 25.

15. Jacques Lacan, *The Ethics of Psychoanalysis 1959–1960*, trans. Dennis Potter (London: Routledge, 1992), p. 298.

16. Ibid., pp. 318 and 280.

17. Ibid., p. 281 (translation modified).

18. Ibid., pp. 281, 295, and 298.

19. Ibid., p. 279.

20. Julia Kristeva, *Desire in Language*, trans. and ed. Leon Roudiez (New York: Columbia University Press, 1980). Among the psychoanalysts who have elaborated on

prenatal life we can mention R. D. Laing, *The Voice of Experience* (New York: Pantheon, 1982), and Sandor Ferenczi, *Thalassa: A Theory of Genitality* (London: Karnac Books, 1989).

21. This point is necessary for the understanding of women's claim over their pregnant body and their legitimate rights to keep or abort their fetus. From the point of view of the matrixial, speculating on a fetus' "needs" separately from the mother-to-be's desires, as some anti-abortion militants are doing when trying to oppress women and limit their rights by means of the phallic imaginary, makes no sense. This imaginary posits the fetus mistakenly as a "separate" entity with separate desires that they then pretend to defend against the mother's desire. I emphasize that the feminine-matrixial configuration supports a woman's full response-ability for any event occurring with-in her own not-One corpo-reality and it disqualifies phallic regulations of it. The fetus is not a separate entity. It differentiates itself only in co-emerging with a woman's body-phantasy-desire complexity, and its "fate" is inseparable from this complexity.

22. Freud, "The Uncanny," pp. 244 and 248.

23. Bracha L. Ettinger, *The Matrixial Gaze* (Leeds, UK: Feminist Arts & Histories Network, 1995).

24. In several footnotes Freud continuously claimed that we must see the difference between birth-separation and other types of separations. Freud indirectly addressed Otto Rank's idea of the trauma of birth. For Freud this separation concerns the pre-Oedipal period only; whatever is formulated as intra-uterine complex, with its distinct apparatus, disappears by inclusion in the castration complex with the solution of the Oedipus complex. Yet, because girls are not supposed to follow the same route as boys (boys move from Oedipus to castration, says Freud, while girls move from castration to Oedipus, and because for men the pre-Oedipal territory "dissolves" while for girls it persists in the unconscious), a matrixial complex should, I argue, be treated as a feminine sex-difference issue that concerns female and male subjects, with a special supplementary implication for female subjects. See my "The Feminine/Pre-Natal Weaving."

25. Levinas in conversation with the author. Unpublished, 1991.

26. The "too early and too late," is an expression used by the poet Paul Celan to describe poetry. For Gilles Deleuze, the time of "too late" is related to aesthetics.

27. Lacan has endlessly repeated through many years of teaching, the idea that "there is no Other of the Other." I suggest that this is limited to the phallic field and that in the matrixial sphere *there is an Other of the Other*. In his very late writing, when discussing James Joyce (*Le Sinthome*, unedited seminar from 1975–1976), Lacan enigmatically delimits this statement only to the phenomenon of jouissance. Saying as usual "there is no Other of the Other," he adds, "at least there is no *jouissance* of the Other of the Other." I propose that he hereby intends the possibility of certain exceptions to his usual claim. Such exception may concern a beyond-the-phallus zone, such as the matrixial.

28. The question of the possibility of such a transmission via art, and particularly women's art, is a major theme in Griselda Pollock's recent writings. See, for example, Griselda Pollock, "Gleaning in History or Coming after/behind the Reapers: *The Feminine, the Stranger and the Matrix in the Work and Theory of Bracha Lichtenberg Ettinger*," chap. 15 in *Generations and Geographies in the Visual Arts* (London: Routledge, 1996).

29. See Dori Laub, "An Event without a Witness: Truth, Testimony and Survival," in *Testimony: Crises of Witnessing in Literature, Psychoanalysis, and History,* ed. Shoshana Felman and Dori Laub (New York: Routledge, 1992), pp. 75–92.

30. Lacan, *The Ethics of Psychoanalysis*, p. 295.

31. Jean-Francois Lyotard, "L'Anamnèse," in *Doctor and Patient*, ed. Marketta Seppälä (Pori Art Museum Publication, Porin Taidemuseo, 1997), p. 109.

11

Antigone

Limit and Horizon

Julia Kristeva

1. Who are you Antigone? A child (*pais, néais*), a girl (*koré*), the offspring (*gennêmo*) of Oedipus, a fiancé (*nymph*), a virgin (*parthenos*), finally and only called the latter by your lover, Haemon, when you have achieved the deathly state he desires? Haemon, who is your cousin, but also the son of your enemy, Creon. The latter who suspects you yourself of being a man: "I swear I am no man and she the man," exclaims your maternal uncle, this tyrant, whose reason you oppose by defying his edict: the interdiction against burying your brother, Polyneices.[1] This makes you an outlaw, a criminal, a rebel, certainly, but you are no warrior: you bear no relation to Joan of Arc, nor to Corneille's heroines of duty. You offer a wild resistance to tyranny, which inevitably topples the logic of the State, and perhaps even political thought in general in so far as they ignore this "absolute individuality" in which you take up residence and which you claim for your brother. It is here, your sacredness, prepared by the indestructible desire for death, the "divine use" of which does not escape you.

Are you an indomitable loner? Fearless? Rigid, cold, frigid even, if one believes your adversary, Creon, who undoubtedly detests you (although he will end up caving in, collapsing in a sort of pitiful chiasmus, doubly inverted by your annihilation—but for this we will have to wait until the end of the play). "Do not, my son, banish your good sense," Creon warns Haemon, who wants to marry you (a funny idea—you, the virgin fiancée of death!), "since you know that the embrace grows cold when an evil woman shares your bed and home." For Creon you are the girl who "repulses" everyone to the point of having to seek "to marry someone in Death's house" (650ff.).

This chapter was translated by Ella Brians. It was written for this volume and has not been published in French. All foreign words in parentheses were included by the author. French terms in brackets have been included by the translator in cases where no exact English equivalent exists.

But perhaps, Antigone, this view of you is incorrect, and you are, on the contrary, a charitable person who comes to the aid (*ophelein*) of the dead (559–560)? Not to all of them of course—that would be to claim too much. You have your favorite, one of your brothers, which is natural, being as you are the descendents of the incestuous Oedipus and Jocasta. Your favorite is Polyneices, by chance, *Poluneikes,* the one who, as his name indicates, "is full of discord," who delights in attacking his own city, his *father-motherland,* and who is, to speak frankly, an anarchist who would like to destroy his own family. So be it: that does not prevent you from being a charitable person in your own manner, an Ophelia if we hear the Greek word *ophelein* while thinking of Shakespeare; and turned, like her, entirely toward death, a full twenty centuries before she will drown herself for love of Hamlet.

Are you a black Eros compressed into sudden flashes, a "radiant desire" (*imeros enargés*) that enchants the old members of the chorus who are seduced by the "eyes of the girl good to bed" (795)? Does this radiance, however, exist side by side a certain psychic rigidity that you employ to defend yourself from the incestuous relations so prized in Labicides' family? Creon claims that the "savage spirit of a savage father shows itself in this girl" (472), and warns you that "[i]t is the toughest iron baked in the fire to hardness"; that "you may see most shattered, twisted, shivered to fragments" (475). Are you no more than an "unhappy girl . . . disobedient to the royal edict" (375–385), a "little guilty Antigone"? Worse, could you be resistant [*rétive*] to all civilization, crude (*omos*) (471), which is to say wild, inhuman? You are, after all, so cruel to Ismene, your prudent sister, "the one who knows," because in naming her this way your father destined her to wisdom. Enough blindness already in this family . . .

No? Indeed, perhaps not. You think of nothing except Polyneices. You are divided, torn—I would say *cleft*—between the city *and* Hades, the world of Creon *and* that of death, the logic of the political *and* that of your own blood, but if and only if it is the blood of a rebel, of an insurgent, of an instigator of transgressions (the most active of which is obviously murder). And so it is the blood of Polyneices, who has launched a civil war, that claims your loyalty—very well! In one of those oxymorons, whose genius you share with Sophocles, you define yourself as a sister, "a criminal—but a religious one," desiring simply to rest near her brother, "loving him as he loved me," in the purity of a *postmortem* wedding night (*noces*) (74–75). To Creon, who takes your funereal compassion for a kind of hatred and an absence of friendship (*philos*), you retort with another definition of yourself, which will surprise those who do not understand you: "My nature is to join in love (*symphilein*), not hate" (523). And we will no longer accept the word of those romantics who proclaim, from age to age, your mystical antimarriage: poets, feminists, melancholy spirits!

To illustrate this ambiguity between love and death, let us begin with the guard who catches you in your second criminal act, washing and covering

Polyneices' dead body with dust to protect it from the sun, the birds, and the dogs. The brave servant cannot help but sympathizing with you, maybe even rejoicing, despite Creon's edict: "We charged her with what she had done, then and the first time. She did not deny a word of it—to my joy, but to my pain as well" (430–440). His feelings, which are in reality yours in the moment of this act of funereal love, are clearly also shared by the chorus, since it is the mouthpiece of Dionysius himself—in such a way that this first *kommos* of the tragedy that bears your name draws the audience completely into your emotional state, where sadness and exultation ally together only to annul one another. Creon, on the other hand, will not have a right to the empathy expressed in the *kommos* that is consecrated to him at the end of the play. It is you who are the victor, Antigone, and we ask ourselves once again what this might mean.

An unfathomable, indefinable figure; lacking a fixed identity in your very authenticity; you escape yourself, Antigone. I understand that you prefer the obscurity of the underworld, for you are not of this world. Yet, there is nothing of indecision in your evasion: you make the law (*nomos*) for yourself, all alone! In your insolent autonomy as a daughter of Oedipus the transgressor, you know in advance that you are excluded from political justice, which is to say from human norms. But your knowledge (which testifies all the same that you "exist within" this social world, at least in part) does not bother you at all. On the contrary, you persist in your obstinate, invincible, sublime certainty. "She did not deny a word of it" (436); "Yes, I confess; I will not deny my deed" (443). And in doing so, you bewilder Creon, who cannot accept the fact that someone dares to defy the law, not because she is ignorant of it, but precisely in order to meet death in full consciousness: "Did you know the proclamation against your action?" Antigone: "I knew it; of course I did. For it was public" (445ff.).

No, she is not mad, our little Antigone. Or rather, she is mad, but with a madness that reveals a superior logic, limpid and intrinsic, that reveals itself as contagious—perhaps even eternal, universal?

2. Is Antigone the way she is because she is the fruit of incest? And because she suffers the consequences of that incest? And because she brings those consequences to their acme and their tragic end at a time before the customs of the city would come to redefine the scope of these confused passions of the familial clan, and before Plato's *Laws* established, in complete lucidity, a familial and political order that already prefigures our own? Is her story a vestige of the past, good only for the archives of psychoanalysts?

Or rather, is Antigone Antigone because she is a woman? Does her mineral solitude, her deathly desire, and her persistence in the "no" that she launches against good sense reveal specifically feminine traits that serve to permanently corrode the social bond—even more dangerous than the "eternal irony of the community" that Hegel will diagnose?

What then to make of this "no" that she opposes to the laws of Creon? (Is it against his totalitarian abuses or against political good sense? This is an enormous subject that the democrats who specialize in human rights still have not managed to clarify.) Is it a dynamic, prospective, Faustian, or dialectical "no"? Or rather, in revealing the limit where the human exceeds itself and of which the sacred is so fond, does Antigone's defiance condemn itself to prove the existence of the uncompromising death drive, which Freud bequeathed to us with neither sufficient precision nor precautions?

The death drive is not that virile aggressivity that belongs to both sexes, which eroticizes the life and death struggle under the guise of desire, and which provides an inventory of erotic tortures like the one that flows from the pen of the Marquis de Sade, for example, as the ultimate cunning of the Supreme Being, above all when *it* bumps up against the numb toughness of the victims. No, Antigone uncovers a placid energy that cuts the bonds and effects a de-binding [*déliaison*] that annuls identities and differences in order to install the subject, beyond loss, depression, and suffering, in the *pathos of dispassionating*. This suicidal *laissez-faire* is not distinct here from endurance; indifference can flash out even in the midst of care, and the abjection of life can perpetuate itself in an insane disobedience that regenerates the social bond. A blank psychosis? Or the triumph of sublimation at the edge of an originary repression, at the frontier of life, that the speaking individual experiences as a going outside of the self—the limit state of an indivisible identity. Mature, sovereign.

3. Because it is woven of incestuous bonds and overlappings, the world of the Labdacids is dominated by the obsessive quest of the *auto* and the *homo*.[2] But this world does not seem to know the *other*, except as stranger, murderer, or instigator of civil wars. The union of self-birthing between the mother-wife and the son-husband, autoengendering, autoaffection, automutilation: this belongs to, happens within, and depends on the *same* family, the *same* womb, the *same* hand. *Sameness* circulates uninterrupted within the same blood and only reflects itself in reciprocity, producing an inverse image through the reversible kinship relation [*parenté*] between the issue of the same bowels, who share an improbable identity (*autos*) that is mobile, problematic, and virtual. This identity is capable, nevertheless, of going deeper into its own self-discovery, into the permanence of the self, as Antigone does by passing beyond the limits of self-knowledge (*autognotos*) (875), all the way toward that metallic certitude of the self for which Creon begrudges and reproaches her. Sovereignty obtained by means of exclusion (*anti*) is always ready to abolish itself in a sudden annul-

ment of itself, but only in the tragic act, as Antigone does not fail to do by *dying to herself*, strictly speaking. As if she had murdered—always already and in herself—the parent(s) with whom she fatally identifies, and whom she only knows how to rejoin for good in the nuptial tomb (*authentês*, the murderer, would be above all the one who commits the act—murder being the act par excellence—against a parent, the double of oneself, as Nicole Loraux and Louis Gernet recall[3]). But finally, which of her kin does she rejoin, with and through Polyneices and their identitary overlappings?

In this labyrinth of identification-disidentification, the losses and recoveries of the same in the enclosure of "*sameness*" [*mêmeté*], *homo* insists more on the *similarity* than on the identity (*auto*) and digs deeply into the furrow of reversible relationships. On this side, Antigone makes herself exactly equivalent to her brother Polyneices, who in turn is equivalent to his father Oedipus (both being sons of Jocasta); but also to *man* in his *virility* because in seeing her reflection in the mirror that Polyneices holds up to her, she catches a glimpse of the masculine trait for which her uncle Creon will reproach her, a brother himself, but to the mother of Antigone: the brother of Jocasta.

At last we arrive at the crucial point: Jocasta! The unique, the sole unnamed, unpronounceable center around which the infernal pursuit of *auto* and *homo* turns. Focal point of the tragic imagery of the piece, never explicitly designated, but always elusively evoked: Polyneices is, Antigone proclaims, "of my own blood from father and mother" (513).[4] Let us be clear: *Jocasta, the mother, is the only one* who persists in her own identity because she is the mother of everyone, including Oedipus; while Oedipus, the father, is himself also the child of *this* mother, but not the only one, since he is not the father of Jocasta.

Curiously, Antigone prefers not to remember that this Universal Mother is also the lover of the son/father, and thus her (Antigone's) Only Rival, at the same time that she (Jocasta) is the Only Mother. Antigone censures the desire and pleasure of Jocasta in order to think of her only as a generative source [*génitrice*]. That is, she thinks of the fecund blood of the womb, and of the one and only maternal blood that lends itself both as reality and as a metaphor that engenders (literally and figuratively) the fluid identities of the consanguineous. The maternal blood produces amorous and murderous identities because, like the blood, these siblings are doomed to procreation and carnage, never one without the other. The confused and confusing identities of these brothers of the "same blood" (*homaimos*), produce an incestuous brotherhood that cannot manifest its autonomy in similarity save by spilling shared blood in a war among brothers. Unless one term puts an end to fecundity? And, only in that way, to its double—war?

Heroine of self-analysis, Antigone, you reveal to us the secrets of tragedy. But you don't announce it; you only persist obstinately in your act of de-binding [*déliaison*]. Strangled by the enclosure of the incestuous family, those trapped in this sameness [*les "mêmes"*], interwoven between *auto* and *homo*, are condemned to regeneration *and* to murder: the engendering and murderous family. Worse, suicidal, because to kill a single body of the same blood in the consanguineous labyrinth of equivalences, equivalent ricochets and reflections, is—for this family here—to kill [*à suicider*] its "*sameness*" [*mêmeté*], to kill *itself*: the deaths of and in the family are the suicide of the family. The internecine intra- and inter-familial wars drag on for ages, under the form, moreover, of endless political conflict: your brothers Polyneices and Eteocles confront one another in a civil war, their cousin Haemon pays with his life for this inexorable cycle of deadly generations, of maternal [*matriciel*] blood . . . Again, today, the wars between national and religious "communities" fall pray to the same tragic logic of suicidal threats, a logic concealed in their allegedly symbolic "*sameness*" [*mêmeté*].

4. This implicit fact, which weaves the tragic fabric of Antigone, must have inevitably led someone—necessarily a woman, a descendent of Jocasta—to change the course of fate by cutting the thread [*fil*] of the inextricable descent of *auto* and *homo*. Such would, in effect, be the solution of Anti-gone (*anti-engendering*): face to face with a death that endures forever; and the chorus is there to remind us that death is the one and only situation in which the human species, for all its sly and cunning, manifests its fateful impotence (360–364). In opposing the *gonê*, in refusing to produce any descendents, you find a "trick"/charm/remedy: you domesticate death. This is no blasphemy against the place of the maternal, nor is it matricide; let's leave that to Orestes. You content yourself with repudiating (*anti* = against) motherhood and, "in its place" (the other meaning of *anti*), you impose a certain reflexive resemblance to it, according to the same logic of *auto* and *homo* of which it is the fruit. But you do so in another world, one that is no longer part "of this world," living by the force of the matrix [*matrice*].

You see all of this clearly, fixed in your subterranean universe on the banks of the Acheron, nevertheless you still nurture the desire for motherhood. Aren't you aware that you give yourself away, divulging your maternal vocation? No, that can't be. Don't you recall the funereal care that you lavished on your brother/father/son, his mortal flesh bathed and swaddled in dust, purified and protected: doesn't this betray a maternal solicitude? Or better yet: "Had I been a mother . . ." (904): Didn't you let these words slip? The moans that you utter before the despoiled body of your Polyneices, are these not "the shrill cry of an embittered bird that sees its nest robbed of its nestlings and the bed empty"

(425–427)? And finally, Antigone, doesn't your death ("hanging by her neck" [1120]) correspond to the hanging of Jocasta?

And yet, Antigone doesn't hang visibly onstage, the messenger only testifies to a "she," third person impersonal, a nonperson: an ambiguity that can only make life difficult for commentators. Who has hung her? Herself? With her own hands? Or not? I prefer to think that this vision of the messenger was only a rhetorical figure employed by Sophocles to say that "she," Antigone, in her opaque and absolute coolness, plotted from the very beginning a mute compressed vengeance against the nonprohibiting mother: the Only Mother, the All Mother. A mother to be killed and whom, in the toxic tides of "*samenesses*" [*mêmetés*], you replace, becoming a corpse in her place.

It was, therefore, necessary that the desire to reunite with your family in death, foreshadowed at the beginning of the play (74–75), already be inscribed in the name of the heroine: against the Mother [*contre la Mère*] and/or *in her place*. In order to be free, or at least autonomous, you consecrate yourself, Antigone, to incarnating the death of the desire for life, Eros' double [*doublure*]. Even though this logic leads you to become one of the suicides in this incestuous family that we discussed above, this death of the desire for life is neither a black sun of melancholia nor a theology of nothingness. It has nothing to do with the groans of that dark poet, Nerval, nor with the praise of non-being so dear to the forked tongue of an Angel of Foligno (even though your terse style irresistibly suggests this), nor with the peaceful content of a Zen monk whose meticulous garden you will never know.

Antigone triumphs over Jocasta in taking her son from her, in whom she does not find the blind sage of Colonus, but rather a discordant Oedipus, finally appeased in the form of a dead baby. On this condition alone, the shadow of the melancholy object has no need to fall on her, but crystallizes itself in *the endurance of the death drive.* I mean: the death drive in the strict sense that Freud gives it in the second topography, which is not to be confused with the eroticization of aggressivity and suffering that one calls sadomasochism. They have nothing to do with one another. For Antigone, as we have seen, Thanatos has cut the ties—decidedly erotic—with the living. Intent on surpassing the limit (*Atè*) of the human, the daughter of Jocasta and Oedipus finds herself at once pulled towards and yet already *at* the limit: atrocious (according to Lacan), being in effect in the "between" of the death drive.[5]

Prior to narcissism, even before autoeroticism, in a radical de-binding [*déliaision*]. Refusing neurotic depression, remaining outside of the masochistic "*père-version*" from which the tormented object derives a fatal pleasure [*dont jouit à mort*]—to the point of becoming insensible to the pact between master and slave—Antigone escapes the neuroses of humanity. Divine Antigone? The chorus advances this hypothesis in an antistrophe that our offended recluse violently challenges. Because she knows that her sovereignty is a merely human one, although fully human, exceptionally human.

In place of the mother, Antigone gives birth to an imaginary universe: she makes up for the loss of her own family by recreating the imaginary world in which life is possible at the limit, within the *Atè* itself. Those who step past this threshold usually sink into madness, lose their human contours, and pass away. Not Antigone. She triumphs in her deathly [*cadavérique*] construction because in it she discovers the benefit of consummating her love for her brother in tender acts of care, in maternal gestures. It is only necessary to die to herself [*mourir à soi*] and in her body (and Creon makes himself the unwitting accomplice of this Antigonean desire that precedes his edict) to accomplish not the *gestation* of a baby, but the *maternal vocation* of tenderness and care: *the sublimation inherent in the maternal vocation.* This is the profit of her sacrifice. Antigone does not know it because the world of tragedy had not yet invented the *infant-subject.* We must wait for the Bible and the Gospels. She struggles in the inextricable interweaving [*tressage*] of Eros and Thanatos, and she defends herself in this struggle, paralyzed by the love that exists outside of time between a dead brother and a sister ready to die to preserve their autonomy and their equivalence [*homologation*].

5. At the site of the de-binding [*déliaison*], if one does not become mad, if one does not lose the limits of language in the mental confusion, then it is the pathos of solitude that paralyzes the one who lives. (S)he is elsewhere, on this side or beyond, an inaccessible Self, an indestructible diamond. But her mortifying narcissism, triumphant and sure of itself, can also free itself [*se rendre disponible*], which confers on her this enigmatic brilliance perceived by the chorus. A contemplative and icy freedom, that of the saint, or occasionally of a highly efficient nurse, Ophelia recovered from the waters and in her role as caretaker. No suffering, pity, or compassion. She feels nothing: "If I shall die before my time, I count that a profit . . . to face such a fate as this is pain that does not count. But if I dared to leave the dead man, my mother's son, dead and unburied, that would have been real pain" (463ff.). The death of the self, as the apotheosis of the *auto*, finally relieved of the weight of living reproductive relations and held tightly in the shroud of the knowledge of its limits, of The Limit: Could this be the ultimate "profit"?

A profit for the manic-depressive psychosis, I might have said, if we must content ourselves with the psychiatric diagnosis, which despite being insufficient is nonetheless real. But this does not explain how the pathos of Antigone not only fails to become pathological, but also rebounds on Creon, and causes him to put on the costume of a plaintive neurotic: "I am no more a live man than one dead" (1322). Throughout this time, Antigone, although invisible from now on, hanging offstage, doesn't cease to fascinate and make herself felt in the heart of spectators and readers—both those present and those to come—as the only heroine of this eponymous piece.

The magisterial solitude of Antigone reaches its climax when her auto-analysis of her own cohabitation with the death drive makes her rebel, not only against the political spirit (of Creon), but also against the gods themselves. Lacan was right: it is not to Creon that Antigone denies the right to identify with Zeus; it is *she herself* who disassociates both from Zeus ("it was not Zeus that made the proclamation" [450]), and from the *dikè* of the gods.[6] Her de-binding [*déliaison*] does not accept their "laws" because these "are not written laws," but a sort of trace without representation, which a human being cannot transgress. More or less than the *dikè* of the gods, it would only be a question of a horizon (*oros*) that Antigone allows herself to aim for, to the point of reflecting it in the radiance of her sovereign identity. A region that absorbs her identity, because it/Id is only thinkable as transversal to language, to the rules, and to the laws, even as it/Id is delimited/fixed by them: the horizon of sensible time, of affect, of the drive at the crossroads of biology and meaning.

Certain of aspiring to the limit of the living and of being drawn [*être aspiré*] to it—while always being inhabited by an (Oedipal) desire to know the truth: a desire bequeathed to her by her parents, through their crime [*faute*] and its revelation—Antigone is sure of her experience. Doesn't it make her intimately familiar with the power of the "programmed death," which biologists today tell us is at work in life from the moment it begins? We can read her debate with Creon over *dikè* in this way: alone in the apprehension of the ebb and flow of the life drive that is a surrogate for the death drive, Antigone situates herself as this blinding, illegible double [*doublure*] for laws that could be the unwritten laws of the gods—there, where the Id [*ça*] neither dictates nor forbids, but where it is felt, where it is tested, where it lives and dies in itself. At the limit of madness, the horizon of psychic sovereignty can be opened.

6. The chorus, though Dionysian, seems to stagger at the sight of her pretension, reminding us that humans ensnared by death do no more than "escape *in* the sickness" (360–364). By taking up and expanding Lacan's reading, I propose a new interpretation of the Greek text, which breaks with the usual translations: in effect, Sophocles speaks of an escape *into* sickness (*nosôn d' amêkhanôn phugas xumpephrastai*) and not of a flight *from* sickness, and in such a way that this "sickness" becomes, definitively, *impossible* (*amêkhanôn*). Here we find a reading of sickness that is already psychoanalytic, but which the common sense of various translators (before Lacan) could not admit, since

they usually, and wrongly, assume that human beings can only "flee *from* the disease." What strikes the Dionysian chorus about our heroine is precisely that, contrary to ordinary human beings, Antigone *does not flee from sickness*. More important, what "common sense" considers a sickness is for her more than a defense: it is a case of a pseudo-sickness, "a sacred trick" (*amêkhanôn*), adds Lacan, as the symptom of an unconscious revolt or of an unbearable desire, through which the daughter of Oedipus escapes from both human and divine laws. Therefore, she is not sick at all: her pathos, shining with all the brilliance of a diamond, has nothing to do with pathology! The confusion of the guard, beyond the fear of being killed because he is bearing bad news, is perhaps also due to the enigma that is this girl, who in her disturbing and yet so familiar strangeness is not mad at all. How could this be possible?

7. Let us suppose, to start with, that the truth of Antigone, which she proclaims from the depths of her nuptial tomb, is no more than a historically dated truth: that of the *tragic advent of the individual* in the suffocating net of an incestuous family that has not yet discovered how to submit to the incest prohibition. The history of Indo-European vocabulary demonstrates that the identity of the Self [*Soi propre*], the foundation of the free Individual, can only be constituted *outside* of the lines of familial lineage, only in the exogamous alliances of consanguineous relations. Thus, the Sanskrit root "*swe*" from which we derive *soi* (in French), *self* (in English), *svoy* (in Russian), and so forth, has its Greek equivalent in "ally/relative" (*étes*) and in "ethics" (*éthos*).[7] The slow and uncertain emergence of free subjectivity. . . . The laws of political society, whatever they were at that time, had to replace and stand guard against the incestuous customs of familial clans, but they did not have the power to cut through the tragic entanglements in which *identity* sought to construct itself, by itself. Wasn't that, precisely, the tragic? And its delicious seduction.

This will be the strength of God the Creator of monotheism, who will replace the *sacrifice* and the *self-sacrifice* with the *separating prohibitions* (alimentary, sexual, moral), thus guaranteeing *the emergence of the subject* in man. The text of the Jewish Bible and the ritual rigor of its people consecrated this historical change by the "election," in which the self is determined only in the face of the Other, this One to be attested to and witnessed in all the others; and simultaneously by *the imperative of procreation* [*génération*]—one that will be pursued to infinity in *Numbers*—in order to guarantee the perpetuation of alterity. Adonai and Yahweh had to put an end to the confusion in the consanguineous *sameness* [*mêmeté*] of the pagan family, which was more or less matriarchal, by prohibiting the shedding of blood (Thou shall not kill!): blood that was necessarily impure; blood spilled in carnage; blood spilled in menstruation. All this to encourage—via the mothers—the perpetuation of the paternal line from fathers to their sons: nominal identities in the generational succession of the elected.

And it is with Christ that not only the (Oedipal) murder of the father will be confessed (as Freud discovered in his study of Moses), but also that Antigone's exploration of the death drive will be reprised, recognized, and metamorphized—a fact that Freud omits. Situated as the focal point of the imaginary, the desire for death/the desire for the death of the subject Son/Father who is beaten to death does not reduce itself to the putting to death of a victim by the tribunal of the rival religion.[8] The experience of mortality allows us to recognize that this might not be the end of life, but rather death's permanent cohabitation in the temporality of the living. From this fact, and beyond the sadomasochistic experience of death and suffering, even of the feminine passivity [*passivation*] in which the passion of the cross excels, we can add the annihilation (*kénose*) of the Son/Father, who in dying descends to hell only to reascend to his place at the right hand of the Father, thus evoking the grave adventure [*aventure tombale*] of Antigone, buried as a result of her desire to rejoin Polyneices, her brother/father beyond the *Atè*.

As for Antigone-mother in the place of the generative source [*génitrice*], the Virgin Mary accomplishes this displacement spectacularly in an eternal return that culminates in the Pieta that attaches her to Jesus, such a young woman, a descendant of the Sulamite who would have dreamt of Antigone.

With the exception—and the difference here is radical—that the fable of a reunion in death will be surpassed by that of the resurrection, in which the incestuous love for and of the Son/Father is finally sanctioned, rehabilitated at the expense of sublimation. Antigone, the sublime, was not unaware of the uncompromising work [*œuvre absolue*] of the drive, which changes its goal (this being the love of death instead of, and in the place of, the erotic ties), but she could not imagine that it was possible to accomplish the work of this drive by speaking/painting/singing, in place of *dying a living death in a tomb-like dungeon*. Following the day of the Christian Passion, when the tragic chalice is emptied to the dregs,[9] the tragic dimension will be transcended yet preserved in the body of the Son-Father, which will only become a corpse in order to be sublimated, a glorious body seated at the right hand of the Father.

Christ and Mary, differently and together, recognize, in short, the sovereign lucidity of Antigone, but they wrest it away from the tragedy in order to found, in the place of and diametrically opposed to the reproductive world, the myth of the possible love in the afterlife, eternally. And they invite all women, natural mothers of the species, not to halt the flow of childbearing but to join with them (Jesus and Mary) at one of the possible crossroads of Greek and Jewish memory.

This adventure has far too often laid the burdens of the cross on the female body. It has nonetheless thereby encouraged the spiritual or sublimatory development of women that accompanies the history of Christianity (from female monastics, passing through the storytellers, epistolaries, writers, witches, warriors, and other revolutionaries, all the way to feminists and female leaders [*présidentes*] of every kind). The ecstasy of Theresa of Avila and her jubilant writings are inseparable from the death of the self [*à soi*] in the agonizing trials of the cloister and in the likewise passionate identification that abandons itself to the Son/Father who is beaten to death. The incestual fantasy now confessed is sublimated and finally relieved in this new Judeo-Christian promise that the Greek world did not know: the Love of the Other who elects and pardons. From that moment forward, the death drive is no longer solely tragic; it now inserts the tragic as the other face of love.

8. Shall I suggest to you yet another, final, hypothesis, contrary to the last? Far from being a relic of the past, the universality of Antigone resonates in the psychic life of women today. I would suggest that beyond the "classical" family—one that respects the incest prohibition, either willingly or unwillingly, that has been drawn away from Judaic and Christian dogma through secularization, and that is endlessly reconstructed under the pressure of reproductive techniques, the emancipation of the "second sex," and the intermingling of diverse religious and cultural traditions (as Judith Butler discusses in *Antigone's Claim*)—the anthropologically universal dimension of *feminine solitude* confronted with the drive of de-binding [*déliaison*] still makes itself evident today in clinical observation, as well as in social behavior. Solitude and de-binding [*déliaison*], neither necessarily reject motherhood, but rather demand and accompany it. Feminine depression and, at the extreme, a variety of maternal crimes bear witness to it. This cannot make us forget, however, the emerging strength of those women who have the opportunity and the capacity to generate a new understanding, skill, or even a way of life or survival out of it: a remarkable consequence of the emancipation of women that is still in process.

In effect, *Oedipus prime* (the primary Oedipal phase), which attaches the little girl to her mother in the precocious mother-baby bond, marks the psychosexuality of the woman with a primary, endogenous homosexuality that is "unwritten" because it is prelinguistic, sensorial, quasi-indivisible. *Oedipus bis* (the secondary Oedipal phase), which directs her instead towards the father, introduces the subject-woman into the world of language, of the ideal, and of the social superego without thereby reducing her earlier form of dependency. Formed in this bi-face Oedipus, the inconsolable mourning of the primary Oedipal phase (*Oedipus prime*) and the improbable completion of the secondary Oedipal phase (*Oedipus bis*), make woman an eternal stranger to the political community, inexorably exiled from the initial osmosis with her generative source [*génitrice*].

Homosexuality will offer the occasion to relive the delights and the discords of this lost continent. Motherhood will provide a chance to step outside of her *Self*, to love finally—as herself—*someone else*: the child of a third person, the father. This is the miracle of the *maternal vocation*, but we can see how it is threatened by maternal madness, this recurrent pathos of the autoerotic, narcissistic "*sameness*" [*mêmeté*] in the persistence of the Oedipus complex. It is also the miracle of symbolic motherhood that renounces the cycles of reproduction of the body and forms itself, like Antigone, at the limit of the human, at the limit of language. In contrast to Antigone, however, this symbolical maternity looks for meaning in this existence at the limit, in order to shed light on the death drive in the *dispassionating* of sublimation.

There is an Antigone in every mother who successfully liberates her children from herself. Like Antigone I risk my neck every time I take on a work [*œuvre*] that exceeds or surpasses me. Because, with or without the experience of motherhood, and above all in the current efforts to construct a modern discourse on maternal passion relevant to the present, it becomes possible, perhaps, for women to approach the limits of the living at which they confront the ambiguities of their Oedipal experiences. Here these heroines of self-analysis confront the internal limits of their sexual identity (the psychic bisexuality endogenous to women); the life of their children (always fragile and the object of solicitude); the new cataclysms that threaten the life of our planet; and the new techniques for the reproduction of life that play at the limits of knowledge without sufficient precaution for life and death.

The diverse apocalyptic events that we witness today, and even the infanticidal acts of some mothers, do not erase the growing number of women who confront the limit states of human experience with the indestructible serenity of Antigone. And who reveal themselves as a horizon—for better and for worse. A horizon at which the laws themselves, because this all takes place in the social order, are susceptible of being transformed; but this transformation takes place first in the depth of the psyche, before being consecrated, eventually, by political justice.

This can be achieved only provided that we develop the language, the thought, an interpretation of our solitary solidity in its cohabitation with the death drive. If not, then we are only left with the barbarism of frozen embryos, of children violated or sold in the traffic of human organs, of sterilized or scorned pregnancies, of women repressed or denied.

9. Antigone "in place of" the mother? At the heart of Winnicott's joyous mother lies an Antigone. She has severed her ties, she has traversed her *auto* and *homo*, she is dispassionate: a certain annulation. What is a good mother? She knows

that the "other" surges out of the limit where its identitary ambition to her is eclipsed, and thereby opens the horizon of possible alterities, of veritable singularities. Against the pathos of the mother and in her place: maternal love, limit state, and inaccessible horizon.

You have already practiced, Antigone, the conditions of this accession by taking the risk of existing at the limit. You are the vestal virgin of the death drive, who verges on crime, but who also purifies herself in the identitary emancipation inherent to the work of art and to that work of art that is the unbearable *dispassionating* of maternal care. Your experience is elusive, but nevertheless concise: defying good sense, but with an absolute rigor and with a mysterious obviousness. You recognize the necessity of silence and the justice of the voice that intones the death of the self, nurtures the hatching forth of the other that takes place in the child, leaves open, and frees the interpretations[10]: open, personal, traced because foreseen, but imprescriptible. Like these unwritten nonlaws of the gods. A musical guide. Sublime.

Notes

1. Sophocles, *Antigone*, line. 484. Hereafter references to this text are given parenthetically within the text by line number and are taken from the following translation: *Antigone*, in *The Complete Greek Tragedies: Sophocles I*, trans. David Grene, ed. David Grene and Richard Lattimore (Chicago: University of Chicago Press, 1991). The French translation used is: *Antigone*, trans. Paul Mazon, ed. and with an introduction by Nicole Loraux, Classiques en poche (Paris: Les Belles Lettres, 2006). While I only rarely quote other thinkers here, my reading draws from several works—my own and those of others. Most importantly, I engage with Jacques Lacan, whose interpretation of *Antigone* appears in Seminar VII, *The Ethics of Psychoanalysis 1959–1960*, trans. Dennis Porter, ed. Jacques-Alain Miller (New York: Norton, 1988). See also G. W. F. Hegel, *Phenomenology of Spirit*, trans. A. V. Miller (Oxford, UK: Oxford University Press, 1977); Friedrich Hölderlin, *Hölderlin's Sophocles: Oedipus and Antigone*, trans. David Constantine (Tarset Valley, UK: Bloodaxe Books, 2001); Judith Butler, *Antigone's Claim: Kinship between Life and Death* (New York: Columbia University Press, 2000); Julia Kristeva, *Tales of Love*, trans. Leon S. Roudiez (New York: Columbia University Press, 1987); Julia Kristeva, *The Sense and Non-Sense of Revolt*, vol. 1 of *The Powers and Limits of Psychoanalysis*, trans. Jeanine Herman (New York: Columbia University Press, 2000); Julia Kristeva, *This Incredible Need to Believe*, trans. Beverley Bie Brahic (New York: Columbia University Press, 2009); and Julia Kristeva, *Seule une femme* (Paris: Editions de l'Aube, 2007).

2. Nicole Loraux, "La main d'Antigone," introduction to the French edition of *Antigone*. Also published in *Métis*, vol. 1 (1986), pp. 165–196.

3. Ibid., p. 108. See also: Louis Gernet, "Authentês," *REG*, vol. 22 (1909), reprinted in *Droit et société dans la Grèce ancienne* (Paris: Recueil Sirey, 1955), p. 33.

4. Trans. note: The French translation of this passage stresses the singularity of the mother: "Il [Polyneices] est mon sang, d'une *seule* mère et du même *père*."

5. Ed. note: Jacques Lacan discusses *Atè* at length in his reading of *Antigone*. He defines it as "the limit that human life can only briefly cross." As Kristeva notes, he describes Antigone as "atrocious" because, he claims, she "goes beyond the limits of the human," which for Lacan implies that "her desire aims at the following—the beyond of *Atè*." Lacan makes an etymological connection between *Atè* and atrocity. The Greek term *Atè* also signifies madness. On Kristeva's reading, however, Antigone is importantly *not* pathological. See Lacan, *The Ethics of Psychoanalysis*, pp. 262–264.

6. Lacan examines the Greek text word by word: "Translated word for word, it means, 'for Zeus is by no means the one who proclaimed those things to me.' Naturally Antigone is understood to have said, 'It's not Zeus who gives you the right to say that.' But she doesn't, in fact, say this. She denies that it is Zeus who ordered her to do it. Nor is it *dikè*, which is the companion or collaborator of the gods below. She pointedly distinguishes herself from *dikè*. 'You have got that all mixed up,' she says in effect. 'It may even be that you are wrong in the way you avoid the *dikè*. But I'm not going to get mixed up in it; I'm not concerned with all these gods below who have imposed laws on men.' " See Lacan, *The Ethics of Psychoanalysis*, p. 278.

7. Emile Benveniste, *Le vocabulaire des institutions indo-européennes*, vol. 1 of *Économie, parenté, société* (Paris: Les éditions de Minuit, 1969), p. 331.

8. Ed. note: See Julia Kristeva, "A Father is Beaten to Death," in *The Dead Father: A Psychoanalytic Inquiry*, ed. Lila J. Kalinich and Stuart W. Taylor (New York: Routledge, 2009), pp. 175–187.

9. Trans. note: The French expressions "Boire jusqu'à la lie," and "Boire jusqu'à le calice," have biblical connotations. Literally meaning "to drink to the bitter dregs," they suggest the idea of "going to the ultimate limit of tragic experience." See Psalms 75:9, and Matthew 20:22 and 26:39.

10. Ed. note: See Julia Kristeva, *Female Genius: Colette* (New York: Columbia University Press, 2004), p. 210. Quoting Colette, Kristeva here refers to hatching in relation to flowering—a kind of rebirth.

Bibliography

The following is an extensive, but not exhaustive, bibliography of essays and books relevant to feminist scholars working on *Antigone*. While not all these texts are explicitly feminist, they do all centrally or indirectly address questions of sexual difference. Also included are those canonical interpretations with which feminist readers of *Antigone* tend to engage. I have not included adaptations for the stage. For an extensive list of the latter, see Moira Fradinger's references in the prologue of this book.

Acker, Kathy. *Pussy, King of the Pirates*. New York: Grove Press, 1996.

Arkins, Brian. "Women in Irish Appropriations of Greek Tragedy." In *Amid Our Troubles: Irish Versions of Greek Tragedy*, edited by Marianne McDonald and J. Michael Walton, 198–212. London: Methuen, 2002.

Athanasiou, Athena, and Elena Tzelepis. "Mourning (as) Woman: Event, Catachresis, and 'that other face of discourse.' " In *Re-Writing Difference: Luce Irigaray and the Greeks,* edited by Athena Athanasiou and Elena Tzelepis. Albany, NY: SUNY Press, forthcoming.

Augst, Therese Ahern. "Difference becomes Antigone: Hölderlin and the Ethics of Translation." *Seminar* 38, no. 2 (2002): 95–115.

Bacon, Helen. "Woman's Two Faces: Sophocles' View of the Tragedy and His Family." *Science and Psychoanalysis: Decennial Memorial Volume* (1966): 10–24.

Barker, Derek W. M. *Tragedy and Citizenship: Conflict, Reconciliation, and Democracy from Haemon to Hegel*. Albany, NY: SUNY Press, 2009.

Battersby, Christine. "Antigones of Gender." Chap. 6 in *The Phenomenal Woman: Feminist Metaphysics and the Patterns of Identity*. Cambridge, UK: Polity Press, 1998.

Benhabib, Seyla. "On Hegel, Women, and Irony." In *Feminist Interpretations and Political Theory,* edited by Mary Lyndon Shanley and Carol Pateman, 129–145. University Park: Penn State Press, 1991. Reprinted in *Feminist Interpretations of Hegel,* edited by Patricia Jagentowicz Mills, 25–44. University Park: Penn State Press, 1996.

Bennett, W. Blake, and Larry J. Tyrrell. *Recapturing Sophocles' "Antigone."* New York: Rowman and Littlefield, 1998.

Bergo, Bettina. "Commentary on Tina Chanter's 'Antigone's Excessive Relationship to Fetishism.' " *Symposium: Canadian Journal of Continental Philosophy* 11, no 2 (2007): 261–273.

Bergoffen, Debra. "Sophocles' *Antigone* and Freud's *Civilization and Its Discontents.*" *American Imago* 43, no. 2 (1986): 151–167.

Bernadete, Seth. *Sacred Transgressions: A Reading of Sophocles' "Antigone."* South Bend, IN: St. Augustine's Press, 1999.

Bollack, Jean. *La mort d'Antigone: La tragédie de Créon*. Paris: Presses Universitaires de France, 1999.

Bush, Andrew. "María Zambrano and the Survival of Antigone." *Diacritics* 34, nos. 3–4 (2004): 90–111.

Butler, Judith. *Antigone's Claim: Kinship between Life and Death*. New York: Columbia University Press, 2000.

Cavarero, Adriana. *Stately Bodies: Literature, Philosophy, and the Question of Gender.* Translated by Robert de Lucca and Deanna Shemek. Ann Arbor: University of Michigan Press, 2002.

Changfoot, Nadine. "Hegel's *Antigone*: A Response to the Feminist Critique." *Owl of Minerva* 33, no. 2 (2002): 179–204.

Chanter, Tina. "Antigone's Dilemma." In *Re-Reading Levinas*. Edited by Robert Bernasconi and Simon Critchley, 130–146. Bloomington: Indiana University Press, 1991.

———. "Eating Words: Antigone as Kofman's Proper Name." In *Enigmas: Essays on Sarah Kofman,* edited by Penelope Deutscher and Kelly Oliver, 189–202. Ithaca, NY: Cornell University Press, 1999.

———. "Looking at Hegel's *Antigone* through Irigaray's *Speculum.*" Chap. 3 in *Ethics of Eros: Irigaray's Rewriting of the Philosophers*. London: Routledge, 1995. Republished in *Between Ethics and Aesthetics: Crossing the Boundaries*. Edited by Dorota Glowacka and Stephen Boos, 29–48. Albany, NY: SUNY Press, 2002.

———. "Tragic Dislocations: Antigone's Modern Theatrics." *Differences: A Journal of Feminist Cultural Studies* 10, no. 1 (1998): 75–97. Reprinted in *Styles of Piety: Practicing Philosophy after the Death of God,* edited by S. Clark Buckner and Matthew Statler, 151–170. New York: Fordham University Press, 2006.

———. "Antigone's Excessive Relationship to Fetishism: The Performative Politics and Rebirth of Eros and Philia from ancient Greece to modern South Africa." *Symposium: Canadian Journal of Continental Philosophy* 11, no. 2 (2007): 231–260.

———. *Whose Antigone?: Philosophy, Psychoanalysis, Imperialism* (working title). Albany, NY: SUNY Press, forthcoming.

Cohler, Bertram, and Robert Galatzer-Levy. "Freud, Anna, and the Problem of Female Sexuality." *Psychoanalytic Inquiry: A Topical Journal for Mental Health Professionals* 28, no. 1 (2008): 3–26.

Copjec, Joan. "The Tomb of Perseverance: On *Antigone.*" Chap. 1 in *Imagine There's No Woman: Ethics and Sublimation*. Cambridge, MA: MIT Press, 2002.

Davis, Clifford. "The Abject: Kristeva and the *Antigone.*" *Paroles Gelées: UCLA French Studies* 13 (1995): 5–25.

DeBoer, Karin. "Hegel's *Antigone* and the Dialectics of Sexual Difference." *Philosophy Today* 47 (2003): 140–146.

Derrida, Jacques. *Glas*. Translated by John P. Leavey and Richard Rand. Lincoln: University of Nebraska Press, 1986.

Des Bouvrie, Synnøve. *Women in Greek Tragedy: An Anthropological Approach*. Oslo: Norwegian University Press, 1990.

Dietz, Mary G. "Citizenship with a Feminist Face: The Problem with Maternal Thinking." *Political Theory* 13, no. 1 (1985): 19–37.

Di Nicola, Giulia Paola. *Antigone: Figura femminile della trasgressione*. Pescara, Italy: Edizioni Tracce, 1991.

Diprose, Rosalyn. "In Excess: The Body and the Habit of Sexual Difference." *Hypatia* 6, no. 3 (1991): 156–171.

Donougho, Martin. "The Woman in White: On the Reception of Hegel's Antigone." *Owl of Minerva* 21, no. 1 (1989): 65–89.

Douzinas, Costas. "Law's Birth and Antigone's Death: On Ontological and Psychoanalytical Ethics." *Cardozo Law Review* 16, nos. 3–4 (1995): 1325–1362.

duBois, Page. "Antigone and the Feminist Critic." *Genre* 19, no. 4 (1986): 370–383.

Duroux, Françoise. *Antigone encore: Les femmes et la loi*. Paris: Côté des femmes, 1993.

Elden, Stuart. "The Place of the Polis: Political Blindness in Judith Butler's *Antigone's Claim*." *Theory and Event* 8, no. 1 (2005).

Elshtain, Jean Bethke. "Moral Woman and Immoral Man: A Consideration of the Public-Private Split and Its Political Ramifications." *Politics and Society* 4, no. 4 (1974): 453–473.

———. "Antigone's Daughters." *Democracy* 2, no. 2 (1982): 46–59. Reprinted as "Antigone's Daughters: Reflections on Female Identity and the State." In *Families, Politics, and Public Policy: A Feminist Dialogue on Women and the State,* edited by Irene Diamond, 147–197. New York: Longmans, 1983. Reprinted again in *Freedom, Feminism, and the State: An Overview of Individualist Feminism*, edited by Wendy McElroy, 61–75. New York: Holmes and Meier, 1991.

———. "Antigone's Daughters Reconsidered: Continuing Reflections on Women, Politics and Power." In *Life-World and Politics between Modernity and Postmodernity: Essays in Honor of Fred Dallmayr,* edited by Stephen K. White, 222–235. Notre Dame, IN: University of Notre Dame Press, 1989.

Ettinger, Bracha L. "Transgressing With-In-To the Feminine." *Women's Philosophy Review* 25 (2000): 56–85. Reprinted in *Differential Aesthetics: Art Practices, Philosophy and Feminist Understandings*, edited by Penny Florence and Nicola Foster, 183–210. London: Ashgate, 2000.

Euben, J. Peter. *The Tragedy of Political Theory: The Road Not Taken*. Princeton, NJ: Princeton University Press, 1990.

———. "*Antigone* and the Language of Politics." Chap. 6 in *Corrupting Youth: Political Education, Democratic Culture, and Political Theory*. Princeton, NJ: Princeton University Press, 1997.

Feral, Josette. "Antigone or the Irony of the Tribe." Translated by Alice Jardine and Tom Gora. *Diacritics* 8 (1978): 2–14.

Fleming, Katie. "Fascism on Stage: Jean Anouilh's *Antigone.*" In *Laughing with Medusa: Classical Myth and Feminist Thought*, edited by Vanda Zajko and Miriam Leonard, 163–186. Oxford: Oxford University Press, 2008.

Foley, Helene P. "The Concept of Women in Athenian Drama." In *Reflections of Women in Antiquity,* edited by Helene P. Foley, 127–168. Philadelphia: Gordon and Breach, 1982.

———. "Tragedy and Democratic Ideology." In *History, Tragedy, Theory: Dialogues on Athenian Drama,* edited by Barbara Goff, 131–150. Austin: University of Texas Press, 1995.

———. "Antigone as Moral Agent." In *Tragedy and the Tragic: Greek Theatre and Beyond,* edited by M. S. Silk, 49–73. Oxford, UK: Oxford University Press, 1998.

——— *Female Acts in Greek Tragedy*. Princeton, NJ: Princeton University Press, 2002.

Fox, Mary-Jane. "The Idea of Women in Peacekeeping: Lysistrata and Antigone." *International Peacekeeping* 8, no. 2 (2001): 9–23.

Gauthier, Jeffrey A. "Historically Emergent Agency: Antigone and Creon." Chap. 1 in *Hegel and Feminist Social Criticism: Justice, Recognition and the Feminine*. Albany, NY: SUNY Press, 1997.

Goff, Barbara. "The Women of Thebes." *Classical Journal* 90, no. 4 (1995): 353–365.

———, and Michael Simpson. *Crossroads in the Black Aegean: Oedipus, Antigone, and Dramas of the African Diaspora.* Oxford, UK: Oxford University Press, 2008.

Goldhill, Simon. "Greek Drama and Political Theory." In *The Cambridge History of Greek and Roman Political Thought,* edited by Christopher Rowe, Malcolm Schofield, Simon Harrison, and Melissa Lane, 60–88. Cambridge, UK: Cambridge University Press, 2000.

———. "Antigone and the Politics of Sisterhood." In *Laughing with Medusa: Classical Myth and Feminist Thought,* edited by Vanda Zajko and Miriam Leonard, 141–162. Oxford, UK: Oxford University Press, 2006.

Grenier, Louise, Suzanne Tremblay, and Janick Auberger, eds. *Le projet d'Antigone: Parcours vers la mort d'une fille d'Œdipe*. Montreal, Canada: Liber, 2005.

Hartouni, Valerie. "Antigone's Dilemma: A Problem in Political Membership." *Hypatia* 1, no. 1 (1986): 3–20.

Hawkesworth, Mary. "The Semiotics of Premature Burial: Feminism in a Postfeminist Age." *Signs* 29, no. 4 (2004): 961–985.

Hegel, G. W. F. *Phenomenology of Spirit*. Translated by A. V. Miller. Oxford, UK: Oxford University Press, 1977. See esp. chap. 6, "Spirit."

———. *Aesthetics: Lectures on Fine Art.* Translated by T. M. Knox, vol. 2. Oxford, UK: Clarendon Press, 1988.

Heidegger, Martin. *Hölderlin's Hymn "The Ister."* Translated by William McNeill and Julia Davis. Bloomington: Indiana University Press, 1996.

———. *An Introduction to Metaphysics.* Translated by Gregory Fried and Richard Polt. New Haven, CT: Yale University Press, 2000.

Hester, D. A. "Sophocles the Unphilosophical: A Study in the *Antigone*." *Mnemosyne: Bibliotheca Classica Batava* 24, no. 1 (1971): 11–59.

Hoff, Shannon. "Law, Right, and Forgiveness: The Remains of Antigone in the *Phenomenology of Spirit*." *Philosophy Today* 50, no. 1 (2006): 31–38.

———. "Restoring Antigone to Ethical Life: Nature and Sexual Difference in Hegel's *Phenomenology of Spirit*." *Owl of Minerva* 38, nos. 1–2 (2007): 77–100.

Hölderlin, Friedrich. *Hölderlin's Sophocles: Oedipus and Antigone*. Translated by David Constantine. Tarset Valley, UK: Bloodaxe Books, 2001.

Holland, Catherine A. "After Antigone: Women, the Past, and the Future of Feminist Political Thought." *American Journal of Political Science* 42, no. 4 (1998): 1108–1132.

Honig, Bonnie. "Antigone's Laments, Creon's Grief." *Political Theory* 37, no. 1 (2009): 5–43.

Humphreys, Sarah C. *The Family, Women, and Death: Comparative Studies.* London: Routledge and Kegan Paul, 1983.

Huntington, Patricia. "The Couple Must become Spiritualized: A Response to Changfoot." *Owl of Minerva* 33, no. 2 (2002): 233–249.

Hutchings, Kimberly. "Beyond Antigone: Towards a Hegelian Feminist Philosophy." *Bulletin of the Hegel Society of Great Britain* 41, no. 2 (2000): 120–131.

———. "Re-thinking the Second Sex." Chap. 4 in *Hegel and Feminist Philosophy.* Cambridge, UK: Polity Press, 2003.

Ierulli, Molly. "The Politics of Pathos: Electra and Antigone in the Polis." *South Atlantic Quarterly* 98, no. 3 (1999): 477–500.

Irigaray, Luce. "The Eternal Irony of the Community." Chap. 10 in *Speculum of the Other Woman.* trans. Gillian C. Gill. Ithaca, NY: Cornell University Press, 1985.

———. *An Ethics of Sexual Difference.* Translated by Carolyn Burke and Gillian C. Gill. Ithaca, NY: Cornell University Press, 1993a. See esp. chap. 7, "Love of Same, Love of Other," and chap. 8, "An Ethics of Sexual Difference."

———. "The Universal as Mediation." Chap. 8 in *Sexes and Genealogies,* trans. Gillian C. Gill. New York: Columbia University Press, 1993b.

Jacobs, Carol. "Dusting Antigone." *MLN* 111, no. 5 (1996): 890–917.

Johnson, Patricia J. "Woman's Third Face: A Psycho/Social Reconsideration of Sophocles' *Antigone.*" *Arethusa* 30, no. 3 (1997): 369–398.

Just, Roger. *Women in Athenian Law and Life.* New York: Routledge, 1989.

Kain, Philip J. "Hegel, Antigone, and Women." *Owl of Minerva* 33, no. 2 (2002): 157–177.

———. "The Ethical Order, Women, and Oppression." Chap. 4, section 2, in *Hegel and the Other: A Study of the Phenomenology of Spirit.* Albany, NY: SUNY Press, 2005.

Keuls, Eva C. *The Reign of the Phallus: Sexual Politics in Ancient Athens.* New York: Harper and Row, 1985.

Lacan, Jacques. *The Ethics of Psychoanalysis 1959–1960: The Seminar of Jacques Lacan,* book 7. Translated by Dennis Porter. Edited by Jacques-Alain Miller. New York: Norton, 1992.

Lane, Warren J., and Ann M. Lane. "The Politics of Antigone." In *Greek Tragedy and Political Theory,* edited by J. Peter Euben, 162–182. Berkeley: University of California Press, 1986.

Lee, Theresa Man Ling. "Rethinking the Personal and the Political: Feminist Activism and Civic Engagement." *Hypatia* 22, no. 4 (2007): 163–179.

Leonard, Miriam. "Antigone, the Political and the Ethics of Psychoanalysis." *Proceedings of the Cambridge Philological Society* (2003): 130–154.

———. "Lacan, Irigaray, and Beyond: Antigones and the Politics of Psychoanalysis." In *Laughing with Medusa: Classical Myth and Feminist Thought,* edited by Vanda Zajko and Miriam Leonard, 121–140. Oxford, UK: Oxford University Press, 2006.

Loraux, Nicole. "La Main d'Antigone." *Métis* 1 (1986): 165–196.

———. *Tragic Ways of Killing a Woman.* Translated by Anthony Forster. Cambridge, MA: Harvard University Press, 1987.

———. *The Experiences of Tiresias: The Feminine and the Greek Man.* Translated by Paula Wissing. Princeton, NJ: Princeton University Press, 1995.

———. *Mothers in Mourning*. Translated by Corinne Pache. Ithaca, NY: Cornell University Press, 1998.

———. *The Mourning Voice: An Essay on Greek Tragedy*. Translated by Elizabeth Trapnell Rawlings. Ithaca, NY: Cornell University Press, 2002.

Lykke, Nina. "Questing Daughters: Little Red Riding Hood, Antigone and the Oedipus Complex." In *Daughtering and Mothering: Female Subjectivity Reanalysed*, edited by Janneke van Mens-Verhulst, Karlein Schreurs and Liesbeth Woertman, 15–25. London: Routledge, 1993.

Mader, Mary Beth. "Antigone's Line." *Bulletin de la Société Américaine de Philosophie de Langue Française* 15, no. 1 (2005): 18–40.

———. "Antigone and the Ethics of Kinship." In *Re-Writing Difference: Luce Irigaray and the Greeks*, edited by Elena Tzelepis and Athena Athanasiou. Albany, NY: SUNY Press, forthcoming.

Markell, Patchen. *Bound by Recognition*. Princeton, NJ: Princeton University Press, 2003a.

———. "Death, Lies, and Recognition: Action and Identity in *Antigone* and Aristotle." *Political Theory* 31, no.1 (2003b): 6–38.

McDonald, Marianne. "Rebel Women: Brendan Kennelly's Versions of Irish Tragedy." *New Hibernia Review* 9, no. 3 (2005): 123–136.

Menke, Christoph. *Tragödie im Sittlichen: Gerechtigkeit und Freiheit nach Hegel*. Frankfurt am Main, Germany: Suhrkamp, 1996.

Miller, Elaine P. "The 'Paradoxical Displacement': Beauvoir and Irigaray on Hegel's Antigone." *Journal of Speculative Philosophy* 14, no. 2 (2000): 121–137.

Mills, Patricia Jagentowicz. "Hegel's *Antigone*." *Owl of Minerva* 17, no. 2 (1986): 131–152. Republished in *Feminist Interpretations of G. W. F. Hegel*, edited by Patricia Jagentowicz Mills, 59–88. University Park: Penn State Press, 1996.

———. *Woman, Nature and Psyche*. New Haven, CT: Yale University Press, 1987. See esp. chap. 1.

———. " 'Hegel's Antigone' Redux: Woman in Four Parts." *Owl of Minerva* 33, no. 2 (2002): 205–221.

Muraro, Luisa. "Female Genealogies." In *Engaging With Irigaray: Feminist Philosophy and Modern European Thought*, edited by Carolyn Burke, Naomi Schor, and Margaret Whitford, 317–333. New York: Columbia University Press, 1994.

Murnaghan, Sheila. "*Antigone* 904–20 and the Institution of Marriage." *American Journal of Philology* 107 (1986): 192–207.

Neuburg, Matt. "How Like a Woman: Antigone's 'Inconsistency.' " *Classical Quarterly* 40, no. 1 (1990): 54–76.

Nower, Joyce. "A Feminist View of Antigone." *The Longest Revolution* 8 (February/March 1983): 6.

Nussbaum, Martha C. "Sophocles' *Antigone*: conflict, vision, and simplification." Chap. 3 in *The Fragility of Goodness: Luck and Ethics in Greek Tragedy and Philosophy*. Cambridge, UK: Cambridge University Press, 1986.

Oliver, Kelly. "Antigone's Ghost: Undoing Hegel's *Phenomenology of Spirit*." *Hypatia* 11, no. 1 (1996): 67–90.

———. "Animal Body Mother." Chap. 1 in *Family Values: Subjects between Nature and Culture*. New York: Routledge, 1997.

Pollock, Griselda. "Beyond Oedipus: Feminist Thought, Psychoanalysis, and Mythical Figurations of the Feminine." In *Laughing With Medusa: Classical Myth and Feminist Thought*, edited by Vanda Zajko and Miriam Leonard, 67–117. Oxford, UK: Oxford University Press, 2006.

Pomeroy, Sarah B. *Goddesses, Whores, Wives, and Slaves: Women in Classical Antiquity*. New York: Schoken, 1975.

Pritchard, Annie. "Antigone's Mirrors: Reflections on Moral Madness." *Hypatia* 7, no. 3 (1992): 77–93.

Purvis, Jennifer. "Generations of Antigone: An Intra-Feminist Dialogue with Beauvoir, Irigaray, and Butler." *New Antigone* 1, nos. 1–2 (2006): 2–10.

Raji, Wumi. "Africanizing Antigone: Postcolonial Discourse and Strategies of Indigenizing a Western Classic." *Research in African Literatures* 36, no. 4 (2005): 135–154.

Ravven, Heidi Miriam. "Has Hegel Anything to Say to Feminists?" *Owl of Minerva* 19, no. 2 (1988): 149–168. Reprinted with minor revisions in *Feminist Interpretations of G. W. F. Hegel*, edited by Patricia Jagentowicz Mills, 225–252. University Park: Penn State Press, 1996.

———. "Further Thoughts on Hegel and Feminism: A Response to Philip J. Kain and Nadine Changfoot." *Owl of Minerva* 33, no. 2 (2002): 223–231.

Reed, Valerie. "Bringing Antigone Home?" *Comparative Literature Studies* 45, no. 3 (2008): 316–340.

Saxonhouse, Arlene. "From Tragedy to Hierarchy and Back Again: Women in Greek Political Thought." *American Political Science Review* 80, no. 2 (1986): 403–418.

———. *Fear of Diversity: The Birth of Political Science in Ancient Greek Thought*. Chicago: University of Chicago Press, 1992.

———. "Another Antigone: The Emergence of the Female Political Actor in Euripides' 'Phoenician Women.' " *Political Theory* 33, no. 4 (2005): 472–494.

Schwab, Gail. "Mothers, Sisters, and Daughters: Luce Irigaray and the Female Genealogical Line in the Stories of the Greeks." In *Re-Writing Difference: Luce Irigaray and the Greeks*, edited by Athena Athanasiou and Elena Tzelepis. Albany, NY: SUNY Press, forthcoming.

Seaford, Richard. "The Imprisonment of Women in Greek Tragedy." *Journal of Hellenic Studies* 110 (1990): 76–90.

Seery, John Evan. "Acclaim for *Antigone's Claim* Reclaimed (or, Steiner, contra Butler)." *Theory and Event* 9, no. 1 (2006).

Segal, Charles. "Sophocles' Praise of Man and the Conflicts of the *Antigone*." *Arion* 3 (1964): 46–66.

———. "The Female Voice and Its Contradictions." In *Religio Graeco–Romana: Festschrift für Walter Pötcher*, edited by Joachim Dalfen, 66–72. Graz, Austria: Institut für Klassische Philologie, 1993.

———. "Lament and Closure in *Antigone*." Chap. 5 in *Sophocles' Tragic World: Divinity, Nature, Society*. Cambridge, MA: Harvard University Press, 1995.

———. "*Antigone:* Death and Love, Hades and Dionysos." Chap. 6 in *Tragedy and Civilization: An Interpretation of Sophocles*. Norman: University of Oklahoma Press, 1999.

Singh, Frances B. "Antigone's Changed Punishment: Gynaecology as Penology in Sophocles' Antigone." *Australian Feminist Studies* 18, no. 40 (2003): 7–16.

Sjöholm, Cecilia. "Family Values: Butler, Lacan, and the Rise of Antigone." *Radical Philosophy* 111 (2002): 24–32.

———. *The Antigone Complex: Ethics and the Invention of Feminine Desire*. Stanford, CA: Stanford University Press, 2004.

Sorum, Christina Elliot. "The Family in Sophocles' *Antigone* and *Electra*." *Classical World* 75, no. 4 (1982): 201–211.

Sourvinou-Inwood, Christiane. "Assumptions and the Creation of Meaning: Reading Sophocles' *Antigone*." *Journal of Hellenic Studies* 109 (1989): 134–148.

Stalpaert, Christel. "The Mind Taken Hostage. Antigone's Corporeal Memory in 'Mind the Gap.' " *Mosaic: A Journal for the Interdisciplinary Study of Literature* 41, no. 3 (2008): 137–152.

Starret, Shari Neller. "Critical Relations in Hegel: Woman, Family and the Divine." In *Feminist Interpretations of G. W. F. Hegel*, edited by Patricia Jagentowicz Mills, 253–273. University Park: Penn State Press, 1996.

Steiner, George. *Antigones*. New Haven, CT: Yale University Press, 1996.

Stone, Alison. "Sexing the State: Familial and Political Form in Irigaray and Hegel." *Radical Philosophy* 113 (2002): 24–36.

———. "Hegel's Dialectic and the Recognition of Feminine Difference." *Philosophy Today* 47 (2003): 132–139.

———. "Irigaray and Hegel on the Relationship between Family and State." Chap. 5 in *Luce Irigaray and the Philosophy of Sexual Difference.* Cambridge, UK: Cambridge University Press, 2006.

Story, Amy. "Simone de Beauvoir and Antigone: Feminism and the Conflict between Ethics and Politics." *Mosaic: A Journal for the Interdisciplinary Study of Literature* 41, no. 3 (2008): 169–183.

Tyrrell, W. Blake. "Antigone's Unnoticed Rite of Passage." In *Rites of Passage in Ancient Greece: Literature, Religion, Society*, edited by Mark W. Padilla, 148–157. Lewisburg, PA: Bucknell University Press, 1999.

Tzelepis, Elena, ed. *Antigone's Antinomies: Critical Readings of the Political.* Athens, Greece: Ekkremes, forthcoming.

Vernant, Jean-Pierre, and Pierre Vidal-Naquet, eds. *Myth and Tragedy in Ancient Greece.* Translated by Janet Lloyd. New York: Zone, 1988.

Walsh, Lisa. "Her Mother Her Self: The Ethics of the Antigone Family Romance." *Hypatia* 14, no. 3 (1999): 96–125.

Weber, Samuel. "Antigone's 'Nomos.' " Chap. 4 in *Theatricality as Medium*. New York: Fordham University Press, 2004.

Weineck, Silke-Maria. "The Abyss Above: Philosophy, Tragedy, and Madness in Hölderlin's Encounter with Sophocles." *Seminar* 36, no. 2 (2000): 161–181.

Werner, Laura. "The Impure Heroine: Antigone, the Family, and the State." Chap. 5 in *'The Restless Love of Thinking': The Concept of Liebe in G. W. F. Hegel's Philosophy.* Helsinki, Finland: Helsinki University Press, 2007.

Wiersma, S. "Women in Sophocles." *Mnemosyne* 37, nos. 1–2 (1984): 22–55.

Willett, Cynthia. "Hegel, Antigone, and the Possibility of Ecstatic Dialogue." *Philosophy and Literature* 14, no. 2 (1990): 268–283.

———. "Hegel, Antigone and the Possibility of a Woman's Dialectic." In *Modern Engendering: Critical Feminist Readings in Modern Western Philosophy*, edited by Bat-Ami Bar On, 167–181. Albany, NY: SUNY Press, 1994.

Willner, Dorothy. "The Oedipus Complex, Antigone, and Electra: The Woman as Hero and Victim." *American Anthropologist* 84, no. 1 (1982): 58–78.

Wilmer, Steve, and Audrone Zukauskaite, eds. *Interrogating Antigone: From Philosophy to Performance*. Oxford, UK: Oxford University Press, forthcoming.

Winterer, Caroline. "Victorian Antigone: Classicism and Women's Education in America, 1840–1900." *American Quarterly* 53, no. 1 (2001): 70–93.

Wohl, Victoria. "The Mystical Foundation of the *Polis*: Sexual Difference and the Aporia of Justice in Sophocles' *Antigone*." In *Bound by the City: Greek Tragedy, Sexual Difference, and the Formation of the Polis*, edited by Denise McCoskey and Emily Zakin. Albany, NY: SUNY Press, forthcoming.

Zambrano, María. *La Tumba de Antígona*. Madrid, Spain: Mondadori, 1989.

Zeitlin, Froma I. "Playing the Other: Theater, Theatricality, and the Feminine in Greek Drama." In *Nothing to Do with Dionysos? Athenian Drama in Its Social Context*, edited by John J. Winkler and Froma I. Zeitlin, 63–96. Princeton, NJ: Princeton University Press, 1990a. Reprinted as chap. 8 in *Playing the Other: Gender and Society in Classical Greek Literature*. Chicago: University of Chicago Press, 1995.

———. "Thebes: Theater of Self and Society in Athenian Drama." In *Nothing to Do with Dionysos? Athenian Drama in Its Social Context*, edited by John J. Winkler and Froma I. Zeitlin, 130–167. Princeton, NJ: Princeton University Press, 1990b.

Zelenak, Michael X. "A Woman's Place is in the Tomb: Sophocles' Antigone." Chap. 6 in *Gender and Politics in Greek Tragedy*. New York: Lang, 1998.

Zerilli, Linda M. G. "Machiavelli's Sisters: Women and 'the Conversation' of Political Theory." *Political Theory* 19, no. 2 (1991): 252–276.

Žižek, Slavoj. "From Antigone to Joan of Arc." *Helios* 31, nos. 1–2 (2004): 51–62.

———. *Enjoy Your Symptom! Jacques Lacan in Hollywood and Out*. New York: Routledge Classics, 2007.

———. *The Sublime Object of Ideology: The Essential Žižek*. London: Verso, 2009.

Contributors

J. M. Bernstein is Distinguished Professor of Philosophy at the New School for Social Research. He received his Ph.D. from Edinburgh University in 1975 and has taught at several institutions, including the University of Essex, the University of California at Berkeley, and Vanderbilt University. Among his books are *The Fate of Art: Aesthetic Alienation from Kant to Derrida and Adorno* (Penn State Press, 1992), *Recovering Ethical Life: Jürgen Habermas and the Future of Critical Theory* (Routledge, 1995), *Adorno: Disenchantment and Ethics* (Cambridge University Press, 2001), and most recently, *Against Voluptuous Bodies: Late Modernism and the Meaning of Painting* (Stanford University Press, 2006). He is currently working on a project on torture.

Judith Butler is Maxine Elliot Professor of Rhetoric and Comparative Literature at the University of California, Berkeley. She received her Ph.D. in Philosophy from Yale University in 1984. She is the author of numerous books, including *Gender Trouble: Feminism and the Subversion of Identity* (Routledge, 1990), *Bodies that Matter: On the Discursive Limits of "Sex"* (Routledge, 1993), *The Psychic Life of Power: Theories of Subjection* (Stanford University Press, 1997), *Excitable Speech* (Routledge, 1997), *Antigone's Claim: Kinship between Life and Death* (Columbia University Press, 2000), *Precarious Life: Powers of Violence and Mourning* (Verso Press, 2004), *Undoing Gender* (Routledge, 2004), and *Giving an Account of Oneself* (Fordham University Press, 2005). Her most recent book is *Frames of War: When Is Life Grievable?* (Verso Press, 2009).

Adriana Cavarero, currently Professor of Political Philosophy at the University of Verona, received her doctoral degree in Philosophy at the University of Padua in 1971. She has been a visiting professor at Harvard University, the University of California at Berkeley and Santa Barbara, New York University, and the University of Warwick. She has published several books, of which the following have been translated into English: *In Spite of Plato* (Routledge, 1995), *Relating Narratives* (Routledge, 2000), *Stately Bodies* (University of Michigan Press, 2002), *For More than One Voice: Toward a Philosophy of Vocal Expression*

(Stanford University Press, 2005), and most recently, *Horrorism: Naming Contemporary Violence* (Columbia University Press, 2008).

Tina Chanter is Professor of Philosophy at DePaul University, Chicago. She is author of *Ethics of Eros: Irigaray's Re-writing of the Philosophers* (Routledge, 1995), *Time, Death and the Feminine: Levinas with Heidegger* (Stanford University Press, 2001), *Gender* (Continuum Press, 2006), and *The Picture of Abjection: Film, Fetish, and the Nature of Difference* (Indiana University Press, 2008). She is editor of *Feminist Interpretations of Emmanuel Levinas* (Penn State Press, 2001), coeditor of *Revolt, Affect, Collectivity: The Unstable Boundaries of Kristeva's Polis* (SUNY Press, 2005), and coeditor of *Sarah Kofman's Corpus* (SUNY Press, 2008). She is also editor of the Gender Theory series at SUNY Press. Her current book project is titled, *Whose Antigone?: Philosophy, Psychoanalysis, Imperialism.*

Bracha L. Ettinger is an artist and Visiting Professor of Psychoanalysis and Art at the Media and Communications Division of the European Graduate School. She received her Ph.D. from the University of Paris VIII in 1996. She works at the intersection of art, psychoanalysis, and aesthetics. Her solo exhibitions have been featured at art institutions around the world, including the Drawing Center (New York, 2001), Palais des Beaux Arts (Brussels, 2000), Museum of Art (Pori, 1996), the Israel Museum (Jerusalem, 1995), the Museum of Modern Art (Oxford, 1993), Museum of Calais (1988), Nouveau Musée de Villeurbanne (1992), Centre Pompidou (Paris, 1987), Freud Museum (London, 2009), the Finnish Academy of Fine Arts (Helsinki, 2009), Tapies Foundation (Barcelona, 2010), and Freud's Dream Museum (St. Petersburg, 2010). Her paintings have been exhibited at major museums, including Kiasma (Helsinki, 2006), Göteborgs Konstmuseum (Gothenburg, 2003), Villa Medici (Rome, 1999), Israel Museum (Jerusalem, 1999), Stedelijk (Amsterdam, 1997), Centre Pompidou (Paris, 1996), ICA (Boston, 1996), and Museum of Art (Tel Aviv, 1991). Ettinger is the author of several books and more than eighty psychoanalytical essays on what she has named "matrixial trans-subjectivity." Her book *The Matrixial Borderspace* collects many of these essays from 1994 to 1999 (University of Minnesota Press, 2006). Based in Paris and in Tel Aviv, Ettinger is a practicing psychoanalyst (member of World Association of Psychoanalysis, Nouvelle Ecole Lacanienne de Psychanalyse, and Tel Aviv Institute for Contemporary Psychoanalysis) and an activist against the Israeli occupation of Palestinian territories through her work with the Physicians for Human Rights, Israel.

Moira Fradinger is Associate Professor of Comparative Literature at Yale University. She holds a Ph.D. in Comparative Literature from Yale University, an

M.A. in Women's Studies from the Institute for Social Studies in Holland, and a Licenciatura in Psychology from the University of Buenos Aires in Argentina. Her research interests include Latin American and Caribbean fiction and film, ancient Greek and modern tragedy, psychoanalysis, feminism, film studies, and political philosophy. Her first book is entitled *Binding Violence: Literary Visions of Political Origins* (Stanford University Press, 2010). She is currently working on two book-length projects, one on Latin American adaptations of Sophocles' *Antigone* in the twentieth century and another on the anarchist imagination.

Catherine A. Holland received her Ph.D. in Political Science from the New School for Social Research in 1996 and currently holds an appointment in Women's and Gender Studies at the University of Missouri-Columbia. She teaches courses in feminist political theory and interdisciplinary feminist thought. Her book *The Body Politic: Foundings, Citizenship and Difference in the American Political Imagination* was published by Routledge in 2001. She has published articles in *Political Theory, Theory and Event, Studies in American Political Development, American Political Science Review*, and the *American Journal of Political Science.*

Luce Irigaray is Director of Research in Philosophy at the Centre National de la Recherche Scientifique, Paris. She is the author of more than twenty books, most of which have been translated into English, including *Speculum of the Other Woman* (Cornell University Press, 1985), *This Sex which Is Not One* (Cornell University Press, 1985), *An Ethics of Sexual Difference* (Cornell University Press, 1993), *The Way of Love* (Continuum, 2002), and *Between East and West: From Singularity to Community* (Columbia University Press, 2002). Her most recent book in English is *Sharing the World* (Continuum, 2008). She is a trained psychoanalyst, and holds two doctoral degrees, one in Linguistics and one in Philosophy.

Julia Kristeva is Professor of the Institut Universitaire de France and teaches at the University of Paris VII, Denis Diderot. She is a member of the Paris Psychoanalytic Association and the International Psychoanalytic Association, as well as the Council for Social and Economic Affairs in France, the American Academy of Arts and Sciences, and the British Academy. She is the author of many books, most of which have been published in English with Columbia University Press. Among her most distinguished works are *Powers of Horror* (1982), *Revolution in Poetic Language* (1984), *Tales of Love* (1987), *Black Sun* (1989), *Strangers to Ourselves* (1991), *New Maladies of the Soul* (1995), *Female Genius. Life, Madness, Words: Hannah Arendt* (2001), *Melanie Klein* (2002), *Colette* (2004), and *This Incredible Need to Believe* (2009). Her most recent book is *Thérèse mon amour* (Fayard, 2008), a monograph on Teresa of Ávila. Kristeva has published several novels, most recently *Murder in Byzantium* (2006), and she is the recipient of prestigious honors such as the inaugural Holberg Prize (1994) and the Hannah Arendt Prize (2006).

Mary Beth Mader, Associate Professor of Philosophy at the University of Memphis, has a Ph.D. in Philosophy from the University of Texas at Austin. She is the author of *Sleights of Reason: Norm, Bisexuality, Development* (SUNY Press, forthcoming) and articles on the work of Luce Irigaray, Michel Foucault, and Sarah Kofman. She is the translator of Luce Irigaray's *The Forgetting of Air in Martin Heidegger* (University of Texas Press, 1999).

Cecilia Sjöholm is Professor of Aesthetics at Södertörn University and holds a Ph.D. in Literature from Stockholm University and a Ph.D. in Philosophy from Nijmegen University. She has published two books in English: *The Antigone Complex: Ethics and the Invention of Female Desire* (Stanford University Press, 2004) and *Kristeva and the Political* (Routledge, 2005).

Fanny Söderbäck, currently working on a Ph.D. in Philosophy at the New School for Social Research, is writing her dissertation on temporality and difference in the work of Julia Kristeva and Luce Irigaray. She received an M.A. in Comparative Literature from Södertörn University in 2003. She has been an adjunct professor at Eugene Lang College, the New School for General Studies, Pace University, and SUNY Purchase College. In 2010–2011 she holds a position as Visiting Assistant Professor at Siena College.

Index

aberration, 9, 134, 139, 142, 161, 163
abjection, 85, 93, 218
abortion, 213n21
Accarino, Bruno, 62n18
action. *See also* agency
  and speech, 6, 28, 35–36, 38–40, 66–73, 79n11, 80n18, 134–135, 137–138, 149, 150, 152n9
  Arendt on. *See* Arendt, Hannah
  ethical, 7, 100, 113, 117, 120–125, 129n8
  feminist, 30, 32, 33, 40
  in the public sphere, 6, 28, 29, 40, 67, 69, 148
  kinship as principle for, 133–134, 161, 166
  of Antigone, 4, 7, 9, 28, *passim* 30–39, 42–43n19, 51, 55, 56, 69–77, 86–87, 96n6, 103, 115, 118–119, 121, 126, 133–136, 140, 146–147, 150, 156–157, 161–162, 164–165, 172n27, 191, 217
  of Creon. *See* Creon
  political, 56, 58, 62n16, 66, 69, 71–73
  soul as a principle for, 5, 58
  tragic, 48, 49, 65, 72, 75, 136, 176, 186, 188–191, 219
  transgressive, 120–121, 126, 127, 137
activism, 2, 29
adaptations of *Antigone*, 6, 15–23, 84, 85, 88–93, 94, 133
Addams, Jane, 29
adoption, 9, 35, 97n8, 141–142, 172n22
Aeschylus, 174
  works by,
    Agamemnon, 189
    Oresteia, 31, 34, 37, 168
    Seven against Thebes, 70, 75, 80n24
aesthetics, 3, 12, 82n48, 114–118, 189, 198–211, 213n26. *See also* art
Agamben, Giorgio, 149
Agamemnon, 189
agency, 11, 75, 112, 123, 126, 139, 160, 165, 169, 175–176, 180–184, 190–191. *See also* action
Alcoff, Linda, 152n15
anarchy, 77, 125, 216
animal,
  Antigone compared to an, 54, 80n17, 220
  human as continuous with, 5, 46, 53–55, 60
  human as different from, 3, 52–55, 210, 158
  feasting on the corpse of Polyneices, 52–54, 97n13, 102, 157, 217
anomaly, 47, 49
  Antigone as an, 73–74
Anouilh, Jean, 95
Antigone, *passim*
Aphrodite, 181–183, 187–188, 190
Apollo, 34, 42n18
après-coup, 107, 136, 138–139
arche, 54. *See also* origin
Arc, Joan of, 215

Arendt, Hannah,
  feminist readings of, 81–82n38
  on action, 40, 66–73, 77, 80n19, 82n47
  on beginnings, 67, 76–77
  on courage, 70, 80n18
  on freedom, 72–73, 81n31, 81n33
  on judgment, 77, 82n48
  on narration, 71–72, 80n28, 82n47
  on power, 67–69, 78–79n8, 79n11
  on sexual difference, 6, 73–74, 81n38, 149
  on theater/art, 77
  on the private/public realms, 5–6, 66–71, 73, 79n14, 80n21, 81n33, 149
  works by,
    Between Past and Future, 82n49
    Human Condition, The, 66, 67, 74, 76, 77, 79n11, 149
    Lectures on Kant's Political Philosophy, 82n48
    Life of the Mind, The, 82n48
    On Violence, 67, 78n8
Argos, 17, 34, 36
Aristotle, 30, 65, 68, 158, 176
  works by,
    Nichomachean Ethics, 62n16
    Poetics, 62n13
    Rhetoric, 155
art, 3, 12, 65, 77, 94, 113, 114, 186, 201, 203–211, 213n28, 228. *See also* aesthetics
Artemis, 42n18
Athens,
  absence of women in, 38, 48, 84, 174
  as democratic order, 34, 35, 48, 67, 69–70, 94
  as scene for tragic drama, 84, 85
  contrasted with Thebes, 4, 28, 34–35, 37, 69
Augst, Therese Ahern, 156
authority, 3, 28, 29, 36, 42n7, 56, 86–88, 97n9, 117, 118, 125, 128, 148
autonomy, 72, 105, 109, 120–121, 140, 152n9, 185, 188–189, 217, 219, 221, 222
Avila, Theresa of, 226

beauty, 7, 199–201, 205–211
  beautiful death. *See* death
  beautiful/ethical ideal, 8, 114–124
  end of, 123–124
  Lacan on. *See* Lacan
  Plato on. *See* Plato
Beauvoir, Simone de, 129n3
Being, 108, 109, 149, 218
  Antigone's proximity to, 151n7
  Being-for-itself, 100, 101, 104
  Being-there, 100, 107, 108
  Hegel on. *See* Hegel, G. W. F.
  Heidegger on (Dasein). *See* Heidegger, Martin
  Lacan on. *See* Lacan, Jacques
  non-being, 138, 186, 221. *See also* destruction
Bell, Vikki, 153n15
Benhabib, Seyla, 7, 81n38, 129n2
Bernstein, J. M., 6–8, **111–130**, 130n17
Bhabha, Homi, 42n8, 152n9
Bible, the, 222, 224, 229n9
bird. *See* animal
birth, 13, 49, 2, 55, 62n14, 130n21, 143, 159, 204, 209, 211, 218
  and death, 49, 52, 62n14, 143
  Antigone giving, 13, 43n25, 77, 222
  of the subject/self, 7, 51, 55, 59, 112, 117
  prebirth/prenatal, 11, 199, 202–207, 212n20
  rebirth/second birth, 77, 83–84, 94–95, 229n10
  trauma of, 213n24
blindness, 6, 91, 95, 127, 195, 200–201, 209, 216
  blind spot, 6, 74, 81n38
  of Oedipus. *See* Oedipus
  of Tiresias. *See* Tiresias
Bloch, Maurice, 151n8

blood, 18, 52, *passim* 99–110, 151n7
consanguineity, 47–51, 55, 59, 101, 219–220, 224
flesh and, 52, 60
incestuous, 34, 49–51, 58, 168, 218–219
menstrual, 52, 99, 101, 219, 224–225
relations, 31, 34, 36, 39, 49–51, 56, 58–59, 68, 86, 99–110, 125, 144, 151n7, 156, 216, 219, 220. *See also* kinship
shedding/loss of, 99, 102–109, 128, 219, 220, 224–225
woman/mother associated with, 7, 45, 49–52, 100, 101, 108, 168, 219, 220
body, 3, *passim* 45–63, 137–138
and soul, 5, 47–48, 52–53, 57, 58, 60, 178
animal, 53–54, 210
dead, 5, 16, 17, 18, 37, 46–48, 52, 53, 56–60, 60n1, 67, 79n11, 100, 135, 165, 221, 225. *See also* Polyneices
expulsion of, 5, 45–46, 48, 59, 60
female, 5, 54–56, 60, 203, 204, 209, 211, 213n21, 225
human, 5, 199, 201, 210
male, 5, 18, 209
mastery of, 176–179
maternal. *See* mother
of Antigone, 5, 15, 45, 138, 173, 222
political, 5, 46, 48, 55, 58–59
sensuous, 180–184, 190
soma, 46, 48, 53, 58, 60n1
transcendence of, 58, 183
woman associated with, 45, 48–49, 51, 54–55, 60
Borneman, John, 153n17
boundary, 9, 34, 47, 52, 54, 66, 75, 84, 93, 94, 202–203, 205, 209
Antigone as crossing, 12, 71, 74. *See also* transgression
between life and death, 147
between private and public, 30, 74, 80n17, 149. *See also* Arendt, Hannah; Greece; private sphere; public sphere
Bourdieu, Pierre, 152n8
Brecht, Bertolt, 15, 95
brother, 9–10, 59, 86–87, 96n6, *passim* 155–171
Antigone as, 136–137, 140, 148, 219
Antigone honoring/defending her, 2, 16, 30, 37, 38, 71, 72, 77, 87, 103, 111, 135, 163, 215, 216
as superior to husband and child, 9–10, 96n6, 115–116, 135, 155–157, 159–160, 169, 171n1
Creon as. *See* Creon
Eteocles as. *See* Eteocles
Hegel on brother-sister relation. *See* Hegel, G. W. F.
Lacan on brother-sister relation. *See* Lacan, Jacques
Oedipus as. *See* Oedpius
Polyneices as. *See* Polyneices
burial, *passim* 16–19, 47, 158, 170, 145
Creon's edict against. *See* Creon
Hegel on. *See* Hegel, G. W. F.
of Antigone, 60, 68, 71, 97n13
of enemies, 57–58
of Eteocles. *See* Eteocles
of Oedipus. *See* Oedipus
of Polyneices. *See* Polyneices
rites, 3, 15, 18, 47, 54, 70, 72, 75, 79–80n17, 126
women as responsible for, 57, 70, 99–100
Butler, Judith, 84, 85, **133–153**, 157, 160–162, 169
on Arendt, 74
on kinship, 8, 9, 12, 97n9, 160–162, 170
on Lacan, 88
on performativity, 8, 92, 161, 170
works by,
Antigone's Claim, 8, 73–74, 80n26, 95n1, 97n9, 129n2, 160–162, 170, 226, 228n1

Butler, Judith, works by *(continued)*
"Competing Universalities," 152n14
Gender Trouble, 9
Giving an Account of Oneself, 81n28

cadaver. *See* body
Cadmus, 42n11, 103, 124
canon. *See* tradition
Canovan, Margaret, 68
catharsis, 188
Cavarero, Adriana, 5–6, 12, **45–63**, 81n28, 129n2
Celan, Paul, 213n26
change, 1, 3–4, 13, 18, 35, 67, 95, 97n9, 158, 159, 173, 178, 185, 220, 224
Chanter, Tina, 6, 82n46, **83–98**, 129n2, 171n12
choice, 16, 18, 68, 102, 121, 122, 139, 146, 170, 184, 185, 186, 190, 191
chorus, 36, 125
as Dionysian, 217, 223, 224
as female, 75
"Hymn to Eros," 184–185, 190
"Hymn to Man," 2, 52–53, 220, 184–185, 223
in *Hippolytus*, 189–190
in *Oedipus at Colonos*, 137, 150n5
on Antigone, 51, 61n7, 133, 148, 172n27, 216, 217, 221–222, 224
on Polyneices, 54, 61n7, 146
Christ, 1, 225
Antigone compared with, 1–2, 111
body of, 225
passion of, 225
Christianity, 16
and desire/sexuality, 179
and free will, 81n31
and love, 226
and motherhood, 225–226
history of, 226
citizen/citizenship, 3, 4, *passim* 30–37, 42n7, 57, 125–126, 149
Athenian, 48, 69, 72, 73
male, 84, 109, 112
civil disobedience, 77, 118
class, 6, 18, 19, 93
Clastres, Pierre, 151–152n8
Clinton, Bill, 142, 152n13
Clytemnestra, 31, 189
Collier, Jane Fishburne, 143, 151n8, 153n17
colonialism, 16, 17, 85
Comaroff, John, 151n8
community, 7, 57, 77
and individuality, 8, 100, 122–127
destruction of, 75, 109
eternal irony of. *See* Hegel, G. W. F.
of the living and the dead, 125–128
women excluded from the, 74, 79n11, 108, 109, 140, 149, 226
conscience, 118, 120, 127, 128
consciousness, 74, 100, 101, 106–109, 112, 120, 128, 129n8, 181, 217
ethical, 118, 122
constitutive outside, 5–6, 74–75, 82n44, 83, 85, 93, 149. *See also* exclusion; other
convention. *See* tradition
corporeality. *See* body
corpse. *See* body
courage, 70, 77, 80n18, 80n23, 102, 160
Creon,
action of, *passim* 67–70, 104, 121
and death, 36–37, 68, 71, 127
as a lonely character, 67, 70, 79n11, 104
as a misogynist/patriarch, 8, 32, 36, 51, 55–56, 60, 124–125
as a tyrant, 39, 54, 56, 58, 60, 67, 215
as brother of Jocasta, 36, 86–87, 101, 219
as representative of human law, 5, 65, 68–69, 104, 118–119
as representative of the private sphere/ the family, 6, 9, 67–71
as representative of the public sphere/ the state, 37, 48, 54, 65, 67, 169–170, 216

Creon *(continued)*
as womanly/feminine, 56–58, 70–71, 175
conflict with Antigone, 30, 31, 35–39, 43n22, 47–48, 54–60, 118–119, 124, 140, 215–218, 223
crime of, 37, 60
edict against burying Polyneices, 15, 36, 47, 58, 83, 86–87, 111, 119, 127, 128, 155, 165, 215–218
etymological analysis of, 67
killing/burying Antigone, 19, 67–68, 71, 87, 97n13
power of, 36, 43n23, 68–69, 71, 73, 86–87, 104, 175
speech of, 36, 55–56, 124–125
crime, 12, 38, 39, 103, 106–107, 121, 139, 152–153n15, 176, 185, 188, 226. *See also* transgression
of Antigone, 6, 31, 70, 111, 135, 143, 147–148, 150, 215, 216, 228
of Creon. *See* Creon
of Jocasta. *See* Jocasta
of Oedipus. *See* Oedipus
crisis, 1, 3, 8, 13, 78n3, 95, 143
cross-dressing, 3, 85, 90
culture, 3, 5, 53–54, 83–84, 92, 126, 134, 142–144, 147, 166, 175, 200, 203, 226
ancient Greek. *See* Greece
contrasted with nature, 2, 3, 11, 52–53, 65, 99–100, 108, 111–112, 114, 126, 188–191
curse, 138–139, 147
gender as a, 136
of Antigone/Polyneices by Oedipus, 133–136
of Oedipus. *See* Oedipus
of Phaedra, 187–188
of Thebes. *See* Thebes
custom. *See* tradition
Cutrofello, Andrew, 192n3

daimon, 174, 184, 185
Dasein. *See* Heidegger, Martin
Davis, Angela, 144
death, 52, 53, 60, 71, 83, 100–101, 144, 184–185, 199–201, 206, 209–210, 220, 223, 225
Antigone and, 10, 11–12, 16, 43n25, 55, 62n20, 74, 76–77, 102–103, 110n3, 121, 127, 135, 140, 146–147, 151n7, 157, 173, 200–201, 215–217, 220, 225
beautiful, 70, 80n20
birth and. *See* birth
Creon and. *See* Creon
desire for. *See* desire
drive, 62n20, 76, 77, 187, 193n27, 200–203, 209, 218, 221, 223, 225–228. *See also* Freud, Sigmund; Lacan, Jacques
Hegel on. *See* Hegel, G. W. F.
Lacan on. *See* Lacan, Jacques
of Antigone, 37, 39, 67–68, 70–71, 73, 76–77, 87, 102–103, 110n3, 188, 191, 210, 221
of God/Jesus, 78n3, 225–226
of Polyneices. *See* Polyneices
women associated with, 10, 12, 200–201, 210
deed. *See* action
deinon. *See* uncanny
Deleuze, Gilles, 213n26
democracy, 3, 28, 32, 56
Athenian. *See* Athens
limited, 78n7, 79n11, 94
Theban. *See* Thebes
Derrida, Jacques, 153n24
desire, 10, 101, 104, 107, 125, 153n24, *passim* 173–191, *passim* 195–214
erotic/sexual, 92, 100–101, 104, 173, 175–176, 179–180, 187–191. *See also* Eros; sexuality
female, 10–11, 108–109, 174, 175, 181, 185, 196, 203–204. *See also* jouissance
for death, 10, 76–77, 135, 173, 215, 217, 221, 225. *See also* death; Freud, Sigmund; Lacan, Jacques

desire *(continued)*
for knowledge/truth, 176, 179–181, 223
incestuous, 46, 135, 162, 170, 201–202, 226
maternal. *See* mother
of Antigone, 76–77, 100, 103, 108, 135, 146, 191, 201, 206–207, 216, 221, 222
Sappho on. *See* Sappho
Schelling on. *See* Schelling, F. W. J.
unconscious. *See* unconscious, the
destiny. *See* fate
destruction, 10, 67, 74, 75, 79n14, 100, 104, 114, 122, 126, 140, 146, 173, 184, 190
self-destruction, 75–76, 79n11, 140, 185
dialectic, 1, 7, 66, 101, 105, 107, 112, 113, 120, 123, 124, 140, 152n9, 176, 218
master-slave. *See* Hegel, G. W. F.
negative, 140
Dietz, Mary, 4, 28, 29–33, 35, 40, 42n7
Diotima, 173
disobedience. *See* obedience; civil disobedience
dog. *See* animal
dream, 1, 112–117, 120–122, 129n5, 225. *See also* Hegel, G. W. F.
dualism. *See* opposition
duBois, Page, 180–181, 183
duty, 1, 99, 100, 106, 109, 118, 215

Eden, 106, 120
Elshtain, Jean Bethke, 4, 28, 29–33, 35, 40, 42n7
emancipation, 3, 226, 228
endogamy, 49–51
enemy, 5, 16, 36–37, 55–60, 63n26, 74, 75, 106, 127, 130n22, 162, 215. *See also* friend; Polyneices
Engels, Friedrich, 143
enigma,
Antigone as, 1, 2, 13, 55, 84, 174, 196, 222, 224
of death, 199, 210
of lines 905–914 in *Antigone*, 9, 96n6, 155–172
of women/the feminine, 6, 11, 76, 200, 210, 211
enmity. *See* enemy
equality, 30
between the races, 85, 88, 93
between women and men, 30, 74, 85, 87, 93, 105–106, 109, 123, 199
inequality, 73, 85
in the public sphere, 73, 79n11
Eros, 11, 86, *passim* 173–193, 216, 221, 222. *See also* desire; love
power of, 173–174, 180–184, 189–190
Eteocles, 36
as brother of Antigone, 102, 146, 148
as friend of the state, 56, 127
as manly/masculine, 102–103
as mirror image of Creon, 75
at war with Polyneices, 71, 75, 103, 134–135, 137, 220
burial of, 165
eternal return, 4, 34, 37, 38
Ettinger, Bracha L., 10–13, **195–214**
Euben, Peter, 34, 38, 84
Euripides, 48, 174
works by,
Bacchae, 124
Hippolytus, 11, 185, 187–190
Medea, 189
Eurydice, 70
evil, 2, 16, 56, 120, 127–128, 176, 186, 215
exclusion, 6, 34, 40, 60, 75, 80n21, 85, 93–94, 107, 141, 149, 204, 205. *See also* constitutive outside; other
of Antigone, 6, 12–13, 73–76, 83, 93–94, 140, 150, 217, 218–219
of the body. *See* body
of women. *See* woman
exogamy, 49, 145, 224

family, 4, 48–49, 87, 125, 141–144, 160. *See also* blood; father; kinship; mother; private sphere
Antigone as a representative of, 5, 9, 29–30, 33–34, 47–48, 69, 85–86, 161, 184
incestuous, 10, 12, 35, 49, 96n6, 101–102, 140, 152n15, *passim* 162–171, *passim* 218–224
in relation to the state, 7, 9, *passim* 28–35, 48, 65, 66, 68, 75, 85–86, 102, 111, 114, 115, 122, 126, 156–157, 224. *See also* Arendt, Hannah; private sphere; public sphere
of Oedipus. *See* Oedipus
woman as a representative of. *See* woman
fantasy, 8, 113–114, 120, 203–205, 209, 226. *See also* dream
fate, 72, 114, 122, 173, 175–176, 180, 184, 187–191, 201, 213n21, 220
of Antigone, 39, 86, 133, 135, 140, 143, 201, 222
of Oedipus. *See* Oedipus
of Polyneices. *See* Polyneices
of Thebes. *See* Thebes
of Tiresias. *See* Tiresias
father, 5, 30–31, 67, 69, 97n9, 102, 105, 134, 141–142, 161, 225–226. *See also* patricide
law of the. *See* law
Oedipus as. *See* Oedipus
paternal filiation/lineage, 31, 32, 50, 59, 102, 103, 133, 135, 143, 144, 165, 168, 202, 219, 225
fear, 1, 12, 19, 49, 51, 56, 60, 79n11, 92, 100, 102, 104, 168, 182, 195, 205, 224
fearlessness of Antigone, 2, 215
female. *See* woman
femininity. *See* woman
feminism, *passim* 2–10, 27–33, 39–41, 76–77, 111–112, 129n3, 141, 143–145, 160, 216, 226
Ferenczi, Sandor, 213n20
fetishism, 1, 84, 96n2
Fitts, Dudley, 171n4, 172n26
Fitzgerald, Robert, 171n4, 172n26
Foligno, Angel of, 221
forgiveness, 1, 111, 120, 128
Fortes, Meyer, 151n8
Foucault, Michel, 38
technologies of the self, 174, 177–178, 184, 192n6
works by,
Archeology of Knowledge, 152n9
History of Sexuality, 10–11, 174, 176–180, 183, 192n6
Fradinger, Moira, 3–4, **15–23**
fratricide, 58–59, 71, 75, 103, 134–135, 166, 220
freedom, 3, 10, 11, 30, 34, 39, 48, 59, 72–73, 81n31, 88–90, 101, 108, 116, 120, 127, *passim* 176–191, 221, 222, 224
Arendt on. *See* Arendt, Hannah
Hölderlin on. *See* Hölderlin, Friedrich
contrasted with necessity, 2, 65, 72, 81n31, 81n33, 176, 185, 187
Schelling on. *See* Schelling, F. W. J.
Freud, Sigmund,
on castration, 187, 195, 205, 213n24
on melancholia, 148–149
on the death drive, 187, 193n27, 218, 221
on women/feminine sexuality, 11, 196
works by,
Beyond the Pleasure Principle, 193n27
"Fetishism," 96n2
Moses and Monotheism, 225
"The Uncanny," 187, 193n27, 205
friendship, 30–32, 89, 92, 144, 160, 169–170, 186
and enmity, 5, 36, 56–59, 63n26, 127, 130n22
Antigone as lacking, 39, 73, 103, 216. *See also* solitude
Fugard, Athol, Winston Ntshona, John Kani, 85, 95
works by,
Island, The, 17, 85, 88–93, 95, 97n13

funeral. *See* burial

Galilei, Galileo, 76
Gehlen, Arnold, 62n18
gender, 3, 8, 9, 80n20, 85, 136, 141–143, 150, 153n17, 166, 178, 182–183, 209, 211. *See also* sexual difference
  ambiguity, 28, 37–38, 56–58, 70–71, 80n23, 85, 90–93, 102–103, 107, 175, 182, 195, 198–199
  Antigone and, 43n25, 73, 80n23, 93, 136–138, 146, 148, 175
  as passive/active distinction, 178–180, 183, 190–191
  complementarity/dualism, 8, 35–38, 111–112, 115–116, 121–125, 127, 141, 180
  conflict/hierarchy/oppression, 6, 11, 19, 85, 89, 93, 181, 183
  in tragedy, 174–175, 180, 189, 191
genealogy, 9, 10, 36, 49, 84, 165, 168, 169, 176, 180
German Idealism, 116, 176, 190
Gernet, Louis, 219
Glowacki, Janusz, 95
  works by,
    Antigone in New York, 18, 95
Godelier, Maurice, 152n8
goddess, 18, 182
Goethe, Johann Wolfgang von, 113, 114, 156, 157–158
good, 2, 29, 127, 128, 181, 191
grave,
  of Antigone, 7, 17, 39, 68, 76, 97n13, 103, 146–147, 173, 219, 224, 225
  of Oedipus. *See* Oedipus
  mass, 16, 104
Greece, 15
  as locus for the birth of subjectivity, 47, 117, 224
  culture in ancient, 7, 62n16, 114, 174, 181
  customs and political life in ancient, 57, 60, 86, 78n3
  ethical life in ancient, 112–128
  mythology, 42n18, 43n23, 11–12, 47, 49, 62n16, 69, 195, 210
  private/public distinction in ancient, 48–49, 66–67, 78n7, 79n14, 80n21, 81n33, 149. *See also* Arendt, Hannah; private sphere; public sphere
  sexuality in ancient, 174–191
  views on death in ancient, 47
  views on women in ancient, 45, 70, 75, 78n7, 84–85, 124, 174, 178, 188
grief. *See* mourning
guilt, 60, 68, 89–90, 101, 103, 106, 111, 121, 148, 185, 186, 188, 216

Hades, 38, 71, 102–103, 134, 156, 216, 217
Haemon,
  death of, 10, 37, 87, 173, 175, 220
  relationship with Antigone, 43n22, 73, 161–162, 173, 215
  relationship with Creon, 56, 67, 73, 81n32, 161–162, 175
Halperin, David, 84
Hamlet, 216
Harris, H. S., 120, 128, 129n9, 130n14
Hartouni, Valerie, 39
Heaney, Seamus,
  works by,
    Burial at Thebes, The, 19, 95
Hegel, G. W. F.,
  as a misogynist (feminist critique of), 3, 7–8, 111–112, 123–125, 130n21
  "eternal irony of the community," 74, 123–125, 218, 226
  feminist defense of, 6–8, 112–128
  Hegelian dream, 8, 101–105, 112–117, 120–122, 129n5
  master-slave dialectic, 97n10, 221
  on Being, 126
  on burial/death, 116–117, 125–126, 166
  on recognition, 8, 97n10, 101, 102, 105, 106, 109, *passim* 112–128

Hegel, G. W. F. *(continued)*
on Spirit/ethical life, 7–8, 112–128, 129n8
on the brother-sister relation, *passim* 101–107, 112, 115–116, 121, 130n13, 153n24, 163, 166
on tragedy, 65, 174, 176, 186
reading of *Antigone*, 1, 6–8, 48, 99–109, 111–130, 146, 153n24, 166, 174, 190
works by,
Aesthetics, 65, 78n4, 153n24
Phenomenology of Spirit, 7, 78n4, *passim* 99–109, *passim* 111–128, 129n5, 153n24, 228n1
Philosophy of Nature, 99
Philosophy of Right, 153n24
Heidegger, Martin,
on Being (Dasein), 184–185
on Hölderlin's translation of *Antigone*, 151n7
on the uncanny, 53, 84, 184–185
on tragic eros, 174
Hellenism, 116–117
Hera, 195
Herder, Johann Gottfried, 65, 69
Herodotus, 155
Hesiod, 53
heterosexuality. *See* sexuality
Hippolytus, 185, 187–188. *See also* Euripides
HIV/AIDS, 144–145
Hölderlin, Friedrich, 62n14, 113, 114, 176, 228n1
aesthetic Hellenism of, 116
on freedom, 190
on the uncanny, 53, 151n7
reading/translation of *Antigone*, 61n10, 137–138, 151n7, 155
Holland, Catherine A., 4, **27–43**
Homer,
on fate, 190
on funeral rites, 47
on *soma*, 60n1
homophobia, 89–92, 142
homosexuality. *See* sexuality
horror, 12, 51–52, 54, 128, 133, 142, 163, 170, 199, 205
hubris, 127, 148
Hutchings, Kimberly, 7, 129n2
"Hymn to Eros." *See* chorus
"Hymn to Man." *See* chorus
hysteria, 102

imaginary, the, 4, 49, 96n2, 113, 197, 213n21
imagination, 13, 15, 16, 18, 20, 27, 32, 34, 40, 89, 126, 159, 166, 173, 186, 188, 203, 222, 225
immortality, 5, 52, 72, 77, 182
incest,
Antigone as a fruit of, 2, 4, 9, 12, 48, 51, 54, 76, 143, 163, 165, 216, 217
brother-sister, 141, 161–162, 170, 172n23
desire. *See* desire
family marked by. *See* family
kinship marked by. *See* kinship
of Oedipus. *See* Oedipus
prenatal, 11, 203–207
taboo, 10, 88, 89, 139, 141, 142, 147, 152n8, 152–153n15, 169, 176, 186, 201–202, 224, 226. *See also* Freud, Sigmund; Lacan, Jacques
undoing, 10, 87, 96n6, 164–167, 170, 225
individuality. *See* subjectivity
inequality. *See* equality
injustice. *See* justice
intersubjectivity, 3, 11, 208
Irigaray, Luce, 6–8, 31, 68, 84, **99–110**
critique of Hegel, 8, 112, 115, 121–123
on matriarchy/the maternal, 12, 81n35
on sexual difference, 8, 85, 121–123
works by,
Speculum of the Other Woman, 6, 61n6, 80n26
Ismene, *passim* 16–19, 29, 104, 165
Antigone's disavowal/repudiation of, 38, 148, 161

Ismene *(continued)*
as Antigone's sister, 17, 29, 50, 61n9, 102, 148, 161, 170, 216
as different from Antigone, 70, 118–119, 121, 173, 191
as failing/refusing to help Antigone, 51, 73, 74
as last survivor of the Oedipal family, 43n23
as manly/masculine, 80n23, 136–137
as womanly/feminine, 39, 74, 80n23, 102, 121
etymological analysis of, 216
love for Antigone, 161
isolation. *See* solitude

Jason, 189. *See also* Euripides
Jesus. *See* Christ
Jocasta,
Antigone compared with, 12–13, 220–221
as Creon's sister, 36, 58, 70, 86–87, 219
as maternal figure, 12, 50, 133, 219
as originator of a blood line, 50, 219, 220
incest/crime of, 12, 50, 86, 103, 147, 161–166, 168, 172n23, 172n29, 201–202, 206, 216, 223
jouissance, 102–103, 109, 203–204, 206
Lacan on. *See* Lacan, Jacques
judgment, 41, 77, 82n48, 116, 120, 189
Just, Roger, 75, 78n7, 79–80n17, 82n44
justice, 35, 74, 85, 127, 217, 227, 228
Antigone instigating, 3, 16, 17, 77
injustice, 3, 17, 77, 8, 127

Kafka, Franz, 76
Kant, Immanuel, 7, 113
aesthetic judgment, 77, 82n48
morality/moral law, 113–115, 118
works of,
Critique of the Power of Judgment, 82n48
Critique of Practical Reason, 82n48
Kennelly, Brendan, 95
kinship,
and race, 9, 88–89, 97n11, 143–144
Butler on. *See* Butler, Judith
incestuous, 48–50, 58–59, 133, 139–141, 143, 146, 150n5, 161–168, 172n29, 216, 218–221, 224
in relation to state power, 9, 35, 79n14, 87, 149, 152n8
norms/laws, 9–10, 36–37, 43n23, 45, 49, 66, 86–88, 101, 104, 133–134, 138–144, 150, 151–152n8, 153n17, 160–161, 164–170
performative, 133, 161, 170
queer/alternative, 9, 141–145, 139
relations, 36, 68, 87, 96n6, 144–148
Knox, Bernard, 130n11, 130n12, 155–157, 170
Kristeva, Julia, 12–13, 204, **215–229**
works by,
"A Father is Beaten to Death," 229n8
Female Genius: Colette, 229n10
Female Genius: Hannah Arendt, 71
Seule une femme, 228n1
Sense and Non-Sense of Revolt, The, 228n1
Tales of Love, 228n1
This Incredible Need to Believe, 228n1

Lacan, Jacques,
as a misogynist (feminist critique of), 3, 9, 160
fetishization of Antigone, 84
Moebius strip, 197
on beauty, 199–201
on Being, 158–159, 196
on death (drive), 11–12, 62n20, 199–202, 221
on jouissance, 195–197, 200, 213n27
on the brother-sister relation, 157–160, 202
on the incest taboo, 88, 204
on the symbolic order, 88, 97n9, 134, 142, 145, 195–198, 204
on Tiresias, 195, 197, 199, 206

Lacan, Jacques *(continued)*
  on women/feminine sexuality, 11–12, 175, 195–197, 200, 202, 209, 212n6
  reading of *Antigone*, 11–13, 84, 88, 151n7, 156–160, 169, 174, 199–202, 221, 223–224, 229n5
  works by,
    Ethics of Psychoanalysis, The, 12, 82n45, 157, 159, *passim* 195–211, *passim* 215–228, 228n1, 229n5, 229n6
Laing, R. D., 212–213n20
Laius, 36, 38, 41, 106, 172n29
  curse of, 135, 137, 186
  House of, 34, 36
law, 19, 105, 152n12
  against burying Polyneices. *See* Creon; Polyneices
  Antigone's own, 10, 13, 51, 96n6, 166–169, 217
  apartheid, 85, 88–90
  divine/family/unwritten, 5, 47, 65, 69, 83, 100–102, 106–107, 114–116, 119, 121, 127, 151n7, 157, 158, 162, 167, 171n14, 223, 224, 228, 229n6
  ethical/moral, 107, 113, 114, 122, 127
  funeral, 79–80n17, 118
  human/state/written, 2, 5, 29, 30, 32, 34–35, 51, 65, 68–70, 73, 100–107, 114–115, 119, 121, 148–149, 156, 224
  kinship. *See* kinship
  maternal. *See* mother
  nomos, 134, 138, 217
  of nature, 53, 200
  of the Father, 9, 97n9, 145
  phallic, 12
  transgression/violation of, 2, 35, 70, 73, 77, 87, 96n6, 106–107, 111, 117–119, 128, 139–143, 149, 155, 156, 158–159, 162, 167, 186, 188, 200, 215, 217, 218, 223
Leach, Edmund, 151n8
legislation, 68, 85, 94, 118
Lessing, Gotthold Ephraim, 113
Levinas, Emmanuel, 207, 212n2
Lévi-Strauss, Claude, 141, 143, 144, 151n8, 166
Lewinsky, Monica, 142, 152n13
libido, 196, 200
logocentrism, 52, 55
loneliness. *See* solitude
Loraux, Nicole, 80n20, 188, 219
loss, 66, 74, 135, 141, 148, 181, 205, 210, 218, 219, 222
love, 59, 78n4, 111, 112, 135, 147, 157, 161–162, 173, 177, 179, 181, 190, 195, 215–216. *See also* Eros; desire
  maternal. *See* mother
  of death/the dead, 127–128, 135–136, 146, 173, 191, 225
  of the impossible, 173, 175
  of truth, 173, 179, 181
  Plato on. *See* Plato
  sibling, 59, 83, 86, 106, 116, 135, 146, 161–162, 216, 222
Luther, Martin, 76

Mader, Mary Beth, 9–10, 12, 84, 86–87, 96n6, 130n11, **155–172**
madness, 13, 102, 196, 217, 222–224, 227, 229n5
Markell, Patchen, 84, 97n10, 130n16
marriage, 10, 36, 49, 87, 88, 92, 101, 103, 153n17, 180
  gay, 141–143, 152n12
  inter-racial, 89
  of Antigone, 10, 37, 43n22, 43n25, 54, 76, 146, 215, 216
Marx, Karl, 143
Mary, Virgin, 225
master-slave dialectic. *See* Hegel, G. W. F.
maternal. *See* mother
Mathews, Aidan, 95
matriarchy, 74, 81n35, 101, 102, 112, 224
matricide, 31, 32, 176, 220
matrixial, 11–12, *passim* 198–214

McDonald, Marianne, 95
Medea, 18. *See also* Euripides
melancholia, 104, 105, 136, 147–149, 221
memory, 53, 71, 111, 128, 141, 180, 198, 203, 205, 206, 209, 210, 225
  commemoration, 71, 72, 77, 31, 33, 111, 202
Menke, Christoph, 130n13
metaphysics, 123, 176, 177, 179, 181, 183, 190–191
Michaux, Henri, 212n12
Miller, Jacques-Alain, 142
Mills, Patricia Jagentowicz, 7, 129n2
Mitchell, Juliet, 145
misogyny, 51, 61–62n12, 56. *See also* woman
  of Creon. *See* Creon
  of Hegel. *See* Hegel, G. W. F.
  of Lacan. *See* Lacan, Jacques
modernity, 4, *passim* 15–19, 27–28, 47, 48, *passim* 65–69, 76, 78n3, 86, 113–114, 120, 128, 173, 184, 191
Montesquieu, Baron de, 79n11
mother. *See also* matricide; matrixial
  Antigone as, 10, 12–13, 49–50, 51, 54, 61n6, 89, 103, 143, 146, 220–222, 225, 227–228
  good, 227
  Jocasta as. *See* Jocasta
  lesbian, 141–143
  maternal body, 4, 11–12, 51, 52, 55–56, 59–60, 156, 170, 213n21
  maternal desire, 50, 61n6, 103, 201–202, 205, 213n21, 219–220
  maternal filiation/lineage/origins, 3, 6, 7, 12, 31, 49–52, 55–56, 59–60, 61n7, 102–103, 165, 168, 198–199, 201, 203, 207, 210, 219, 220
  maternal law, 51, 103
  maternal love, 116, 205, 228
  maternal power, 50–51, 59, 62n14, 101
  maternal vocation, 220, 222, 227, 228
  motherhood, 226–227
  of the Plaza de Mayo, 29
  single, 9, 141
mourning, 17, 42n18, 66, 70–71, 73, 75, 80n17, 80n23, 103, 105, 148, 168, 175, 210, 226
myth, 5, 16–18, 53, 59–60, 65, 93, 96n2, 101, 111, 112, 196, 200, 225
  ancient. *See* Greece
  of origin. *See* origin

narration, 35, 54–55, 60, 71, 77, 80–81n28, 137, 138, 143
nature, 2, 7, 45, 46, 53, 55, 59, 60, 62n14, 75, 82n44, 100, 106, 109, 115, 119, 121–123, 126, 143, 144, 186, 189, 200
  contrasted with culture. *See* culture
  laws of. *See* law
necessity, 10, 29, 73, 80n21, 92, 94, 107, 111, 113, 116, 121, 126, 127, 135, 136, 138, 139–140, 142, 151n7, 160–161, 164, 169, 186–189, 228
  contrasted with freedom. *See* freedom
negation, 69, 76, 100, 106, 111, 113, 116–120, 140, 146
Nerval, Gérard de, 221
Nietzsche, Friedrich, 78n3, 83, 192n3, 207
  works by,
    Beyond Good and Evil, 62n18
    Untimely Meditations, 32–33
    Use and Abuse of History, The, 40
Niobe, 38, 42n18
nomos. *See* law
nonviolence. *See* violence
nostalgia, 4, 55, 60, 104
Nussbaum, Martha, 42–43n19, 129n2, 157

Obama, Barack, 1
obedience, 28, 51, 102, 108, 120, 124, 180, 216, 218
Oedipus,
  Antigone's identification with, 168
  as brother of his own children, 10, 35, 50, 87, 133–137, 140–141, 143,

Oedipus *(continued)*
146, 148, 150n5, 162, 164–165, 172n23, 219
as father, 10, 35, 40, 50, 80n23, 87, 102, 133–135, 150n5, 158, 164–166, 168, 219
as tragic figure, 37, 75, 176, 186
as womanly/feminine, 91, 97n15
blindness of, 50, 67, 91, 187, 221
burial/death of, 135, 165, 172n25
complex, 9, 11, 97n9, 133, 142, 145–146, 173, 196, 203, 213n24, 226–227
curse/fate of, 34, 38, 39, 75, 91, 133–139, 157, 167, 168, 172n26, 186–188
cycle, 12, 34–35, 134, 136, 185, 189. *See also* Sophocles
family/lineage of, 10, 12, 35, 36, 39, 43n23, 50, 61n7, 87, 91, 96n6, 101–102, 133, 137, 140, 146, 156–157, *passim* 162–171, 215, 219
grave of, 172n25
incest/crime of, 9–10, 12, 34–35, 38, 50, 86–87, 102, 134–135, 137, 147, 158, 162, 164–169, 172n23, 172n29, 176, 186, 202–203, 206, 217, 223, 225
oikos. *See* family
Oliver, Kelly, 7
ontology, 8, 10, 28, 32–33, 40, 66, 117, 147, 149, 158, 159, 164, 190–191
Ophelia, 216, 222
opposition, 5, 30, 36–37, 66, 107, 113, 116
between Antigone and Creon, 5–6, 47–48, 54, 69, 85–86, 102, 109, 119, 167, 127. *See also* Creon
between friend and enemy, 36, 56. *See also* enemy; friend
between human and divine law, 5, 65, 69, 106, 114, 158. *See also* law
between humans and animals, 52–53. *See also* animal
between individual and state, 51
between man and woman, 7–8, 45, 55, 65, 99, 102, 104, 105, 106, 107, 114, 121, 122, 125. *See also* woman
between private and public, 5, 6, 69, 78n7, 79n11, 85–86, 122, 169. *See also* Greece; private sphere; public sphere
tragedy as a set of, 46, 65
oppression, 3, 30, 77, 85, 94–95, 124, 213n21. *See also* woman
Orestes, 31, 35, 37, 220. *See also* Aeschylus
origin, 35, 38, 54, 124, 138, 143, 168, 184, 201, 211
maternal. *See* mother
myth of, 34, 42n11, 46, 120
natural/animal/material, 5, 32, 46, 53–54, 60, 62n14
Òsófisan, Fémi, 95
works by,
Tègònni, 3, 18, 97n11
other, 6, 7, 28, 69, 83–86, 88–90, 93–95, 108, 146, 169, 174, 176, 181, *passim* 196–211, 212n6, 213n27, 218, 224, 226, 228. *See also* constitutive outside; exclusion
woman as. *See* woman
otherness. *See* other
Ovid, 195

pathology, 3, 115, 140, 205, 222, 224, 229n5
pathos, 106, 108, 218, 222, 224, 227, 228
patriarchy, 8, 30–34, 40, 42n7, 55, 61n6, 70, 74, 81n35, 101–102, 123, 144, 152n15, 180, 188
patricide, 34, 102, 134, 137, 176, 186, 225. *See also* Oedipus
Patterson, Orlando, 144, 153n20
Paulin, Tom, 95
performativity, 6, 9, 84–85, 92, 133, 137, 138, 150, 161, 170
Butler on. *See* Butler, Judith
kinship as. *See* kinship
perversion, 9, 10, 35, 74, 103, 140, 145, 152n9, 203

Phaedra, 185, 187–188, 191. *See also* Euripides
phallus, 11–12, *passim* 196–211, 212n6, 212n8, 212n9, 213n21, 213n27
phantasy. *See* fantasy
philia. *See* friendship
Pinkard, Terry, 129n7
pity, 51, 103, 222
Plato, 5, 68
  on beauty, 181
  on body and soul, 47, 58, 181, 183
  on enmity, 57–59
  on eros/love/sexuality, 173, 179–183, 185, 191
  on (search for) truth, 173, 176–177, 179, 181
  works by,
    Laws, The, 179, 217
    Phaedrus, 181, 183
    Protagoras, 62n16
    Republic, 57–58
plurality, 67, 72, 79n11, 178
Pollock, Griselda, 213n28
Polyneices,
  as an enemy of the state, 56–58, 75, 127, 162, 216
  as Antigone's brother, 86–87, 89, 96n6, 101–103, 112, 135, 146, 158–168, 216, 219
  as representative of a patriarchal order, 55
  as womanly/feminine, 80n23, 103
  at war with Eteocles, 71, 75, 103, 134–135, 137, 220. *See also* war
  burial of, 10, 54, 56, 70–72, 86, 90, 118–119, 126, 127n27, 128, 134, 135–136, 148, 155–166, 216–217
  corpse of, 5, 15, 17, 45–50, 52–55, 58, 68, 97n13, 128, 148, 157, 217, 220
  cursed by Oedipus, 134–135
  death of, 59, 135, 166
  etymological analysis of, 216
  fate of, 47, 135
  individuality/singularity of, 47, 126, 146, 148, 156, 158–163, 168, 202
  unburied/denied burial, 5, 45–47, 52, 87, 111, 148
power, 18, 67, 137, 151–152n8, 177–178
  Arendt on. *See* Arendt, Hannah
  female, 29, 30, 45–47
  maternal. *See* mother
  of Antigone, 29, 33
  of Creon. *See* Creon
  of Eros. *See* Eros
  of the body, 47–49
  of the negative, 116–117, 120
  patriarchal, 31, 32, 101–102, 149
  state, 3, 9, 29, 37, 67, 102, 103, 109
prepolitical, 27, 67, 68, 81n33, 84, 149
private sphere, 3, 5–6, 12, 29–30, 65–77, 78n7, 79n11, 81n33, 104, 149, 156. *See also* Arendt, Hannah; Greece; opposition
Prometheus, 62n16
Proust, Marcel, 76
psyche. *See* soul
psychoanalysis, 9, 11, 12, 96n2, 133, 138–141, 145–146, 160, 174, 176, 197, 205, 212–213n20, 217, 223–224. *See also* Freud, Sigmund; Lacan, Jacques
public sphere, 3, 5–6, 12, 29–30, 38, *passim* 65–77, 78n7, 79n11, 147, 149. *See also* Arendt, Hannah; Greece; opposition
punishment, 42n18, 67, 93, 102, 137, 195
  of Antigone 68, 103, 106, 147

queer, 9, 141–145

race, 1, 3, 6, *passim* 16–19, 85, 88–94, 143–144
  and kinship. *See* kinship
Rank, Otto, 213n24
rape, 102, 106, 107, 144, 188
Rapp, Rayna, 151n8
Ravven, Heidi M., 6, 129n2
Real, the, 142, 197–198, 204, 207, 210–211, 212n6

rebirth. *See* birth
recognition, 7–8, 47, 86–88, 93, 96n6, 142, 145, 147, 149, 167–169, 172n29, 181, 225
  Hegel on. *See* Hegel, G. W. F.
Reiss, Timothy, 95
religion, 1, 3, 6, 66, 93, 100, 115, 127, 216, 220, 225, 226
repression, 7, 8, 32–33, 75, 107–109, 123–124, 158, 197–198, 204, 218, 227
reproduction, 3, 8, 35, 139, 143–144, 148, 151–152n8, 227
resistance, 18, 32, 67, 77, 85, 94, 105, 108, 196, 215, 216
revolt. *See* revolution
revolution, 1, 3, 17, 70, 103, 104, 109, 145, 224, 226
riddle, 2, 41, 60, 140, 176
  of the Sphinx. *See* Sphinx
Rivière, Joan, 212n9
Rome, 122–123
Rosaldo, Michelle, 143
Rousseau, Jean-Jacques, 113
Rubin, Gayle, 143

Sade, Marquis de, 218
Sahlins, Marshall, 151n8
Sappho, 11, 174, 180–184
  as Platonic intertext, 181, 183
  on eros/desire, 11, 180–184, 190–191
  works by,
    Hymn to Aphrodite, 182–183
Saxonhouse, Arlene, 39, 43n25
Scheherazade, 19
Schelling, F. W. J., 113, 185–191
  aesthetic Hellenism of, 116
  on eros/desire/sexuality, 11, 175–176, 186–191
  on freedom, 11, 176, 185–191
  on the sublime, 188–189
  works by,
    Philosophical Inquires into the Nature of Human Freedom, 185, 186
    Philosophical Letters (*Briefe*), 186
    Philosophy of Art, 185, 186, 188
Schiller, Friedrich, 113, 114, 176, 186, 189
  on the sublime, 188–189
Schlegel, August Wilhelm, 113, 186, 190
Schlegel, Karl Wilhelm Friedrich, 186
Schmitt, Carl, 56–57
Schneider, David, 133, 143, 151n8
Segal, Charles, 130n12
self-consciousness, 8, 95, 100, 111, 112, 117–119, 123, 129n8
self-destruction. *See* destruction
Sestili, Antonio, 61n9
sexism. *See* misogyny; woman
sexual difference, 3–4, 6, 7–8, 31, 37–39, 56, 65–66, 73–74, 107, 122–123, 141, 145, 196. *See also* gender
sexuality, 6, 8, 11, 46, 85, 91, 93, 140, 146, *passim* 173–191, 193n27. *See also* desire; Eros
  bi-, 102, 227
  female/feminine, 3, 10, 11, 174, 195–196, 200, 226–227
  hetero-, 9, 143, 146
  history of, 10–11, 174–180, 191. *See also* Foucault, Michel
  homo-, 91–93, 142, 152n12, 178, 226–227
Shakespeare, William, 216
shame, 103, 161, 166, 170, 188, 200
singularity, 8, 35, 51, 107–109, 112, *passim* 117–128, 142, 153n24, 162, 163, 228, 228n4
  of Antigone, 2, 118–121, 126, 130n13
  of Polyneices. *See* Polyneices
Sipylus, 42n18
sister,
  Antigone as, 10, 12, 49, 51, 54, 72, 87, 89, 164, 216
  Hegel on brother-sister relation. *See* Hegel, G. W. F.
  Ismene as. *See* Ismene
  Jocasta as. *See* Jocasta
  Lacan on brother-sister relation. *See* Lacan, Jacques

Sjöholm, Cecilia, 10–11, 70, 74, **173–193**
works by,
Antigone Complex, The, 10, 80n20, 129n2
slavery, 49, 73, 79n11, 81n33, 91, 103, 104, 144, 149, 153n20, 178
master-slave dialectic. *See* Hegel, G. W. F.
Socrates,
Antigone compared with, 1–2, 111
as a master of truth, 179
on the burial of enemies, 57–58
Söderbäck, Fanny, **1–13**, 5–6, **65–82**
solitude, 19, 51, 60, 66, 73, 79n11, 103, 104, 106, 119, 217, 222–223, 226. *See also* friendship
Solon, 79–80n17
soma. *See* body
Sophist, 1
Sophocles, 48, 58, 61n6, 65, 69, 102, 115, 118, 127, 174, 216, 221
works by,
Antigone, *passim*
King Oedipus, 185, 189
Oedipus at Colonus, 37, 80n23, 134–139, 150n5, 165, 221
sorrow. *See* mourning
soul, 46–48, 52, 105, 109, 120, 189, 199, 205, 206, 208, 210, 227
as a principle of action, 5, 58
body and. *See* body
lack of, 126
sovereignty, 72–73, 80n23, 86, 87, 102, 104, 140, 146–147, 152n9, 162, 218–219, 222–223
speech, 13, 57, 104, 134, 137–138, 141, 149, 167, 182, 218, 225
action and. *See* action
feminist/political, 17, 28, 30–31, 39–40, 59
of Antigone, 15, 28, 30–38, 50, 54, 61n7, 73–74, 87, 89, 103, 115–116, 134, 135, 140, 147, 148, 150, 155, 156, 162–163
of Creon. *See* Creon
unspeakable, the, 147–149
Speight, Allen, 130n13
Sphinx, 97n15
riddle of the, 91
Spirit. *See* Hegel, G. W. F.
Stack, Carol, 143
Steiner, George, 43n23, 61n9, 77, 80n23, 129n1, 133, 171n11
strangeness, 5, 33, 37, 41, 43n23, 46, 47, 57, 134, 147, 201, 208
of Antigone, 28, 37–39, 43n19, 156, 224
Strathern, Marilyn, 151n8
Stone, Alison, 7
subjectivity, 7, 10, 11, 13, 47, 50, 58, 104, 105, *passim* 112–128, 130n13, *passim* 174–185, 189–191, *passim* 196–211, 224
birth of. *See* birth; Greece
female, 3, 7, 55, 59, 108, 196, 204, 213n24
male, 55, 105, 175, 177, 181, 204, 213n24
sublation, 8, 100, 101, 105–108, 113, 122–123, 128
sublimation, 12, 218, 222, 225–227
sublime, the, 83, 176, 188–190, 196, 217, 225, 228
suicide, 10, 31, 37, 39, 43n22, 76, 103, 188, 218, 220, 221
Svenbro, Jesper, 181
symbolic order, 45, 49, 55, 88, 94, 97n9, 101, 111, 139, 141, 142–143, 202, 204, 207
Lacan on. *See* Lacan, Jacques

Tantalus, 42n18
techne, 53, 179
Tègònni. *See* Òsófisan, Fémi
temporality. *See* time
terror. *See* horror
Thanatos, 221, 222
kalos thanatos, 70
Thebes, 4, 15, 17, 33–39
as ancient nondemocratic order, 34, 39, 67, 69
as democratic order, 30, 39
city walls of, 46, 52, 59

Thebes *(continued)*
contrasted with Athens, 28, 34, 35, 37, 69
curse/fate of, 4, 34, 37, 39, 43n25, 75
downfall of, 75
foundation of, 42n11
kinship in, 49–50, 67
Oedipus' return to, 134–135
role in Athenian tragedy, 28, 34
the people of, 40, 43n19, 73, 172n27
women in, 38
Theseus, 134, 135
time, 34–40, 43n22, 133–138, 195, 200, 204–209, 211, 212n2, 213n26, 223, 225
timelessness, 2, 83, 159, 185, 208–209, 222
Tiresias, 67, 124
blindness of, 195, 200
compared with Antigone, 200, 202, 210–211
fate of, 195, 211
sexual identity of, 11, 195, 197, 198, 199, 206, 210–211
tomb. *See* grave
totalitarianism, 16, 218
tradition, 16, 32, 46, 120, 122, 141, 147, 226
ancient, 30, 34, 36, 37, 47–49, 52, 57–58, 70, 86, 118, 136, 146, 177–178, 181, 183, 191, 217, 224
Antigone and, *passim* 30–38, 41, 81n32, 134, 158, 165
feminist, 29, 40
Western/patriarchal, 4, 5, 27–29, 30–31, 39–40, 94, 111, 166, 175, 176, 178, 180, 181
transcendence, 51, 181, 183
transgression, 47, 56, 66, 120–121, 128, 143, 176, 186, 223
matrixial, 11–12, 198–203, 206–211
of Antigone, 7, 9–10, 11–12, 38, 70, 71, 73, 77, 111, 117–118, 120–121, 126–127, 188, 201, 216
of Oedipus. *See* Oedipus
of the law. *See* law
transgressive action. *See* action
trauma, 138, 140, 198, *passim* 203–221, 213n24
truth, 1, 100, 104, 119, 120, 125, 173, *passim* 176–183, 185, 191, 196, 223, 224
tyranny, 32, 33, 39, 56, 70, 79n11, 215
of Creon. *See* Creon

uncanny, the, 2, 12, 18, 20, 45, 46, 52, 53, 60, 84, 184–185, 187, 193n27, 205
deinon, 45, 62n16, 174, 184, 187
Freud on. *See* Freud, Sigmund
Heidegger on. *See* Heidegger, Martin
Hölderlin on. *See* Hölderlin, Friedrich
unconscious, the, 7, 106–109, 146–147, 176, 202–203, 205, 207, 209–210, 213n24, 224
desire/fantasy, 100, 108
underworld. *See* Hades
universality, 7, 74, 92, 97n9, *passim* 100–109, *passim* 110–128, 156, 163, 166, 181, 212n6, 217, 226

vengeance, 1, 221
violence, 31, 45, 53, 67, 69, 81n33, 100, 137, 144, 148, 149, 185
nonviolence, 67, 106, 137
virginity, 10, 102, 190, 215, 228
voice. *See* speech

war, 1, 15, 16, 17, 19, 36, 56–57, 100, 106, 126, 130n20, 189, 219, 220
between Polyneices and Eteocles, 71, 75, 109, 134, 219, 220. *See also* Polyneices
civil, 12, 16, 57, 216, 218, 220
of the sexes, 101, 112. *See also* misogyny; woman
Warner, Michael, 145
Werner, Laura, 7, 78n4, 80n26
Weston, Kath, 144
wife, 179, 180, 189
Antigone as, 10, 12, 51, 102, 146, 161
Eurydice as, 70, 104

wife *(continued)*
  husband and, 89, 101, 116, 164, 172n21
  Jocasta as, 36, 50, 86–87, 101, 103, 105, 133, 218
Winckelmann, Johann Joachim, 113, 114
Winnicott, Donald, 227
Wolin, Sheldon, 27, 41
woman. *See also* gender
  Antigone as, 2, 3–4, 5, 28, 29, 32, 37–38, 55–56, 70, 73–75, 80n23, 87–88, 102–103, 217–218, 220
  and politics, 1, 27, 66, 70, 75, 83–84, 125, 226
  as a representative of the family, 7, 29, 100, 108, 111–112
  as derivative of man, 11, 107–108, 196–197
  as other, 5, 27, 55, 75, 105–107, 114, 134, 176
  associated with death/burial, 12, 100, 108, 200
  body of. *See* body
  Creon as. *See* Creon
  in Greek tragedy, 124, 180, 188
  Ismene as. *See* Ismene
  Lacan on. *See* Lacan, Jacques
  Oedipus as. *See* Oedipus
  oppression/repression/exclusion of, 5–8, 27, 36, 45, 48, 51, 56, 74, 76, 79n11, 82n44, 83–84, 87–88, 102, 108–109, 123, 124, 226
  Polyneices as. *See* Polyneices
  Tiresias as. *See* Tiresias
womb, 12, 52, 55, 99, 100, 103, 108, 158, 159, 169, 202–205, 209, 210, 219, 220
Wyckoff, Elizabeth, 157

Yanagisako, Sylvia Junko, 143, 151n8

Zeitlin, Froma I., 4, 34, 38, 43n25, 69, 71, 174
Zerilli, Linda, 4, 28, 30–33, 36, 40, 42n7
Zeus, 151n7, 182, 190, 195, 223, 229n6
Žižek, Slavoj, 84
  works by,
    Enjoy Your Symptom!, 140–141
    "From Antigone to Joan of Arc," 96n1
    Sublime Object of Ideology, The, 43n23